DO ECONOMISTS MAKE MARKETS?

DO ECONOMISTS
MAKE MARKETS?

On the Performativity of Economics

Edited by
Donald MacKenzie,
Fabian Muniesa,
and Lucia Siu

PRINCETON UNIVERSITY PRESS PRINCETON AND OXFORD

Published by Princeton University Press, 41 William Street, Princeton,
New Jersey 08540

In the United Kingdom: Princeton University Press, 6 Oxford Street, Woodstock,
Oxfordshire OX20 1TW

Third printing, and first paperback printing, 2008
Paperback ISBN: 978-0-691-13849-7

The Library of Congress has cataloged the cloth edition of this book as follows

Do economists make markets? : on the performativity of economics / edited by
Donald Mackenzie, Fabian Muniesa, and Lucia Siu.
p.   cm.
Includes bibliographical references and index.
ISBN-13: 978-0-691-13016-3 (alk. paper)
ISBN-10: 0-691-13016-7 (alk. paper)
1. Economics. 2. Markets. I. Mackenzie, Donald, 1950– II. Muniesa, Fabian,
1972– III. Siu, Lucia, 1971– IV. Title: On the performativity of economics.
HB71.D55   2007
381—dc22   2006038670

British Library Cataloging-in-Publication Data is available

This book has been composed in Sabon

Printed on acid-free paper. ∞

press.princeton.edu

Printed in the United States of America

10 9 8 7 6 5 4 3

Contents

Illustrations, Boxes, and Tables

Acknowledgments _____

First drafts of most of the chapters in this book were presented to a workshop held at the Ecole Nationale Supérieure des Mines de Paris in August 2004. The workshop was made possible by support from the Centre de Sociologie de l'Innovation and from a Professorial Fellowship on Social Studies of Finance awarded to Donald MacKenzie by the UK Economic and Social Research Council (RES-051-27-0062). We are deeply grateful for helpful comments to all the participants in the workshop, and to three anonymous referees for Princeton University Press.

Chapter 2 is based on an article that appeared in French in *Actes de la Recherche en Sciences Sociales* 65 (1986); an earlier version of chapter 3 appeared in the *Journal of the History of Economic Thought* 28 (2006); and chapter 8 is a much-revised version of an article that appeared in *Sosiologisk Årbok* 8/1 (2003). We are grateful to the copyright holders for permission to reuse this material here, and to John Law for his translation of the main part of chapter 2.

DO ECONOMISTS MAKE MARKETS?

Chapter 1

Introduction

DONALD MACKENZIE, FABIAN MUNIESA, AND LUCIA SIU

Monetary Theory at Thirteen Thousand Feet

La Paz, January 1986. The young Harvard economist who arrives at the airport has visited twice before, so he knows what to expect: the thin air of Bolivia's capital, three and a half kilometers above sea level, which will leave him short of breath throughout his visit; the extreme poverty; the beauty of the mountains; the hyperinflation that is beginning. He goes from the airport directly to the Banco Central de Bolivia, where he discovers that the money supply had sharply increased in December.

The economist, Jeffrey Sachs, goes on to deliver his advice to Bolivia's planning minister and then its president. The advice may seem dangerous—Sachs was to be summoned by the International Monetary Fund to explain himself—but for Sachs it was a straightforward implication of what his discipline teaches about the theory of money. If inflation is to be brought under control, the pesos that are flooding the economy must be taken out of circulation, even at the cost of spending Bolivia's precious, limited reserves of foreign currency to buy them up.

Later, Sachs was to muse on his meager understanding of the country to whose leaders he gave his crucial advice. It was only in a conversation a couple of years after his 1986 visit that he realized that Bolivia's physical geography was a fundamental feature of its economic situation, not merely an incidental fact. "Of course I knew that Bolivia was landlocked and mountainous. . . . Yet I had not reflected on how these conditions were key geographical factors, perhaps the overriding factors, in Bolivia's chronic poverty. . . . Almost all the international commentary and academic economic writing about Bolivia neglected this very basic point. It bothered me greatly that the most basic and central features of economic reality could be overlooked by academic economists spinning their theories from thousands of miles away" (Sachs 2005, p. 105).

Nevertheless, commented Sachs, a meager knowledge of the context had not stopped his advice on monetary policy being successful. Bolivia's hyperinflation did come to an end. "Monetary theory, thank goodness, still worked at thirteen thousand feet" (Sachs 2005, p. 105).

The Question of Performativity

Sachs's advice to the government of Bolivia is unusual in that it marked the beginning of an exceptional degree of individual influence. Sachs and his former student David Lipton went on to draw up what became the plan of first Solidarity and then the Polish government to shape the economic structure of postcommunist Poland; they attempted, much less successfully, to repeat the exercise in Yeltsin's Russia; Sachs now advises the United Nations and world leaders on how to end poverty in Africa. In other respects, however, Sachs's Bolivian trips were simply one manifestation of a far more general phenomenon: the move of economics from the journals, textbooks, and lecture theaters into "the real economy." In Chile, for example, the "Chicago boys"—Chilean economists trained at the University of Chicago—were reshaping Chile in the 1970s and 1980s in a fashion more fundamental than Sachs's influence on Bolivia (Valdés 1995). The phenomenon is not restricted to Latin America, to the former Soviet bloc, or to matters of government policy: economics is built into the modern world far more pervasively than that.

The shaping of economies by economics can be viewed as a triumph for the truths discovered by the discipline, or it can be condemned as the damaging imposition of an abstract and unrealistic worldview; such matters remain fiercely controversial. At a minimum, however, what is made clear by the cases of Bolivia, Poland, Russia, and Chile, as well as by those discussed in the chapters that follow, is that economics is at work within economies in a way that is at odds with the widespread conception of science as an activity whose sole purpose is to observe and study, that is to "know" the world.

The issue that needs to be tackled in relation to economies and economics is not just about "knowing" the world, accurately or not. It is also about producing it. It is not (only) about economics being "right" or "wrong" but (also, and perhaps more important) about it being "able" or "unable" to transform the world. Economics swings between representation and action, between science and policy, between academic inquiry and political intervention, both as a discipline and in the careers of many individual economists; Sachs is far from alone in this respect. Economics often seems abstract (to some of its proponents, as well as to its critics), yet it also articulates with, influences, is deployed in, and restructures concrete economies in all their messy materiality and their complex sociality. How can we confront such a cumbersome object? In this volume, we discuss the potential of the notion of *performativity*.

For the philosopher J. L. Austin, a performative utterance was a specific kind of statement or expression that establishes its referent through the very act of uttering (Austin 1962). In saying, for instance, "I apologize," I am not reporting on an already existing state of affairs. I am bringing that state of affairs into being: to say "I apologize" is to make an apology. "I apologize" is, thus, a performative utterance.

Although (as far as we are aware) it was Austin who coined the term "performative," the notion partakes of a long pragmatist tradition (nourished by the work of authors such as Charles S. Peirce, William James, John Dewey, Charles W. Morris, and more recently John R. Searle)[1] for which a central issue is the way in which actions, entities, and representations are intertwined. Performativity is not achieved by words alone. Even in the case of a simple utterance such as "I apologize," the speaker can undermine the performative effect by adopting a sarcastic tone of voice or sneering facial expression. Then the words no longer constitute an apology: they do not bring into being that of which they apparently speak. More generally, the "conditions of felicity" that make an utterance successfully performative are social as well as linguistic and bodily, as the sociologist Pierre Bourdieu pointed out (Bourdieu 1991). In the Middle Ages, a monarch could make someone an "outlaw" by declaring that person to be such, but only if his right to do so was accepted sufficiently widely.

Although the origins of the notion of performativity lie in philosophy, the concept has been taken up in the social sciences and humanities more widely. Judith Butler, for example, has taken it into the mainstream of feminist theory (1990, 1997). The diverse fields that have adopted Robert K. Merton's (1949) notion of the "self-fulfilling prophecy"—in which the release and social circulation of a description or prediction enhances its validity—can be seen as investigating a version of performativity.

One area in which the notion has been particularly widely drawn upon is science studies. Historians, sociologists, philosophers, and anthropologists of science have used performativity or similar intuitions to understand the nature of scientific claims and practices. For instance, Ian Hacking (1983) showed how the sciences' representations of the world can be understood only in their close entanglement with intervention in that world. Andrew Pickering (1995) suggested that a "performative idiom," more attentive to activity than to knowledge alone, could surpass the limitations of the "representational idiom" that is common in the scholarly appraisal of science. Barry Barnes (1983) pointed to the performative nature of the feedback loops between certain terms—which he calls "social kind" terms—and their referents. These approaches connect to larger considerations of the reflexive nature of modernization and of the complex interactions between science and society (see, for example, Beck et al. 1994).

Michel Callon, whose work is grounded in the field of science studies, proposed elucidating explicitly the performative character of economics; that is, he proposes considering economics not as a form of knowledge that depicts an already existing state of affairs but as a set of instruments and practices that contribute to the construction of economic settings, actors, and institutions (1998a). In Callon's words, "economics ... performs, shapes and formats the economy, rather than observing how it functions" (1998b, p. 2). As Callon makes explicit in his chapter in this book, in formulations such as this "economics" refers to the full range of disciplines, specialties, technologies, and forms of knowledge with which economic actors and their markets are equipped. He nevertheless includes in particular the academic discipline of economics, seeing its role as performative rather than descriptive. Callon's proposal has generated intense debate. It has been perceived as a compelling tool for analyzing the social impact of economics (e.g., MacKenzie 2003; MacKenzie and Millo 2003) but also as a dangerous threat to the sociological critique of economics (e.g., Fine 2003; Miller 2002). This collection of essays is an attempt at pursuing the debate and at fleshing out with empirical evidence and theoretical considerations this inquiry into the performativity of economics.

What does it mean to say that economics is performative? This whole volume is an attempted answer to that question, and many authors not directly represented here (including economists as well as sociologists and philosophers) have contributed much to the discussion.[2] Nevertheless, let us give a relatively simple example to introduce the notion of "the performativity of economics" for those encountering it for the first time. Consider the efficient-market hypothesis: the proposition that prices in financial markets "always 'fully reflect' available information" (Fama 1970, p. 383). The hypothesis, given definitive form by University of Chicago economist Eugene Fama, became the centerpiece of modern financial economics: "I believe there is no other proposition in economics which has more solid empirical evidence supporting it than the Efficient Market Hypothesis," wrote Michael Jensen (1978, p. 95).

The efficient-market hypothesis is not simply an analysis of financial markets as "external" things but has become woven into market practices. Most important, it helped inspire the establishment of index-tracking funds.[3] Instead of seeking to "beat the market" (a goal that the hypothesis suggests is unlikely to be achieved except by chance), such funds invest in broad baskets of stocks and attempt to replicate the performance of market indexes such as the S&P 500. Such funds have become major investment vehicles, and their effects on prices can be detected when stocks are added to or removed from indexes (see MacKenzie 2006, pp. 104–105, and the literature cited there).

Consider, too, the many empirical tests of the efficient-market hypothesis, which generally have taken the form of the analysis of databases of securities prices (and of ancillary events such as corporate earnings announcements) to discover whether an investment strategy can be found that systematically offers excess risk-adjusted returns; the existence of such a strategy would seem to indicate that some price-relevant information is *not* being incorporated into prices. It has in fact been fairly common for tests to seem to reveal such a strategy. When this happens, one possible conclusion that could be drawn is that the "anomalies" (as they are called) indicate that the efficient-market hypothesis is false; it might even be concluded that "orthodox" financial economics should be replaced by "behavioral finance" (which suggests that investors' psychological biases give rise to anomalies).

It will, however, surprise no one with a background in science studies that a variety of other responses to an apparently failed test of the efficient-market hypothesis are possible.[4] From the viewpoint of performativity, the most interesting response has been for researchers themselves (or market participants who are close to such researchers) to move from simulating the results of investment strategies to employing those strategies in practice in order to profit from the anomalies their tests have revealed. The typical effect of such exploitation, when it becomes at all widespread, is to reduce or eliminate anomalies (MacKenzie 2006, pp. 98–105; Schwert 2002).

Thus financial economics in the form of the efficient-market hypothesis has not simply been "applied" (for example, in the form of index funds): "failed" tests of the hypothesis have given rise to practical action that generally has had the consequence of tending to restore the hypothesis's empirical validity. It is this kind of interweaving of "words" and "actions"—of representations and interventions—that the concept of "performativity" is designed to capture.

Note that to emphasize the performativity of economics is not necessarily to be committed to a causal role of "ideas" (in the sense, for example, of Weber 1930; see, e.g., Blyth 2002). Certainly, ideas from economics are often drawn upon to argue for one policy rather than another, or to defend or criticize an institution. When such efforts seem successful, we must, however, always ask whether it was the appeal to economics, rather than any other factor, that led to the outcome. Furthermore, to view economics as a body of ideas is far too narrow, for economics also consists of people, skills, datasets, techniques, procedures, tools, and so on.

An emphasis on performativity does not imply an evaluation, positive or negative, of the "effects" of the aspect of economics in question. The chapters that follow sometimes show economics "working" in the sense that the market participants involved see themselves as applying economics, view their uses of economics as having effects, and evaluate those effects as desirable. But unanimity on all these points may well be the exception, and the chapters also describe cases where such matters are the subject of sharp disagreement.

Multiple Performativities

The notion of "performativity" is, therefore, a complex one and needs to be unfolded in its many varieties. To speak at a high level of generality about the "effects" of economics on economies is a dangerous shortcut. Are these effects direct? Of what kind are they? Economics (both in the broad sense of the wide variety of specialties and technical forms of knowledge deployed in markets and also in the narrower sense of the academic discipline) can relate to and act upon its objects in many ways: by observing them, by measuring them, by predicting them, by providing theories to explain them or instruments to regulate them, by spreading some functional technique about them (or just some suggestive vocabulary to deal with them), by designing them in a laboratory, by inventing them, and so on. And, symmetrically, the "object" of economics (the many economic entities that are taken into account by economics) can react to this science in many ways: by mimicking it, by using it for profit, by believing it (and possibly by funding it!), by inadvertently operating it, but also by fighting it, by undermining its validity, and so on. Such interactions can change how resources are produced, organized, exchanged, and consumed, as illustrated by the Bolivian example.

When dealing with the performativity of economics, it is thus important to bear in mind the multiple ways in which economics may "perform." Plainly, markets can function perfectly well (and historically have done so) without drawing on economics in the academic sense; the technical and conceptual equipment of market participants is very varied. Furthermore, economics, even in just the academic sense, can have many forms. Economic theory is only one form among others, and it may cohabit with empirical knowledge and operational tools of many sorts. In some cases, the intervention of economics may translate into the intervention of economists themselves, as in the case of academic economists who are employed by or appointed as consultants to a particular firm, marketplace, government, or regulatory body. In other cases, economists may not circulate, but they may produce tools and instruments (such as pricing formulas or macroeconomic models) that market actors or policy makers can embrace and put to use. The influence of a particular economic doctrine or procedure can be understood as a matter of persuasion, beliefs, and states of mind. But it can also correspond to a matter of institutional and technological setting in which economics has no direct psychological impact. For example, traders—human beings and even capuchin monkeys (Chen et al. 2006)—may behave in a "neoclassi-cal" manner when put in the proper environment, without being schooled in or believers in neoclassical economics. Finally, economics can be put into practice—and its proposals enforced—through specific political decisions and policies (from regulatory bodies to audit agen-cies), but it can also spread through use and possibly enter into—more or less accidentally and spontaneously—processes of path dependence and irreversibility (Arthur 1994, David 1985).

To identify the varieties of performativity is difficult. The purpose of this book is not—and could not be—to propose a systematic typology. The performativity of economics is still under construction. The aim of this collection of essays is rather to put the notion of "the performativity of economics" to the test of bringing it to bear on various aspects of eco-nomic life and economic science. For that purpose, we brought together a series of contributions that discuss the problem of the performativity of economics from backgrounds ranging from the history and the philos-ophy of science to economic sociology and political science. The contrib-utors to this book are not all of one mind—some embrace the notion of performativity; others sharply oppose it—but all believe that the notion needs to be taken seriously.

Outline of Chapters

Chapter 2 is Marie-France Garcia-Parpet's study of the introduction of a computerized market for table strawberries at Fontaines-en-Sologne, a village around ten miles southeast of the river Loire in the Loir-et-Cher region of France. Apparently a modest case study of a development of only local significance, Garcia-Parpet's chapter (which is the first English translation of a 1986 article that was an important inspiration of Callon's work) raises an issue central to this book: how economic sociology and anthropology should analyze markets.

One traditional sociological and anthropological approach to markets involves investigating ways in which concrete, specific marketplaces such as that at Fontaines-en-Sologne differ from economists' "abstract" mod-els of markets. Such differences certainly existed prior to the introduction of the computerized strawberry market, and some differences persisted, but the new market was a reasonable approximation to economists' views to a "perfect market," with relatively homogeneous commodities, low bar-riers to entry, and competitive buyers and sellers all with fairly complete knowledge of the quantities and prices on offer.

Instead of invoking social factors to explain the remaining differences between the "ideal" market and the concrete marketplace, Garcia-Parpet focuses on how at Fontaines-en-Sologne the new marketplace was consciously shaped to approximate to the ideal. The process was not the "spontaneous appearance of a mechanism for liberating economic energies," writes Garcia-Parpet. It was a deliberate, planned creation, among the designers of which was an adviser well-versed in economics, and it was also a material artifact. The desire for a market in which supply and demand would find a competitive equilibrium was inscribed into the computerized auction system and even into the very architecture of the building constructed to house the market, which had separate rooms of buyer and sellers, both visible to the auctioneer but not to each other. However, Garcia-Parpet's study should not be interpreted either as an account of the discovery of the most efficient way to trade strawberries or as the permanent victory of a particular market model. In later fieldwork, summarized in a postscript written specially for this volume, she found further evolution of the strawberry market, one aspect of which was that the relationships between producers and shippers had become characterized by what she calls "a more solidarity-oriented attitude." As Callon notes in his chapter, the economists' "ideal market," the construction of which Garcia-Parpet had documented, seemed to be becoming more like the markets posited by economic sociology.

Garcia-Parpet's chapter is paradigmatic in its suggestion that economic sociology and anthropology should focus on how markets are constructed and maintained (and on the role of economic theory, material devices, procedures, physical architectures, linguistic codes, and so on, in the construction and functioning of markets), rather than focusing simply on demonstrating ways in which concrete marketplaces differ from economists' "abstract" markets. Chapters 3 and 4 take up this argument for financial models and financial markets, especially the markets for financial derivatives. A "derivative" is a contract or security whose value depends on the price of an underlying asset, or on the level of an index or interest or exchange rate. As recently as 1970, trading in financial derivatives was sparse, and to trade many modern derivatives would have been illegal. By June 2005, derivative contracts totaling $329 trillion were outstanding worldwide—a figure that corresponds to roughly $51,000 for every human being on earth.

In chapter 3, Donald MacKenzie focuses on the theory of options, which are derivatives contracts that give their holder the right, but not the obligation, to buy (or, in an alternative form of option, to sell) an underlying asset such as a block of stock at a set price on, or up to, a given future date. Option theory is high-status, Nobel Prize–winning economics, but it is more than that, argues MacKenzie: it is built into the infrastructure of options markets. It helped make those markets seem legitimate; it provided a guide to the pricing of options and to hedging the risk they entail; and it has become incorporated into the way market participants talk and think about options.

MacKenzie is specially interested in two subsets of the performativity of economics. The first he calls "Barnesian performativity" (the reference is to the sociologist of science Barry Barnes). In this, the use of economics—for example, in the form of material artifacts incorporating economic models—alters economic processes and/or their outcomes to make them more like their depiction by economics. In the other subset examined by MacKenzie ("counterperformativity"), the effect is opposite in direction: the use of economics undermines its claims to empirical accuracy. Both Barnesian performativity and counterperformativity are to be found in the history of option pricing, argues MacKenzie.

In chapter 4, Vincent-Antonin Lépinay discusses today's complex financial derivative products, which are in a sense the descendants of the options discussed by MacKenzie in chapter 3. Lépinay focuses on the "languages" or "codes" used to articulate the properties of these products. These products are hard to grasp, conceptually and materially, and this chapter describes the difficulties faced by actors trying to understand them in a stable and profitable manner. Sometimes, these products' properties are expressed using mathematics, especially—but not exclusively—the mathematics of partial differential equations such as the Black-Scholes equation discussed by MacKenzie. However, mathematics is not sufficient: the traders at the bank that was Lépinay's fieldwork site also need to express the properties of a derivative in terms of a set of existing, specific products that will hedge it, and this requires financial intuition and fine-grained market experience. Furthermore, a bank that sells derivatives needs to develop a software-implemented "pricer" for them (the calculations involved go beyond what can reasonably be done by hand), and this requires the translation of mathematics into detailed algorithms in specific computer languages. Finally, a derivative is also a legally binding contract with very specific economic features, and Lépinay describes the efforts to develop both an in-house language for expressing those features and an industrywide markup language to specify the properties of derivatives in a standard, easily portable way.

A conventional approach in the sociology of language would be to analyze the diversity of languages by identifying interest groups deploying their preferred linguistic codes: former physicists scornful of the overly formalistic approach of "quants" with backgrounds in pure mathematics; computer programmers impatient with the inability of those in mathematical finance to specify their models with sufficient exactitude that they can be translated into algorithms; and so on. However, while Lépinay's analysis hints at features of this kind, he seeks to go beyond it, defending a realist view of market languages against sociological reductionism. It is not the case that "anything goes" in the articulation of the properties of financial products: the languages of finance have to function effectively as "grips for action and levers of understanding." What we need, concludes Lépinay, is a "poetics of codes" that understands that the "technologies of language have their own qualities." No language is simply a mirror of what it sets out to articulate, but neither should languages be reduced to the social interests of those deploying them.

Chapters 5, 6, and 7 move to different areas of economics, focusing in particular on modern experimental economics and its uses in the design of markets. In chapter 5, Francesco Guala argues that experimental economics offers more than a way of checking whether economic theories are empirically correct. Alongside that "theory-testing" approach runs another strand of experimental economics that Guala calls the "institution-building" approach.

From a theory-testing viewpoint, performativity can seem to be a problem. A common worry about the validity of economic experiments is, for instance, that the experimental subjects playing in "laboratory" markets are often students of economics, who may be influenced by what they have learned about "correct" behavior. From an institution-building viewpoint, however, performativity is a resource. "Economic rationality," writes Guala, "is not like Newton's laws, which are supposed to be at work everywhere in the universe. It is a fragile property that must be carefully preserved by creating a hospitable environment." What the institution-building approach seeks to do is to design markets so that they constitute an environment precisely of that kind, one in which, in Guala's words, "rational choice models can work." This is not simply an academic enterprise. Market designs informed by economics are now of considerable commercial and public-policy importance, most famously in the auctions of the communications spectrum that in the late 1990s and early 2000s earned tens of billions of dollars for the governments of the United States, United Kingdom, and other countries from the mobile telephone industry.

However, the use of economics to inform market design does not constitute fully fledged performativity, argues Guala. It is akin to a phenomenon that philosophers and sociologists of science such as Nancy Cartwright, Ian Hacking, and Bruno Latour have argued is widespread in the natural sciences: the deliberate creation of a laboratory setup or other "niche" for which theory is an adequate empirical description. Genuine performativity occurs, Guala claims, only when economics directly affects individual behavior, instead of (or as well as) shaping that behavior by influencing the design of the environment in which it takes place. Although both forms of performativity are likely to play a role in market design, Guala argues that for various practical and theoretical reasons it may be difficult to disentangle them in concrete instances.

In chapter 6, Fabian Muniesa and Michel Callon note that any experimenter "performs" in the sense of bringing things into being "by assembling them in a particular manner (in a particular site, through particular trials, and for a particular audience)." What is observed in the experimental setting is indeed provoked or produced through it. Of special interest to Muniesa and Callon is a classic topic of the "Actor-Network Theory" tradition founded by Callon and his colleague Bruno Latour. That topic is the relationship between the paradigmatic experimental site—the laboratory—and what is "outside" it: in the case of science, nature "in the wild," or in the case of economic experiments, the "real economy."

Laboratories achieve their results—for example, "niches" within which theories work—by tightly controlling both material entities and human beings (in Actor-Network Theory, the term "actor" normally encompasses both). How then can laboratory results be translated from these niches to the outside? The classic Actor-Network Theory answer is: by transforming the world outside the laboratory so that it better resembles the laboratory (e.g., Latour 1983). In their chapter, Muniesa and Callon continue this sort of analysis by focusing on what they call "economic experiments" at large. This encompasses laboratory economics, but also other kinds of experiments, performed in real-scale markets as well as in laboratories. All instances of economic experiments can be characterized by features such as their localized setting, the manipulative techniques used to generate information, and the extent to which experiments provide public proof on which to base further action. But these features will evolve differently in an experimental auction performed in an academic classroom, in a consumer test performed by a consumerist association, and in an experimental economic measure implemented in a national economy.

In particular, Muniesa and Callon consider experimental sites in which the distinction between inside and outside is less strict than in the classic laboratory setting. Some of the economic experiments they discuss are performed in vivo: not in a laboratory but in real markets. Other cases—"platforms" is what Muniesa and Callon call them—are intermediate: more open than laboratories; more closed than in vivo experiments. They hint at an inherent trade-off between the manipulative thoroughness of these experimental settings and the kind of public proof they produce. A closed setting facilitates the "purification" and manipulation of experimental entities but creates problems in moving a result into the wild. An open setting weakens experimental control but facilitates processes of translation, as it blurs the divide between the inside and the outside of the experimental setting.

In chapter 7, Philip Mirowski and Edward Nik-Khah offer a skeptical analysis of an apparently prime case of the performativity of economics, the use of game theory and of experimental economics in the U.S. communications spectrum auctions, and they deploy this analysis to attack existing understandings of performativity. What previous analyses have missed above all, they argue, is the role played by key political and corporate actors: the Federal Communications Commission (which, as they note, had to decide what game theory "implied") and especially the large telecommunications companies. Orthodox modern "neoclassical" economics is so flawed, argue Mirowski and Nik-Khah, "that it cannot be made to 'work,'" other than very temporarily, even via the mechanisms of performativity. Overattention to performativity misses the way in which outcomes are shaped by big socioeconomic and political interests.

Indeed, Mirowski and Nik-Khah see the flaws that they diagnose in analyses of performativity as symptoms of a deeper fault in the intellectual tradition from which many of those analyses (especially Callon's) spring: Actor-Network Theory. That tradition rejects the explanation of scientific developments in terms of social factors, preferring to analyze those developments as the simultaneous construction of both "nature" and "society." Social structures are, however, more durable and more potent than this, argue Mirowski and Nik-Khah. Those who ignore their durability and their potency are naive.

Chapter 8, however, offers a defense of Callon and of a broadly Actor-Network perspective. In it, Petter Holm discusses an analysis of the relationship of "economics" to the "economy" that is often counterposed to Callon's: Daniel Miller's theory of "virtualism" (Carrier and Miller 1998), also discussed more briefly by Didier in chapter 10.[5] Like many of the contributors to this book, Miller believes that "economists and other agents of abstract models such as audit and consultancy" have "the increased ability . . . to transform the world into closer approximations of their theories and models." Unlike most of this book's contributors, however, Miller regards this transformation as in a sense superficial and "ideological" (hence his label: "virtualism"). "Actual disembedded markets" as posited by economists have not come into being, he argues. In Miller's view, the thesis of performativity as advanced by Callon mistakes the "culture of representation" in economics and other abstract modeling for "ordinary economic . . . practice." Instead, argues Miller, "we have . . . to radically separate out the market as a ritual and ideological system constructed by economists and the actual practice of economies" (Miller 2002, pp. 218, 224, 230).

Models are not abstractions, insists Holm; they are "constituent parts of market practices." The case he discusses is the construction of a market by the introduction of individual transferable quotas (ITQs) in fisheries. ITQs turn fisherpeople into "owners and investors," and fish, once "regarded as a common heritage of the coastal people" become in effect private property. It is a story that can be told along virtualist lines (Helgason and Pálsson 1998), but Holm draws instead on Actor-Network Theory, delving into how the foundations of ITQs were laid by the use of science and technology to transform a fish from an elusive wild creature into a "fish-as-fit-for-management . . . a true cyborg: part nature, part text, part computer, part symbol, part human, part political machine."

The focus of chapter 9, by Timothy Mitchell, is a different set of efforts at market construction, those inspired by the work of Hernando de Soto, founder of the Institute for Liberty and Democracy in Peru. De Soto offers a diagnosis of, and proposed solution to, the problem of underdevelopment that has been endorsed by leading economists, such as Ronald Coase and Milton Friedman, and that has influenced law and policy in many developing countries. Throughout the Third World, de Soto argues, most of the possessors of land and houses lack formal legal title to them, and so cannot sell them or use them as collateral for loans. If systems were set up to register and enforce rights of ownership, much wealth that is currently "outside" the market economy could be brought within it, greatly enhancing the prospects for economic development.

Mitchell points out the lack of evidence that de Soto's project has been or is likely to be successful, either in its original Peru or in Egypt (which is Mitchell's empirical focus). Assets are held without formal property relations for good reasons, such as a desire to avoid the threat of dispossession. Experience of previous efforts in Egypt to extend formal property arrangements suggests that such extension will probably promote speculation in property and in land, rather than productive investment, and thus is likely to benefit privileged members of this generation at the expense of the poor of this and future generations.

Mitchell argues that behind the blindness of de Soto and those influenced by him to the likely drawbacks of the extension of formal property arrangements lies a set of errors. One is a worldview in which a clear boundary between markets and what lies outside them is assumed. Markets do not have boundaries, suggests Mitchell; at most, they have contested frontier regions, which are always disputed, morally and politically as well as "economically." Another error is to see projects such as de Soto's as ways of representing, in the form of property, wealth that lacks adequate representation. "What economics does," argues Mitchell, "is not to represent what was previously unrepresented, but to try and reorganize the circulation and control of representations." De Soto misrepresents the nonmarket world as deficient, Mitchell concludes, but he also warns de Soto's critics not to stop at exposing this misrepresentation: misleading as de Soto's ideas might be, they are part of a potentially powerful apparatus for redistributing access to, and control over, assets.

In chapter 10, Emmanuel Didier takes up the topic of economic statistics, a prime intermediary between "economics" and the "economy," drawing on his historical research on the agricultural statistics produced in the United States in the early twentieth century. Didier shows that those statistics were designed to have an effect on the economy: by generating and circulating "objective" data on production and market prices, the statistical division of the U.S. Department of Agriculture hoped to protect farmers from the deliberately false reports disseminated by speculators.

Didier argues, however, that to have effects on the world (as statistics did and does) is not the same as to be performative. He argues that some proponents of the notion of performativity (notably MacKenzie and Millo 2003) seem to be asserting that facts are created "out of thin air" by a direct effect of theory: by an Austinian, linguistic, performative act, akin to the priest's utterance "I baptize you." This is quite implausible, suggests Didier. The notion of performativity is an unsatisfactory stopgap.

Instead of performativity, Didier prefers—at least in the context of economic statistics—the notion of "expressing," which he draws from the work of Deleuze (1968). "Expressing" is not to be read as "representing" or "portraying": the sense in which it is used by Deleuze and by Didier is more that of "pressing out." Pressing out is a material process: Didier nicely illustrates the material aspects of the production of statistics. However, what is pressed out is not what was there all along. As Didier puts it: "Expressing takes place when various elements (at least two) are gathered in a particular way, and this particular relation evidences a new feature of the whole composed by that coming together." He suggests the analogy of the encounter with soil of a particular kind permitting the making of wine in which characteristics potentially present in vinestocks are expressed. Didier believes that the subtle notion of expressing captures well the way in which economic statistics alters the entities enumerated and affects the economy, without being a simple creation "out of nothing."

In chapter 11, Michel Callon, whose edited collection *The Laws of the Markets* (Callon 1998a) initiated the current discussion of the performativity of economics, reflects on the notion, on the debates around it, the alternatives to it, and on the contributions made by the previous chapters. He locates performativity within the broad tradition of pragmatism. Instead of regarding statements as true or false, pragmatism conceptualizes them as successful or failed. Actor-Network Theory adds to the pragmatist tradition a distinctive focus on the *agencements* that generate success and failure. (*Agencements* are the assemblages or arrangements—which are simultaneously human and nonhuman, social and technical, textual and material—from which action springs.)

The study of innovation in science and technology indicates what to expect with respect to the performative role of economics, suggests Callon. Many elements have to be added to laboratory science to make it successful "at large" or "in the wild," and much needs added to "confined economics" (the economics of the laboratory for experimental economics, the seminar room, the academic journal, and the textbook) for it to perform economies. The heterogeneous elements, struggles, and rivalries found in the chapters by Holm (elements from biology and engineering) or by Mirowski and Nik-Khah (politics and struggles for industrial dominance) are just as anticipated, as is MacKenzie's counterperformativity.

Callon argues for going beyond an Austinian emphasis on "doing things with words," and in his chapter he often prefers the term "performation" to "performativity." The latter can too easily be read in Austinian fashion as a property of statements, and Callon's chapter suggests that that is too a narrow a view, even when "statements" are understood broadly as including formulas, methods, tools, and instruments as well as verbal formulations. "Performation," in contrast, is an action: it is performativity as an activity or a material operation. This activity is collective (that is, heterogeneous and multifaceted): economics in the academic sense is at most only one of the elements at play. The norm is not the smooth performance of economics but conflicts, upsets, crises, and competition between different "programs," including programs seeking to perform a human being different from *Homo economicus*, the calculative egoist often posited by economics. Performativity is therefore best thought of, Callon suggests, as "co-performation": that formulation highlights both this collective aspect and the fact that performativity is an activity, not just a property of statements.

Attention to performativity as co-performation (in this sense) leads Callon to consideration of economic experiments, understood in a broad way that includes, for example, experiments in cooperative production such as that at Mondragón. The choice posited by Marx between interpreting the world and changing it need not constrain us, concludes Callon: the task of the analyst is, in alliance with economic actors, to multiply possible worlds.

That, it seems to us, is entirely the correct conclusion. Consider, for example, the emerging markets for carbon dioxide emissions permits. The proposals for markets in pollution permits emerged from economics, but economists have not been unanimous in advocating them as the best means of slowing global warming—there has, for example, been persuasive advocacy of carbon taxes—and many factors beyond academic economics are involved in the shape the new markets are taking.

These factors range from the exigencies of metrology (there are complex problems to be solved in producing credible baselines against which to measure reductions or increases in emissions, and in measuring the extent of emissions and of carbon sequestration by forests, etc.) to international and domestic politics, industry lobbying, and much else. Whether a world market in carbon will emerge is still unclear, and if it does, its ecological and other consequences will depend on its design: outcomes could range from powerful incentives to reduce emissions to a fig leaf allowing "business as usual." Nothing is settled, and there is much need for intervention of the kind Callon advocates.

To expect that Callon's reformulation of the notion of the "performativity of economics" will settle controversy about it would be quite unrealistic (indeed, in their chapter Mirowski and Nik-Khah already signal their dissent). Nor would we wish for such an outcome, for we see this volume not as ending a debate but as encouraging it. Empirical work on the performativity of economics is in many ways still sparse, as is indicated, for example, by the absence of any work so far on carbon markets informed by the notion, with the exception of Lohmann (2005). Such empirical work must surely go hand in hand with further theoretical development. We do not pretend to know where this will lead, but of two things we are sure: that economics (in the academic sense as well as in the wider senses indicated by Callon) is built into the societies of high modernity, and that analysis of this is still in its infancy.

Notes

1. See, e.g., James (1907/1975); Morris (1971); Searle (1969).
2. Sociologists, economists, and historians of economics have started to elucidate the reflexive nature of economic knowledge (Steiner 2001), to scrutinize the interaction between economic models and policy making (Evans 1999; Morgan and Den Butter 2000), to analyze the connection between economics and computing (Mirowski 2002), to explore the "mediating" capabilities of models (Boumans 2005; Morgan and Morrison 1999), and to study how economic and statistical knowledge can turn into a technology of governance (Desrosières 1998; Miller 2001; Power 1996). Economists themselves (including prominent authors such as John Maynard Keynes, William Baumol, Alan Blinder, Robert C. Merton, and William Sharpe) have also sketched various ways in which economics can be considered an integral part of the economy; see, e.g., Blinder (2000); Faulhaber and Baumol (1988); Keynes (1936/1964, pp. 383–384); Merton and Bodie (2005); Sharpe (1990). A recent essay tried to systematize the idea (Ferraro et al. 2005).
3. There is a sense in which the idea that "ought" to have inspired index funds was the Capital Asset Pricing Model (which postulates that the optimal portfolio

of risky assets is the market as a whole), but in practice it was simpler efficient-market intuitions that were the inspiration. See Bernstein (1992) and MacKenzie (2006).

4. For example, an apparent anomaly might be a statistical artifact, or (since testing for excess risk-adjusted returns requires an asset-pricing model), it could be that a "failed" test indicates a deficiency in the asset-pricing model rather than the presence of a market inefficiency.

5. Readers interested in how Miller might respond to criticisms such as Holm's should turn to his reflections on his debate with Callon (Miller 2005).

References

Arthur, W. B. 1994. *Increasing Returns and Path Dependence in the Economy*. Ann Arbor: University of Michigan Press.

Austin, J. L. 1962. *How to Do Things with Words*. Oxford: Clarendon.

Barnes, B. 1983. "Social Life as Bootstrapped Induction." *Sociology* 17: 524–545.

Beck, U., A. Giddens, and S. Lash. 1994. *Reflexive Modernization: Politics, Tradition and Aesthetics in the Modern Social Order*. Cambridge: Polity.

Bernstein, P. L. 1992. *Capital Ideas: The Improbable Origins of Modern Wall Street*. New York: Free Press.

Blinder, A. S. 2000. "How the Economy Came to Resemble the Model." *Business Economics* 135:16–25.

Blyth, M. 2002. *Great Transformations: Economic Ideas and Institutional Change in the Twentieth Century*. Cambridge: Cambridge University Press.

Boumans, M. 2005. *How Economists Model the World into Numbers*. London: Routledge.

Bourdieu, P. 1991. *Language and Symbolic Power*. Cambridge: Polity.

Butler, J. 1990. *Gender Trouble: Feminism and the Subversion of Identity*. New York: Routledge, Chapman & Hall.

Butler, J. 1997. *Excitable Speech: A Politics of the Performative*. London: Routledge.

Callon, M., Ed. 1998a. *The Laws of the Markets*. Oxford: Blackwell.

Callon, M. 1998b. "Introduction: The Embeddedness of Economic Markets in Economics." Pp. 1–57 in *The Laws of the Markets*, edited by M. Callon. Oxford: Blackwell.

Carrier, J. G., and D. Miller, Eds. 1998. *Virtualism: A New Political Economy*. Oxford: Berg.

Chen, M. K., V. Lakshminarayanan, and L. R. Santos. 2006. "How Basic Are Behavioral Biases? Evidence from Capuchin Monkey Trading Behavior." *Journal of Political Economy* 114:517–537.

David, P. A. 1985. "Clio and the Economics of QWERTY." *American Economic Review* 75:332–337.

Deleuze, G. 1968. *Spinoza et le problème de l'expression*. Paris: Minuit.

Desrosières, A. 1998. *The Politics of Large Numbers: A History of Statistical Reasoning*. Cambridge MA: Harvard University Press.

Evans, R. J. 1999. *Macroeconomic Models: A Sociological Appraisal*. London: Routledge.

Fama, E. F. 1970. "Efficient Capital Markets: A Review of Theory and Empirical Work." *Journal of Finance* 25:383–417.

Faulhaber, G. L., and W. J. Baumol (1988). "Economists as Innovators: Practical Products of Theoretical Research." *Journal of Economic Literature* 26:577–600.

Ferraro, F., J. Pfeffer, and R. I. Sutton. 2005. "Economics Language and Assumptions: How Theories Can Become Self-Fulfilling." *Academy of Management Review* 30:8–24.

Fine, B. 2003. "Callonistics: A Disentanglement." *Economy and Society* 32: 478–484.

Goffman, E. 1959. *The Presentation of Self in Everyday Life*. New York: Doubleday.

Hacking, I. 1983. *Representing and Intervening: Introductory Topics in the Philosophy of Natural Science*. Cambridge: Cambridge University Press.

Helgason, A., and G. Pálsson (1998). "Cash for Quotas: Disputes over the Legitimacy of an Economic Model of Fishing in Iceland." Pp. 117–134 in *Virtualism: A New Political Economy*, edited by J. G. Carrier and D. Miller. Oxford: Berg.

James, W. 1907/1975. *Pragmatism*. Cambridge, MA: Harvard University Press.

Jensen, M. C. 1978. "Some Anomalous Evidence Regarding Market Efficiency." *Journal of Financial Economics* 6:95–101.

Keynes, J. M. 1936/1964. *The General Theory of Employment, Interest and Money*. New York: Harcourt, Brace.

Latour, B. 1983. "Give Me a Laboratory and I Will Raise the World." Pp. 141–170 in *Science Observed: New Perspectives on the Social Studies of Science*, edited by K. D. Knorr-Cetina and M. Mulkay. London: Sage.

Lohmann, L. 2005. "Marketing and Making Carbon Dumps: Commodification, Calculation and Counterfactuals in Climate Change Mitigation." *Science as Culture* 14:203–235.

MacKenzie, D. 2003. "An Equation and Its Worlds: Bricolage, Exemplars, Disunity and Performativity in Financial Economics." *Social Studies of Science* 33:831–868.

MacKenzie, D. 2006. *An Engine, Not a Camera: How Financial Models Shape Markets*. Cambridge, MA: MIT Press.

MacKenzie, D., and Y. Millo. 2003. "Constructing a Market, Performing Theory: The Historical Sociology of a Financial Derivatives Exchange." *American Journal of Sociology* 109:107–145.

Merton, R. C., and Z. Bodie. 2005. "Design of Financial Systems: Towards a Synthesis of Function and Structure." *Journal of Investment Management* 3:1–23.

Merton, R. K. 1949. *Social Theory and Social Structure*. New York: Free Press.

Miller, D. 2002. "Turning Callon the Right Way Up." *Economy and Society* 31:218–233.

Miller, D. 2005. "Reply to Michel Callon." *Economic Sociology: European Electronic Newsletter* 6/3:3–13. Available at http://econsoc.mpifg.de/archive/esjuly05.pdf, accessed June 19, 2006.

Miller, P. 2001. "Governing by Numbers: Why Calculative Practices Matter."
    Social Research 68:379–396.
Mirowski, P. 2002. *Machine Dreams: Economics Becomes a Cyborg Science*.
    Cambridge: Cambridge University Press.
Morgan, M. S., and F. Den Butter, Eds. 2000. *Empirical Models and Policy Mak-
    ing: Interaction and Institutions*. London: Routledge.
Morgan, M. S., and M. Morrison, Eds. 1999. *Models as Mediators: Perspectives
    on Natural and Social Science*. Cambridge: Cambridge University Press.
Morris, C. W. 1971. *Writings on the General Theory of Signs*. The Hague:
    Mouton.
Pickering, A. 1995. *The Mangle of Practice: Time, Agency and Science*. Chicago:
    University of Chicago Press.
Power, M., Ed. 1996. *Accounting and Science: Natural Inquiry and Commercial
    Reason*. Cambridge: Cambridge University Press.
Sachs, J. D. 2005. *The End of Poverty*. London: Penguin.
Schwert, G. W. 2002. "Anomalies and Market Efficiency." Cambridge, MA:
    National Bureau of Economic Research, Working Paper 9277.
Searle, J. 1969. *Speech Acts: An Essay in the Philosophy of Language*. Cam-
    bridge: Cambridge University Press.
Sharpe, W. F. 1990. Capital Asset Prices with and without Negative Holdings.
    Nobel Prize Lecture, December 7.
Steiner, P. 2001 "The Sociology of Economic Knowledge." *European Journal of
    Social Theory* 4:443–458.
Valdés, J. G. 1995. *Pinochet's Economists: The Chicago School in Chile*. Cam-
    bridge: Cambridge University Press.
Weber, M. 1930. *The Protestant Ethic and the Spirit of Capitalism*. London:
    Unwin.

Chapter 2 _____

The Social Construction of a Perfect Market

THE STRAWBERRY AUCTION AT FONTAINES-EN-SOLOGNE

MARIE-FRANCE GARCIA-PARPET

In 1981 a marketplace for table strawberries trading was created at
Fontaines-en-Sologne—a market which now (1986)[1] attracts a large part
of the strawberries that are grown in the region of Sologne and Grande
Sologne in France. The strawberry exchange attracts strawberry growers, but also wholesalers and shippers from the region. These funnel the
strawberries to Rungis (the central agricultural wholesale marketplace
near Paris), to major purchasing centers, and to foreign markets.

The marketplace is characterized by the way in which it makes use of
up-to-date technology—transactions are performed through an electronic
scoreboard, and take the form of a descending-price or "Dutch" auction
(*marché au cadran* in French), in which the auctioneer starts with a high
price and then gradually lowers it until the goods in question are sold. Information about the goods on offer and about the bids made for them is
immediately available to everyone involved, without direct bargaining or
interaction between buyers and sellers. The creation of an exchange of
such a kind precisely in what the Mansholt Report[2] referred to as the
"lungs" of Paris is interesting in its own right. But another reason makes
this market interesting sociologically: our data suggest, that this market
is, in some sense, a concrete realization of the pure model of perfect competition, a model that occupies pride of place in economic theory.[3] The
model of perfect competition remains an ideal, something to be achieved,
rather than a reality. Nevertheless, the concept of pure competition is
widely used for its broad explanatory power (e.g., Ferguson and Gould
1975; Samuelson and Nordhaus 1973). In this model the "social" always
appears as a residual variable, an obstacle to the aim of bringing pure
competition into being.

In this chapter, I assume that the auction market constructed at
Fontaines-en-Sologne, the *marché au cadran*, may be treated as a practical realization of the model of pure competition, and I will consider
whether "social factors" should indeed treated as residual variables
which can be used, after the event, to account for the differences between the observable facts and those predicted by the model, or whether

they are better seen as intervening all across the practical process of making up this, the purest of "economic" markets. In short, I will try to determine the social conditions for the creation and operation of this market.

The Day-to-Day Operation of the Market at Fontaines-en-Sologne

Fontaines-en-Sologne's strawberry auction venue is in the middle of the countryside, not far from a main road. It consists of a building with two parts. On the one hand there is a hall, where the growers (i.e., the sellers) display their strawberries, appropriately wrapped and labeled. On the other, there is a salesroom where the auction is carried out.

The salesroom is divided in turn into three parts. First there is a cabin, with a computer, a telex, and a microphone. This is where the "auctioneer" conducts the auction.[4] Second, on the outside wall of the cabin, there is an electronic board which displays information about the "lots" that are to be sold. This identifies which one is being auctioned, together with its current price. It also displays the prices at which previous lots were sold, together with the identification of the buyer. Third, opposite to the cabin there are two separate rooms, one for the buyers and one for the sellers. The sellers' room has benches and rectangular tables, scales, a blackboard with various messages, and a range of specialist publications with daily strawberry price quotations in different national and international markets. The buyers' room, which is above that of the sellers, has a series of raised steps which allow a good view of the electronic scoreboard. Each buyer has a desk with an electronic switch which can be used to stop the bidding, and so to signify a willingness to buy the lot in question at the current price. Both the buyers and the sellers have a perfect view of the auctioneer's cabin and the electronic board, where the bids are made. On the other hand, buyers and sellers cannot see one another.

At about half past twelve in the afternoon during the strawberry season, the producers or members of their families bring their produce to the market. The strawberries are in baskets of 500 grams, laid out in trays which are stacked up. These stacks vary in height, depending on the quantity of strawberries and the number of lots that the producer has on offer. Each crate carries a label which indicates the variety of strawberry, its quality measured in terms of criteria laid down by one of the region's regulatory bodies, the Comité Economique du Val de Loire (economic committee of the Val de Loire), and a mark to indicate its origin. The sellers then go to the auctioneer's cabin and give him a slip of paper with the exact description of the products laid out in the hall (the

Figure 2.1 The auction warehouse at Fontaines-en-Sologne

Figure 2.2 The auctioneer's cabin

Figure 2.3 The buyers' room

number of lots, their type, and their weight). The auctioneer enters these data into the computer and creates a catalogue which is distributed to the buyers who arrive at about one o'clock and start to walk round the hall inspecting the produce. After half an hour the auctioneer announces the opening of business by sounding a bell, and everyone takes his or her place for the sale. The auctioneer starts by announcing the category of strawberries to be sold, and enters instructions about the maximum and

Figure 2.4 The sellers' room

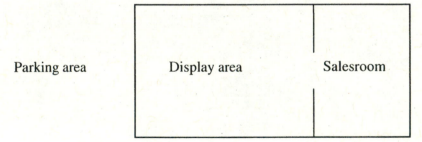

Figure 2.5 Upper view of the auction venue

minimum prices into the computer.[5] As noted, the actual sale of each lot
follows a descending auction procedure: it starts at the highest price, and
the computer is programmed to reduce the price per kilo progressively
until a buyer is found. The producer or seller of the lot indicates by hand
whether he or she accepts or rejects sale at the given price. If he or she
does not agree with the price displayed on the electronic board, the lot is
offered for sale again at the end of the auction. If he or she still thinks
that the price is not satisfactory, then the market, in the person of its

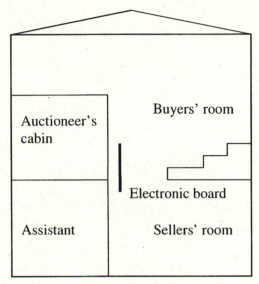

Figure 2.6 Vertical cross section of the auction venue

president, may refuse permission for it to be offered for sale a third time. Each lot is sold in turn in this way. The transactions are completed without words, apart from the announcements made by the auctioneer.

Once the buying and selling is completed, buyers and sellers leave the salesroom and there is general discussion and conversation. Producers tend to complain when the prices seem to them to be too low. Usually the buyers do not respond to such complaints, though sometimes they justify themselves by arguing that there are a few outlets willing to take strawberries at higher prices, or by claiming the fruit on offer is of poor quality. Finally the producers depart, and the buyers are left loading their purchases onto their lorries.

A Perfect Market?

The model of perfect competition defined by economists assumes the operation of four conditions:[6]

    1. Each economic agent acts as if prices were given. In other words, none of the buyers or sellers should be strong enough to be able to exercise a noticeable influence over prices. This is called the condition of atomicity.

2. The product is homogeneous. This means that it should have the same significance for all concerned, and that it should be identifiable without considering its seller.

3. The market is fluid. This means that exchange counterparties are free to enter or to exit the market.

4. The market is transparent. In other words, economic agents should have perfect knowledge of the quantity, quality, and price of the products on offer.

To what extent are these conditions fulfilled by the strawberry market described above? Each day, the market brings about thirty-five producers and ten buyers together. Clearly the numbers involved are not large enough to guarantee atomicity of supply and demand. There are so few participants that some have more power than others, and individuals are able to influence the level of prices. Nevertheless, the practice of breaking the auction up into lots does fragment supply and demand and makes it possible for producers to avoid letting a single low price affect the price for the whole of their production that day. In addition, it puts the buyers into competition with one another as often as there are numbers of lots on offer. In this way, then, the sale of a lot represents a relatively small part of supply and demand, and the parties to the exchange have little power to determine overall prices.[7]

The product exchanged in the market seems to satisfy the second condition, that of homogeneity. Table strawberries correspond to a single and established social use. The criteria of freshness, appearance, and quality that they need to meet are more defined than those required by food-processing industries. In addition, these criteria are independent of the identity of the producers, and they take the form of a label of origin, variety, and quality that is recognized by the Comité Economique du Val de Loire.

With respect to fluidity, as noted earlier, if the price proposed by the buyer is felt to be inadequate by the producer, the producer may refuse to sell and offer the lot again at the end of the day's market for a second, or even a third, time. If the strawberries are withdrawn at the end of the day, the producer or administrator of the market may store them in a cold room until the following day in the hope of a favorable movement in prices. Such changes result from seasonal and weekly variations in the market, and they are revealed in the statistics calculated by market administrators and in the weekly publications about strawberries issued by the Association Française des Coopératives de Fruits et Légumes (French Association of Fruits and Vegetables Cooperatives). But producers can also reprocess strawberries in order to sell them to the food industry[8] or simply stop the sale by ceasing to gather them—a solution which, though apparently irrational, in fact makes sense according to producers because picking them accounts for one-third of the cost of production, and losses may occur if the price is too low. Thus when prices fall, producers may phone home and order that the gathering of strawberries should stop forthwith. This is possible because the great majority of the workforce is hired by the day. On the demand side, the same freedom to enter and leave the market is also encountered. Buyers are not obliged to purchase, and the decision to acquire a particular lot is independent of the acquisition of other lots. In addition, buyers often come to the market in the family car and telephone home for a small van or a lorry (depending on the quantity bought) if necessary. They do this even though they know roughly how many strawberries will be on offer before they set out in the morning.[9]

Finally, the unity of time and place of the transactions ensures that the market is transparent. The display of strawberries in the hall and the catalogue makes it possible to have precise knowledge of the quantity and quality that are on offer. As the auction progresses the state of demand becomes public knowledge: the buyers and the sellers know about all the transactions that are agreed, together with their prices and the quantities involved.

Here, then, we find that the four conditions for a perfect market are fulfilled. Thus we can consider the market of Fontaines-en-Sologne a kind of concrete realization of the economic model of perfect competition. However, if we look a little more closely, we see that not all of these conditions are strictly fulfilled.

Though there are many producers and lots at the height of the season, with both substantial daily production and competition between buyers, at the end of the season production declines, often only a few sellers appear at the market, and overall daily production is only a few tonnes. Under such circumstances there are only a few buyers, and those that are most active dominate the market. I saw evidence of this when, on one occasion, the time for the auction was shifted from one o'clock to five o'clock because this suited one of the buyers who was taking about half the daily production at the end of the season.

We have seen how growers may withdraw their product from the market when they consider that the prices being offered do not cover their production costs. Under such circumstances the various stratagems of the growers (no picking, storing fruit in the cold room, converting it for industrial jam-making) which may be practiced on a large scale can have a momentary stimulating effect on the level of prices so long as there is also a corresponding demand. In fact, these techniques are not necessarily an admission of defeat, but rather a way of minimizing losses.

Such differences between the abstract model of the market and its concrete realization are familiar to economists and should not be

treated as undermining the efficacy of the model. Even in the view of
those who defend it, the model of perfect competition is not fully realistic. But this does not mean that the model cannot be used to provide
plausible explanations or accurate predictions about phenomena in the
real world.

However, it is not such differences between theory and reality that I
wish to explain sociologically. These can, after all, be explained by distinguishing between the market as a principle (determination of price by
supply and demand) and its concrete realization in a specific marketplace (Polanyi 1957). My interest lies, rather, in the existence of "social
factors" that are involved in the creation of a marketplace with the characteristics described in the model of perfect competition. Accordingly, I
will analyze the social conditions for the construction and operation of
this market: What capital was needed, in particular, for the purchase of
the computer and the building? What agents contributed to the creation
of this market in practice, and in terms of its rules of operation? What
are the economic and social characteristics of its users, the buyers and
sellers? What is the character of the commercial network brought into
being in this way? To what extent does its existence reflect continuity
with the networks that previously existed, and to what extent does its
represent a break with the past?

The Networks of Commercialization before 1979

Though strawberries have been grown for personal consumption in
Sologne for a long time, it was not until the 1920s and the 1930s that
the first commercial strawberry fields were planted. According to Lucien
Perroux, it was "the shippers, local cooperatives, and vendors from Les
Halles of Paris [the central wholesale marketplace], who moved to
Sologne between 1900 and 1930, who stimulated production. This followed the growth of the commercial production of asparagus in
Sologne. The cultivation of strawberries allowed them to increase the
volume of produce they were handling, and so to make better use of
commercial networks. Accordingly, the shippers encouraged their asparagus growers to experiment with strawberries" (Perroux 1967).

In some communes of the region (especially Fontaines-en-Sologne)
strawberries are widely cultivated. They are grown in open fields, are
often intended for industry, and the methods that are used in their production have hardly evolved since the early 1960s. In such cases they represent only a supplementary source of income for the grower. However,
for a relatively small number of producers, strawberry cultivation represents an important, if not the most important, source of income. These

growers concentrate on table strawberries, which sell at a relatively high price, and use modern techniques—plastic greenhouses, plastic sheets laid on the ground to keep the fruit clean, the use of selected plants and their rapid replacement to increase productivity and maintain quality, and a four- or five-year rotation.

Strawberries are also grown in other areas of France. Thus in the southwest and in the Rhône-Alpes region, strawberries were being produced in the 1970s using methods that were modern and well adapted to the demands of consumers. By contrast, the strawberries of Loir-et-Cher, which were highly thought of at Les Halles in the 1950s, were no longer considered to be of especially good quality in national and international markets by the beginning of the 1970s.

In 1980, some 75 percent of the production of table strawberries was sold by producers directly to brokers, shippers, or agents.[10] Brokers, small local merchants working for a commission, channeled production to the main wholesale market at Rungis, but they also practiced production themselves, collected vegetables, or ran a cafe or a grocery shop. Shippers were larger scale local merchants who worked partly on behalf of dealers at Rungis but mostly on their own account. Agents were merchants based in Rungis.

Before the auction market was launched, brokers and shippers collected the produce themselves, whereas for agents it was sent to Rungis by the producers. But from a sociological point of view the transactions involved were similar. At the time of striking the bargain, the grower did not know the price at which his produce would sell in Rungis, and he would only learn about this a week or two later. Payment would be yet further delayed—according to the growers for several months. In return, the wholesalers often made advance payments to the growers and bought not only the strawberries, but all the other produce grown. The producers had confidence that the wholesaler would take everything that he grew. Cooperatives were responsible for about 25 percent of the table strawberries grown. Though they remained an important commercial network until the 1960s, they are now in a phase of marked decline.[11] Their commercial policies do not allow them to compete with brokers and shippers, and they are sometimes dependent on the latter for access to certain markets, particularly international markets.

Though it is not a commercial network in the full sense, the local strawberry growers' union should also be mentioned: the Syndicat des Producteurs de Fraises du Loir-et-Cher. It was created in 1973 on the initiative of a councilor in the Chambre d'Agriculture, the local representative body of agricultural professionals. The union did not offer many direct commercial services to its members (apart from group-buying facilities). But it served as a venue for conflict resolution between shippers and producers and facilitated the use of a "brand" image for the strawberries grown in the region.

The technical staff and members of the Chambre d'Agriculture linked to this project were interested in stimulating production and enabling growers to match the quality and appearance of the strawberries grown in the major producing areas in France. To achieve this, certain producers and technical staff launched a communication campaign and edited brochures describing the "13 commandments" for good strawberry growing. These were intended to reduce the number of varieties grown, to stop the practice of mixing different varieties in the same tray, and to impose some uniformity on methods of packing. In 1976 this effort was rewarded. A label of quality for "Strawberries from Sologne" was introduced by the Loir-et-Cher section of the Syndicat des Producteurs de Fraises (the national union of strawberry growers) with the approval of the national committee. This translated into economic advantages for growers (they received a subsidy equal to 5 percent of the selling price if their produce met the label's quality criteria) as well as symbolic advantages: it put the strawberries, now labeled "Strawberries from Sologne," on an equal footing with those from other regions of quality production such as the southwest, Rhône-Alpes, and Lorraine.

The Syndicat des Producteurs also tended to help in building links between growers from different areas on the basis of their common interests. This was to prove crucial for the establishment of the auction marketplace, and it lies at the root of the "homogeneity" of the produce bought and sold in the market at Fontaines-en-Sologne. As we have seen, the latter is one of the conditions assumed in the model of perfect competition. Homogeneity is not a characteristic that exists in and of itself. Rather, it is the end product of an effort to organize and stimulate production. The latter depended, in this case, on subsidies, together with sanctions for poor production. Thus a councilor involved in the process said "we went to war for the 'Strawberries from Sologne' label."

To summarize, this was the commercial context in which the auction market at Fontaines-en-Sologne was created: transactions which followed the lines of personal links with brokers, shippers, and agents; and cooperatives which were poorly adapted commercial networks for growers in the areas that they covered. The producers had been dissatisfied with the commercial networks of the region for a long time, and some of them nursed the hope of being able to create a "little Rungis at Fontaines-en-Sologne" one day—a primitive model for the market that was actually created in 1981. We will now consider the factors that contributed to the developing discontent with the traditional commercial networks, factors that were to lead to their rapid destruction.

LA MARQUE DE QUALITE "FRAISE DE SOLOGNE"

Pour mieux rentabiliser les fraises de qualité, une marque de qualité « Fraise de Sologne » a été créée par le Comité Interprofessionnel de la Fraise du Loir-et-Cher, récemment constitué.

Cette marque, utilisée dès la campagne 1973, permettra de rendre plus homogènes les lots de fraises du Loir-et-Cher, d'entreprendre des actions de publicité. Elle facilitera le choix des acheteurs recherchant la qualité.

Un macaron normalisé appliqué sur les plateaux par le producteur, permettra de distinguer ces lots.

Caractéristiques des lots vendus avec la marque de qualité :

— provenir de cultures paillées (paille ou plastique),

— variétés : GORELLA, RED GAUNTLET, BELRUBI,

— stade de récolte : 2 jours avant maturité optimum,

— catégorie EXTRA (étiquette rouge) et 1 (étiquette verte),

— emploi d'emballages neufs :

- barquettes : le bois est conseillé ; les autres sont tolérés pour 1973,
contenance : 250 et 500 g uniquement.

- plateaux : préférer le format 57 x 34, mais le 50 x 30 est accepté. Hauteur : 8-12 cm.

Les personnes qui voudront utiliser cette marque devront respecter les conditions ci-dessus et accepter les visites effectuées par le Comité Interprofessionnel, avec le concours des techniciens du C.T.I.F.L.

Document diffusé
par la Chambre d'agriculture de Loir-et-Cher

LES 13 COMMANDEMENTS DU PRODUCTEUR DESIREUX D'OBTENIR DES FRAISES DE QUALITE

*

1 - Choisir un sol sain, frais ou irrigable, pas trop calcaire.

2 - Choisir 2 ou 3 variétés ayant fait leurs preuves dans la région : actuellement GORELLA et RED GAUNTLET.

3 - S'approvisionner en plants sains et sélectionnés chez un pépiniériste agréé.

4 - Prévoir des durées de plantation inférieures à 3 ans.

5 - Maintenir la culture propre.

6 - Protéger la culture des parasites par des traitements appropriés.

7 - Pailler le sol obligatoirement avec du film plastique ou de la paille.

8 - Alimenter la plante en eau et en engrais.

9 - Récolter à un stade de maturité permettant le transport et la commercialisation dans de bonnes conditions.

10 - Former, encadrer, intéresser le personnel à récolter des fruits de qualité.

11 - Prévoir un tri conforme aux normes et surtout sans fardage.

12 - Dès la récolte, entreposer les lots dans un local frais ou si possible réfrigéré.

13 - Utiliser des emballages de qualité suffisante.

Figure 2.7 The "Strawberry from Sologne" quality label

The Social Characteristics of the Promoters of the Auction Market

The creation of the computer-assisted descending-auction market seems to have been the result of a meeting between an economic adviser to the Chambre d'Agriculture and a number of local producers who shared an interest in promoting this new method of buying and selling.[12]

In 1979, a young economic adviser was appointed to Loir-et-Cher with the task of reorganizing the production of fruits and vegetables in the Sologne and the Val de Loire. This adviser had more educational capital than other members of the Chambre d'Agriculture including the director. He had studied at the Ecole Supérieure d'Agronomie at Nancy and had two degrees, in biology and in law. It was doubtless as a result of his training in economics, which he had received as a law student, that he was familiar with the neoclassical theory that was to guide his actions. Thus it was his view that policies bringing growers together were justified "in order to get competitive mechanisms working again."

The economic organizations concerned with the commercialization of fruit and vegetables did not differ greatly from those concerned specifically with strawberries. There was a regional section of the FNSEA (National Federation of Agricultural Unions) for fruit and vegetables, though this had only a nominal existence. Cooperatives were in a precarious position. The adviser first tried to call for a reorganization of the

Figure 2.8 "Quality strawberries say where they come from" (advertisement)

whole of the fruit and vegetable market through the regional section of the FNSEA for fruit and vegetables and through the cooperatives. This was unsuccessful. He explained this and the lack of welcome it received by invoking the inertia and the conservatism of the administrative councils and members. By contrast, a small number of growers (six in all, of whom five were from Fontaines-en-Sologne) found his proposal appealing and showed some interest in organizing a centralized auction market.

The growers who were involved in the creation of Fontaines-en-Sologne's auction venue were among the largest producers in the region. They cultivated areas of between 30 and 80 hectares each, whereas overall 77 percent of the full-time growers had under 35 hectares. Five of the growers in question had one or more employees in a region in which only 25 percent of the producers were employers. They were up-to-date professionals who were among the first in the region to use contemporary techniques for the production of strawberries on which they depended for most of their income. They also cultivated strawberry plants, seed corn, and tobacco, or they raised cattle—all activities which demanded considerable technical knowledge and were relatively lucrative. Though they were representative of the agricultural population in terms of age, being between 45 and 55, they differed by being better educated (a technical diploma in one case, and past attendance at an agricultural school in the others).[13] In addition, the creation of an auction market was important for at least five of these up-to-date growers for a further reason: they had children who might take over the business, and the only way in which this could be assured was by making the business viable. This implied the production of greater yields of better quality but, most of all, a more effective commercial network. Conquering new markets and producing in order to sell better—to do this was to undertake an operation similar to that accomplished by their fathers when they were young and introduced mechanization: modernizing their production in order to keep their children on the land. But the feature which most distinguished them from other producers was the fact that they had more, and more frequent, links outside the region through professional organizations, seed producers, and connections with other strawberry growers elsewhere in France. In addition, locally, they were often in positions of leadership, in part because of their professional competence.

Among these growers was a member of the board of a national association of corn seed growers, a member of the board of the regional section of the national union of strawberry growers, and the president of the local union (the Syndicat des Producteurs de Fraises du Loir-et-Cher). Two of them participated in the "national strawberry seminars," the yearly meetings where national strategy and subsidies are discussed. Some of them were also engaged into local politics. Two were deputy mayors at Fontaines-en-Sologne's town council. Most of them were also members of the board of local associations and charities.

A number of these actors (three brothers at Fontaines-en-Sologne and the president of the local union of strawberry growers) were active in the business of strawberry seedlings, which was vital from the point of view of acquiring knowledge about the production of strawberries and its potential intensification. These producers grew selected plants, which they sold in several regions, and especially in the southwest, which was the dominant strawberry-growing region in France. In this way, in the course of much traveling, they learned all about agriculture in this region. In particular, they learned that strawberry growing was not a traditional form of agriculture in that region, a region whose soils were less appropriate to it than those of the Sologne. Despite this, the majority of southwest growers had incomes greater than or equal to those of the most successful producers in the Sologne. This discovery transformed the perspective of the Sologne strawberry-seedling producers, which had

previously been limited by their proximity to the growers of the Beauce.
The latter, who were their immediate partners in the professional and
political organizations, had been their sole point of reference: they cultivated rich soils which lent themselves well to the growth of cereals. By
comparison, the Sologne, which was classified as a "disadvantaged
area," looked like a poor region.

Indeed, the Sologne, considered one of the poorest regions of France
since the nineteenth century,[14] was categorized as a "disadvantaged area"
in 1976 by the European Council of Ministers—a position which gave it
a status similar to that of mountainous regions. This status is based on
criteria such as low demographic density, production per hectare below
80 percent of the national average, and returns per member of the active
population below 80 percent of the national average.

In the nineteenth century large estates—often more than 1,000
hectares—dominated the area. The peasants only rarely owned the land
that they worked. They were "tenants," agricultural laborers who were
allocated a patch of land while they were attached to an estate. During
the twentieth century most of these large estates were broken up, and the
tenants or their children were able to buy or rent small areas. The old
landowners kept only their houses and the hunting woods. In 1979,
when the Fontaines-en-Sologne auction market was only a project,
70 percent of the properties situated in what became later the perimeter
of the Fontaines-en-Sologne market had under 50 hectares. Half of this
area was owned directly, and half rented. According to the General Agricultural Census, in the 1980s some 10 percent of these farms specialized
in cereal growth, 30 percent obtained more than 80 percent of their revenue from stock rearing (producing milk or meat), and the remainder
practiced mixed farming (cereals, stock rearing, and vegetables). The soil
was poor, and its combination of sand and clay exacerbates the effects of
periods of drought or rainfall, often endangering the harvest. The market for land was heterogeneous, and plots of land were acquired as much
for hunting, fishing, and second homes as for agriculture. The FNSEA,
which is the largest professional agricultural organization in the region,
found it difficult to elect new delegates from the communes, because the
average age of farmers was particularly high (67 percent were more than
45 years old).

The contact with other regions, and especially the southwest, thus encouraged growers to think of their context in a new way. They became
aware of the fact that they had better soils for growing strawberries than
the producers in Lot-et-Garonne, for instance, and of the fact that they
were themselves producing the strawberry plants that were the basis of
the property of that region. In other words, they realized that they could
produce strawberries equally profitably if they chose to do so.

The Work of Creating the Auction Market

In 1979, an auction market which increased both prices and the quality of production was created at Verg, in the Lot-et-Garonne province.[15] The strawberries of Loir-et-Cher, already considered inferior to those from the south, were thus doubly disadvantaged. It was in this context that regional leaders and the economic adviser, who were convinced that creation of an auction market was desirable, started to try to persuade both the producers and the shippers that this should be done. Their basic object was not to replace the shippers who were already working in the region. Rather, it was to create a new context in which competition would operate more freely. This would, it was hoped, henceforth reflect the operation of supply and demand, rather than being imposed by the shipper or the broker.

First, they contacted some shippers in the region who would be likely to buy at the auction, instead of collecting the produce on site. Most of the shippers reacted strongly to the creation of the new market, and collectively rejected this new trading system. They also sought to dissuade producers by spreading counterinformation. But for certain buyers the creation of an electronic market made the penetration of new markets possible. Thus the shippers in the region of Saint-Romain, who were short of locally produced strawberries, had an interest in marketing a product that would bridge the gap between the production of asparagus in the spring and the vegetable season, which started in July. Others shippers came to the conclusion that this would allow them to take control of a large part of the production that was currently sold directly to agents. In this way, the notion of competition triumphed, with a handful of shippers agreeing to play the game proposed by the producers and thereby to disorganize the system within which the shippers worked.

To persuade the growers, trips were organized by the Syndicat des Producteurs de Fraises to look at the way in which other auction-based trading systems worked. Educational meetings were organized in the area. When the growers in favor of the electronic market judged that they were sufficiently numerous, a general meeting of the Syndicat des Producteurs de Fraises decided to create the market within the union. The drawing up of rules and regulations and the approaches to government for assistance and subsidies were facilitated by the economic adviser, who also assisted in the process of buying the auction computer and recruiting the auctioneer.

In May 1982, the new market started operation in a former school in Fontaines-en-Sologne. In the following year the market obtained administrative and financial autonomy from the Syndicat des Producteurs de Fraises and moved to a custom-built warehouse. It brought together

Box 2.1
The objectives of economic organization: Excerpts from the economic adviser's report

The objective of economic organization is to manage the market, i.e. to give producers a true economic power in their relations with buyers. . . . The efficacy of trade requires that they behave as entrepreneurs with bargaining power. In order to gain such power, they need to restore conditions of competition between the buyers. . . .

a) Facing concentrated networks
To respond to the demand of a highly concentrated industry, producers need to modify the balance of power, and provide an offer powerful enough to become an economic force. . . .

b) Restoring market transparency
The clarity of transactions, the control of quality and quantities, and the assessment of financial and production flows require a circuit of organized information for producers. . . .

c) Obtaining references on homogeneous products
In order to offer the quality demanded by commercial circuits, to enter international markets, and to get better sale conditions, producers need to talk the same language and implement standards. They also have to watch the homogeneity of their production, using standardized packaging. This is how new markets open. . . . Once competition is enhanced and sale conditions furthered, the gaining of bargaining power needs to be based on the protection of producers' income. . . .

d) Free trade born out of free discussion
The worst consequence of the distortions that hinder competition is the lack of liberty in commercial transactions. If the producer lacks information, it cannot enter into a fair, equilibrated interaction with the buyer. The latter, its commercial counterparty, is the one that finally sets the price. . . .

twenty one producers (eleven from Fontaines-en-Sologne joined the new commercial organization).[16] On average, these mostly cultivated about 50 hectares and produced a large proportion of "table strawberries." Indeed, only those producers with many strawberries, and a van, were able to travel in order to sell their produce—and even they needed free time, which in turn depended on the assistance of members of the family who were responsible, for instance, for supervising the strawberry picking while the boss was away.

Among the members of the auction market, three worked with their sons and twelve had children who had a basic diploma of agricultural technician and might follow their fathers into agriculture. Seventeen grew other crops in addition to strawberries (tobacco maize, or strawberry seedhings, and some reared cattle), which they sold into commercial networks while avoiding middlemen. They were, accordingly, more independent from brokers than the others. It is significant that the only producer who broke the rule that the entire crop had to be brought to the auction market (and sold part of it to brokers instead) combined the production of strawberries with that of vegetables.

On the side of the buyers, the data that I have at present permit only a few tentative hypotheses. The brokers who did not have enough economic capital to manage their own enterprises were excluded from a system where it was necessary to pay on the spot. It was thus the shippers—and in particular those who were the strongest economically—who entered the market. They had the necessary funds to deposit the bankers' guarantees required by the producer-organizers of the market.

Thus the creation of the new auction-based trading mechanism at Fontaines-en-Sologne should be seen as a social innovation resulting from the work of a number of individuals interested, for different reasons, in changing the balance of power between the growers and the buyers. By contrast, it should not be seen as the spontaneous appearance of a mechanism for liberating economic energies which came into being because of the rationality and efficiency of its procedures. Because this market implies a rupture with existing practices, its creation represents a cost in material and psychological investment. It also represents political work undertaken to persuade the economic actors to join, together with confrontation with the shippers in order to convince them that they should participate. It is not, therefore, a simple development of preexisting trade relations—the outcome of a mechanism which would have perfected itself as interactions between those involved in exchange developed and unfolded. The practices which constitute the market are not market practices.

"Invisible Hand" or "Continuous Creation"?

In 1985, the new market was in operation, though its creation had shaken friendships of long standing between brokers and producers and had led to stormy arguments within families in which some members entered the new market, while others continued to defend the traditional networks vigorously. Now that the market was in operation, did

Box 2.2

The role of the economic adviser: Excerpts from an interview with Bernard Foucher, the economic adviser in charge of the Fontaines-en-Sologne market project

I was the one who first contacted all the potential partners, the associations, the ministry. But it was they who took the decisions. . . . Between April and May, we needed to write the rules and regulations, to get the telephone wires plugged-in, get the computer, etc. The shippers didn't want to come. There were some negotiations. . . .

I helped them a lot, but they took the decisions themselves. It wouldn't have worked without that embryo of willingness, not even with heavy means of persuasion. I did not come with "the idea" of the auction. I had this idea in mind, yes, but this was not the only idea. This method happened to crystallize around this group of people. . . . I first thought that they had to further the system of co-operatives, but they did not want to. . . .

I was into the field twelve hours a day. As soon as I felt some positive feedback, some dynamic people, there was no reason not to help them. And I keep on doing it. The stronger always wins, so they need to remain strong. Otherwise they will disappear. Some people would be perfectly happy with that, especially the shippers. Or the cooperatives, which were a little bit shaken by all this and did have to question themselves. Or some families that did not play a leading role. Someone could also be pleased at the national level. You know, there is a "two-speed" agriculture. Someone could ask: how come those guys developed this market in a zone that is not really fit for intensive agriculture? Why did they dare to develop this supersophisticated thing in Sologne? . . .

I was very involved in all this. It was an exciting experience. . . . But, contrary to the producers, I did not have much at stake. I mean that there is a difference between a producer who puts his business at risk and a technician who commits only with the quality of his job. But well, this may have other implications later.
[In 1986, Bernard Foucher became president of the Chambre d'Agriculture de Loir-et-Cher.]

the establishment of price levels result, as predicted by Adam Smith (1776/1976), from the operation of an "invisible hand"? An invisible hand that ensures the development of an equilibrium between supply and demand because each person pursues his or her own interest? An invisible hand that leads to equilibrium only if conditions of perfect competition are met, as Samuelson (Samuelson and Nordhaus 1973, p. 43) would assume? Rather, the functioning of the market needs to be seen as the object of perpetual vigilance on the part of its organizers, who have to struggle against all kinds of actions that market participants deploy to intervene in the market process. Thus, though the creation of this market put the shippers in competition with one another, since 1980 the shippers have attempted to reorganize themselves and make alliances in order to regain their former power. Their attempts include the daily exchange of information by telephone about developments in the market and secret agreements whose effects may be noticed when, for example, a lot is put on sale for the second time because the producer felt that the price being offered was too low and buyers stop the auction at the same price as in the first auction round.

The administrative council of the Fontaines-en-Sologne market has taken certain measures to inhibit the growth of such collusive practices. Thus the renewal of the buyers' memberships—which should occur automatically according to the 1981 rules—is, in fact, examined each year. This opens the way to redefining what is required of the buyers. In addition, expulsion is theoretically possible according to the rules, and though it has occurred on only one occasion (as a result of lack of solvency), it is certainly frequently used as a threat.

The producers also must be carefully watched. Not all of them abide by the rules, either because they do not think that this is in their interests, or because they don't fully understand what is involved. Some try to profit from the two systems by selling in the auction market one day and to shippers directly the next. They disobey the rule that all fruit must be brought to the market and, in so doing, undermine the new relations of power and reduce the transparency of the market. Others act clumsily because they don't know enough about the level of demand in other markets. Though silence is observed while transactions are taking place at the Fontaines-en-Sologne market, later, when producers and buyers emerge from the hall, they often engage in more or less heated debate. For example, growers accuse buyers of abusing their power and reducing the level of their bids and threaten them with expulsion from the market or with stopping harvesting. These hostile comments directed at shippers when prices fall, even if this is only the result of overproduction, risk undermining the cordial climate necessary for the conclusion of transactions and the proper playing of the game. As a result, those producers who are most familiar with the overall national market are expected to explain details about prevailing prices to others and to limit their protests. The president or the treasurer of the market organization is present each day to observe, advise, and enforce the rules in order to maintain the desired good relations and "family spirit." After each session of the market the auctioneer, the secretary, and the president of the market (or his delegate) hold an informal meeting to discuss the conduct of the day's transactions.

The Social and Economic Effects of the Auction Market

The creation of the new market has had a positive effect on the level of strawberry prices in the area. According to figures from the union of strawberry growers, before 1981 these were always substantially below national levels. Since 1981 this tendency has been reversed. On average, prices are typically equal to or above these, and the difference can be as much as 40 percent. This noticeable increase in prices has taken place not only in the new market, but also in the traditional networks, because the creation of the market has modified older networks. In particular, it has created a standard for the growers, a reference point. The latter are now able to learn about market prices by attending the auction or reading the local press, in which prices are regularly published. In this way, shippers and brokers found that they had no choice but to align their prices to those in the Fontaines-en-Sologne's market. Indeed, they were often obliged to raise their prices above those in the market in order to stop producers from joining the market in large numbers, and so further weaken the position of the buyers. Overall, exports of strawberries from the region increased from 9,495 tonnes in 1980 to 89,758 tonnes in 1981.

The price increase is not simply a function of the trading method. It is also a consequence of the stimulating effect of displaying different kinds of strawberries side by side. The homogeneity of the product and the transparency of the market reveal differences in quality and quantity between produce that were not visible when collections were made locally. "The first year," said the producers, "we were horrified. The new market taught us how to work. We looked at our neighbors' strawberries and we thought—we don't want to be taken for someone who grows strawberries that will be made into jam." But while intensifying competition over quality between producers, the auction market was also a source of information—information about the best techniques. Information about how and how much plants and fruits are sprayed tends to remain secret, but much information is nonetheless circulated about plant and fruit diseases and their remedies.

As strawberry growing has become more profitable, this has led to an increase in the area under cultivation. In particular, in the commune of Fontaines-en-Sologne, the area increased threefold between 1981 and

1985. In addition, the market has increased the range of produce being brought for sale. Asparagus have been sold in this way since 1982, and leeks since 1984.

This way of institutionalizing the sale of strawberries has modified the status of the products as well as that of the producers. During the 1970s, in Loir-et-Cher, strawberries represented for most growers no more than a way of supplementing income. Because of the new market, strawberries from Sologne have acquired both a label of quality and regional recognition. The local press, and especially the *Nouvelle République* and the *Petit Solognot*, have published a series of articles highlighting the quality of strawberries from the Sologne. Strawberry growing has thus become a symbol of dynamism, as is witnessed by the organization of a "strawberry fair." In 1984 and 1985, a leisure association for young people in Sologne organized such a fair with games, sideshows, and an exhibition about the market and the sale of strawberries. According to the press, 15,000 people attended this fair at Fontaines-en-Sologne—a village with only 848 inhabitants. The festival brought with it a level of excitement reportedly never before experienced in Fontaines-en-Sologne, while at the same time contributing to the creation of the regional image of the Sologne strawberry.

It is the display of produce at the auction site that is responsible for the differential prices but also may confer symbolic profits.[17] The presentation of products at a single time and place makes differences in quality and quantity apparent. These are a function of differences between the areas cultivated and of differences in techniques, which are in turn a function of differences in the economic and cultural capital of producers. The public character of information about prices and quantities makes it possible to know the economic standing of the different members.

The creation of the new market has also reinforced existing links, and created new links, between producers. The long evenings spent bringing it into being, the group travel, the work required to build the warehouse, the communal acceptance of the risks involved—such group efforts created an "auction market identity," something that is reinforced on every occasion the market is held. Thus each working day the growers are brought together in a space which is distinct from that of the shippers. They grumble together about the buyers, help each other to unload, exchange information about agriculture—but at the same time they are involved in social contacts. The new market has become a particularly dynamic network for communication in a region in which the growers are very spread out, and in which Sunday mass and the marketplace have lost their weekly social role. Links extend beyond the auction market, and often, when the children of a grower get married, they invite other members of the market to a celebratory drink in the market salesroom. In this way, the distinction between the growers who are members of the market and those who are not becomes more obvious.

With the creation of the market, new sources of power and prestige have come into being. The market is managed by an administrative council, which is elected by its members. The leaders of the market have built up new links with the banks and an up-to-date technology. According to the economic adviser who assisted them in its creation, this change is symbolized by a shift in their conduct within the regional branch of the bank (the Crédit Agricole). "Do you know the Crédit Agricole? It's an office block five stories high. The counter is on the ground floor. The office of the manager is on the fifth floor. Before the market started the growers only went to the ground floor. Now they don't feel embarrassed to go up five floors."

The new market, which has the legal form of a service cooperative, has increased in prestige so much that in 1982 the annual strawberry meeting organized by the national union of strawberry growers was held in Sologne, at Cour-Cheverny. At the same time, the local union (the Syndicat des Producteurs de Fraises du Loir-et-Cher, which got the market started) has lost its most active members, who are now entirely committed to the work of the market. Indeed, some of the latter believe that it is only a matter of time before their union entirely disappears.

The Evolution of the New Market

Between 1981, when the marked started, and 1984, the number of members of the market increased by 65 percent, the volume of strawberries sold by 55 percent, and the area planted with strawberry plants by 66 percent, according to the market's own statistics. At first sight it would appear that what has happened is that the producers have reacted to an increase in demand, and so in their profits, either by becoming members of the market or (in the case of those who were already members) by increasing the area of strawberries under cultivation. But it seems unlikely that the increase in anticipated income fully explains these changes.[18] Thus a detailed study of the distribution of membership suggests that other factors have also played a part in the decision about whether to join.

For instance, in general members of cooperatives have not joined the new market, even though membership would have been highly profitable. Cooperatives impose tight rules on their members. They are most widely established in communes in which vegetables and grapes (both mainly sold through cooperatives) constitute the most important produce. Those who grow vegetables and grapes are dependent on the cooperatives, which act as more or less exclusive brokers for these kinds of produce.

In addition, the cooperatives are legally able to require their members to sell all their produce (including strawberries) through the cooperative system. The manager of the cooperative of Contres (which is close to Fontaines-en-Sologne) was also the mayor of the commune until 1981. If he had opted to join the new market, then this would have had much more significance than a simple change in economic habits.

In addition, a certain number of general councilors and technicians from the Chambre d'Agriculture did not seem to favor the market. No doubt this was because they had supported the development of cooperatives, and they were suspicious of a more efficient form of economic organization which called their support for cooperatives—and even the cooperatives themselves—into question. In other cases, the decision not to join the economic market appeared to be linked to local circumstances, for example, family or personal relations, local competition, and disagreement.

Yet again, in some communes (Montrieux, Romorantin) the level of membership was high, whereas others (Courmemin, Fresnes) with considerable strawberry growing which were closer to the market were underrepresented. The data that I have available only suggest possible explanations for this. It seems, for example, that at Fresnes there was a particularly well-established broker who had kinship links with many of the producers, and this led the producers to maintain the traditional form of selling.

At Courmemin, one leading grower who was deputy mayor and one of the largest producers in the whole of France—and a substantial strawberry nursery gardener—did not join the market. Why? There are various explanations that have to do with competition with the president of the auction exchange. Both were substantial producers of strawberry plants. And both were hoping to become the manager of the union of strawberry plant producers. Thus his nonmembership of the market is, perhaps, a strategy for trying to limit the success of the market and the prestige of its president—and all the more so because if he had joined his example would probably have been followed by a large number of other strawberry producers, and especially plant growers who were subcontracted to him.

A Custom-Built Market for Custom-Made Farmers

In a case study such as this, which seems to fit the conditions of competition defined by Samuelson and Nordhaus (1973), it is possible to explore such conditions in a way somewhat different from that of economists, and in particular to consider the social conditions that make such a market possible at all. If we look at it this way, then social variables are not a residue to be used to explain why the market measures up only imperfectly to the conditions defined in the model. Instead, they allow us to explain how the market was brought into being, and how it is sustained.

The market at Fontaines-en-Sologne was not established in a social vacuum. Rather, it was developed in opposition to existing social links—a network in which some individuals had not found their place. Thus the creation of the market becomes fully explicable only if we take account both of prior social links between brokers, shippers, and farmers and of the difficulties encountered by the cooperatives in the region. The trading practices that characterize this market were not given in advance. Rather, they were the product of work, of investment in two senses of the term. First, there was financial investment in a site, a building, and personnel.[19] Such investment would not have been possible on the part of purely isolated individuals (producers or shippers). Second, then, there was a further form of psychological investment: the work that went into creating an association and a collective identity for its members. This psychological investment was just as important: the enterprise required the creation of collective belief in the possibility of success—a consensus and mutual confidence on the part of all the participants.

Furthermore, if trade is reduced to variations in prices capable of adjusting the relationship between supply and demand, it is precisely because the whole organization of the market was conceived with this idea in mind. The spatial structure of the building, the daily sequence of activity—the whole arrangement was designed to ensure that buyers and sellers are able to see prices only as they appear on the computer-driven auction board during the descending-auction process. The language and even the expressions used by the participants are highly codified. Everything to do with the quality and quantity of strawberries has to take place before the sale actually begins. During the sale, the catalogue acts as the concrete reference point at each transaction. The architecture of the salesroom mimics the representation of the curves of supply and demand, which are created independently of one another. The building separates the buyers from the sellers, who are arranged so that no direct communication—no nods or winks, no signs or gestures indicating approval or disapproval—may pass between them during the auction. Everything has been designed so that "social factors" do not enter to disturb the free matching between supply and demand and their mutual accommodation in the form of price.

However, if daily practices of the market have secured strict correspondence to those posited by economic theory, then this is because the latter served as the framework of reference for the design of each detail of the market,[20] especially concerning the rules that define what is admitted and what is not.[21] Thus the "perfect" market at Fontaines-en-Sologne is the end product of a process of social and economic construction. And the whole process was possible only because a certain number of social agents (in particular, producers whose children might benefit in the long run) had a particular interest in altering the balance of power between brokers, shippers, and farmers, and because they were able to do so, assisted by an economic adviser with converging interests,[22] who allowed the enterprise to benefit from his legal and social capital.

It is important to note that the particular form and structure of this market cannot be reproduced everywhere, for all forms of production, and for all kinds of producers. Thus at present prices for most agricultural products, including those of cereals and milk, are fixed politically. Those for which prices obey such a thing as the law of supply and demand are quite unusual. Again, locally, this market is only indirectly linked to producers as a whole, and those farmers who belong to the market are socially and economically quite unlike the majority of those who grow strawberries.

While the new auction market has established a spatial distinction between exchange counterparties, it has tended to reinforce the social identity of buyers and sellers. Though the producers are in competition with one another, they nevertheless share a certain number of common experiences (the anxious wait for the daily opening of the market, the discovery of the daily prices, leaving together at the end of the sale, collective complaints about the level of prices). And it is the same with the shippers. Thus, it is easy to imagine that the auction market has increased the level of competition between them (for before it began each shipper more or less had a monopoly in a given geographical area). On the other hand, the way in which they meet, and the common character of their daily round at the market, has enabled them to develop links that are more effective than those that they previously had through their union. Accordingly, the market has formalized groups with interests that are simultaneously antagonistic and complementary, and its creation alongside the brokers and the cooperatives has redefined the character of possible alliances and conflicts. But it is not only objective social positions that have changed in this way; the representations that are associated with them have changed as well. Thus with the birth of the market, being a strawberry grower became a legitimate identity, one that is the symbol for the agriculture of the future in a region previously considered backward, suitable only for hunting.

The "perfect" functioning of the market is due not to market mechanisms or to an "invisible hand" that has been restored by the application of noninterventionist principles of laissez faire. Instead, it is the result of the work of a number of individuals with an interest in the market, together with acceptance by others who have also found it to their advantage to obey to the rules of the game. Thus the market is better conceived as a field of struggle than as the product of mechanical and necessary laws inscribed in the nature of social reality—laws that are occasionally distorted by "social factors." The creation of the auction market has shaken the different sales networks and reshaped the patterns of social distinction. In part, it was produced by (and served the interests of) a limited group of agents with particular characteristics and interests. But it is also located in the broader field of commercial networks as a whole. Indeed, it is in a relationship of dependency with this. The equilibrium of this field might be undermined at any time, as the relations of power between producers, shippers, cooperatives, and government unfold and alter.

Postscript: Fontaines-en-Sologne Revisited

At the end of the 1990s, I again became interested in descending-price auctions. In my 1986 article on the auction market at Fontaines-en-Sologne, whose English translation makes up the previous sections of this chapter, I suggested that this market institution, despite the fact that it was unknown beforehand in Sologne, was the transposition of an already legitimized mechanism—the descending or Dutch auction—that was already used in Brittany. Wishing to analyze further this institutional innovation, I inquired about the status of this form of exchange. I was told by economists that this trading mechanism was "outdated" because it prompted undue price volatility, and that I would do better to focus on futures contracts—a particularly pervasive market format used in mass wholesale.

Media coverage of the crisis of descending-price auctions and a shifting perception of their value among economists made me aware of the fact that this market form was threatened. I restarted fieldwork, not to return to the hypotheses explored in the article (other work such as Callon [1998] has helped to validate the approach I took), but rather to complete the analysis by taking into account wider changes in commerce and growing importance of the mass retail of strawberries, its concentration, and its effect on the strawberry market. At the time I wrote the article, the Fontaines-en-Sologne market had just been born, and the hypothesis of a possible shift in the balance of power between producers, shippers, and regulatory bodies was considered only as a logical evolution of the market, its power struggles, and its dynamic processes.

When I again conducted fieldwork in 1998 (with further interviews in 2002), the *cadran de Sologne*, the computerized descending-price auction, was still in operation, and still presented as a highlight of the region.

Figures confirmed this impression. The number of members remained almost unchanged—from 35 in 1986 to 44 in 2002, of which 32 were strawberry traders. Many young producers were involved, which can be taken as evidence of the success of the market's promoters, who wanted to keep their children in the strawberry business. In 2002, some 80 percent of local strawberry production was sold through the Fontaines-en-Sologne auction. The rest was traded directly by shippers. The total area devoted to strawberry production increased from 57 hectares in 1986 to 101.5 hectares in 2002, of which 3.5 hectares were "hanging gardens." In 2002 again, about 2,000 tonnes of strawberries were traded at Fontaines-en-Sologne (almost five times more than at the market's start). The market contained nine authorized buyers. In 1992, a more convenient, air-conditioned display venue had been built. Sologne-labeled strawberries reached especially high average prices in 1997. In 2002, prices were not as good. But producers were entering a diversification process to better respond to demand. Along with asparagus trading, other services were offered to the market community, such as group-buying facilities for phytosanitary products.

But, in spite of such encouraging signs, the group in charge of the market expressed concerns. The market's good shape was felt to be an exception in a landscape in which an increasingly large number of producers in other regions were abandoning auction mechanisms in favor of sale cooperatives or even forward contracts with the mass retail sector.[23] These recent changes in pricing and trading methods were accompanied by a fall in prices and problems of overproduction. The price of strawberries from Sologne did not entirely follow this trend. But producers became increasingly concerned about a potential fall in prices. Several tensions arose from 1995 on. These were partially due to a shift in the commercial policy of large retailers, a sector that represented more than 40 percent of Fontaines-en-Sologne's sales.[24]

The growth of large retailers and their impact on commercialization networks became increasingly visible in the management of the logistics of fruit distribution, particularly in the case of strawberries. Before 1995, shipping and distribution firms purchased produce autonomously and could handle day-to-day variations in prices—such as those that characterize auction markets—more easily. The increasing concentration of these firms, and the concomitant standardization of commercial practices, promoted other kind of arrangements, such as weekly prices fixed in advance, as a way of better scheduling promotional offers and meeting expected demand. Logistics and pricing required more and more regularity, which caused much pressure on shippers who were tied to daily price variations, including those of strawberries.[25] The most important shipper who was buying at the Fontaines-en-Sologne's auction—he bought an

average 30 percent of the produce sold there—was selling entirely to
the mass retail sector. Another two shippers—buying 5 percent each—were
selling half of their commodity to mass retail. The other shippers were dealing with wholesalers, public contractors, or exporters and turned to mass
retail central buying offices only exceptionally. Central buying offices had
insistently tried to convince the Fontaines-en-Sologne's managers to deal
directly without the intermediation of shippers, but they faced refusal for a
long time.

On the other hand, competition among buyers at the Fontaines-en-
Sologne's market resulted from the confrontation of actors who were not
focused only on the strawberry business. Strawberries were produced in
a limited part of the year, and their growers also produced other fruits
and vegetables (apples, asparagus, pickles, etc.). Leeks played an important role in balancing the activity of shipping firms. They were not very
profitable per se, but fresh leeks were available at least nine months a
year, which allowed fuller utilization of personnel and trucks. Moreover,
whereas strawberries had to meet tight quality criteria, leeks in the region were not subjected to such constraints and indeed could barely
meet the standards of the central buying offices. Leeks from the Landes
or La Manche were more competitive, in that sense. Difficulties in the
leek business—a fall of 30 percent in profit in 1998—rendered shipping
firms more dependent on strawberry business and thus more fragile.

Eventually, central buying offices imposed the use of 250-gram plastic
baskets with plastic wrapping, when strawberries had usually been
packed into unwrapped 500-gram wooden baskets.[26] Plastic wrapping
translated into increasing costs for shippers and increasing asymmetries
among them (four shippers were already handling 72 percent of purchases). Most of the shippers' customers were somewhat reluctant to see
such changes and thought that altering the strawberries' presentation
could threaten their high-quality image. All these circumstances translated into increasing constraints on buyers. Producers had difficulty in
profiting from price variations, as their exchange counterparties were reduced to a handful of buyers. Shippers dealing with mass retail central
buying offices could hardly cope with the dissonances produced by a
dual system: daily price variations on the producers' side, and weekly
predefined prices on the side of central buying offices. For shippers, the
Fontaines-en-Sologne's auction system was outdated, no longer compatible with their needs. They were urging a change in market organization.

A close look at shippers revealed that some of them—usually family-
run firms—had to leave the business. Newcomers were basically small
buyers who could not access the mass retail sector. Three of the more important buyers were over 55 years old, and two of them did not have
any children in the business. Some market managers and shippers were

agreeing on the fact that "the shipping business was dying." Market competition on the purchase side, which had been carefully designed and nurtured by the market promoters,[27] was threatened by a decreasing number of buyers and an increasing product differentiation. Forty percent of sales was directed toward mass retail, and was through only three shippers.

The construction of the auction market formed groups, crystallized identities. The antagonism of opposing producers and shippers that I described earlier was still alive. But my new observations pointed out the emergence of a more solidarity-oriented attitude. Shippers were recognizing that the Fontaine-en-Sologne's auction system—combined with the quality labeling of strawberries—allowed producers to exist as such. Producers who engaged in the early crusade for market transparency— that is, for a furthering of competition among shippers—were reluctant to enter into trade directly with mass retailers' central buying offices. Without a "reference price," they would find themselves ill-equipped for a defense of their interests in the market. They also thought that new market arrangements would be too demanding in terms of logistics for a product with a short growing season. Besides that, a transformation of market practices would challenge the economic disposition that they acquired with the auction market—the stimulation of production through systematic monitoring and comparison of prices.

Market managers were trying to defend shippers, for instance, asking central buying offices not to bypass shippers. When they published advertisements about the market, they added contact details of the shippers who were acknowledged members of the market. When clients got in touch directly with the Fontaines-en-Sologne market, managers redirected them to the members—"we have known *our* shippers for a long time," a manager said.

However, solidarity was somewhat less pronounced in the case of younger generations, confronted with other logics of social reproduction. Producers' new family arrangements could prevent the producer from leaving his or her farm during auction days, because no other family member was available to replace him or her. Shippers who were not dependent on traditional circuits and who were engaged in business with mass retailers were also somewhat disconnected from a defense of the auction system. The identity of the "strawberry from Sologne" started to be questioned, as its quality was based more on a competitive tension than on a standardized assessment. Recently, and as a response to an audit process in 1999, market managers decided to rebrand Sologne strawberries. The *fraises du cadran de Sologne* have become the new *Miam-Miam Sologne* strawberries. Besides the fact that this new brand name may not raise much enthusiasm, it is noticeable that

the word *"cadran,"* that is, the auction identity, is no longer part of
the identity of Sologne's strawberries, at least not as they are now
marketed.

In short, the Fontaines-en-Sologne's auction market was threatened
less by the shippers' collusive strategies against the producers' move of
fostering competition than by the transformation of commercial networks, the rise of agrofood mass retail, and their economic justifications.
Competition between commercial networks seems to be playing a crucial
role in legitimating certain market institutions and delegitimating others.
The logic of market relations cannot be grasped only through the logic
of market interactions. At the origin of markets there are never rootless
and detached individuals. The history embodied in the different actors
that intervene in the construction of a market and the history materialized in the preexisting circuits of exchange delineate the space of constraint of any new social construction.

Notes

1. This chapter appeared originally as Marie-France Garcia, "La construction
social d'un marché parfait: le marché au cadran de Fontaines-en-Sologne," *Actes
de la Recherche en Sciences Sociales*, no. 65, November 1986, 2–13 (special issue
on the "social construction of the economy"). The translation is by John Law,
and has been revised by Fabian Muniesa (who also has translated the postscript).
Fontaines-en-Sologne is a village located in the Loir-et-Cher department, in the
province of Val de Loire.

2. At the end of the 1960s, the Mansholt Report (a document issued by the
Club of Rome, which aimed at setting the bases for the European agricultural
integration) shared a dominant view according to which regions that were not
naturally fit for highly productive agriculture (such as the Sologne) should be
devoted to intensive rearing, forest facilities, or tourism.

3. In John Hicks's *Value and Capital* (1946), a key reference for many contemporary economists, perfect competition is considered as a concept without which
economic theory would fall apart: "It has to be recognized that a general aban-
donment of the assumption of perfect competition, a universal adoption of the
assumption of monopoly, must have very destructive consequences for economic
theory. Under monopoly, the stability conditions become indeterminate and the
basis on which economic laws can be constructed is therefore shorn away"
(pp. 83–84). In a foreword to a Spanish edition of his book, Hicks tempers
his statement and says that not all economic theory is shorn away, only that of
"general equilibrium" (1954, p. 10).

4. This "auctioneer" is a technician who was been recruited by producers to
operate the electronic auction board. He is also expected to take charge of the
auction sessions.

5. Maximum and minimum prices are set on the basis of prices obtained the day before at the Fontaines-en-Sologne market or at other marketplaces (whose prices are transmitted by telex). Some other criteria can be taken into account, such as the day of the week or the period of the year (for example, buyers and producers agree on the fact that strawberries do not sell well when there is a long holiday weekend).

6. According to Gould and Ferguson's manual, first published in 1966, then reprinted in 1969, 1972, 1975, and 1980 in the United States, translated into French and printed in 1980 and 1984, perfect competition implies the following assumptions: each economic agents acts as if prices were given, as if goods were homogeneous, as if resources were perfectly mobile, as if firms could enter and exit the market freely, and as if economic agents had complete and perfect knowledge (Ferguson and Gould 1975, pp. 222–225).

7. For the three sales we observed during the height of the strawberry season (July 7, 17, and 18, 1985) we counted, respectively, 62, 59, and 61 lots, with an average weight between 100 and 500 kilos each.

8. The price paid for strawberries in the processed or canned food sector is rather low. In 1985, these "industrial" strawberries were sold at an average 4.50 francs, whereas the minimum price for table strawberries was set at 6 francs. To switch from the table strawberry market to the industrial food market made sense only if already-harvested strawberries remained unsold at the Fontaines-en-Sologne auction. In that case, strawberries were transferred from their 500-gram baskets to bigger bulk cases and driven to a canning factory.

9. The administration of the market phones the producers each morning in order to estimate the quantity that will be put up for sale that day.

10. Some 31 percent of the table strawberry production was sold directly to these intermediaries, 44 percent was sold through the Fontaines-en-Sologne auction, and 25 percent was handled through cooperatives. Only one cooperative member switched to the auction market, so it is possible to infer roughly that 75 percent of the production was sold bilaterally to intermediaries. It is difficult to assess the proportion handled respectively through brokers, shippers, or agents. As far as the latter are concerned, 22 growers among the 122 members of the strawberry growers' union (which controlled about 60 percent of the region's production) were selling directly to agents. The relations between growers and agents were established in the last generation, the latter often being descendents of Sologne migrants who had settled in Paris after World War II.

11. In the mid-1980s, after the closure of the Noyers and Vineuil cooperatives, only some cooperatives were still active in Contres, Soings-en-Sologne, and Les Montils.

12. The descending auction (*marché au cadran*) is far from being a recent invention. Descending auctions were in use in Holland in the nineteenth century and were introduced in France first at Saint-Pol-de-Léon in 1961 (Elegoët 1984), and then successively in Brittany, in the north (Vaudois 1980) and in the southwest.

13. The social properties of these actors do not differ from that of the leaders of agricultural professional organizations studied by Sylvain Maresca in

Meurthe-et-Moselle and Charente: "Those who have to enact the dominant representation of peasantry poorly match peasantry's dominant reality" (Maresca 1983, p. 49).

14. Christian Poitou (1985) gathers an interesting set of historical material that emphasizes the poverty of this region.

15. We will return later to the impact of the auction mechanism on price formation.

16. Determining exactly the total number of strawberry producers in the region is difficult since most available sources provide only aggregate data for "fresh fruits and vegetables." We know that the local union of strawberry growers (Syndicat des Producteurs de Fraises) counted 122 members in 1980. Most of them were big producers. Knowing that strawberry production was quite widespread in the region, we can estimate that the total number of producers was higher than 300.

17. The public exhibition of strawberries is also a matter of honor for producers. Seeing the quality of strawberries furthers the public's recognition of the producers who have mastered the techniques of strawberry growing. This process is not so different from the Trobriander display of yams described by Malinowski (1922).

18. Pierre Bourdieu (1979) shows that income alone cannot explain economic orientations. Albert Hirschman (1970) points to the fact that firms do not necessarily seek to maximize profit.

19. I do not have precise data about these financial costs. One informant mentioned figures of approximately 200,000 francs, without considering the auction warehouse.

20. Pierre Bourdieu (1984) calls the contribution of scientific formulations to the construction of a social world the "theory effect."

21. Max Weber's (1978) general considerations about the role of market rules in the establishment of market competition are of particular relevance here.

22. The professional career (and, eventually, the political trajectory) of the economic adviser depended on the success of the Fontaines-en-Sologne project.

23. This was especially true for the chicory markets of Boursies and Phalempin and the strawberry markets in the southwest. The latter case raised a particularly strong concern among Sologne' producers.

24. Estimates from 1995 indicate that about 40 percent of buyers were large and medium retailers, 20 percent were exporters, and 40 percent were wholesalers (Bourdais 1995).

25. Strawberry prices are particularly volatile. At the end of the 1990s, the price of 1 kilogram could suffer a 10-franc variation from one day to the other.

26. See Barrey et al. (2000) for an analysis of the importance of packaging devices in the construction of markets.

27. The Fontaines-en-Sologne's market managers were always actively preventing shippers from collusion. A few years after the birth of the market, they stopped considering membership renewal as an automatic process. In 1992, they introduced the possibility of the market structure acting as a buyer, precisely as a way of destabilizing possible agreements between buyers.

References

Barrey, S., F. Cochoy, and S. Dubuisson-Quellier. 2000. "Designer, packager et merchandiser: Trois professionnels pour une même scène marchande." *Sociologie du Travail* 42(3):457–482.

Bourdais, A. 1995. *Audit stratégique et organisationnel de la filière fraise: Le cadran de Sologne.* Audit report, Angers, Ecole Supérieure d'Agriculture d'Angers.

Bourdieu, P. 1979. *La distinction: Critique sociale du jugement.* Paris: Minuit.

Bourdieu, P. 1984. "Espace social et genèse des 'classes,'" *Actes de la Recherche en Sciences Sociales* 52–53:3–12.

Callon, M. 1998. "Introduction: The Embeddedness of Economic Markets in Economics." Pp. 1–57 in *The Laws of the Markets*, edited by M. Callon. Oxford: Blackwell.

Elegoët, F. 1984. *Les révoltes paysannes en Bretagne.* Saint-Pol-de-Léon: Editions du Léon.

Ferguson, C. E.. and J. P. Gould, 1975. *Microeconomic Theory.* Homewood, IL: Richard D. Irwin.

Foucher, B. (1981), *Etude sur la promotion de l'organisation légumière en Loir-et-Cher.* Research report, Conseil general de Loir-et-Cher.

Hicks, J. R. 1946. *Value and Capital: An Inquiry into Some Fundamental Principles of Economic Theory.* Oxford: Clarendon.

Hicks, J. R. 1954. *Valor y capital: Investigación sobre algunos principios fundamentales de teoría económica.* Mexico City: Fondo de Cultura Económica.

Hirschman, A. O. 1970. *Exit, Voice, and Loyalty: Responses to Decline in Firms, Organizations, and States.* Cambridge MA: Harvard University Press.

Malinowski, B. 1922. *Argonauts of the Western Pacific.* London: Routledge.

Maresca, S. 1983. *Les dirigeants paysans.* Paris: Minuit.

Perroux, L. 1967. *La culture du fraisier en Loir-et-Cher.* Blois: Chambre d'Agriculture de Loir-et-Cher.

Poitou, C. 1985. *Paysans de Sologne dans la France ancienne: La vie des campagnes solognotes.* Le Coteau: Horvath.

Polanyi, K. 1957. "The Economy as Instituted Process." Pp. 243–270 in *Trade and Market in the Early Empires: Economies in History and Theory*, edited by K. Polanyi, C. M. Arensberg, and H. W. Pearson. Glencoe, IL: Free Press.

Samuelson, P. A., and W. D. Nordhaus, 1973. *Economics.* New York: McGraw-Hill.

Smith, A. 1776/1976, *An Inquiry into the Nature and Causes of the Wealth of Nations.* Oxford: Oxford University Press.

Vaudois, J. 1980. "Le développement des marchés au cadran dans la région du Nord." *Etudes Rurales* 78-79-90:113–134.

Weber, M. 1978. *Economy and Society.* Berkeley: University of California Press.

Chapter 3

Is Economics Performative?

OPTION THEORY AND THE CONSTRUCTION OF DERIVATIVES MARKETS

DONALD MACKENZIE

The thesis discussed in this book—that economics is "performative" (Callon 1998)—has provoked much interest but also some puzzlement and not a little confusion. The purpose of this chapter is to examine from the viewpoint of performativity one of the most successful areas of modern economics, the theory of options, and in so doing hopefully to clarify some of the issues at stake.[1] To claim that economics is performative is to argue that it *does* things, rather than simply describing (with greater or lesser degrees of accuracy) an external reality that is not affected by economics. But *what* does economics do, and what are the effects of it doing what it does?

In this chapter I focus on "economics" in the academic sense, rather than on the wider practices included by Callon within the scope of the term, and examine in particular the theory of options. That this is an appropriate place in which to look for performativity is suggested by two roughly concurrent developments. Since the 1950s, the academic study of finance has been transformed from a low-status, primarily descriptive activity to a high-status, analytical, mathematical, Nobel Prize–winning enterprise. At the core of that enterprise is a theoretical account of options dating from the start of the 1970s. Around option theory there has developed a large array of sophisticated mathematical analyses of financial derivatives. (A "derivative" is a contract or security, such as an option, the value of which depends on the price of another asset or on the level of an index or exchange or interest rate.)

Also since the start of the 1970s, financial markets themselves have been transformed. In 1970, many modern financial derivatives were still illegal, and trading in others was sparse. By June 2005, financial derivatives contracts totaling $329 trillion were outstanding worldwide,[2] an astonishing figure that corresponds to roughly $51,000 for every human being on earth. The figure overstates the economic significance of derivatives in a variety of ways, but even if we take account of that by reducing it by a factor

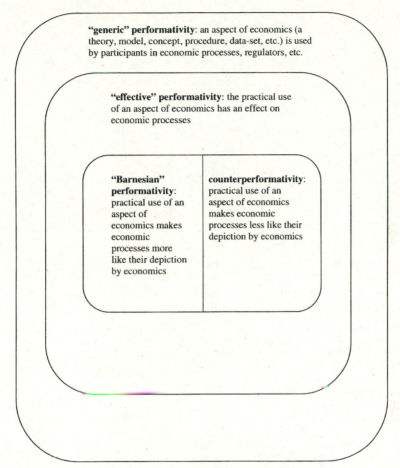

Figure 3.1 A possible classification of the performativity of economics. The depicted sizes of the subsets are arbitrary; I have not attempted to estimate the prevalence of the different forms of performativity.

of a 100—which is probably the order of magnitude of an appropriate correction—financial derivatives remain one of the world's most important markets. What is the connection between these two developments? In particular, what has been the role of the theory of options and of similar derivatives in the transformation of the markets for derivatives?

This chapter proceeds as follows. First comes a brief account of its substantive subject matter: the economic theory of options. A second section discusses, in the context of option theory, two basic versions of the thesis that economics is performative: the versions that I call "generic performativity" and "effective performativity" (see figure 3.1). The former describes cases in which an aspect of economics such as option theory is used in economic practice. The latter designates the subset of cases in which the use of economics "makes a difference": for example, economic processes in which economics is drawn upon are different from those from which it is absent. The section illustrates "generic" and "effective" performativity by discussing how option theory was used in option trading, focusing on the key material mediator between the theory and the crowded trading floors of options exchanges (paper sheets of theoretical prices), on the legitimatory role of option theory, and on the incorporation of the theory into market vernacular.

The chapter's third section distills out from effective performativity a particular, strong version of the thesis of performativity that I call "Barnesian performativity" (the reference is to the social theorist and sociologist of science Barry Barnes) and argues that the notion is applicable to option theory. In Barnesian performativity, an effect of the use in practice of an aspect of economics is to make economic processes more like their depiction by economics. In MacKenzie (2004) I called this "Austinian performativity," but that invocation of the philosopher J. L. Austin had the disadvantage of seeming to imply that it was a purely linguistic process. Indeed, the fourth section of the chapter invokes the critique of Austin by sociologist Pierre Bourdieu in order to examine *why* option theory was able to have the strong effects suggested by the preceding sections. The fifth section examines the extent to which the use of the theory played a role in making its assumptions (originally greatly at odds with the empirical reality of markets) less unrealistic. The penultimate section of the chapter, however, examines ways in which classic option theory became "less true" after the 1987 stock market crash, and briefly points to the possibility (discussed in more detail in MacKenzie 2004) that a practical application of the theory—so-called portfolio insurance—exacerbated the crash. If it did, it would be an instance of what I call "counterperformativity": the use of a theory or model making economic processes *less* like their depiction by economics.[3] The chapter's seventh section is its conclusion.

Theories of Options

An option is a contract that gives the right, but does not impose the obligation, to buy (or, in an alternative form of the contract, to sell) a set quantity of a particular asset at a set price on, or up to, a given future date. If the contract is an option to buy, it is referred to as a "call" option; an option to sell is a "put" option. If the option can be exercised at any point up to its expiration, it is called an "American" option; if it can be exercised only at its expiration, it is "European."[4] The asset in question is classically a block of stock (typically 100 shares), but options can also be written on many other assets: gold, oil, wheat, and other physical commodities; stock indexes and other more abstract assets; and so on.

A central question for the theory of options is how the cost of options is established. Intuition suggests certain parameters that can be expected to play a role in determining the cost: the current price of the underlying asset; the option's strike or exercise price (the price at which it permits the underlying asset to be bought or sold); the length of time to the option's expiration; the level of interest rates; whether the price of the underlying asset tends to be stable or to fluctuate considerably (in other words, the "volatility" of the price of the underlying asset); and whether the price of the underlying asset is expected to rise or to fall. Unaided intuition is, however, not sufficient to go beyond this list to a formula for the option price. Nor is practical experience decisive in this respect. Options have been traded since at least the seventeenth century, and market practitioners developed rules of thumb for pricing options, but those rules of thumb did not add up to a precise or comprehensive theory.

Although efforts to construct a theory of options were presented in Europe around the turn of the twentieth century,[5] the key developments from the viewpoint of this chapter took place in the United States starting in the late 1950s. As a new specialty of "financial economics" coalesced (Bernstein 1992; MacKenzie 2006; Mehrling 2005; Whitley 1986a, b), particular attention was placed on stock-price movements. Those movements, it was suggested, had the form of what statisticians call a "random walk": the change in the price of a stock could be viewed as a random (probabilistic) variable. The precise statistical form of that random walk was a matter of some controversy (of which more below), but increasingly one particular form, the log-normal random walk, was regarded as canonical. In other words, changes in the natural logarithms of stock prices were modeled as following the normal distribution, the well-known "bell-shaped curve" of statistical theory.

With a well-established mathematical model of stock-price changes, working out the value of an option seemed a tractable problem. Several researchers (including economists Paul Samuelson, Case Sprenkle, and James Boness, and mathematician and arbitrageur Edward Thorp) used the log-normal model to construct formulas for the value of an option (see MacKenzie 2003). Unfortunately, their solutions involved parameters whose values were extremely hard to determine empirically, notably investors' expectations of returns on the stock in question and the degree of investors' risk aversion (the extent to which they demand a higher expected return from an investment with an uncertain payoff than from one whose payoff is sure).

By the start of the 1970s, however, work by financial economists Fischer Black and Myron Scholes, with key additional input from their colleague Robert C. Merton, produced what has become the canonical theory of options (Black and Scholes 1973; Merton 1973). Although there were significant differences among the trio in how they approached the problem (MacKenzie 2003; Mehrling 2005), their core argument can be expressed as follows. They assumed that the stock "pays no dividends"; that its price fluctuates log-normally (with a fixed level of volatility); that both stocks and options can be bought or sold at any point in time without incurring transaction costs or causing market prices to move; that options are European; that money can both be borrowed and lent at an identical, constant "riskless" rate of interest; and that short selling (sale of a borrowed asset) incurs no financial penalty (Black and Scholes 1973, p. 640). They showed that in this model it was possible to construct a portfolio of an option and a continuously adjusted position in the underlying asset and lending/borrowing of cash that was riskless: changes in the value of the option would be canceled out exactly by changes in the value of the position in the asset and cash. Since this perfectly hedged portfolio was riskless, it must earn exactly the riskless rate of interest. If not, there would be an opportunity for arbitrage: a way of making a profit that demands no net outlay of capital and involves no risk of loss. Such an opportunity could not persist: option prices would adjust so that it disappeared.

This argument sufficed to derive the famous Black-Scholes option pricing equation, a differential equation linking stock price, option price, stock volatility, the riskless rate of interest, and time (equation 1 in the appendix to this chapter). The characteristics of the option in question (put or call, exercise price, expiration date) enter in the form of a boundary condition. There are complications—a correction for dividend-paying stocks needed to be developed, and the analysis had to be extended from European options (for which there is a simple boundary condition) to American options, the analysis of which can be much more difficult because of the possibility of early exercise (see Merton 1973)[6]—but in at least the simpler cases explicit closed-form mathematical solutions were found. The key such solution, the Black-Scholes formula for the price of a call option on a stock that pays no dividends, is given in the appendix (equation 2).

The Black-Scholes-Merton model was an elegant piece of reasoning that swept away many of the complexities of earlier work on options. Critical is the fact that the mechanism imposing Black-Scholes-Merton option pricing is arbitrage. The extent of investors' risk aversion and whether investors expect stock prices to rise or fall are irrelevant: if the price of an option deviates from its Black-Scholes value, a risk-free profit opportunity that demands no net capital investment is created.

The Black-Scholes-Merton model is a defining—perhaps *the* defining—achievement of modern financial economics, winning Scholes and Merton the 1997 Nobel Prize (Black died in 1995, and the prize is never awarded posthumously). Of course, option theory did not end with their canonical work. It was elaborated rapidly and successfully by them—especially by Merton—and by others. A development of particular practical importance was the binomial model elaborated in Cox, Ross, and Rubinstein (1979), which especially lent itself to computerized numerical solution. It incorporated Black-Scholes-Merton as a special case and facilitated the analysis of American options. Black-Scholes-Merton analysis was broadened to stochastic processes other than the log-normal and to more general "martingale" models. To the analysis were added features such as variable rates of interest, differential rates for borrowing and lending, and stochastically fluctuating levels of volatility. The analysis was extended to corporate securities other than options (for example, debt securities). Indeed, the pricing of options and of related "derivative" securities has become the central topic of modern quantitative finance (see, e.g., Hull 2000), while the theory of "real options" (decisions that involve implicit options) is of wide interest as a methodology for the analysis and improvement of decision making.

In one sense the Black-Scholes-Merton model, in the long run, has been less important to quantitative finance than the novel methodology involved in its derivation by Scholes and Merton.[7] (In brief, to value a derivative, identify a "replicating portfolio" or perfect hedge—in other words, a continuously adjusted portfolio of more basic assets that has the same payoff as the derivative in all states of the world—and then invoke the fact that a position that consists of a perfectly hedged derivative is riskless, and thus can earn only the riskless rate of interest.) In a sense, this methodology is invoked when practitioners use the cost of hedging to price a derivative, which they do all the time.[8] Nevertheless, the fact that this methodology had a canonical product—the Black-Scholes-Merton option model—is helpful from the viewpoint of this chapter, because it enables us to give a specific focus to an enquiry into the performativity of option theory.

Generic and Effective Performativity

Economics, argues Callon (1998), is among the practices that perform markets. What does this claim mean? The most basic level of its meaning is what I call "generic performativity": an aspect of economics (a procedure, a model, a theory, a data set, or whatever) is used in economic practice. However, though that is in principle something that can be determined simply by observing the economic process in question, it is not in itself of great interest. For a claim of performativity to be interesting—for the use of economics to constitute what I call "effective" performativity—an aspect of economics must be used in a way that has effects on the economic processes in question. The incorporation of the aspect of economics into the collective calculation devices (Callon and Muniesa 2003) that constitute markets must *make a difference*: economic processes incorporating the aspect of economics must differ from their analogues in which economics is not incorporated.

To what extent was option theory used in economic processes, and what effects did that use have? The first modern organized options exchange opened in Chicago on April 26, 1973. The key paper (Black and Scholes 1973) had not yet appeared in print (it was in the May–June issue of the *Journal of Political Economy*) but before or immediately after the options exchange opened at least two participants—Mathew Gladstein (see below) and arbitrageur Ed Thorp (MacKenzie 2003)–were aware of the model and ready to employ it. Within a couple of years, they were joined by many others.

The Black-Scholes-Merton model's core was a differential equation (equation 1 in the appendix) that would have been opaque to anyone without college-level training in mathematics. Even in the simple case of a call option on a non-dividend-bearing stock (appendix, equation 2), an unaided human being cannot realistically be expected to calculate a Black-Scholes price. At the very least, a table of natural logarithms and of the distribution function of a normal distribution are needed.[9] However, calculating prices manually in this way is clearly both time-consuming and tedious. It was far more attractive to program computers (or the programmable calculators that were becoming available in the mid-1970s) to produce Black-Scholes prices.

Both computers and calculators had limitations, however, as material mediators between the Black-Scholes-Merton model and the key arenas within which options were bought and sold, the "open-outcry" trading floors of Chicago and of the other options exchanges, in which contracts were made by voice and by hand signals. The computer systems of the 1970s could not in practice be used while trading on such floors, and—despite a widespread impression to the contrary in sources such as Passell (1997)—most traders seem to have regarded the calculators as too slow; even the few seconds needed to input parameter values and obtain a solution could mean loss of profitable trading opportunities. Few "use [programmable calculators] regularly for option evaluation after the initial novelty wears off" (Gastineau 1979, p. 270).[10]

I UNITED STATES STL CORP	EXPIRATION	ANN INT	ANN DEV	DIV AMT	EX DATE	AMEX I 2 OF 7
	JLT 16 76	5.650%	21.00%	5.8700	8/ 4/76	
	OCT 15 76	6.230%	21.00%	5.8700	11/ 3/76	
	JAN 21 77	6.630%	21.00%			

——— 06/04/76 ———	*——— 06/11/76 ———*	*——— 06/18/76 ———*	*——— 06/25/76 ———*	*——— 07/02/76 ———*

Figure 3.2 One of Black's sheets. The numbers on the extreme left-hand side of the table are stock prices, the next set of numbers are strike prices, and the larger numbers in the body of the table are the Black-Scholes values for call options with given expiry dates (e.g., July 16, 1976) on the Fridays of successive weeks (e.g., June 4, 1976). The smaller numbers in the body of the table are the option deltas. The data at the head of the table are interest rates, Black's assumption about stock volatility, and details of the stock dividends.

Instead, an old technology formed the key mediator between the model's mathematics and the shouting, sweating, gesticulating, jostling human bodies on the trading floors: paper. Away from the hubbub, computers were used to generate Black-Scholes prices. Those prices were reproduced on sets of paper sheets which floor traders could carry around, often tightly wound cylindrically with only immediately relevant rows visible so that a quick squint would reveal the relevant price. While some individual traders and trading firms produced their own sheets, others used commercial services. Perhaps the most widely used sheets were sold by Fischer Black himself (see figure 3.2). Each month, Black would produce computer-generated sheets of theoretical prices for all the options traded on U.S. options exchanges, then have them photocopied and sent to those who subscribed to his pricing service. In 1975, for example, sheets for 100 stocks, with three volatility estimates for each stock, cost $300 per month, while a basic service with one stock and one volatility estimate cost $15 per month (Black 1975b).

At first sight, Black's sheets look like monotonous arrays of figures. They were, however, beautifully designed for their intended role in "distributed cognition" (Hutchins 1995a, b). Black included what options traders using the Black-Scholes-Merton model needed to know, but no more than they needed to know—there is virtually no redundant information on a sheet—hence their easy portability. He found an ad hoc but satisfactory way of dealing with the consequences of dividends for option pricing (an issue not addressed in the original version of the model), and devoted particular care to the crucial matter of the estimation of volatility.[11] Even the physical size of the sheets was well-judged. Prices had first to be printed on the large computer line-printer paper of the period, but they were then photoreduced onto standard-sized paper, differently colored for options traded on the different exchanges.[12] The resultant sheets were small enough for easy handling, but not so small that the figures became too hard to read (the reproduction in figure 3.2 is smaller than full scale).

How were Black's sheets and similar option pricing services used? They could, of course, simply be used to set option prices. In April 1976, options trading began on the Pacific Stock Exchange in San Francisco, and financial economist Mark Rubinstein became a trader there. He found his fellow traders on the new exchange initially heavily reliant on Black's sheets: "I walked up [to the most active option trading 'crowd'] and looked at the screen [of market prices] and at the sheet and it was identical. I said to myself, 'academics have triumphed'" (Rubinstein interview, June 12, 2000).

To find such a close fit between the "sheets" and market prices was unusual. However, if there was a divergence, sheets such as Black's could be employed to identify overvalued options to sell (and sometimes also undervalued options to buy). None of the option pricing models directly yielded a theoretical option price; all required input of parameters whose values had to be determined by empirical estimation and sometimes by judgment. Black-Scholes-Merton was the most parsimonious in this respect, but even it requires an estimate of stock volatility that cannot be formed solely by analysis of past stock-price fluctuations, since it is *future* volatility that matters to the price of an option. There were, however, cases—plentiful, for example, in the early months of the operation of the Chicago Board Options Exchange and in the ad hoc New York "put and call" market that preceded it—in which, according both to contemporary testimony (Wellemeyer 1973) and to retrospective accounts (in the oral history interviews drawn on in this chapter),[13] a clear discrepancy appeared between the market prices of options and the Black-Scholes prices generated by plausible volatility estimates. Typically, market prices tended to be substantially *above* Black-Scholes prices.

The Black-Scholes-Merton model and many of its successors (its predecessors were generally less explicit in this respect) did more than provide a guide to option prices: they also suggested how the risks involved in taking positions in the options market could be minimized. The continuously adjusted offsetting position in the underlying asset and cash invoked in the mathematical derivation of the Black-Scholes equation could, at least in principle, be constructed in reality, via the practice that market participants came to call "delta hedging." The requisite size of the position in the underlying asset is determined, in the Black-Scholes analysis, by the option's "delta," the constantly changing but readily calculable partial derivative of the option price with respect to the stock price. As seen in figure 3.2, the subscribers to Black's option service received not just theoretical prices but also delta values. A delta of 96, for example, indicated to a trader who had sold a call option (on a block of 100 shares) that the number of shares that had to be bought to hedge the call was 96.

Because deltas constantly changed, the practical implementation of more than a rough proxy for delta hedging would in most cases incur excessively high transaction costs. However, even an options market participant who would find delta hedging using stock too expensive could nonetheless draw on the Black-Scholes-Merton model to perform the arbitrage operation that participants called "spreading" (see, for example, Galai 1977, pp. 189–194). This operation—which appears to have been widely used—relied on the model to identify pairs of options on the same underlying stock, in which one option was, according to the model, underpriced relative to the other. Traders could then buy the underpriced option and sell its overpriced counterpart, and a simple modification to the Black-Scholes analysis showed how to minimize exposure to the risk of fluctuations in the price of the underlying stock by making the sizes of purchases and sales inversely proportional to the options' deltas.

Although spreading was in use before Black began his option service, the introduction to it that Black provided to its subscribers told them, in his characteristically clear and straightforward prose, how to use the sheets to exploit opportunities for spreading:

> An investor who wants to set up a spread between two maturities or two striking prices can use the [sheets'] option values to decide when to do the spread, and the delta factors to decide how many contracts to have on each side. A spread makes sense if the short side [the options to be sold] is overpriced and the long side [the options to be bought] is underpriced; or if the short side is more overpriced than the long side; or if the short side is less underpriced than the long side.
>
> To find out how many contracts to use on each side of a spread to make it low in risk for small movements of the stock, divide the two delta factors. If a

January option has a delta factor of 15, and the corresponding April option has a delta factor of 30, then a low risk spread between these two options would involve two January contracts for each April contract. (Black 1975b, p. 7)

Spreading was a direct, instrumental use of option theory. The theory could also be drawn upon to defend the legitimacy of the very idea of a market in options. Throughout their history, options had often been suspected of being simply wagers, bets on stock-price movements. In the United States in the 1960s and 1970s, this suspicion was a basis for hostility on the part of regulators to permitting an options exchange (MacKenzie and Millo 2003). However, the Black-Scholes-Merton analysis disentangled options from the moral framework in which they were dangerously close to gambling, and showed how they could be priced and hedged as part of the normal operations of mature, efficient capital markets. Burton R. Rissman, former counsel to the Chicago Board Options Exchange, told me in an interview on November 9, 1999:

> Black-Scholes was really what enabled the exchange to thrive. . . . [I]t gave a lot of legitimacy to the whole notions of hedging and efficient pricing, whereas we were faced in the late 60s–early 70s with the issue of gambling. That issue fell away, and I think Black-Scholes made it fall away. It wasn't speculation or gambling, it was efficient pricing. I think the SEC [Securities and Exchange Commission] very quickly thought of options as a useful mechanism in the securities markets and it's probably—that's my judgment—the effects of Black-Scholes. I never heard the word "gambling" again in relation to stock options traded on the Chicago Board Options Exchange.

Option theory was thus used as a guide to trading and to hedging, and also to legitimate options markets. For these uses to qualify as effective performativity, economic processes with the theory being used must differ from processes without it being used. It could be, for example, that option theory did no more than capture patterns in market prices that were already empirically present before the theory was developed. If that were so, the performativity involved would be so weak that the term that Didier in his chapter in this volume draws from Deleuze—"expression"—could well be preferable, option theory would just be expressing patterns that were already there, in the markets, in a "state of potentiality." Alternatively, it could be that economists were operating as "hired hands" whose intervention did not change economic processes in any truly significant way.[14] If either were the case, we would be dealing only with generic, not effective, performativity.

As Moore and Juh (forthcoming) and Mixon (2006) showed, broad features of the Black-Scholes-Merton model were indeed already present in the patterns of prices in option markets prior to the formulation of the model; indeed, Moore and Juh claim that "long before the development of the formal theory, investors had an intuitive grasp of the determinants of derivative pricing" (forthcoming, p. 1). However, significant discrepancies often appeared between the model and preexisting price patterns. For example, one of Scholes's students obtained access to the diaries of a broker in the ad hoc put-and-call market for the years 1966–1969, and Black and Scholes used the prices recorded in the diaries to test the model, finding that "in general writers [the issuers of options] obtain favorable prices, and . . . there tends to be a systematic mispricing of options as a function of the variance of returns of the stock" (1972, p. 413). Similarly, when the Chicago Board Options Exchange opened for trading "initially prices were not in line with prices predicted from using the Black-Scholes model" (Scholes 1998, p. 486).

These discrepancies suggest that the Black-Scholes-Merton model did more than simply express price patterns that were already there: as I shall argue below, there is reason to think that the use of the model altered price patterns. The model also provided capacities for coordinated action that did not exist prior to its development. This is clearest with respect to the notion of "implied volatility." In this, Black-Scholes-Merton or a similar option pricing model is run "backward," to work out by iterative solution the level of volatility of the underlying asset consistent with the price of options on the asset. The procedure condenses considerable complexity (a plethora of differently priced put and call options with different strike prices and different expiration dates, and perhaps more complex forms of option as well) to a single set of easily compared and easily understood numbers. In the case of most stock-index options, for example, implied volatilities of 15 percent per annum or less currently indicate "normal" conditions; volatilities much above 20 percent per annum indicate serious disquiet about the future; 40 percent per annum indicates deep crisis.

"Implied volatility" is an inherently theoretical notion: its values cannot be calculated without an option pricing model. By simplifying the options markets' complexity to a common metric, implied volatility allowed the burgeoning trading firms of the 1970s, such as O'Connor and Associates, to expand and extend their activities by coordinating teams of floor traders operating on geographically dispersed options exchanges. What was being traded on these exchanges, the firms reasoned, was the Black-Scholes-Merton model's fundamental parameter: volatility. O'Connor traders were provided with sheets from which they could calculate the implied volatilities of the options being bought and sold on trading floors. They would report these implied volatilities by hand signals to the O'Connor booths beside the trading floors and thus to the firm's headquarters: for example, "I can buy Arco [oil company Atlantic

Richfield] on a 15," or, in other words, purchase options the price of which implied a 15 percent per annum volatility of Atlantic Richfield stock. As the trader who told me this put it, there would be "two or three people sitting upstairs saying 'Mickey can buy Arco on a 15. Someone in San Francisco can buy Santa Fe on a 13.' They're both big oil companies . . . if you thought all oil stocks were similar . . . you'd certainly rather buy one on 13 than a 15. . . . [So] they'd say 'don't buy any.'" Coordination was greatly facilitated by the way in which strategies involving a multiplicity of transactions could be talked about very simply: "We would have a morning meeting, and [Michael] Greenbaum [founder of O'Connor and Associates] would say, 'The book isn't long enough volatility. We're looking to buy some,' or 'We bought too much yesterday. We're looking to be less aggressive.'"[15]

Later, paper sheets were replaced by more sophisticated material mediators between option pricing models and floor traders, such as the "Autoquote" system described in MacKenzie and Millo (2003). The key point, however, is that option theory was and is embedded in artifacts that play essential roles in the operation of options exchanges. Just as "speed cards" and "speed bugs" are part of "How a Cockpit Remembers Its Speeds" (Hutchins 1995b), so material implementations of the Black-Scholes-Merton model and of the developments and variants of it became part of how an options exchange calculates options.

Barnesian Performativity

The facts that patterns of option prices in the United States in the late 1960s and early 1970s did not correspond closely to the Black-Scholes-Merton model and that the model was then widely used as a guide to trading raise the intriguing possibility that the model was performative in an especially strong sense: its use brought about a state of affairs of which it was a good empirical description. Let me call this possibility Barnesian performativity.

"I have conceived of a society," writes Barnes, "as a distribution of self-referring knowledge substantially confirmed by the practice it sustains" (1988, p. 166). Consider a simple example: money.[16] A metal disk or piece of paper is not money by virtue of its physical properties alone; it is money because it is believed to be a medium of exchange and store of value, and that belief is validated by the practices it informs. Our shared belief that the pieces of paper we call "dollar bills" are money leads us to treat those pieces of paper in ways that make them constitute money.

Space prohibits exploration of the underlying social theory advanced by Barnes (see Barnes 1983, 1988). Instead, I use the term "Barnesian" simply as a label for a particular subset of the performativity of economics: the subset in which an aspect of economics is used in economic practice, its use has effects, and among these effects is to alter economic processes to make them more like their depiction by economics.

The Black-Scholes-Merton model would have been performative in the Barnesian sense if practices informed by the model altered economic processes toward conformity with it—for example, if they shifted patterns of market prices toward what the model postulated—thus making the model an instance of "knowledge substantially confirmed by the practice it sustains."

Another way of expressing Barnesian performativity is in the idiom of Actor-Network Theory. As Bruno Latour puts it: "Knowledge . . . does not reside in the face-to-face confrontation of a mind with an object. . . . The word 'reference' designates the quality of the chain in its entirety. . . . Truth-value circulates" (1999, p. 69, emphases in original deleted). The suggestion that the Black-Scholes-Merton model may have been performative in the Barnesian sense is the conjecture that the use of the model was part of the chain by which its referential character—its fit to "reality"—was secured.

That this might be the case is suggested by the way in which the discrepancies between model and market seem to have diminished rapidly in the years after the model's publication in 1973. The key difficulty in judging the fit between model and market is the need to input an estimate of volatility before the model yields an option price. As noted above, what is at issue is not past volatility, which can be measured statistically, but market participants' estimates of future volatility, which are not observable. The resultant difficulty was neatly sidestepped by Mark Rubinstein (1985), who—in the most thorough test of the fit of the Black-Scholes-Merton model to 1970s' prices—judged the fit without independently estimating volatility.

Using a subset of a huge database of nearly all Chicago Board Options Exchange price quotations and transactions between August 1976 and August 1978, Rubinstein constructed from matched pairs of observed option prices the estimate of volatility that minimized deviations from Black-Scholes values and calculated the maximum deviations from the Black-Scholes prices implied by the deviation-minimizing volatility estimate. In the case of options on the same stock with the same time to expiration but different strike prices, Rubinstein found typical deviations of around 2 percent. The fit of the model was by no means exact—some residual discrepancies were much higher than 2 percent—but by social-science standards it was strikingly good. When index options were introduced in the 1980s, the fit improved further: residual discrepancies for index options fell to around 1 percent (Rubinstein

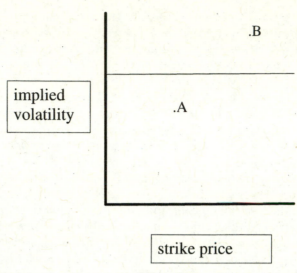

Figure 3.3 If the Black-Scholes-Merton model is correct, the implied volatility of all options on the same stock with the same time to expiration should be the same, so the graph of implied volatility against strike price should be a flat line. Rubinstein used this as a test of the empirical validity of the model. "Spreaders" used it as a way of profiting from price discrepancies. They used the model to identify relatively cheap options to buy (such as point A on the graph) and, simultaneously, relatively expensive options to sell (point B). Such trading could be expected to have the effect of flattening the graph.

1994, p. 774). By 1987, it could with some justice be said that: "When judged by its ability to explain the empirical data, option pricing theory is the most successful theory not only in finance, but in all of economics" (Ross 1987, p. 332).

Although the evidence is only circumstantial, it seems plausible that the "spreading" strategy helps explain the way in which the Black-Scholes-Merton model largely passed its key econometric tests by Rubinstein. In respect to strike prices, Rubinstein's test is essentially whether the graph of implied volatility against strike price is a flat line, as it should be on the model (see figure 3.3). It was precisely deviations from that flat line that "spreaders" were looking for, exploiting, and thus probably causing to diminish. Indeed, even the chief elegant feature of Rubinstein's test—its avoidance of the need independently to estimate volatility— had its counterpart in a practical virtue of spreading: the strategy of constructing offsetting options positions was "less sensitive to the estimated volatility of the stock" (Black 1975a, p. 40) than strategies that required taking a position in the stock. The crucial econometric test of the Black-Scholes-Merton model was thus isomorphic with the practical use of the model in spreading.

Conditions of Felicity

The philosopher J. L. Austin coined the term "performative" to designate utterances that *do* something: if I say "I apologize," or "I name this ship the *Queen Elizabeth*," or "I bet you sixpence it will rain tomorrow," then "in saying what I do, I actually perform the action" (1970, p. 235). There is a sense then that in invoking the notion of performativity one is always also invoking the critique of Austin by Pierre Bourdieu.

To analyze performative utterances using only linguistic philosophy is (as Didier's chapter in this volume suggests) to treat them as "magic." The "conditions of felicity" of a performative utterance "are social conditions," as Bourdieu (1991, p. 73) rightly points out. Only by analyzing these conditions can we understand the difference between the successful performance when a member of the Royal Family names a ship the *Queen Elizabeth* and the unsuccessful performance when a shipyard worker seeks to name it the *Mr Stalin* (Austin 1962, p. 23).

Thus, that sheets based on the Black-Scholes-Merton model were available does not explain why they were bought and used. Even if the use of sheets was thought necessary—and not all options traders believed it was (MacKenzie and Millo 2003)—Black's sheets were not the only options advisory service available in the late 1970s. Gastineau's *Stock Options Manual* (1975) listed three such services; the book's second edition (1979) listed 15. Of the latter, six did not offer option values, so were not directly comparable with Black's service. Five services, including Black's, offered theoretical prices generated from the Black-Scholes-Merton model or variants thereof. The remaining four services, however, used a different approach, offering option values based not on theoretical reasoning but on econometric analyses of observed price patterns; these analyses seem mainly to have been variants of the econometric work of Sheen Kassouf (1965).

Why might an options market participant in the 1970s have chosen to use Black's sheets or another material implementation of the Black-Scholes-Merton model? The answer might simply be because the sheets were a good guide to market prices, but, as noted above, the fit between model and market was not always close, especially in the earlier part of the decade. Although it is difficult to be certain of the reasons for the dominance of the Black-Scholes-Merton model, a number of factors seem likely to have been significant. One factor—perhaps the factor closest to Bourdieu's emphasis on the interrelations of language, power, legitimacy, and cultural hierarchy—was the authority of economics. Financial economists quickly came to see the Black-Scholes-Merton model as superior to its predecessors. As noted above, it involved no nonobservable parameters except for volatility, and it had a clear theoretical basis, one closely linked to the field's dominant viewpoint: efficient market theory. The Black-Scholes-Merton model thus "inherited" the general cognitive authority of financial economics in a political culture in which economics was a useful source of legitimacy, and in which, in particular, the status of financial economics was rising fast (MacKenzie 2006).

That the Black-Scholes-Merton model thus embodied the most authoritative account of what options "ought" to cost might well have been a factor for market participants with links to academia. However, while there were a number of such participants, Chicago floor traders in general were and are not in awe of professors. From their viewpoint, however, the model had the advantage of "cognitive" simplicity. The underlying mathematics might be complicated, but the model could be talked about and thought about relatively straightforwardly; its one free parameter—volatility—was easily grasped, discussed, and reasoned about. Kassouf's model, in contrast, involved a regression equation with six coefficients that required econometric estimation (Kassouf 1965, p. 55). An options pricing service based on Kassouf's model would perform the requisite calculations, but from the user's viewpoint such a model was a black box; it could not be reasoned about and talked about in as simple a way as the Black-Scholes-Merton model could. Many of the variants of, modifications of, and alternatives to Black-Scholes-Merton that quickly were offered by other financial economists also had a crucial drawback in this respect, since they typically involved a mental grasp of, and estimation of, more than one free parameter—often three or more. As *The Stock Options Manual* put it, "The user of these complex models is called upon to deal with more unknowns than the average human mind can handle" (Gastineau 1979, p. 253).

Another factor underlying the success of the Black-Scholes-Merton model was simply that it was publicly available in a way many of its early competitors were not. As U.S. law stood in the 1960s and 1970s, an options pricing model was unlikely to be granted patent or copyright protection, so there was a temptation not to disclose the details of a model. Keeping the details private may have been perfectly sensible for those who hoped to make money from their models, but it was a barrier to the adoption of those models by others. Black, Scholes, and Merton, however, did publish the details, as did Sheen Kassouf (whose model was described in his PhD dissertation).[17]

Not only was the Black-Scholes-Merton model public, but the necessary material mediators—especially Black's sheets—were also available

($300 a month in mid-1970s' dollars was no trivial cost, but it was within the means of major market participants, and it could of course be shared, with traders banding together to subscribe and then photocopying the sheets). In contrast, Gary Gastineau (author of *The Stock Options Manual*) developed, along with Albert Madansky of the University of Chicago, a model that Gastineau believed remedied what he felt were the deficiencies of Black-Scholes-Merton (see below). However, not only did he publish only "an outline of the general form" of his model, but he used its results "solely for the benefit of certain individual and institutional clients" (Gastineau 1979, pp. 203, 269), rather than making them available more widely in the form of an options pricing service. So Gastineau was in the paradoxical situation of being a critic of the Black-Scholes-Merton model who, nevertheless, felt compelled to recommend Black's sheets to the readers of his *Stock Options Manual,* which seems to have been the guide most widely used by newcomers to options trading: "Until another weekly service incorporates Black's service, his tables . . . are the best evaluation data available to the average investor" (Gastineau 1979, p. 269).[18]

The situation was perhaps akin to the triumph of the publicly available IBM personal computer (PC) architecture over its proprietary rivals, especially Apple. Whether or not IBM's architecture was better than Apple's can be debated endlessly, but a key factor was that it (like the Black-Scholes-Merton model) was available for others to adopt in a way in which Apple's was not.

These three factors—the Black-Scholes-Merton model's high academic standing, its cognitive simplicity, and its PC-like public availability—were reasons for options traders to adopt it, for example by subscribing to Black's sheets and using them as a guide to trading. Beyond these factors, however, were two ways in which the model's use influenced the behavior of those who did not agree with it and even of those who did not know what it was. (One interviewee at the Chicago Board Options Exchange reported being asked "What's this Black-Scholes?" even in the early 1980s.)

The first such route of influence was competition. As noted above, with plausible estimates of volatility the Black-Scholes-Merton model tended to generate option values that were below the market prices prevalent in the ad hoc put-and-call market and in the early months of the Chicago Board Options Exchange. For a critic of the model such as Gastineau, that was an indication that the model undervalued options. However, it also meant that market competition tended to drive option prices down toward Black-Scholes values. The supply of options is not fixed. Individuals and institutions can "write" (that is, issue) options whenever they believe that the prices for which they can be sold are advantageous.[19] If such individuals or institutions believe that Black-Scholes values are "correct," market prices above those values will be taken to indicate just such a situation.[20]

The process began the very day the Chicago Board Options Exchange opened for trading. Mathew Gladstein of the securities firm Donaldson, Lufkin and Jenrette had contracted with Scholes and Merton to provide theoretical prices ready for its opening:

> The first day that the Exchange opened . . . I looked at the prices of calls and I looked at the model and the calls were maybe 30–40 percent overvalued! And I called Myron [Scholes] in a panic and said, "Your model is a joke," and he said, "Give me the prices," and he went back and he huddled with Merton and he came back. He says, "The model's right." And I ran down the hall . . . and I said, "Give me more money and we're going to have a killing ground here." (Gladstein interview, November 15, 1999).

From Gastineau's viewpoint, the resultant process was alarming—"Widespread use of the Black-Scholes model by institutional investors may have the effect of both depressing and distorting actual option premiums" (Gastineau 1975, p. 200)—but from another viewpoint it was a performative effect of the model. Black-Scholes prices were, in a sense, imposed even on those writers of options who believed such prices to be too low: they either had to lower the prices at which they sold options or see their business taken away from them by the adherents of Black-Scholes.

The second mechanism by which others' adherence to Black-Scholes-Merton influenced the behavior of traders who did not believe in it was via risk-management practices (see Millo 2003). If a trader on an organized options exchange became bankrupt, his or her clearing firm inherited his or her liabilities; if a clearing firm failed, the other such firms bore its liabilities. This created a strong incentive to monitor traders' risk-taking; as one interviewee put it, "If you're guaranteeing people's trades, you don't want them making stupid bets with your money."

Assessing the risks being taken by a trader was far from simple, since he or she might hold dozens of option positions, and perhaps positions in the underlying stock as well. The Black-Scholes-Merton model's deltas could, however, be aggregated to a single measure of exposure to the price movements of a given stock. If a trader's aggregate delta was close to zero, his or her positions were "delta-neutral" and could be considered to a first approximation well-hedged; if the delta was substantial, then the trader's positions were, in aggregate, risky. Sophisticated risk managers learned not to stop at delta, but also to consider the other measures colloquially known as "the Greeks," such as gamma (the second derivative of option value with respect to the price of the underlying asset, in other, words the rate at which delta changes as the price of the underlying asset changes).

Just how effectively the Black-Scholes-Merton model was deployed in the 1970s and 1980s as a "disciplinary" tool of risk management is questionable; a clearing firm that attempted too closely to control its traders' risk-taking faced the possibility of them defecting to a different clearer with a more liberal approach. However, if a trader's clearer cared whether his or her positions were delta-neutral, or had other model-dependent characteristics, then the trader might at least have to consider the matter, which required that Black's sheets or some other instantiation of the model be consulted. Furthermore, the Black-Scholes-Merton model had a *communicative* function in respect to risk (Millo 2003). Unlike its predecessors, from which measures of risk could often be extracted only clumsily,[21] the Black-Scholes-Merton model allowed the risks of options trading to be *talked about* among traders, clearing firms, the Options Clearing Corporation, exchange officials, and regulators.

A Changing World

Given its theoretical elegance and its practical advantages, why might the Black-Scholes-Merton model nevertheless be considered by some to be deficient? The model's developers, and all sophisticated users of it, knew that the market conditions it posited were idealizations. Black repeatedly warned of this (see, for example, Black 1988), and some of Merton's work was directed precisely at supplementing the model: see, for example, Merton (1976), which analyzes option pricing when stock prices can "jump" discontinuously, as they can in actuality but not in the original model.

It was, indeed, straightforward for anyone with experience of the markets of the 1970s to list ways in which the Black-Scholes-Merton model's assumptions were unrealistic. Gastineau, for example, provided such a list, asserting that their aggregate consequence was a tendency for the model to generate theoretical prices that were "on average too low" (Gastineau 1975, pp. 198–200). For example, transaction costs were not zero, and the continuous rehedging posited in the model's derivation was therefore infeasibly expensive. Short selling was often difficult and generally subject to financial penalties: the proceeds on a short sale were held as collateral by the broker from whom stock had been borrowed, and in the 1970s the entirety of the interest on such proceeds was typically retained by the broker. Gastineau especially emphasized a further point: work in financial economics in the 1960s had shown that stock price movements, at least over short timescales, did not follow the log-normal distribution of the Black-Scholes-Merton model. Such movements were "fat-tailed," with extreme movements happening far more frequently than implied by log-normality.

However, during the 1970s and 1980s many of the Black-Scholes-Merton model's assumptions became less unrealistic. Transaction costs generally fell: for instance, New York Stock Exchange commissions on stock transactions (a major transaction cost for any options-market participant other than members of the New York exchange) fell rapidly after a prolonged battle ended with the abolition of fixed commissions on May 1, 1975 (see Seligman 1982). As short selling—stigmatized since the 1930s as an alleged tool of market manipulation and cause of crashes—gradually regained acceptability, and as pension funds began to be prepared to earn extra returns by lending their stock for short selling,[22] the latter's costs also fell, albeit less dramatically than in the case of commissions.

Above all, the introduction in the United States in 1982 of stock-index futures—especially the Standard and Poor's S&P 500 index futures bought and sold on the Chicago Mercantile Exchange—meant that when index options began to be traded in 1983 they inhabited a world in which key Black-Scholes-Merton assumptions had indeed become more realistic. Buying a future permitted the "virtual" purchase of a large block of stock (the stock of the corporations comprising the index), but with much lower transaction costs than incurred in actual purchase, and with the purchase price of the stock being, in effect, borrowed almost in its entirety. Selling such a future was in effect equivalent to short sale of the same block of stock, but with none of the difficulties and little of the expense of conventional short selling.

Most of these changes had little directly to do with the Black-Scholes-Merton model. Factors such as technological change, the growing influence of free-market economics, and the shifting political climate (crystallized in the 1980 election of President Reagan) were more important. Some effects of the model can nonetheless be pointed to. As noted above, the Black-Scholes-Merton analysis helped grant legitimacy to options trading. Another factor was that earlier upsurges of such trading had typically been reversed, arguably because option prices had usually been "too high" in the sense that they made options a poor purchase because they could too seldom be exercised profitably (Kairys and Valerio 1997). The availability of the Black-Scholes formula, and its associated hedging and risk-measurement techniques, gave participants the confidence to write options at lower prices, helping options exchanges to grow and to prosper.

High-volume trading of options in organized options exchanges (rather than in the earlier, much lower volume, ad hoc put-and-call market) permitted far lower transaction costs. The discrepancies between the model and put-and-call market prices identified by Black and Scholes (1972) could not, they noted, be exploited economically—transaction costs were too high. As such costs fell, even small discrepancies could be exploited and so could be expected to diminish. To the extent that the availability of the Black-Scholes-Merton model played a part in the processes reducing transaction costs, the increased capacity to exploit discrepancies was a performative effect of the model: the model facilitated the trading that moved patterns of prices toward its postulates.

The capacity to generate theoretical prices was also important in the growth of the over-the-counter (direct, institution-to-institution) derivatives market, the overall volume of which came to exceed that of exchange-traded derivatives. Many of the instruments traded in the over-the-counter market are highly specialized, and sometimes no liquid market, or easily observable market price, exists for them. However, both the vendors of them (usually investment banks) and at least the more sophisticated purchasers of them can often calculate theoretical prices, and thus have a benchmark "fair" price.

The Black-Scholes-Merton analysis and subsequent developments of it are also central to the capacity of an investment bank to operate at large scale in this market. They enable the risks involved in derivatives portfolios to be decomposed mathematically. Many of these risks are mutually offsetting, so the residual risk that requires hedging is often quite small in relation to the overall portfolio. Major investment banks can thus "operate on such a scale that they can provide liquidity as if they had no transaction costs" (Taleb 1998, p. 36; see also Merton and Bodie 2005). So the Black-Scholes-Merton assumption of zero transaction costs is now close to true for the derivatives portfolios of major investment banks—in part because the use of that theory and its developments by those banks allows them to manage their portfolios in a way that minimizes transaction costs.

Counterperformativity?

All this may seem a smooth tale of performativity—of generic performativity, effective performativity, and probably at least some elements of Barnesian performativity. But the tale has a twist: the gigantic one-day fall of the U.S. stock market on October 19, 1987. The fall was a grotesquely unlikely event on the assumption of log-normality: for example, Jackwerth and Rubinstein (1996, p. 1612) calculate the probability on that assumption of the actual fall in S&P index futures as 10^{-160}. What the crash led to was more than a disembodied rejection of the null hypothesis of log-normality. The fall in stock prices came close to setting off a chain of market-maker bankruptcies that would have threatened the very existence of organized derivatives exchanges in the United States, and perhaps even of the New York Stock Exchange. The subsequent systematic departure from Black-Scholes option pricing—the so-called volatility smile or volatility skew, a pattern of option pricing in which the graph of implied volatility against strike price (figure 3.3) is no longer a flat line—is more than a mathematical adjustment to empirical departures from log-normality: it is too large fully to be accounted for in that way (see, for example, Jackwerth 2000). It can in a sense be seen as the options market's collective defense against systemic risk (MacKenzie and Millo 2003).

The empirical history of option pricing has, therefore, not two phases but three. The initial phase of relatively poor fit between the Black-Scholes-Merton model and market prices was followed by the second phase, described above, in which the fit improved rapidly (in part, I have conjectured, as a performative effect of the model's use). That second phase, and thus the Barnesian performativity of classic option theory, ended on October 19, 1987. In the third phase—from 1987 to the time of writing—option theory is still performed in the generic and effective senses (it is used, and its use makes a difference), but its canonical model has lost its Barnesian powers. When Rubinstein's test (sketched in figure 3.3) was repeated after 1987, the flat line that is the Black-Scholes-Merton model's trace had vanished (Rubinstein 1994). It has not reappeared; the volatility skew that has replaced it seems enduring.

Among the factors exacerbating the 1987 crash, one intriguing possibility is an application of option pricing theory: portfolio insurance. This involves using the theory to synthesize a put option, and thus a "floor" below which the value of an investment portfolio will not fall. The synthesis of a put requires sales of stock (or of index futures) as stock prices fall, and such sales have been cited as a major process in the crash, for example, by the main official inquiry (Brady Commission 1988). That portfolio insurance exacerbated the crash cannot be proved, but neither is there a decisive way of showing it played no part (see MacKenzie 2004). If it did have a role, it would be an instance of what one might call "counterperformativity." This is Barnesian performativity's opposite: the use of an aspect of economics altering economic processes so that they conform less well to their depiction by economics. If portfolio insurance exacerbated the crash, it made at least the classic form of the option theory underpinning the technique not more true, but less.

Whatever the causes of the 1987 crash, that empirical patterns of option prices since 1987 no longer follow the Black-Scholes-Merton model has an analytical advantage from the viewpoint of this chapter. It answers a possible objection: that the model is simply right, that it captures the only stable way a mature, efficient market can price options, and that talk of the model's "performativity" is therefore just a fancy way of saying something that could thus be said much more simply. The existence of the skew since 1987 reveals the historical contingency of what I have suggested is the phase of the Barnesian performativity of the model. In that phase, price patterns followed the model (to at least a fair degree of accuracy) not because they were the only patterns that were possible but, at least in part, because of the model's existence and use. The model made a difference, and if this chapter's conjecture is correct, part of that difference was that market prices moved toward the postulates of the model.

Conclusion

In the societies of high modernity, the generic—and probably also the effective—performativity of economics seems pervasive.[23] Callon and Muniesa argue that markets are collective calculation mechanisms, in other words, sociotechnical apparatuses that allow a good to be made comparable with other goods, to be evaluated, and a "result"—"a price, a classification, a choice"—produced (2003, p. 205). Economic practices such as marketing and accounting clearly play constitutive roles in such mechanisms, and economics in the academic, disciplinary sense is increasingly involved too. The financial derivatives market may be an unusually clear case of the effective performativity of economics—it is hard to imagine today's huge volumes of derivatives trading being possible without the calculative resources that option theory and its many developments provide—but it is surely not unique.

In this chapter, however, I have sought to do more than to document how economic models and their products such as "implied volatility" make it possible to "calculate" derivatives: to legitimate, to compare, to evaluate, to price, and to hedge them. From within the overall domain of the performativity of economics, I have suggested isolating two particular cases: Barnesian performativity, in which the use of an aspect of economics alters economic processes so that they are more like their depiction by economics, and counterperformativity, in which the effect of use is to make those processes less like their depiction.

Are Barnesian performativity and counterperformativity simply new names for self-fulfilling and self-negating prophecies, which are old topics (see Merton 1948)? If, as Krishna (1971) and Barnes (1983) advocate, the notion of self-fulfilling prophecy is generalized beyond the original predominant attention to pathological forms of inference (in which the "true reality" of a social situation is overturned by a widespread misconception, as in a sound bank failing as the result of a bank run), then the notion becomes perfectly applicable to financial markets (see, for example, MacKenzie 2001) and it is one which is, of course, used frequently by economists.

However, the notions of Barnesian performativity and counterperformativity have the advantage that they locate the processes to which they point as subsets of the wider topic of the generic and effective performativity of economics. The notions also avoid the frequent—albeit entirely unnecessary—association of self-fulfilling prophecy with arbitrariness. It would, for example, be quite mistaken to imagine that any arbitrary option pricing formula, proposed by sufficiently authoritative people, could have been performative in the Barnesian sense other than very fleetingly. If, for example, the use of such a formula gave rise to substantial arbitrage opportunities, then it would have been unlikely to "make itself true" in anything other than an evanescent sense. Barnesian performativity is not arbitrary self-fulfilling prophecy.

To invoke Austin's coinage—"performative"—can, of course, give rise to a misconception of a different sort: that we are dealing with some mysterious power of words. Bourdieu's point is essential: we must not imagine we can identify performativity purely as a linguistic process, and we must also always inquire into the social, cultural, and political nature of the "conditions of felicity" of the process. Nor should we forget one of Callon's main arguments: the collective calculation mechanisms that constitute markets are *material*. The Black-Scholes-Merton model could not have been performed in the markets had it remained simply a conceptualization in economists' heads. The reason I have emphasized the role of Black's sheets is to highlight their significance as material means of calculation, as aspects of "distributed cognition," as ways of connecting the apparently abstract mathematics of the model to the sweaty, jostling bodies on exchange trading floors.

While one can be reasonably sure that the generic performativity and effective performativity of economics are widespread, matters are not so clear in respect to Barnesian performativity and counterperformativity, which may be rare and hard to identify unequivocally. The role played by models and other aspects of economics will always be interwoven with other factors. Part of what gave Black-Scholes-Merton its performative power was its linking to the Chicago derivatives exchanges, with their traditions of price transparency and competition among market makers. Take away this linkage, and patterns of option pricing no closer to Black-Scholes-Merton than those of a century ago can still prevail today, as Moore and Juh demonstrate for the case of options sold to retail investors in South Africa: "Mispricing on the modern JSE [Johannesburg Stock Exchange] is at a comparable level with mispricing in the early twentieth century" (forthcoming, p. 21).

Furthermore, what is probably unusual about the case of option theory (one cannot be entirely sure about its frequency until far more empirical work is done) is the existence of a single, stable, canonical form of the theory: the Black-Scholes-Merton model. Option theory developed and diversified, but there remains a sense in which the Black-Scholes-Merton model is the benchmark. The very conceptualization of the empirical phenomenon that undermines it—the post-1987 volatility "skew"—is testimony to the model's canonical role: it is a skew with respect to the Black-Scholes-Merton flat-line relationship between strike price and implied volatility.

If an area of economics is too diverse and is changing too fast, empirical enquiry into Barnesian performativity and counterperformativity becomes very difficult. If different theories or models are used by different participants, and if they are frequently discarded and replaced, then their use may have effects on their "truth," but identifying those effects will be problematic because it will be difficult to know where to start.[24] The circumstances that make the enquiry feasible in the case of option theory—a widely used canonical model, and decades of empirical tests of the model—are probably not unique, but they may not be common.

Although empirical investigations of Barnesian performativity and counterperformativity may therefore be difficult, one virtue of the notions is that in respect to an economic theory or model they prompt us to ask a question additional to the two natural questions (Is the theory or model analytically tractable? and Does it adequately represent some economic process?). The additional question is this: What would be the effects of the widespread use of the theory or model? That third question *was*, for example, asked prior to 1987 of the use of option theory in portfolio insurance, but not often enough and influentially enough (see MacKenzie 2004).

It is possible that in some circumstances the answer to the third question should be given greater weight than the answers to the other two. That, for example, was implicitly the post-1987 judgment of the Options Clearing Corporation, the ultimate guarantor of U.S. exchange-traded options. It adopted a model that mainstream financial economics had rejected: Benoit Mandelbrot's infinite-variance Lévy distributions (see Mirowski 1995). These distributions capture the feature whose absence from the Black-Scholes-Merton model's log-normal random walk had disturbed Gastineau: "fat tails," in other words, the high probabilities of extreme events. However, mainstream financial economics came to view infinite-variance distributions as analytically unattractive (they undermine standard statistical techniques), and as having features that are unintuitive and difficult to square with empirical price data (MacKenzie

2006). After being the focus of much attention in the 1960s, they were discarded from the academic mainstream at the start of the 1970s.

The virtue that the Options Clearing Corporation saw in infinite-variance Lévy distributions twenty years later was, in effect, their potential counterperformativity. An infinite-variance distribution assigns high probabilities to extreme events, so when such events take place the estimators of the distribution's parameters change only modestly. Compared to the normal distribution, the estimator of whose variance is far more sensitive to extreme events, infinite-variance distributions thus have an advantage as the basis for determining the margin deposits demanded from options-market participants (which is the role in which the Options Clearing Corporation uses them). Infinite-variance distributions do not exacerbate a crisis by generating sudden demands for hugely increased margin deposits. By adopting a model that assigns high probabilities to extreme, dangerous events, the Options Clearing Corporation hopes to reduce the chances of such events (see MacKenzie 2006).

As I have acknowledged, Barnesian performativity and counterperformativity can be difficult to investigate, and (in any full sense) they may be rare. They point us, however, to a vital issue. An economic theory or model posits a world, so to speak. It is too simple to ask only if that world is realistic (as in the standard criticism that economics is unrealistic). We must also ask if the widespread use of the theory or model will make the world it posits more real or less real. If either is the case, we need to ask whether that world is to be desired or to be avoided. Sometimes that is easy to answer: few will see a world of frequent financial crises akin to the 1987 crash as desirable, and the Options Clearing Corporation's wish to avoid such a world is entirely understandable. Other cases, however, will be more nuanced and more controversial. Difficult as the resultant issues are, they are too important to be settled by default. The desirability of markets is debated often, but frequently at a high level of generality, while the crucial detail of the collective calculation mechanisms that constitute them usually escapes widespread scrutiny. If attention to the performativity of economics encourages such scrutiny, then it is indeed worthwhile.

Appendix: The Black-Scholes Equation for a European Option on a Non-Dividend-Bearing Stock

The Black-Scholes option-pricing equation is

$$\frac{\partial w}{\partial t} = rw - rx\frac{\partial w}{\partial x} - \frac{1}{2}\sigma^2 x^2 \frac{\partial^2 w}{\partial x^2} \qquad (1)$$

where w is the price of the option, x is the price of the stock, t is time, r is the riskless rate of interest and σ the volatility of the stock price. ("Volatility" is the extent of the fluctuations of the stock price, measured by the annualized standard deviation of continuously compounded returns on the stock. The "riskless rate" is the rate of interest paid by a borrower who creditors are certain will not default.)

The canonical solution to the Black-Scholes equation is for a European call option. Such an option gives the right to buy the stock at price c at time t^*. Its value is thus zero if x^*, the stock price at time t^*, is less than or equal to c, and $x^* - c$ if x^* is greater than c. This known set of values for w at time t^* forms a boundary condition, and equation (1) can then be solved to yield the following expression for the value of a European call option:

$$w = xN\left[\frac{\ln(x/c) + (r + \frac{1}{2}\sigma^2)(t^* - t)}{\sigma\sqrt{t^* - t}}\right]$$
$$- c[\exp\{r(t - t^*)\}]N\left[\frac{\ln(x/c) + (r + \frac{1}{2}\sigma^2)(t^* - t)}{\sigma\sqrt{t^* - t}}\right] \tag{2}$$

where N is the (cumulative) distribution function of a normal or Gaussian distribution, and ln indicates natural logarithm. The result also holds for an American call option with expiration t^*; Merton (1973, pp. 143–44) showed, under quite general conditions, that the early exercise of an American call on a non-dividend-bearing stock is never optimal, so its theoretical value is equal to that of a European call. As noted in the text, however, the analysis of American calls on dividend-bearing stocks and of American puts is considerably more complicated, and in practice seems most often to be treated by computational techniques, based, for example, on the finite-time binomial model of Cox, Ross, and Rubinstein (1979). (The Black-Scholes-Merton model is a limit case of the binomial model.)

Notes

1. An earlier version of this chapter was published in the *Journal of the History of Economic Thought* 28 (2006):29–55, and reports work supported by a Professorial Fellowship awarded by the UK Economic and Social Research Council (RES-051-27-0062). It builds upon three existing papers on option theory and its practical applications: MacKenzie and Millo (2003), MacKenzie (2003), and MacKenzie (2004). For historical details of the case discussed here, the above papers and MacKenzie (2006) should be consulted.

2. Data from Bank for International Settlements, http://www.bis.org, accessed January 3, 2006.

3. Sometimes the crisis of the hedge fund Long-Term Capital Management (LTCM) is viewed as an instance of problems in the practical application of option theory, but this overstates the importance of option theory to LTCM and misses the market dynamics that led to its crisis. See MacKenzie (2006, pp. 211–242).

4. The terms "European" and "American" originally pointed to geographical differences in typical options contracts, but that is no longer the case: European as well as American options are now traded in the United States, and American options are traded in Europe. There are also forms of option more complex than these, but they need not detain us.

5. This early work on option theory includes the now celebrated work of Louis Bachelier (1900) and the more recently rediscovered work of a Trieste actuarial professor, Vinzenz Bronzin (1908; see Zimmermann and Hafner 2004).

6. For example, "There is almost always a positive probability of premature exercising of an American put, and hence, the American put will sell for more than its European counterpart" (Merton 1973, p. 158).

7. The original derivation by Black was a direct invocation of the Capital Asset Pricing Model: see MacKenzie (2003) and Mehrling (2005).

8. "In most . . . derivatives markets, price is determined by hedging cost," write four practitioners (McGinty et al. 2004, p. 20).

9. Experienced options traders can in practice mentally estimate Black-Scholes prices. However, they do not do this by inputting parameter values into formulas such as equation 2 of the appendix; rather, they seem to draw on their long experience of Black-Scholes pricing. Their "mental" solutions are thus in a sense derivative of the "material" solutions described in the text.

10. An additional particular difficulty was making the necessary adjustment to Black-Scholes to take into account the payment of dividends, which "on a hand calculator is difficult and time-consuming" (Gastineau 1979, p. 269).

11. "My initial estimates of volatility are based on 10 years of daily data on stock prices and dividends, with more weight on more recent data. Each month, I update the estimates. Roughly speaking, last month's estimate gets four-fifths weight, and the most recent month's actual volatility gets one-fifth weight. I also make some use of the changes in volatility on stocks generally, of the direction in which the stock price has been moving, and of the 'market's estimates' of volatility, as suggested by the level of option prices for the stock" (Black 1975b, p. 5).

12. I am grateful for this information to Clay Struve, who as an MIT undergraduate in the 1970s earned money doing such tasks for Black's option service.

13. For details of the interviewing, see MacKenzie and Millo (2003) and MacKenzie (2006).

14. See Mirowski and Nik-Khah's chapter in this volume.

15. See MacKenzie and Millo (2003).

16. See also Searle (1996).

17. See Gastineau (1975, p. 184).

18. See also Gastineau (1975, pp. 177–178). A specific factor influencing Gastineau's 1979 recommendation was that Black had been quick to incorporate into his service the results of analysis (by Parkinson 1977) of the pricing of

American puts, a problem to which, as noted above, the Black-Scholes approach did not yield an immediate solution. Initially, the organized options exchanges in the United States were allowed to trade only calls, but in June 1977 put trading began (Cox and Rubinstein 1985, p. 24), creating a need for pricing puts.

19. Assuming, that is, that they have the funds to meet the necessary brokers' commissions and requirements for "margin" deposits.

20. Of course, the question arises of why the "downward pressure" on prices discussed in the text was not counterbalanced, as it appears not to have been, by purchases of options by those who believed that Black-Scholes prices were too low. Among the factors that may have been important were different budgetary constraints on those who were not market makers but used the options exchanges (1) to write options or (2) to buy options. When organized options trading began in the early 1970s, "one of Wall Street's most widely held beliefs is that option buyers consistently lose money and option writers consistently make money" (Gastineau 1975, p. 138), a factor that may explain why in the early years the purchasers of options seem to have been mainly private individuals, with institutional investors involved, if at all, only in writing options. The initial period of organized options trading coincided with a "bear market," so the early experience of buying calls (as noted above, puts were not traded until 1977) is likely to have done little to disturb the above widespread conviction among professionals (Gastineau 1975, p. 138–9, 152).

21. Most mathematical models of the relationship between stock and option prices—Kassouf's, for example—allow the equivalent of delta to be calculated. However, the calculation was often more complicated than glancing at the values of delta on Black's sheets. In the most influential version of Kassouf's model (Thorp and Kassouf 1967), calculating the equivalent of delta involves drawing a graph of the relationship between stock and option price and estimating the slope of the graph at the appropriate point.

22. See Swensen (2000, p. 145).

23. See, for example, Faulhaber and Baumol (1988) and MacKenzie (2006).

24. These difficulties would attend any investigation of whether post-1987 patterns of option pricing are Barnesian performative effects of models other than Black-Scholes-Merton.

References

Austin, J. L. 1962. *How to Do Things with Words*. Oxford: Clarendon.

Austin, J. L. 1970. *Philosophical Papers*. 2nd ed. Oxford: Clarendon.

Bachelier, L. 1900. "Théorie de la spéculation." *Annales de l'Ecole Normale Supérieure*, third series 17:22–86.

Barnes, B. 1983. "Social Life as Bootstrapped Induction." *Sociology* 17: 524–545.

Barnes, B. 1988. *The Nature of Power*. Cambridge: Polity.

Bernstein, P. L. 1992. *Capital Ideas: The Improbable Origins of Modern Wall Street*. New York: Free Press.

Black, F. 1975a. "Fact and Fantasy in the Use of Options." *Financial Analysts Journal* 31:36–41, 61–72.

Black, F. 1975b. "The Option Service: An Introduction." Personal papers of Mark Rubinstein.

Black, F. 1988. "The Holes in Black-Scholes." *Risk* 1/4 (March):30–32.

Black, F., and M. Scholes. 1972. "The Valuation of Option Contracts and a Test of Market Efficiency." *Journal of Finance* 27:399–417.

Black, F., and M. Scholes. 1973. "The Pricing of Options and Corporate Liabilities." *Journal of Political Economy* 81:637–654.

Bourdieu, P. 1991. *Language and Symbolic Power*. Cambridge: Polity.

Brady Commission. 1988. *Report of the Presidential Task Force on Market Mechanisms*. Washington, DC: U.S. Government Printing Office.

Bronzin, V. 1908. *Theorie der Prämiengeschäfte*. Leipzig: Franz Deuticke.

Callon, M., Ed. 1998. *The Laws of the Markets*. Oxford: Blackwell.

Callon, M., and F. Muniesa. 2003. "Les marchés économiques comme dispositifs collectifs de calcul." *Réseaux* 122:189–233.

Cox, J. C., and M. Rubinstein. 1985. *Options Markets*. Englewood Cliffs, NJ: Prentice Hall.

Cox, J. C., S. A. Ross, and M. Rubinstein. 1979. "Option Pricing: A Simplified Approach." *Journal of Financial Economics* 7:229–263.

Faulhaber, G. L., and W. J. Baumol. 1988. "Economists as Innovators: Practical Products of Theoretical Research." *Journal of Economic Literature* 26: 577–600.

Galai, D. 1977. "Tests of Market Efficiency of the Chicago Board Options Exchange." *Journal of Business* 50:167–197.

Gastineau, G. L. 1975. *The Stock Options Manual*. New York: McGraw-Hill.

Gastineau, G. L. 1979. *The Stock Options Manual*. 2nd ed. New York: McGraw-Hill.

Hull, J. C. 2000. *Options, Futures, & Other Derivatives*. Upper Saddle River, NJ: Prentice Hall.

Hutchins, E. 1995a. *Cognition in the Wild*. Cambridge, MA: MIT Press.

Hutchins, E. 1995b. "How a Cockpit Remembers Its Speeds." *Cognitive Science* 19:265–288.

Jackwerth, J. C. 2000. "Recovering Risk Aversion from Option Prices and Realized Returns." *Review of Financial Studies* 13:433–451.

Jackwerth, J. C., and M. Rubinstein. 1996. "Recovering Probability Distributions from Option Prices." *Journal of Finance* 51:1611–1631.

Kairys, J. P., Jr., and N. Valerio III. 1997. "The Market for Equity Options in the 1870s." *Journal of Finance* 52:1707–1723.

Kassouf, S. T. 1965. *A Theory and an Econometric Model for Common Stock Purchase Warrants*. Brooklyn, NY: Analytical Publishers.

Krishna, D. 1971. "'The Self-Fulfilling Prophecy' and the Nature of Society." *American Sociological Review* 36:1104–1107.

Latour, B. 1999. *Pandora's Hope: Essays on the Reality of Science Studies*. Cambridge, MA: Harvard University Press.

MacKenzie, D. 2001. "Physics and Finance: S-Terms and Modern Finance as a Topic for Science Studies." *Science, Technology, & Human Values* 26: 115–144.

MacKenzie, D. 2003. "An Equation and Its Worlds: Bricolage, Exemplars, Disunity and Performativity in Financial Economics." *Social Studies of Science* 33:831–868.

MacKenzie, D. 2004. "The Big, Bad Wolf and the Rational Market: Portfolio Insurance, the 1987 Crash and the Performativity of Economics." *Economy and Society* 33:303–334.

MacKenzie, D. 2006. *An Engine, Not a Camera: How Financial Models Shape Markets.* Cambridge, MA: MIT Press.

MacKenzie, D., and Y. Millo. 2003. "Constructing a Market, Performing Theory: The Historical Sociology of a Financial Derivatives Exchange." *American Journal of Sociology* 109:107–145.

McGinty, L., E. Beinstein, R. Ahluwalia, and M. Watts. 2004. *Credit Correlation: A Guide.* London: JP Morgan. Available at http://www.math.nyu.edu/~cousot/Teaching/IRCM/Lecture10/Base%20correlationJPM.pdf, accessed June 24, 2006.

Mehrling, P. 2005. *Fischer Black and the Revolutionary Idea of Finance.* New York: Wiley.

Merton, R. C. 1973. "Theory of Rational Option Pricing." *Bell Journal of Economics and Management Science* 4:141–183.

Merton, R. C. 1976. "Option Pricing when Underlying Stock Returns Are Discontinuous." *Journal of Financial Economics* 3:125–144.

Merton, R. C., and Z. Bodie. 2005. "Design of Financial Systems: Towards a Synthesis of Function and Structure." *Journal of Investment Management* 3:1–23.

Merton, R. K. 1948. "The Self-Fulfilling Prophecy." *Antioch Review* 8:193–210.

Millo, Y. 2003. "Where Do Financial Markets Come From? Historical Sociology of Financial Derivatives Markets." PhD diss. University of Edinburgh.

Mirowski, P. 1995. "Mandelbrot's Economics after a Quarter Century." *Fractals* 3:581–600.

Mixon, S. 2006. "Option Markets and Implied Volatility: Past versus Present." Available at http://ssrn.com/abstract=889543, accessed June 24, 2006.

Moore, L. and S. Juh. Forthcoming. "Derivative Pricing 60 Years Before Black-Scholes: Evidence from the Johannesburg Stock Exchange," accepted for publication in *Journal of Finance*. Available at http://www.afajof.org/journal/forth_abstract.asp?ref=280, accessed June 24, 2006.

Parkinson, M. 1977. "Option Pricing: The American Put." *Journal of Business* 50:21–36.

Passell, P. 1997. "2 Get Nobel for a Formula at the Heart of Options Trading." *New York Times*, October 15:D1, D4.

Ross, S. A. 1987. "Finance." Pp. 322–336 in *The New Palgrave Dictionary of Economics*, vol. 2, edited by J. Eatwell, M. Milgate, and P. Newman. London: Macmillan.

Rubinstein, M. 1985. "Nonparametric Tests of Alternative Option Pricing Models Using All Reported Trades and Quotes on the 30 Most Active CBOE Option Classes from August 23, 1976 through August 31, 1978." *Journal of Finance* 40:455–480.

Rubinstein, M. 1994. "Implied Binomial Trees." *Journal of Finance* 49: 771–818.

Scholes, M. S. 1998. "Derivatives in a Dynamic Environment." Pp. 475–502 in *Les Prix Nobel 1997*. Stockholm: Almqvist & Wiksell.

Searle, J. R. 1996. *The Construction of Social Reality*. London: Penguin.

Seligman, J. 1982. *The Transformation of Wall Street: A History of the Securities and Exchange Commission and Modern Corporate Finance*. Boston: Houghton Mifflin.

Swensen, D. F. 2000. *Pioneering Portfolio Management: An Unconventional Approach to Institutional Investment*. New York: Free Press.

Taleb, N. 1998. "How the *Ought* Became the *Is*." *Futures & OTC World* Black-Scholes-Merton Supplement:35–36.

Thorp, E. O., and S. T. Kassouf. 1967. *Beat the Market: A Scientific Stock Market System*. New York: Random House.

Wellemeyer, M. 1973. "The Value in Options." *Fortune* 88/5 (November): 89–96.

Whitley, R. 1986a. "The Rise of Modern Finance Theory: Its Characteristics as a Scientific Field and Connections to the Changing Structure of Capital Markets." *Research in the History of Economic Thought and Methodology* 4: 147–178.

Whitley, R. 1986b. "The Transformation of Business Finance into Financial Economics: The Roles of Academic Expansion and Changes in U.S. Capital Markets." *Accounting, Organizations and Society* 11:171–192.

Zimmermann, H., and W. Hafner. 2004. "Amazing Discovery: Professor Bronzin's Option Pricing Models (1908)." Available at http://www.wwz.uni-bas.ch/ finance/publications/2004.html, accessed June 24, 2006.

Chapter 4

Decoding Finance

ARTICULATION AND LIQUIDITY AROUND A TRADING ROOM

VINCENT-ANTONIN LÉPINAY

This chapter[1] analyzes the circulation of a financial product in and out of an investment bank. It uses the notions of articulation and liquidity to characterize the process of products' investigation carried out by the wide variety of actors in the bank. "Articulation" refers to the adjustment of all sorts of linguistic codes to express a novel, not-yet-described product. "Liquidity" refers to the state of a collective in which the products' qualities are temporarily rendered unproblematic. The chapter describes the difficulties faced by financial actors in collectively making sense of novel products for which full descriptions are not yet available. It is not the case that any arbitrary description can capture the products' properties. They keep striking back and hence fuel an endless financial conversation. A large variety of media is used to seize the products and frame their descriptions once and for all, but if their felicitous understanding and manipulation exploit this multiplicity of expression, they also represent a threat to the integrity of the product and to the bank.

Introduction

Industries dealing with innovative products need to invent languages of description to communicate and control their risks. This is particularly true for banks issuing financial products for which payoff uncertainty is great on both sides of the deals. Even when sophisticated blueprints foreshadow the issuance of a novel financial product, the real experimentation entailed by its actual launch on the market brings about unexpected outcomes. In these circumstances, organizations strive to decode their likely consequences and they develop apparatuses to express possible scenarios.

This chapter builds on Callon's work (1998), yet unlike some other contributions in this volume, it does not focus on high economic theory. Rather, it looks at the intricacies of an investment banking blueprint that tried to create new species of economic product. In comparison to the research program launched by Callon (1998), its interest focuses on the difficulties faced by performative enterprises. Callon's daring thesis insists on the role of economists and other agents (accountants, marketers, etc.) who give shape and continuity to economies. When taken literally, "performativity" can be read as a standard theory of action. Yet Callon[2] himself has defended a much more extended version of performativity that attenuates the human-centered approach often based on Austin (1962). Economies are not created *ex nihilo*, rather, they are composed as patchworks of heterogeneous forces. The locus of great interest then is the series of compromises that need to be made for an economy to exist. The "felicity" of an Austinian performative utterance (see MacKenzie's chapter) prompts investigation as much of the world as of the statements and the emotions that it triggers. An aspect of these compromises is the long chain of mediations that need to be established in order to create a world; performing these economies is not a one-way exercise.

This chapter describes the effort of financial actors in an investment bank to make products *speak their risks*. It employs the notion of articulation to characterize these endeavors taking place at several locations, inside and outside the bank. The multiplicity of these articulations puts the bank at risk since it jeopardizes its unity. The flourishing of descriptions leads to a lack of liquidity as it increases uncertainty about the product's real properties. This uncertainty covers several functions and divisions of the bank. It endangers the trading and client-centered "front office" through the likelihood of mispricing overly complex products and through the possibility of miscommunication with clients; it destabilizes the "middle office" as it challenges the integration of the categorizations used within the bank; it slows down the administrative "back office" by lack of a simple standard unifying the industry.

This chapter makes a case for a pragmatic sociology of linguistic codes that would relate to the matter being articulated at the three levels of language, category, and standard. What is being discussed, categorized, and standardized keeps pressing upon these very processes and constantly informs the collective of operatives striving to come to grips with the matter. Hence codes are not, for example, exclusively social strategies intended to create asymmetry between the community of bankers privy to the secret of financial products and unsophisticated laypeople. Access to the products is possible only through codes, and without this access the daily business of investment banks—managing large portfolios of contracts—is unthinkable. As technologies of the products, codes offer operators grips for action and levers of understanding, allowing them to grasp the products' structures.

I start by describing the methodological puzzle raised by the sociology of a description in an environment characterized both by the imperative of accountability and by the dispersed collection of operatives through which the product has to circulate. I discuss the notions of "articulation" and "liquidity" in relation to this heterogeneous collective, made up of the products' technologies of expression and the human actors with their own idiosyncratic bodies of knowledge. I describe five scenarios of articulation showing five different instances of codification (a financial classroom, a financial trading room, the R&D team developing derivatives-pricing software, the development of a different form of software for grasping the characteristics of products, and the effort to develop an industrywide product-description language).

Methodology for a Sociology of Financial Conversation

This chapter draws on fieldwork of several months spent in the trading room (and middle and back office) of a French investment bank. I focus with varying scrutiny on different sequences observed. Changing focus is highly pragmatic. The trading room was a relevant site since it was where the conversation on products displayed moments of friction and where the common world built into words about products set the stage for uncertainty. Similarly, large-scale financial institutions became privileged areas to be investigated when they accommodated negotiation around product categorization. If this very practical principle goes against the grain of conventional divisions (micro vs. macro, actors vs. institutions), it is precisely because the objects I am interested in cross these boundaries and call for a method that follows their scaling up and down.[3] Given the limited space of this chapter, one way of highlighting the fascinating intimate colloquium between actors and codes has been to provide raw descriptions of particular moments, as well as of typical situations. Respect for the ethnographic raw material and discussion of a typified sequence may seem to split this chapter methodologically in two. However, the unity of the object will make up for the disunity of the methods.

A related difficulty for this chapter comes from the problem of the definition of its objects—primarily, capital-guarantee products. Problematic as it may sound, it is not possible for me to define these products. The products borrow as many definitions as there are locations in which they circulate. The dispersion of their definition along the network of operators is a challenge for the social scientist setting out to describe what is at stake here. Any definition that I could offer at the start of my analysis would run the risk of simply producing another competing definition, put forth in another venue (outside the bank). It would do nothing more than add another definition[4] to the chorus of existing definitions.

Definition, after all, is the topic of this chapter.[5] The accuracy of definitions is the bone of contention for the actors involved, be they directly involved, as were the traders selling the products, or more distant, as were the French authorities seeking to ensure the integrity of the market. Nevertheless, it is necessary to start with a preliminary presentation that locates the stakes of the product at hand and situates it vis-à-vis an ecology of financial products already populating the market.[6]

Fieldwork in the market division of the bank opened the door to a world in which languages literally proliferate, but in which the very organization of markets shrank this proliferation to a series of tests, usually coming down to the *profit and loss* (P&L) of trades and of the divisions of the bank. These quasi-experimental conditions, in a world fraught with a large variety of idioms, are a blessing for this study. It submitted these idioms to the test of accuracy and goodness-of-fit with respect to the financial markets.

However, this test, as specific and explicit as it was, could not help remaining open-ended and underdetermined. Even if the indicator profit and loss seems to foreclose the variety of idioms and to be able to bring them to the one-dimensional, scientific, and final account of the return yielded by the financial products, this is far from being the case. The very notion of "profit" is constantly reshaped by conflicting languages; it can span different lengths of time (profit over a year, over a week) and it always needs an apparatus of accounting techniques (Carruthers and Espeland 1991; Miller and O'Leary 1998, 2002) to squeeze multiple financial engagements into a single economic metric. "Profit" is sometimes pure liquidity—the holding of cash in the present, without any claims over the future—but it rarely comes down to this perfect form, as the calculus of profit and loss usually takes place while the assets are still on the market, that is, not yet liquid. They cannot be withdrawn temporarily, measured, and then silently squeezed back into the markets. They are being experimented with in vivo, to use the terminology of Muniesa and Callon's chapter.[7] This characteristic affects all ventures— all "going concerns," in the accountant's terminology—as soon as they exhibit a variety of forms of investment and return. Only the Ricardian fiction (Ricardo 1815/1951) of a producer consuming wheat and returning wheat allows the reduction of languages to one single scientific metric. But the bank had embarked on a Ricardian nightmare, a complex situation that the English economist encounters at the end of the *Essay on Profits* when he considers economies more complex than the fiction of wheat.

Inside the bank, the combination of production factors entails the gathering together of disparate bodies of knowledge not used to collaborating. Communities with different and distinct expertise try to force

Box 4.1
Capital-guarantee products

Capital-guarantee products were and are popular, with hundreds of different product designs issued by banks and other financial institutions. A basic capital-guarantee product will typically promise investors that their capital investment will be returned in full (hence the name) and that they will also benefit from any increase in a particular stock index. A basic product of this kind is easy for a bank to understand and to synthesize. The bank can, for example, use the money received from the investor to buy a low-risk zero-coupon bond that at maturity will pay out a sum equivalent to the capital guarantee. Because it pays no interest, such a bond will currently sell at a discount to that sum, and the bank can use the discount to buy a "call option" (see chapter 3) on the index in question.

There are, however, capital-guarantee products of much greater complexity than this, which combine the basic capital-guarantee feature with more complicated payoff functions, and the product discussed in this chapter was of that kind: its payoff function involved both the average changes in three stock indexes and the performance of the best-performing of the three. This complication meant it was far more difficult to "grasp" the product: it could not, for example, be synthesized in the simple way described above.

their own approach in the definition of the product. To render more visible the chaotic nature of the conversations going on around the products, I highlight these groups.

Closest to the products' formal expression are the trading room's "financial engineers"—its "quants," as they are called. They are responsible for the final version of the contracts entered into between the bank and its clients. They do not create these formulas from scratch. Instead, they inherit them from a complex interaction between the bank's salespeople and traders' experience of the market. But even among the financial engineers themselves, the conversation has to take place to bridge different approaches to what a price is and how mathematical formulations of a financial product should be understood. Mathematicians and physicists come with backgrounds that can make them describe a price as either an equation to be solved or a Brownian motion[8] to be followed.

The traders are in charge of the daily hedging of their portfolios of products. They buy and sell to make sure that the bank will be able to

honor each product's payoff without incurring a loss, and they also seek
to benefit from market opportunities. This activity makes them develop
expertise akin to that of the financial engineers in the trading room: both
groups need to figure out how much a contract will be worth in a week,
a month or a couple of years. Yet their paths to understanding how the
value of these products moves are not always compatible.[9] Traders are
immersed in the market, surrounded by "noises" that they cannot rule
out as probably would a financial engineer working with mathematical
price functions instead of prices. The salespeople in the trading room
work very closely with the traders and the financial engineers when new
products are issued. They believe they know whether it will sell and generate a large profit or go unnoticed, hidden by the growing list of products offered by the bank's competitors. The descriptions adopted by this
prominent group in the room are nevertheless adapted to its primary
interlocutor, the bank's clients. Squeezing themselves, through the proximity of salespeople, into the cozy conversation of the trading room,
clients open it up to the outside world populated by competitors and
other agencies. Clients, too, want to control their risks and to tailor
financial products to their specific needs. For example, when they face
standard financial risks such as currency fluctuations, they do not have
to approach the bank seeking ad hoc products tailored to their needs,
and they can simply resort to liquid securities, precisely the kind of securities, such as exchange-traded futures, which no longer raise definitional
conflicts and which are described in languages that allow the two sides
of a transaction to communicate easily.

Nevertheless, the boundary between liquid, standardized securities
and tailor-made products is not fixed. For example, the diffusion of capital guarantee products has been overwhelming since the mid-1990s. The
appeal to clients, private and institutional, has been simple. This class of
products shared the best of both worlds: security provided by the guarantee, and performance through the basket of underlying securities to
which the payoff was indexed. Lodging this new breed of product
directly between two well-established financial "species" gave the marketing department of the bank and the salespeople many descriptive
resources. They could draw on both repertoires and combine them, creating another language. Still, it was not the final mode of description for
these products.

Banks deal with each other as much as they deal with private and
institutional clients and they have slowly built a community well aware
of their common interests.[10] A trade association, the International
Swaps and Derivatives Association (ISDA), has long tried to promote a
specific language for the exchange of financial derivatives[11] contracts.
The ISDA has thus created a library of products, meant eventually to

cover the broadest spectrum of possible scenarios in which two parties
are willing to swap flows of money on a contingent basis. The ISDA has
been working to reduce the transaction costs burdening banks engaged
in trading customized financial products, but it has also worked at creating a transparent language that breeds trust among market participants.
The shared interests of major investment banks have been highlighted by
the recent upheavals in various sectors of the financial markets, but
maybe more so by an increasing number of disagreements between sellers and buyers of these innovative financial products. These disagreements covered the whole spectrum from a growing sense of distrust of
issuers of new financial products to overt challenges to certain deals'
fairness that ended in lawsuits (such as *Procter & Gamble vs. Bankers
Trust*) and damaged the banking industry's reputation for a commitment
to competitive prices. Many of the conflicts regarding the deals stemmed
from the clients' criticism of an allegedly fuzzy description of the products' profit and loss characteristic.

The ISDA looks after the interests of the financial derivatives industry.
It attempts to cover not products traded on organized national exchanges
but "over-the-counter" derivatives trading which does not occur in
exchanges. Nevertheless, national regulatory bodies also have a say in
the description of derivatives products. Their entry into the discussion
around financial products is through clients and what they supervise as a
whole: national markets. Particularly relevant to my fieldwork were regulators who sought to promote a fair financial market in France. The
Commission des Marchés Financiers (CMF) and Commission des Operations Boursières (COB)[12] looked after the interests of the market
through the enforcement of regulations meant to guarantee proper disclosure from corporations issuing equity or debt. The rise of a new class
of product, derivatives, attracting so much attention and promising such
fantastic prospects, drew the regulatory bodies to add their say to the
chorus of voices. What they termed "formula products" (they introduced the class "*les produits à formules*" to the registry of products
available on French exchanges) were blamed[13] for possibly misleading
small investors. As a consequence, they forced the banks issuing them to
abide by a series of disclosure rules, to make sure that they would not let
fuzzy definitions sneak into the prospectus. The legal departments of
most major French investment banks were in close contact with COB
and CMF officers. They would translate the official requirements to the
sales desks and to the engineers to ensure that they complied with the
rules.

Finally, it must be noted that still another level of regulation played a
role in the definition and disclosure of the product. The Basel Committee
on Banking Supervision, a joint body of the world's leading central banks,

also provides guidelines for actors in the financial markets dealing with complex derivatives. Along with national regulatory bodies and professional associations like ISDA, the Basel Committee works, among other things, to define measures of risks and precautionary asset reserves to prevent bank failures, for example during market downturns. Framing these capital guarantee products as (1) risky investments or (2) insurance against market hazards entailed very different consequences for the banks in terms of the liquid assets that had to be set aside to cover their risks under the Basel framework.

These multiple perspectives on the description of financial products made "financial conversation"—discussion of those products—a tricky nexus linking different groups (mathematicians vs. computer programmers; issuers vs. clients; regulatory bodies vs. issuers) that offered different and to an extent competing ways of describing financial services. Compared to the large body of research falling into the category of "conversation analysis" (Atkinson and Heritage 1984; Gibson 2005; Sacks 1992), my investigation of financial conversation differs because it takes the *content* of that conversation to be crucial in the dynamic of formatting its structure. Financial conversations display specific patterns because they deal with entities—the financial products that keep slipping from the grips of their creators—that affect the proper way of speaking and conversing about them. As a preliminary characterization that needs subsequent refinement, conversation analysis as conventionally pursued focuses on the subtle structure of conversation without much interest in what the conversation is about (the "structural axis," we might call it). My analysis of a financial product circulating among academics, traders, clients, and regulatory authorities focuses on the dynamics of tailoring the most accurate categories that respect the product's own morphology while allowing for the circulation of those categories (the "pragmatic axis").

The frequent issuance of new products prompts the bank to make models and languages proliferate to offer new perspectives on their properties. This is an economic version of language differentiation observed in other contexts.[14] In the context of the bank, differentiation increases the grip on the product but it also immediately jeopardizes the unity of the bank. Each local language draws boundaries around an isolated "clan" and hinders the communication demanded by the very sensitivity of these products. They thrive in a narrow niche with liquid, standardized products on one side and ad hoc, custom-built products on the other. Yet, because of the innovative nature of the niche, an imperative to adjust linguistic codes to faster changing products animates the conversation.

Articulation and Liquidity

The two imperatives of an ever more detailed description ("articulation") and of a description that is liquid, that circulates, are in tension here. In many ways, a process of articulation runs against the liquidity of a transaction. Articulating takes time; it does not facilitate the quick, quasi-impersonal trait of contemporary financial trading. Most of this trading (Millo 2003; Muniesa 2003) deals with goods that are already prearticulated, so that the burden of articulation and spelling out of their characteristics is displaced upstream. The parties to a transaction do not need to worry about the content of what is being circulated precisely because that content has been taken care of by other actors in the long network preceding the transaction itself. These initial investments in forms (Carruthers and Stinchcombe 1999; Thévenot 1986) are what wards off possible disputes.

To examine this, let me turn to an extreme case: money in a nation-state in which the default of the lender of last resort seems to be ruled out—for example, the United States of America when the U.S. dollar seemed as good as gold. The ability unproblematically to exchange money against goods stems from the fact that there seems to be nothing to worry about and nothing to discuss about what is exchanged. The quasi-pure presence of the coin or the dollar bill comes from the general trust in their purchasing power and the general belief that a good will always be "within the reach" of a coin. This great liquidity enjoyed by most developed countries' consumers relies deeply on the institutions that states have built to breed trust and to avoid a time-consuming search for information.

The articulation of state-backed moneys is made all the easier when what is being exchanged is accepted by all consumers as a real proxy for goods available on markets. When it assumes the form of coins and bills, acceptance is almost immediate, but as the medium of exchange begins to involve a conditionality spanning the future—a promise to pay, for example—things become less self-evident. To endow these more future-based media with the same liquidity, the uncertainty (Keynes 1936; Knight 1936/1971) of the events likely to occur between now and a promise's "maturity" (when the bonds will have to be repaid, when the payoff inscribed in a formula will be delivered to the client) must be transformed into a plausible narrative. Transforming uncertainty into risk is one strong form of articulation, a move from the complete lack of information to a probability space which entitles one to forecast. When faced with a real uncertainty—a set of events that cannot even be delineated—nothing can be said about it in quantitative terms, but a lot can be described in other terms.

Articulation

I will return below to the narratives into which uncertainty is transformed in the bank. Before I do so, let me say more about the resources
deployed in this transformation, which we might call "technologies of
expression" (see Didier's chapter and Deleuze 1968). Through plausible
narratives, the qualities of products are expressed: they take form; they
are written down or embodied in some lasting medium. This chapter will
cover a wide range of these technologies of expression, but their shared
element is that they provide the resources with which the relation is
woven between the actors and products whose characteristics are being
made explicit. With this articulation, it is possible to do something with
and to say something about these characteristics.

Consumers pulling a bill out of their pockets to pay in a supermarket
do not engage in a highly articulated discourse about the solidity of their
currency's central bank, the national debt, or prudent economic policy
and its sustainability over a longer term, because all these conditions are
currently being met and are encapsulated in institutions of articulation.[15] If they are interested, they can find out what the central bank's
policy is, its level of accountability, how the public debt challenges the
long term worth of a dollar. Although paper money is most of the time
taken as a black box, it can be traced to the circuitry of the macroecon-
omy and political decisions. It can become a subject of discussion, but
the liquidity enjoyed by consumers will not depend on their skillful
defense of the state's paper money. The task of articulation is carried out
by other entities in the economy and trust is built within these entities.
On the contrary, if individuals with no special records of practical success in the world of finance try to sell a contract to the general public,
they will have to build from scratch the scenario of their innovation:
what it will do when the market collapses, how much it is likely to cost
its consumers, and all the other considerations that can arise in the
exchange of long-term contracts.

An interesting example of articulation was given in the beginning of
the 1980s by Hayne Leland, an economist who devised and promoted
the technique of portfolio insurance described by MacKenzie[16] in his
chapter in this book. As can be inferred from MacKenzie's brief account,
portfolio insurance was an early form of capital-guarantee product that
promised its purchasers a floor below which the value of their stock
portfolios would not fall.

Leland's endeavor to spell out the principles of portfolio insurance
borrowed an interesting technique, which attached the characteristics of
the innovative product to the preferences of the investors. Explaining
how portfolio insurance worked (the convexity of returns, the floor

under which the insurance triggered and guaranteed no loss, etc.) allowed Leland to peg it to a large class of investors, interested in benefit-
ing from the returns offered by equities without being willing to take all
the risks entailed by this market. An excerpt from the introduction to his
article helps understand the paths of articulation:

> The existence of options markets can generate new opportunities for portfo-
> lio management. As Ross (1976) has shown, a complete set of options markets
> on a reference stock or portfolio will enable investors to achieve any desired
> pattern of return conditional on the terminal value of the referent asset. While
> "buy-and-hold" equity strategies allow investors to achieve returns *propor-
> tional* to the terminal value of a reference portfolio, buy-and-hold option
> strategies permit *nonproportional* returns to be achieved. A *nonproportional*
> return of particular interest to some investors is that which provides portfolio
> insurance. Equivalent to a put option [see MacKenzie's chapter] on the refer-
> ence portfolio, portfolio insurance enables an investor to avoid losses, but cap-
> ture gains, at the cost of a fixed "premium." Unfortunately, options markets do
> not currently exist for portfolios of securities and a portfolio of options is not
> equivalent to an option on a portfolio. Even when options markets do not
> exist, however, investors may be able to achieve *nonproportional* returns on
> terminal asset values by following dynamic investment strategies. . . . While the
> theory of option pricing suggests how to value options, and therefore how to
> value portfolio insurance, it does not suggest the nature of investors who
> would benefit from purchasing options or insurance. Unlike traditional insur-
> ance, in which everyone can benefit from a pooling of independent risks, port-
> folio insurance involves hedging against a common (market) risk. For every
> investors buying portfolio insurance, some other investors must be selling it,
> either by writing the appropriate put option, or by following the inverse
> dynamic trading strategy. Who should buy, and who should sell? In this paper,
> we provide a characterization of investors who will benefit from purchasing
> portfolio insurance. (Leland 1980, p. 581)

Articulation and liquidity are achieved by Leland in one and the same
move. The mystery surrounding the new product is dispelled by the
twofold clarification aiming at (1) the working of the dynamic strategy
making up portfolio insurance and (2) investors' preferences.[17] Even in
cases where goods seem basic enough not to call for specific articulation
(cotton, for example), there is actually articulation somewhere in the long
debate (Caliskan 2004) making up the general economy of exchange. In
the case of a consumer's dollar bill, it is probably not in the face-to-face
exchange that articulation is needed but at another end of the paper-
money economy, closer to the Federal Reserve decision making (Abolafia
2002) and the broadcasting of policy choices. But articulation was very
much the day-to-day business of the bank I studied.

"Articulation" is not yet, as far as I know, a sociological concept. To study articulation requires attendance to the technology of persuasion (Rosental 2003) and to the resources mobilized by actors in their attempts to highlight an aspect of the world that they are trying to bring to existence. The notion of "articulation" forms part of a pragmatic analysis of language (see Callon's chapter) and it calls attention to the intermediaries that are used to articulate the characteristics of a good. This definition of a good does not immediately assume a linguistic form. Articulating borrows many different media before coming to a purely linguistic utterance. All these prelinguistic paths are in their own right steps in a process of definition that is never ending. There will always be more to say about a good, more to say about a financial product that can reveal its characteristics only after being subject to a particular market configuration. This is why "articulation" and "accuracy" stand in an interesting relation.

As new questions, new aspects of products, and new challenges arise, the descriptions and definitions that so far have been consistent can become irrelevant or even utterly wrong. "Articulating" does not mean stating once and forever the list of properties of a good. It is simply a way of folding some of these properties into a particular formula that inevitably leaves some other parameters out.

Consider once again the scene of the consumer pulling out coins from his or her pocket.[18] Imagine a store owner refusing to take these coins because they are silver and silver is known for weakening the body's energy, so much so that the cautious store owner does not wear a silver-made wristwatch, ring, or earring. To ensure the completion of the transaction, the consumer now needs to convince her that money (meaning now a piece of conventional standard value inscribed in a coin) is not harmful to its bearer's health. Contrary to the narrative used to work with a sequence involving only the economic agent and the reliability of the medium, it now stretches to the health effect of carrying coins in one's pocket. To win the confidence of the storeowner, the consumer may have to enrich and rearticulate his or her previous narrative so as to encompass new elements that will make the exchange of coins between individuals innocuous. He or she may have to refer to studies by the Food and Drug Administration, in addition to the Federal Reserve Bank's latest reports. Was the first narrative that was told about the coin (a piece of convention backed by the legitimate power of the state) truer than the second (a piece . . . + the material substance that has not been convincingly shown to endanger the health of exchanger)? The questions addressed in the two cases are obviously not the same, but articulating paves the way for questions of accuracy. Each challenge to the quality of a description or definition presupposes a list of characteristics of the good, so that epistemology always comes after the preliminary phase of exploration. The art of articulating develops during that experimental stage.

Liquidity

A stable ontology, however, is what is demanded by liquidity. Understood in its economic dimension, liquidity is a measure of the ability of goods to circulate and also an index of a common world. A liquid market is one in which the quality of goods is not questioned by exchangers (Akerlof 1970) and in which the bid and offer prices are nearly equal. Similar expectations about goods make conversation around these goods easy. It is not even necessary to detail their qualities in many circumstances since their name carries enough to allow a peaceful exchange, or at least a transaction that does not contain the seeds of personal dispute.[19] Like "articulation," "liquidity" is not a specifically sociological concept. It has been harnessed by economists for a long time, but only recently (Baker 1984; Carruthers and Stinchcombe 1999; Zuckerman 1999, 2004) has it been factored into sociology. Yet, even in these latter efforts, liquidity remains an economic concept imported into sociology for lack of a better surrogate concept, and it carries with it a set of assumptions that sociology may not want to endorse so hastily.

Consider Carruthers and Stinchcombe's (1999) article on two cases of the emergence of liquidity. They engage the economists' assumption that liquidity could emerge spontaneously and set out to demonstrate that institutions are necessary. They point to three institutional elements necessary for liquid markets to emerge: continuity of trading, prices organized by a market maker, and homogeneity guaranteed by a standard. Yet they never make space for the heated debates that took place among economists, market designers, and policy makers about what is continuity, with or without a market maker, and how homogeneous goods need to be. On this latter aspect the authors state that "intangible commodities are easier to standardize than tangible ones because one does not have to deal with the inherent variability of the material world" (Carruthers and Stinchcombe 1999, pp. 377–378). Unlike the assumption of this intuitive idea, the case of a new financial product shows that materiality and tangibility are not synonymous. A product that is only a series of words on spec sheets and contracts is as material as a cotton bag or a bushel of grain traded in Chicago. As a result, liquidity is as difficult to ensure for these creations as it is for natural products.

Carruthers and Stinchcombe tend to bracket out what is being exchanged because they presume an "evolutionary social epistemology" behind the question of liquidity. Its problem would only be one of convention and trust in other market participants' next move, not of understanding the actual characteristics of the commodities held in a portfolio. They relate this epistemology to finance: since the value of a security traded on the secondary market depends greatly on the future assessment of its value by prospective buyers, the actual return is of no primary importance. I do not follow this approach because I consider finance an industry for which the imperative of description and understanding is not something that can be sold on a secondary market.

In this chapter, I address the phenomenon of liquidity without assuming any specific agency to the market. Periods of high volatility are moments of high uncertainty around the definition of individuals and goods, moments in which stable ontologies crumble. When uncertainty of this kind strikes the market, the rush for more liquidity drains precious liquid assets—those whose ontologies remain stable—from the market. What were conversations around the values of goods become a silence,[20] resuming only to sell bad debts and seek the solid ground of "real" economy. In his attempt to grasp the psychology of markets, French sociologist Gabriel Tarde (1904, p. 195) remarks how the texture of conversations is indicative of the trust economic agents show to each other. In this daring view, conversation is not just a fancy veil, inconsequential with regard to the structure of markets. Conversation is the very fabric of these markets, inasmuch as it defines the characteristics of goods and the functions of market participants.

Taking Tarde's insight seriously, this chapter captures the volatility of a financial product's definition. It is not a metaphorical but a sociological use of the concepts of "volatility" and "liquidity," because if prices are privileged entry points to capture the dynamics of markets, their seeming self-sustaining nature can also lure the social scientist into bypassing the numerous hesitations and negotiations leading to their formation. Previous historical research (Ackerman 1988; Collman 1968; Galbraith 1990; Metz 1988; Sobel 1968) has described in great detail critical moments of uncertainty when markets almost literally froze because of participants' fears of ending up with worthless assets. Yet these accounts stress mostly the end point of full illiquidity, which is in a continuum that runs to the opposite state of fully liquid markets. Between these two states stand probably the most interesting cases for economic sociologists trying to understand how exchange can be maintained in the face of numerous threats. Although it may not be as dramatic to describe the daily hesitations of exchangers around the characteristics of goods, it is more helpful to capture these mundane sense-making negotiations than to contemplate either the rare moments in which liquidity vanishes or the pure routine of complete liquidity. Those two moments do not lend themselves to an easy analysis of what makes exchange orderly.

These two notions—articulation and liquidity—can now help us follow the chaotic order of products in and out of the trading room. To understand the difficulties of articulating a common ground that respects both the specificity of the product and the need for a shared description, five different sites need to be visited: a classroom; a trading room; the R&D team developing derivatives-pricing software; the development of a different form of software for grasping the characteristics of products; and the effort to develop an industrywide product-description language.

Thinking Financially

Thinking financially emerged early on in my field work as a crucial topic. In the first place, it was the motto of a mathematical finance teacher.[21] Before moving to the trading room, I decided to attend a master's course in stochastic processes applied to finance in order to grasp what was at stake in the very specific pedagogy of this form of applied mathematics. The mathematicians I was going to observe in the trading room would be my fellow students in the classroom. Coming from the most distinguished universities, they were faced with a set of entities that constantly challenged the purity of clean and sleek mathematical functions. This was the ideal site to observe the clash of languages mobilized to describe finance. The question of pedagogy was even made relevant by the field itself thanks to a special course, taught by one of the most promising young specialists in stochastic processes who had worked in trading rooms while obtaining his doctorate. He felt the need to warn the students against the temptation of abstraction. To explain what a good trader needed to do, this professor stressed several times that bringing sophisticated probability theories to the trading desk was not enough. He seized this occasion to highlight what he saw as a specificity of finance vis-à-vis mathematics or, for that matter, even physics. It had to do with intuition and even two forms of intuition: mathematical intuition and financial intuition.

The first form called for a very intimate knowledge of laws, statistical or deterministic, and a deep understanding of the combination of stochastic laws with fixed boundary conditions. He construed it as the ability to manipulate Brownian-motion processes with limits:

> Basically, for the valuation of an option, the intuition comes down to knowing the odds to pay off . . . but the event can be very complex; if you are not used to thinking of the probability of an event, then you are a bit clumsy[22] because you always need to resort to an equation . . . in Finance, the kind of math that you can use is extremely varied. You can do everything in a determinist

framework; there are many people who do everything without knowing what a random variable is. They just solve partial differential equations (PDEs).[23] There are many mathematicians who work very clumsily because they have very little intuition; they can be good but . . . they are clumsy.

He tended to think of this first intuition as a necessary component of a good trader or financial engineer. But he was led to downplay its fruitfulness compared to the second form of intuition, and to assimilate it to a nonstochastic approach to finance. Although he very much looked down on the partial differential equation solutions characteristic of the latter as ways to discover the price of a market security, he was tempted to lump this method together with his own stochastic approach and to differentiate them both markedly from financial intuition. This second brand of intuition did not rely exclusively on mathematical laws to do pricing; instead, it demanded an equally intimate knowledge of the current financial products available on the market for hedging and any other financial strategies. Replying to a comment of mine on the nature of "intuition" in which I assumed that it came down to storing and combining mathematical laws in the mind, he said:

> Having laws in mind, yes. But this is a first intuition, call it a mathematical intuition. Afterwards, you have a financial intuition that is very different and amounts to picking the products you will choose to hedge; to translate every product you design no longer in terms of laws, because this is obvious, but in terms of products available on the markets for the hedge, to be able to say which of these products will make you save money if you design and sell the product. This becomes a financial question and it involves financial operations you make with the money you have at the outset. If you start with 10 francs and the event "I pay 100 francs" occurs, your initial 10 francs must have become 100 francs. The gist is to find out which product will turn 10 into 100. In the market, there are so many products associated with specific events and they give you solutions. It is up to you to find the combination which will keep you balanced: you do not pick the right product, you end up with variance, you can make money but you can also lose a lot and you are not in control any longer.

This second intuition closely resembled a very local skill: being able to find in the market the security or securities that would reduce the portfolio exposure just as a meticulous book collector knows perfectly where a volume or volumes are located on his or her hundreds of shelves. These two forms of intuition lent themselves to different regimes of language. For the trader learning by heart typical stochastic processes, the new products could basically be laid out as mathematical formulas or control theory algorithms; any engineer sufficiently trained in stochastic processes would be able to describe what a product could do when plunged into a market whose stochastic dynamics were known. For the trader more familiar with the ecology of financial products at hand, defining a product would follow a slightly different path. Instead of reducing the product to a mathematical process, he or she would approach it through several *similar* products.

> With a 10-year Spanish inflation-indexed option, I buy Spanish inflation-correlated stocks and OATs[24] indexed on French inflation, but I know it is not a liquid bond, so I do not call it hedging; rather it is betting.

"Likeness," or similarity, is a crucial aspect of this opposition of intuitions. It refers to the skill that is at stake: financial languages are about transporting prices into other processes, hence finding or building likeness between worlds. But if the search for a similar-enough world is difficult, it is not exclusively because of the deeply human underlying layer that makes formal models ill-fitted, but because of the constant change in the population of financial products. A stable ecology would draw neat boundaries within which to search, but financial products of all sorts keep proliferating. If the only way to describe and talk of a product is to refer to it through existing products (financial intuition), any change of these building blocks of the description/discussion jeopardizes the belief in the one best description. The elements which had once been chosen and aggregated with a view to building the best description possible are now outdated by the new composition of the financial population/language elements at hand. This is all the more the case as products that had been conceived as second-degree, derivative financial products have become traded in their own right. They have become part of a population that they were meant to describe and have started swapping qualities with these initial goods.

Talking Finance with a Mathematical Grammar

One way to understand further how the expression of financial products becomes a question is to accompany the "scientists" of a trading room in their daily manipulations. The extraction of the relevant features of a product starts when it is subjected to a series of tests. One of these tests works on the assumption that financial products can be approached as mathematical entities. The conversation that this initial qualification sets off is framed by the discipline of mathematics and by the mathematical equipment used to squeeze information out of it.

When the "quant"[25]—the local name, in France as well as in the United States, for the person who takes responsibility for quantitative approaches—works on the equations of complex models, they are most frequently input into a software package that processes mathematical operations (especially "Scientific Workplace"). When it comes to observing the reactions of a product price through a model, small price variations are usually assessed through partial derivatives (in the calculus sense of "derivative"). As these products carry several sources of risk, these partial derivatives encompass different dimensions, including the sensitivity of a product's price to changes in the interest rate, and the price and price volatility of the underlying stocks. But these derivatives follow strictly mathematical rules that are not necessarily relevant for financial questions. They are as respectful of mathematical disciplines as they are deaf to actual challenges posed by their financial destiny and to the fact that they will be surrounded by other chaotic market entities, not by orderly mathematical functions. Once the software has run and found a solution, the quasi-infinite decomposition into high-order derivatives has to be rearranged into financially meaningful clusters. Some of the derivative terms cancel out; others are rearranged into unexpected[26] financial terms. In many ways, this exploration brings about unexpected outcomes, just as Black and Scholes were surprised by their famous result, described by MacKenzie in his chapter.[27]

In the trading room on which I focused, the chief quant (I shall call him "the Quant") was a physicist by training, a most unusual feature in the French tradition of mathematical domination over other sciences. Most major French banks usually hired young mathematicians to tackle the challenge of increasingly technical products. The Quant was surrounded by some of these young mathematicians, who had all been trained in the "Bourbaki"[28] tradition. When the Quant arrived a couple of years prior to my fieldwork, he tried to implement some changes in the way formal models were written and he attempted to switch to models in the spirit of more physics models and tools closer to experiments than to mathematical proof. But he very soon experienced a gap between what he considered "good" models and what the rest of the quantitative team was used to accepting.

The mathematicians did not share many of the assumptions of the Quant, but they carried with their own assumptions of mathematics something stronger than the fragile fabric of hypothesis: the pieces of software helping them to implement their models were all written in a programming language that they cherished. They felt at home with this equipment in a way that no physicist could. This reified language helped them carry out many of the demonstrations that they would present to the Quant. On this desk, the traders were working with two major sets of software. One—"pricers"—provided them with the price of a portfolio, which they could break down into subportfolios or value groups of products across portfolios. The other—risk analysis software—added more parameters to the pricer. It was meant to help traders make hedging decisions. It had been customized by the engineers and the computer developers with a pragmatic view: market imperfections were coded into the risk analysis software while they were erased from the pricer. But as a well-formalized and well-defined set of assumptions running on a computer platform, the risk analysis software and the pricers also rendered possible the contestlike structure of their results' assessment. Because they were stable statistical rules, any differences between the prices produced by the software and realworld prices put at risk the validity of the software and its existence on the desk.[29]

In itself, theoretical statistics is a very articulate language. However, any misfit between the description and the dynamics of the products questions the modeling choice: does attaching the model to the product help to articulate the model? Is the model a good language to resort to in order to predict what the product will yield? The Quant had a very clear position on these issues:

> Scientific Workplace and Mathematica [another computerized mathematics package] do not understand finance; they both go into endless details, especially when it produces high order expansions[30] of a price function, but they do not provide us with what we need. They miss the nature of finance even, and maybe particularly, when they refine the calculations. They do not think financially.

Decomposing a continuous price function is a language game with its own rules, which the Quant follows to a certain extent. It leads to unanticipated results that sometimes bring out new features of a model. It has a life of its own (Pickering 1995) and raises questions that were not on the agenda until it was run. But it also resonates in a very peculiar way vis-à-vis the products on the market. The Quant feels that it leaves aside the core of what should be the business of a model. At this stage, his feeling is not yet a perfectly articulated idea, because it fights precisely against an existing articulation. It is only a hunch that is fueled by an alternative appraisal of the products in question. This intuition, however, indicates to the Quant a failure of the models that the mathematicians favor, in that they capture very poorly the financial realities behind the model. He experiences a rare conflict of competing articulations. He cannot dismiss bluntly the current models running on the desk because they are sustaining the "conversation" of most young mathematicians on his team. They are also inscribed in their equipment, the software that they are using, and in the conventions that made this community orderly. This language of description is so entrenched that the alternative for which he had been lobbying in the trading room was doomed.

Despite his endless complaints against the irrelevance of partial differential equations, he would still use this mode of representation to interact with his colleagues. The imperative of a common language is too strong to entertain one's own private language.

The Bodily Articulation of Finance

Two theories of description compete here. The first relies on the grammar of stochastic models. But in the opposition that we are constructing, stochastic and determinist models do not differ much; they actually belong to the same realm of models expressing the chaotic nature of financial products. As such, they can tell what price should be assigned to a given deal and they also provide information pertaining to the risks incurred by the bank that issues such a product. But they remain remote from the actual financial products that will turn these risks into strategies. This is where the second form of description appears: instead of being scaled down to Brownian motions, new products are projected onto another level made up of other existing products. The projection is what those involved call the *hedging scenario*. Talking about a product entails building this complex and conditional narrative in which products displaying different properties are summoned, sequentially or simultaneously. Most of the time, these two forms of description and their associated intuitions are not exclusive. They can complement each other in a fruitful way, but they point to skills that are not always easy for one person to develop simultaneously. The first requires a dedicated mathematical and/or statistical training ("one needs to have laws in one's head," as the professor puts it), while the second involves maximizing one's exposure to the behavior of existing products available on the market. Although not mutually exclusive in principle, the two forms of description concentrate their followers into two separate activities.

The finance professor tried in his own way to bridge the gap between these two intuitions and two languages of description. Torn between the expectation of young apprentice mathematicians like his younger self—most of them came from the *Grandes Ecoles* or at least the *Classes Préparatoires*—and the urge to train them in the messy, real world of financial strategies, he would fuse the hedging scenarios (the language of hedging products) and the models (the language of mathematical functions) by embodying the hedging strategies associated with specific products. It was literally a middle way between the blackboard, traditionally accommodating mathematical price functions, and storytelling, depicting hedging strategies. Facing the students, the professor would mimic with his body the price curve of a product and try to replicate the discontinuities associated with special payoffs. From my fieldnotes:

> Drawing in the air, on an imaginary transparent blackboard, he would complement the fleshed out language of functions with stories of events occurring on the market:
>
> "Product X hits its limit barriers, then you know you have to pay the designated payoff. But you do not wait until this very last moment, you anticipate and you use the curve's derivative to hedge."
>
> He joins the fingers of each hand and makes their tips meet around this imaginary point when the trader must start anticipating the payoff. The tips hit each other at an increasing pace as the curve steepens and the closeness to payoff grows. The pace is meant to convey the number of underlying securities bought to hedge. This hitting is accompanied by the story of the strategy.

The professor's body tries to find a common world for two competing languages. It is well-documented that scientific pedagogy (Lave 1988, 1990; Ochs et al. 1994, 1996) is also about bodies interacting with objects rather than a rules-driven mind grasping *in abstracto* these elements. In the classroom, the rigidity of mathematical functions is mitigated by narratives grounded in products. Each language brings in what is absent in the other. To the question "What is needed accurately to describe a product?" it provides an answer that shows how the conventional and quasi-scientific language of finance does not create the product on its own. The market is such that the performativity of financial mathematics is still in need of a body that heals its flaws and its inability to define and to exhaust its object in its language.

In search of the most accurate form of description for these innovative products, the professor had also a more ontological line on markets and models. If the body had to be summoned to provide the students with a description of the dynamics involved, it was also because of the building blocks of the market itself. Behind the figures, behind the lengthy contracts and the formalisms expressing these products, were traders and brokers fighting with their own body language to understand the market and anticipate the changes. The professor insisted that the ultimate intuition had to make sense of the human struggle in a chaotic environment. His body language was well-suited for conveying the strategies and counterstrategies carried out in this environment. It borrowed its very substance from the messy fusion of products and traders hunched over their desks. Hence, in a way, there was only minor distance between the language and the reality to be represented. They had more than a family resemblance: they stemmed from the same bodies. Not a strategic mind plotting behind a screen the next ultimate scheme to beat the market, but a trader trying to survive among a population of highly interrelated products, moving in unexpected directions.

This classroom exercise of a professor facing his students was not confined to this venue. A pedagogy "in the wild" (see Callon's chapter) was taking place in the trading room too, next to the very same instruments that were expressing the products in formalized terms. This room was an unexpected ecology, putting together bodies, tools, and specialized languages in a patterned way that figure 4.1 summarizes. In the close environment of each trading desk, conversations were driven by the products' design.

Coding the Product

The hedging strategies carried out "on paper" in the classroom showed an opposition between financial intuition and mathematical intuition. This opposition is subsequently reiterated, on a different level, when the product and the model[31] leave their initial state of paper form to assume the form that they will have when the traders incorporate them in their portfolios. They need to be coded in order to run on the personal computers and servers in the trading room. They were formulas on paper; they become lines of code written in C or C++.

When one moves further into the pricer, the necessity to understand what "the product says" shifts to another imperative: understanding what the model means. Making a product a model is already a first coding: it must retain the most significant coordinates of the product and leave aside the noise of the market. Yet, once this purification has been realized, there is no way to check its success without running the model daily. The most articulated model is of no use if it cannot be run on a trader's computer. But the next step in this long process of the articulation of products adds another layer of technology, as problematic as Scientific Workplace or Mathematica. In order finally to make the product talk, a programming language must be chosen. In this choice and in the modalities of writing (including the style of the program) are as many possible pitfalls or unexpected solutions to fuzzy expressions of the product.

Ethnography in the bank turned out also to be very fruitful in giving a sense of the challenges and opportunities raised by a model becoming a machine. After the classroom and the trading room, a third venue must be now scrutinized: the pricer R&D team. A member of this team, whom I shall call Franck, was in charge of the coding operations for nonstandard products in the bank. I met him during a conference dedicated to the implementation questions relevant to mathematical finance.

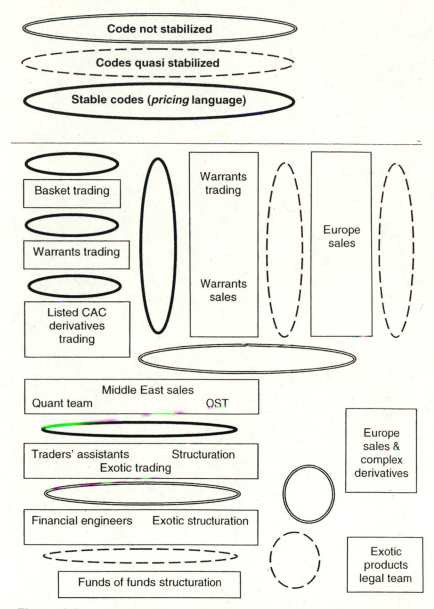

Figure 4.1 "Code zones" in the trading room. This room was an unexpected ecology, putting together bodies, tools, and specialized languages in a patterned way.

It was one of those strange meetings where people are convinced they share a lot and strive to find a common ground but speak in different languages. For a French academic, it was the opposite of the usual meetings, where people meet when they are convinced that they speak exactly the same language but end up disagreeing on everything! Franck had recently received a request from his boss to take charge of the coding of a model developed by Hull and White (1990).[32] Here is how Franck describes his job:

> We rely on the understanding of the product by the research team [the Quant and his assistants: see above]: he [Quant] reads the article, he sends us 20 pages when he has read through the model, it is a synthesis. He describes the model on a very functional basis; he tells you "in this model there are n steps, and we understand it this way. . . ." The [financial] engineers tell you which yield curve model you should use for this model, because they see that it fits well. But sometimes, the passage from the article and the script synthesis that they pass over is not easy. Sometimes we receive something really horrendous, I mean from our point of view, from what we are supposed to do. The mathematicians do not see that part of the model. Recently we had to write a code for a variation around Hull-White. They use a process for the interest rate; it is supposed to represent the interest rate in the model. The tricky part in these models is clearly the calibration of the yield curve. Which algorithm are we supposed to use to calibrate it? Hull and White do not answer, they take it for granted; it is no more than three lines in their article. I bump into this question for days and I have sent them an e-mail but they do not answer: they write an article, it becomes famous, but as for the implementation, these are not prestigious questions. . . .
>
> All the programs have bugs. Negative prices, bad scripts, or even bad memory allotment. Besides technical errors which can be corrected by any computer engineer, there are mistakes where you just screw up your reasoning, and in these cases, it is much more difficult to correct. Then, you have to understand Hull-White.

The code is another technology of the product, but it brings along all the constraints of a previously articulated language, with its own rules of implementation and its own strength and weakness. It also contains the two dimensions that we alluded to earlier: coherence of the code and felicity of its combination with the model.

There are many different ways to code a model, but beyond this openendedness, Franck used to favor one code over another because it conveys more accurately what the product covers. Franck had been trained in C and he was still coding in C when I interviewed him, but he knew that in the long run he would have to turn to C++. He recognized the special family resemblance between object-oriented programming languages such as C++ and the type of questions they had to solve when they dealt with the programming of pricers. The object-oriented programming philosophy seemed more suited to the financial engineering he envisioned. The series of classes defined in C++ was useful for expressing the architecture of products in the information technology system of the bank. From this viewpoint, object-oriented languages were the natural languages of finance.

But Franck was also well aware that C, which is not an object-oriented language, was equivalent to C++ at a certain level of generality. They were both general-purpose programming languages, which could lend themselves to any programming task. Nevertheless, this level was not the one experienced by Franck: a C and a C++ code, although equivalent when considered at the abstract level of a program running on a universal Turing machine, could not be conflated on the living ground of the expression of the characteristics of financial products. Along with the efficiency of the code, its inner consistency as a technology of expression matters equally. One way of expressing an object that is still largely uncharted is to locate a similar enough other object and draw on its articulation to come to think of that of the unknown. The family resemblance between the programming "objects" of C++ and the way in which contracts were defined in the bank weighed on Franck. Unlike the finance professor mentioned previously, he was not making any claim regarding the essence of finance. Yet he too was engaged in a definitional controversy. In a way reminiscent of the opposition between financial and mathematical intuitions, Franck opposed a disembodied description of products that did not attend to its actual existential requirement as it is managed by a trader, preferring the real definition of a product plus a software code plus a machine code.

This shift is not unique. The definition of any product takes place within successive envelopes as it is transported in new environments. Crafting a pricing machine with a new set of constraints is another crucial step in the long process meant to extract a product's properties. It was a misleading abstraction to distinguish a theoretical pricing procedure dealt with by academics from the implementation of a machine that was expected to spit out a price on demand. The material constraints bearing on the machine limited considerably the extent to which the abstract price could actually ever come to existence. In embracing a richer degree of existence for the product and its price—a degree that was a fait accompli because of a bank policy that gave priority to the front office's requirements rather than the bank's technicians' preferences—certain statements about products simply could not be expressed without running the risk of serious inconsistency. Assuming the existence of a price was fine from a mathematical finance perspective, but it became an unsupported claim from the perspective of an engineer whose business it was to reach an actual price when running an algorithm implemented in software on an actual, physical machine.

Articulating a product is very closely related to endowing it with a certain degree of existence. The market price achieved by Hull and White through a series of deductions is not wrong or even misleading. It just points to a set of entities that have a narrow degree of existence. Situated on a spectrum of possible degrees of existence, products do not find an easy solution to the issue of liquidity. Shrinking their qualities into the deductive price of mathematical finance academics would be a solution to the problem of a common language, but only if the skills necessary to understand this form of the price were a common good or a free resource. Yet acquiring these skills was not easy for people with little or no mathematical training. Faced with the scarcity of these esoteric skills, the second solution to the problem of liquidity was to give up these costly investments in articulations foreign to most of those in the trading room. A language that was "natural" and shared by most groups in the room would *do* more than the elite language of a few. But this second solution enhanced liquidity only temporarily and locally at the expense of articulation, and thus it did not solve the problem of building a common world. It even created a new issue around capital guarantee products: from questions of prices and risky strategies, the products started raising questions of costs. The lack of a unified language for these products threatened the economy of this gold mine. This change entailed an articulation radically different from what had been put forth so far.

A Contract Language: Price versus Definition

Nobody knows precisely how to talk about these products. Be it via mathematical languages, or via a more intuitive and grounded-in-the-financial-ecology approach, or via yet another formalized computer language, there is no way out of a technology of expression. One might want to talk of the *product itself*, but before and without its expressive garments, no one could utter anything worthwhile. Yet, this *last word* was dreamt about by the engineers who had to face the puzzle of a wild beast (Steinherr 2000) which kept showing an unexpected profile to its owners: the last word would close, once and for all, the possibilities of controversies triggered by the product. Unfortunately, the last word can never be uttered, at least never sufficiently to sum up what the product attempts to say.

When they started to be sold in large numbers, these capital-guarantee products soon showed how the current information system of the trading room was overstretched by the intense care required. Aware of this flaw in their system, the managers of the room, along with the board of the bank, decided to develop in-house software aimed at solving the overload problems. This new piece of software meant another language, but this time the managers hoped that it would put an end to the everlasting discussions over the products and to the heated controversy among front, back, and middle offices, the accounting department, and all the other departments taking part in this endless conversation. Its main architect explains the philosophy that was behind the software called TRADE (pseudonym):

What I tried to do with TRADE is to separate clearly two things which are usually mixed in people's minds, let alone in the code of products: I tried to differentiate clearly between the definition of a financial contract—what it is—and its pricing—what it is worth. These are two things most people confuse. . . . This is very important, all the finance textbooks start with "a market, let's assume n assets written n_1, n_2 . . . following an integrable submartingale" but this does not matter, it comes afterwards and they should tell me first what a financial contract is. And then comes the definition of a call, and it is Max(0, $S - K$). . . . [33] It is extremely difficult to formalize the notion of a contract independently of its pricing, and in most finance textbooks the contract and the pricing are being confused but these are two different things. There is a flaw on this point.

[I ask him if what he was after was the positivist dream of a financial grammar.]

This is a very algebraic approach; this is a language. I work on a language with a rigorous semantics. A language that distinguishes between a *contract* semantics and a *pricing* semantics [his emphasis]. At the end of the day, in the bank we all agree that we write contracts that are vouched for by the market department lawyers. It is very unusual for a lawyer to understand what a Brownian motion is or what a complex pricing means. And yet they can tell you whether the contract is good or not, and that shows that there are different semantic levels. We must be able to manipulate the notion of "contract" regardless of the notion of "pricing." That is the idea, "if you do X, then Y. . .," but to be able to express this kind of event, we must adopt a very clear formalism that takes into account the passing of time. . . . Take, for example, three-month LIBOR.[34] Ask someone from the front office what it is and you will get the following answer: it is the division of two zero-coupon [bonds] . . . that is what a mathematician will tell you. The back office tells you, for me a three-month LIBOR, this is a market datum, there is a fixing every night and I must be careful to check the accurate data and to input it in the historical database. You have two completely different approaches, but the problem with the mathematician's solution is that it already contains a model; it is already a pricing of three-month LIBOR. When you say "a LIBOR is the relation of two zero-coupons," it is immediately a no-arbitrage reasoning.[35] What you say with this definition is that if you have a [no-arbitrage] model of the dynamics of interest rates, then three-month LIBOR is necessarily equal to this formula. That is true, but this is not a definition of LIBOR. (. . .) Everybody dreams of the long-searched-for front [office]–back [office] integration but nobody asks the good question "What do I need, what description do I need in order to achieve this result?"

The architect of the TRADE language defends the idea that the market price of a product does not exhaust what should be said about it. For him, the language of price ruling on most desks of the front office forms only one aspect of the product, and it does not capture what is in his view specific to financial derivative products: the range of contingent actions that clients can undertake when they buy one of these contracts. A price, even when it is the result of these complex concatenated structures, does not render them visible. Not because the rest of the characteristics of a product would be richer than just this narrow quality,[36] but precisely because price, though the ultimate dimension, is not an articulate language. It depends in so many ways upon all the other characteristics of a product. The language of price is what summarizes the product ex post facto, once the traders' positions are closed. But in the meantime, it cannot be reduced to this dimension alone. Only the whole gamut of a product's qualities can help make sense of the erratic dynamics of its price. Indeed, it is easy to come to an agreement on a price when it is not yet a real price, only a function of other variables that index sums to be paid in the future. But when the variables leave the stage, and actual sums of money need to be paid, it is necessary for the banker to grasp the product in other dimensions.

What is at stake in this new version of the product's articulation is the reference to an environment larger than the sheer market price around which the finance professor and the Quant were struggling. They were focusing on the complexity of a price mainly conditioned by the market magnitudes (rates, market prices of underlying securities). The engineer of the TRADE language highlights another envelope around the products. In addition to their market prices, he also insists that their definition include production prices and that these two cannot be completely detached. Languages suited to capture the front-office side of these products left aside some of their critical outcomes, once viewed from another perspective. This concern for a second dimension of the products did not come out of nowhere. It was informed by a series of clamorous mishandlings and an innumerable series of cost markups following deficient circulation of information. In the face of the organizational and human costs incurred by the complexity of the products, TRADE's architect tended to downplay their financial complexity and insist that the problem was the lack of a structure within which to manage them appropriately:

> We are in an industry where the difficulty is not theoretical; here, it comes from the required provisions in a contingent world, with precise dates to be respected. There are huge amounts of money involved and legal commitments over years, and we do not have the ultimate formalism that would allow us to combine these provisions in response to clients' demands. Each time we have to make loads of analysis and there are battalions of interns doing that.

They were not just interns, but large numbers of fully paid back-office managers and middle-office officers working at reconciling the different versions of the same product, as they were produced in several venues around the bank. The bottom line of the product, once all these additional costs were registered, could differ markedly from the blueprint written up by the front-office financial engineers. What had been left aside in a sketchy description of cost-benefit analysis came back disruptively when other departments of the bank tried to summarize its impact on the balance sheet.

Yet the main difficulty was not internal communication. That could still be solved through a hierarchical principle assigning each department its responsibility. The clients, on the contrary, were not as easy to satisfy and the imperative of serving them properly raised a more difficult issue. The lack of simple framework that could be used to describe transactions would slow down deals and keep many back-office operatives busy. TRADE, which was designed with a view to solving a local standardization issue, slowly evolved toward a strategic move by the bank to create an industrywide standard. Initially designed as an in-house software effort by a team within the R&D department, it became a project conducted outside the bank by a spinoff company funded by the bank itself. The explicit aim was to use a successful example to force the rest of the major banks to adopt this language.

The project of building a language that would put an end to fuzziness in the description of financial products did not appeal only to this bank. The community of bankers was well aware of the dangers associated with a loose definition of the innovative products that were springing to life in so many trading rooms. Adopting a language that would eventually come to be spoken by every partner in these new deals was an outcome dreamt of by more than one leading bank. It was a way of turning what was still a craft to the level of an industrial process. What used to be endless conversations about financial products had to leave the stage in favor of a stricter code, shared by as many institutions as possible.

From Conversations to a Standard: FPML, an Industrywide Language

The Financial Products Markup Language (FPML) was developed with a view to offering this standardization to the industry leaders. With strong ties to the ISDA, the initiative involved some of the biggest actors[37] on the financial market. Like most of the initiatives backed by ISDA, it took the form of a series of working groups putting out proposals subsequently discussed by the participants. The ambition for a language developed in cooperation is most interesting from the viewpoint of the question of financial conversation being tracked in venues around the bank.

Consisting of a series of electronic spreadsheets covering most families of over-the-counter derivatives, FPML aims at making the craft of customizing clients' specific deals irrelevant. The claim of this free-license project is to exhaust all possible products and all possible formulas of exchange between any two market participants.[38] It is tantamount to the dream once entertained by the positivist Vienna Circle (Carnap 1947): putting an end to the confusion entailed by badly coined languages (languages lacking transparency with respect to the matter that they express). It also means that finance, as a subset of economic transactions, has its own grammar that the subsequent flow of innovations will express. The FPML standard targets this level of finance. Its focus against confusion is explicit in its presentation:

> Over-the-counter (OTC) derivative transactions such as swaps have developed rapidly since they were introduced in the early 1980s. These contracts share a number of attributes that make them flexible and effective for solving many complex financial needs for organizations. For example, since they involve only two firms ("counterparties"), these transactions can easily be customized to meet specific customer requirements. As they are over the counter, it is not necessary to get agreement from an exchange or a regulator to change the contract specifications. These characteristics have caused the OTC derivatives market to grow quickly in volume and in product variety. However, the very flexibility and rapid evolution of OTC derivatives has challenged technology. For most of the life of the OTC derivatives industry, technology development has focused on building tools for pricing and risk managing these transactions, functions that are primarily internal to the firms entering these transactions. For this reason, the communication and confirmation of details of these transactions between counterparties has typically been highly manual, and therefore error-prone and frequently of poor timeliness. Firms typically exchange details via fax, and humans read these faxes to compare them with their own firms' representations of these transactions. Whether for initial confirmation of the trades, or for purposes such as settlement or collateral

matching, the lack of an automated mechanism for communicating this information causes significant expense and operational risk, as well as rigidity in
business processes. (http://www.fpml.org/documents/faq.html)

One of the pages of the FPML project Web site contains a PDF document entitled "Chatting in XML Financial Messages." It describes how
XML technology now enables both the solidity of a standard—shared
by a large community—and the fluidity of a chat among partners. The
comparison that is drawn at great length recalls the ages of the telegraph
and of the subsequent revolution brought about by the telephone:

> According to conventional perception, the only way for parties to swap their
> financial transactions is asynchronous exchange of messages . . . each party
> uses its own application software. Applications are almost unrelated and can-
> not talk natively between them. . . . Such communication between applications
> resembles in some manner what happened prior to the invention of the tele-
> phone when, in order to communicate, people send and received telegrams. . . .
> Trends of the business world are now intertwined with trends of the technolog-
> ical world more than ever. While the business world still communicates in an
> asynchronous telegraph-like way, technology has advanced to real-time com-
> munications. (www.fpml.org/resources/**xml**-background/index.asp)

The Web site goes on to depict an ideal system in which traders and
brokers could be linked instantaneously, without even having to engage
in technical and arduous operations. In contrast with the currently flawed
system where business deals take at least three days to be confirmed fully
for lack of smooth technical support, the article describes what could be a
conversation that would instantaneously be mirrored by a similar series
of steps in the software systems of the chat partners. Cumbersome old
software packages would be replaced by a transparent, resistanceless
apparatus that would put an end to the disagreement arising from either
asynchronous applications or conversations that were not grounded in a
strict syntax provided by an order processing software.

The bankers developing FPML are engaged in an exercise of definition
and framing of what the products that proliferate increasingly on the
market do. To keep a hand on these slippery products, the categories constructed try to seize them at their joints, so to speak. This process of articulation entails a language that aims at diluting the complexity of the
product into a smooth object, opposing any resistance to its intelligibility.

Articulation and Manipulation

It may be helpful at this stage to come back to the tension between
Franck's local priorities and the functionality of the code on a larger

scale (ISDA). When Franck spells out his preferences for a code, it is fair to reverse the usual narrative of choice: he is struck by the capabilities of the code of his taste, rather than deliberately choosing this code. His preferences are embedded in this complex process of experimentation with a language that reveals its potentiality in the making. In this respect, he is not different from the traders trying to make sense of the behavior of their portfolios: all are embarked on an uncertain journey, surrounded by other traders also searching for the best move on the market. But the human environment (Knorr Cetina and Bruegger 2002) is not the whole story. It is actually only a small part and only one species within the population that the bank's operatives have to deal with. The resistance coming from the products and their batteries of tools (mathematical functions, computer codes, software) should not be treated separately from human interactions in the market. For bank operatives, achieving the proper articulation of a product turns out to be as demanding as catching the market trend through wise psychology. The task of articulation demands open-mindedness from the operatives;[39] they learn to listen to the products and to let go of their preconceptions derived from different disciplines.

With the ISDA trying to enforce its language, the interests at stake of bankers seem much clearer. Market share is at stake, competition rules the game, and there seems to be no room for hesitation. The building of an industry-standard language creates a network of alliances between partners in a very clear instance of industry's economic strategy (David 1985). However, granted this strategic dimension, can the choice of one articulation, as opposed to another, come down to a sheer arbitrary decision?

Manipulation could be thought of as the alternative to articulation as a way of conceptualizing these matters. In its usual meaning, "manipulation" entails the twisting of a reality with a view to reaching certain objectives. It is actually a category widely used to stigmatize a broad array of practices on financial markets (Hertz 1998; Lépinay and Hertz 2004). Traders manipulate markets through the diffusion of ungrounded information; rogue accountants manipulate the books by making up their contents;[40] banks manipulate the contracts to hide the risks faced by their clients. These narratives of manipulation fit very well with the large literature on asymmetric information, but they are not useful for markets that are structured so clearly around a principle of constant innovation. As such, innovation does not rule out asymmetry and it does not mean that power relations structuring markets do not contribute to the ecologies. What the concept of manipulation offers as a resource is not the opposite of articulation. Rather, manipulation is articulation viewed from the perspective of one group and against the expectations of another group competing with it on the market. Manipulators and articulators share the same expertise (Chateauraynaud and Bessy 1995) in the matter at hand. The referent (the product, for example) is as much an ally—or possibly an impediment—as other market participants, but even the most extreme of manipulators cannot do without referents altogether. The level of investigation necessary might well change as the degree and form of competition change, but the description of a product cannot take on any arbitrary guise.[41]

Conclusion

This chapter challenges the classical tenets of a sociology of language in two ways. It defends a realist theory of language in which the functionality of linguistic categories is not naive preconception, but rather evidence of the pragmatic interaction between codes and an underlying resistant world to which those codes refer. I have elaborated this realist and pragmatist approach through the focus on financial languages and the moving referentiality with which they grapple.

Finance dramatizes the test of accuracy that its languages must take. Each version of the financial languages illustrated in this chapter is subjected to a relentless test—ultimately, profit and loss—that brings about an answer to the question of its accuracy. The competitive context of these languages makes it much easier to attend to their functionality dimension (Jackobson 1971), but it may be the case that the sociology of language has overlooked functionality due to its nearly exclusive interest in the symbolic dimension of languages. Sociology has accepted a limited version of the functionality argument in showing that language always serves social interests. However, while there is undoubtedly an interplay of social interests around financial languages, even in the apparently one-dimensional test-driven environment, it is a case in which another less-explored dimension can be added to this well-documented aspect. Social interests "speak," but so do products.

This chapter also casts light on a second neglected aspect of the interaction between languages and people: languages offer their own characteristics, which are discovered and investigated *in practice*. Linguistic structures envoke no sense of submission; rather, the codes that we have observed around financial products are playgrounds of imagination and tinkering, and not just human imagination—products and codes are among the players in the playground. As one of the computer engineers that I interviewed put it, "A code, it is full of the unexpected, it is easy to be overflowed by some of its reactions."

Once again, this finding goes against the grain of a sociology of language with a structural flavoring. This chapter has placed special emphasis on the intimate colloquium woven between the codes and their users. My analysis makes space for a *poetics* of codes. Even in a highly competitive arena such as financial markets, choices are made that cannot be reduced either to social-strategic positioning (be it symbolic or more materially driven) or to a call from the products themselves (as in our first version of nonsymbolic functionality). These choices play out in the gap between social and natural functionality. Emphasis on social functionality—explanations in terms of social interests, for example—neglects the active role of the real-world referents of codes, while an emphasis on natural functionality (as framed by the indicators of accuracy, primarily profit and loss) risks oversimplifying this role. The poetics of codes that I have sought to exemplify in this chapter avoids both blind alleys, emphasizing that technologies of language have their own qualities, reducible neither to "Society" nor to "Nature."

Notes

1. This chapter has benefited from comments by Donald MacKenzie and Fabian Muniesa as well as a careful reading by the reviewers of Princeton University Press. Harrison White and Peter Bearman have been insightful commentators and Alexandra Vinocur a cautious reader.

2. In his subsequent work, Callon has been increasingly interested in less strategic regimes of action, in which humans are seized by the materiality of the world rather than commanding its structure. See Callon et al. (2000).

3. This chapter follows a network made up of institutions (banks, regulatory bodies, associations, universities) and of products. Yet simply invoking a network topology is not sufficient to highlight what goes on around the quest for understanding the properties of the products. Michel Callon and Bruno Latour (1981; Latour 2005) have illustrated this approach of studying heterogeneous networks in a series of works that also cut through conventional domains of sociology.

4. This puzzle of the description and of the status of social scientists adding their own definition to that of the natives is not my main focus in this chapter. It has received the most extreme solutions in science studies approaches to techno-scientific controversies. Although my concern here recalls the challenge that Garfinkel (1967; Garfinkel and Rawls 2002) addressed to the positivist social sciences à la Parsons, I side more easily with recent Actor-Network approaches to the question (Latour 2005 Law; and Hassard 1999). This is made relevant and easier by the rather narrow network covered by the product. Unlike more controversial issues studied by scholars leaning toward Actor-Network Theory, I did not come across a wide variety of actors trying to voice radically different positions. Even outside the bank, the product did not spark *irreconcilable* definitions.

5. A sociology of the definition is already well in place. Boltanski and Thévenot (1983) have studied the contentions around national registries of professional labels and categories.

6. A solution to this puzzle has been given by Star and Griesemer (1989) with the boundary object notion explaining the agreement of otherwise divided communities around objects lending themselves to as many interpretations as there are outstanding communities. The success of this notion probably comes from it being itself a boundary object. It reconciled science studies scholars interested in the objects of science and technology with social constructivists increasingly aware of the role of objects in social organizations. Yet this coming together may not have clarified positions as extremely separate as these. Social constructivists were happy to encompass boundary objects as they became new receptacles of social meaning, but they would not take any further step in the direction of more realist sociologists of science for whom objects did make a difference in the shape of society and could not be construed as indeterminate conventions. The reason why the notion of a boundary object turned out not to be helpful for this study comes from the very organization of the bank.

7. On the variety of experiments taking place in the bank, see Lépinay (2003).

8. "Brownian motion" is the movement of a tiny particle subject to random collision with the molecules of the fluid or gas in which it is suspended. There are strong similarities between how financial economists model price movements and how physicists model Brownian motion.

9. Olivier Godechot's (2001) early study of traders' skills in a Parisian trading room shows how chartists, mathematically inclined traders, and fundamentalists cannot communicate over the same products. The language that they develop to describe these products' dynamics does not find an easy common ground. But informed by a framework taken from the work of Pierre Bourdieu, Godechot tries to relate these disagreements to macro factors without acknowledging that the lack of a common language can come from the products' variety itself.

10. Sean Flanagan (2001) studied the group dynamics during the rise of the International Swaps and Derivatives Association.

11. A "derivative" is a contract whose value depends on the price of another underlying asset or on the level of an index or exchange or interest rate.

12. They merged in 2003, after the fieldwork was completed, and gave birth to the Autorités des Marchés Financiers.

13. In its 2002 *Facts and Figures* bulletin, the COB released this statement on formula products: "*Framing formula funds*. Faced with the fast development of 'formula funds' which raise difficulties of understanding for investors, the Commission decided in August 2002 to launch a consultation, the outcome of which has been a decision aimed at better controlling those products. As a general rule, the prospectuses of these funds will have to contain certain mandatory information meant to make it easier for subscribers to understand the product. In addition to that, a new national registry category will be created and named 'formula funds.'"

14. Lancaster (1971) has come closest to an economic analysis of this differentiation. In locating the dynamic of competition around small but significant shifts in goods' properties, he bridges the gap between a very abstract economic theory and marketing theories focusing on the local scenes of exchange. See also Callon et al. (2000) for an extension of Lancaster's approach.

15. As this chapter argues, the most fruitful cases to study liquidity and articulation are the disruption of previous orderly regimes. Apart from the introduction

of new species in a population of economic goods, some recent cases of economic disruption have shown how regimes of liquidity and articulation are suspended. The current cases of Argentina and the former Soviet Union are most interesting as they make explicit the taken-for-granted orderliness of currency regimes and what they require to hold against waves of distrust. See Douglas (2005) for early twentieth-century Argentina.

16. A key difference from the products on which I am focusing is that in these the bank guarantees this floor, while most portfolio insurers offered a trading strategy designed to create this floor, but did not themselves guarantee it.

17. The second part of Leland (1980) dwells on the more technical notion of preferences' convexity, but it does it with a view to providing the investor—or his or her finance adviser—with a definite map of his or her interests. Convexity becomes a surrogate of the complex composition of an investor decision. It now clears the hesitations and provides a simple rule to be followed against the threat of distrust.

18. This thought experiment is not far-fetched. Cases of alleged innocuous substances revealing their danger to certain populations are most common and the bread and butter of environmental disputes. Who, in the 1920s, could have guessed that lead was going to be the toddlers' enemy in the 1990s? On these cases of undomesticated goods showing their evil face long after they have been circulated on a large scale, see Latour (2005).

19. There can be a lack of satisfaction for one party to the exchange, but it will not be imputed to a deceptive scheme by the other party.

20. Physical noise is a most interesting indicator of market confidence, but it does not follow a simple rule. When certainty begins to fade, it may be the case that noise goes up and communication goes down.

21. Whether to call this discipline "mathematical finance" or "financial mathematics" was the topic of lively discussion during an interview with another professor whom I interviewed a couple of months after I witnessed this piece of finance pedagogy. For this teacher, who was very attached to the rigorous proofs entailed by the discipline of mathematics, financial mathematics conveyed the idea of a conversion of finance to the rules of mathematics, whereas mathematical finance was simply a more formalized way of writing finance, without touching the content of its subject matter. The first meant to substitute mathematical unknowns with relevant dimensions of finance; the second abstracts these dimensions without forcing them to adopt the language of mathematics.

22. I have translated the French word *lourd* as clumsy. "Lourd" here means not agile, literally heavy, and attached to a trajectory with momentum.

23. The Black-Scholes-Merton equation (equation 1 in the appendix to MacKenzie's chapter) is the prototype of these equations.

24. OATs, Obligations Assimilables au Trésor, are bonds issued by the French Treasury. They are very well rated by most financial agencies.

25. See Derman (2004) for a lively introduction to the life of a quant, a physicist making pricing models in a trading room.

26. I cannot exploit sociologically in detail the consequences of this exploration and the "unearthing" of unexpected results. It is part of the research agenda of a noncritical and noninternalist sociology of mathematics which would

make space for the very peculiar dialectics tying disciplinary rules and innovation. To the best of my knowledge, only Pickering and Stephanides (Pickering 1995), Livingston (1986, 1999), and Rosental (2003) have addressed these questions.

27. One of the apparently most important parameters, the expected return on the underlying security, simply—and to their total amazement—disappeared and simplified greatly the equation, giving it an analytical solution. MacKenzie (2003) describes this in much more detailed terms.

28. "Bourbaki" was a group of French mathematicians who set out to found a most rigorous mathematics and end the fuzziness surrounding mathematics. This legacy is still very much active in the French educational system, particularly in the elite engineering schools.

29. This software could either be bought from companies specializing in financial computing or could be developed in-house. Our bank had chosen the second solution, as will be seen later.

30. High-order expansions permit understanding the behavior of a function around a given value. When it is a price function with variables including interest rates and the price of the underlying asset, the expansions involve higher order derivatives and cross-derivatives of these variables.

31. Mary Morgan (2000) has investigated the complex question of model testing in the social sciences, as opposed to the natural science modes of demonstration.

32. Hull and White are among the best known academics whose models made their way to the market, Hull via his widely read textbook on futures and options (1997). Franck refers to a model that they developed with a volatility structure that must be calibrated to market prices.

33. That is, the value of a call option (see MacKenzie's chapter) at its expiration is zero if the stock price S is below the exercise price K, and it is $S - K$ if $S \geqslant K$.

34. LIBOR is London Inter-Bank Offered Rate, measured each working day by a firm employed by the British Bankers' Association and broadcast via systems such as Bloomberg. LIBOR as ascertained in this fashion is the average rate at which a panel of leading banks report other banks as being prepared to lend them money in a given currency for a fixed period (in this case three months).

35. That is, a form of reasoning in which it is posited that the only patterns of prices that can be stable are those that permit no opportunities to make riskless profits with no net capital outlay.

36. This could be the nonreductionist approach witnessed on some secondary markets for goods, where people can challenge the totalizing nature of the price, and use values overflow prices.

37. Bank of America, BNP Paribas, Citigroup, Crédit Lyonnais, CSFB, Deutsche Bank, Goldman Sachs, Lehman Brothers, JP Morgan Chase, Morgan Stanley, UBS, and many other companies developing back office systems (http://www.fpml.org/participants/index.html).

38. The Web site states: "All categories of over-the-counter derivatives (OTC) will eventually be incorporated into the standard" (http://www.fpml.org/news/factsheet.html).

39. This sense of open mindedness has been studied in detail by Hennion (1993) in his study of amateur musicians. Hennion's approach highlights the regimes of action that these stances entail.

40. The last five years have brought the profession of accountants to front stage. From holders of peripheral boring jobs they have been turned into the ultimate hidden agents of capitalism. They have been described as overt liars.

41. The story of the QWERTY keyboard told by David (1985) is an interesting counterexample but one that comes from a case where the test is not as easy to carry out. It is a much more open-ended situation, involving in particular the user and entailing a joint test of the users' skills and the machine.

References

Abolafia, M. 2002. "Making Sense of Recession: Policy Making at the Federal Reserve." New York Conference on Social Studies of Finance, Columbia University & SSRC, May 3–4, 2002.

Ackerman, K. D. 1988. *The Gold Ring: Jim Fisk, Jay Gould, and Black Friday, 1869.* New York: Dodd, Mead.

Akerlof, G. 1970. "The Market for Lemons." *Quarterly Journal of Economics* 84:488–500.

Atkinson, M., and J. Heritage, Eds. 1984. *Structures of Social Action: Studies in Conversation Analysis.* Cambridge: Cambridge University Press.

Austin, J.L. 1962. *How to Do Things with Words.* Oxford: Clarendon.

Baker, W. E. 1984. "The Social Structure of a National Securities Market." *American Journal of Sociology* 89:775–811.

Bloor, D. 1983. *Wittgenstein: A Social Theory of Knowledge.* New York: Columbia University Press.

Boltanski, L. and L. Thévenot. 1983. "Finding One's Way in Social Space: A Study Based on Games." *Social Sciences Information* 22:631–679.

Caliskan, K. 2004. "Global Market Maintenance and Its Price in the Two Worlds of Commodity Circulation." Paper submitted to the Political Economy Research Center Seminar, October 12, University of Massachusetts at Amherst. Available at http://courses.umass.edu/econ804/caliskan.pdf

Callon, M., Ed. 1998. *The Laws of the Markets.* Oxford: Blackwell.

Callon, M., and B. Latour. 1981. "Unscrewing the Big Leviathan: Or How Actors Macrostructure Reality and How Sociologists Help Them to Do So?" in *Advances in Social Theory and Methodology: Toward an Integration of Micro and Macro-Sociologies*, edited by K. Knorr-Cetina and A. Cicourel. London: Routledge and Kegan Paul.

Callon, M., C. Méadel, and V. Rabeharisoa. 2000. "L'économie des qualités." *Politix* 52:211–239.

Carnap, R. 1947. *Meanings and Necessity: A Study in Semantics and Modal Logics.* Chicago: University of Chicago Press.

Carruthers, B. G., and W. N. Espeland. 1991."Accounting for Rationality: Double-Entry Bookkeeping and the Rhetoric of Economic Rationality." *American Journal of Sociology* 97:31–69.

Carruthers, B. G., and A. L. Stinchcombe. 1999 "The Social Structure of Liquidity: Flexibility, Markets, and States." *Theory and Society* 28(3):353–382.

Chateauraynaud, F., and C. Bessy. 1995. *Experts et faussaires: Pour une sociologie de la perception*. Paris: Métailié.

Collman, C. A. 1968. *Our Mysterious Panics, 1830–1930: A Story of Events and the Men Involved*. New York: Greenwood.

David, P. A. 1985. "Clio and the Economics of QWERTY." *American Economic Review* 75:332–337.

Deleuze, G. 1968. *Spinoza et le problème de l'expression*. Paris: Minuit.

Derman, E. 2004. *My Life as a Quant: Reflections on Physics and Finance*. New York: Wiley.

Douglas, R. 2005. "Moonshine, Money and the Politics of Liquidity in Rural Russia." *American Ethnologist* 32:63–81.

Downey, G. L. 1998. *The Machine in Me: An Anthropologist Sits among Computer Engineers*. New York: Routledge.

Espeland, W. N., and P. Hirsh. 1990. "Ownership Changes, Accounting Practice and the Redefinition of the Corporation." *Accounting, Organizations and Society* 15:77–96.

Flanagan, S. M. 2001. "The Rise of a Trade Association: Group Interactions within the International Swaps and Derivatives Association." *Harvard Negotiation Law Review* 6:211–264.

Galbraith, J. K. 1990. *A Short History of Financial Euphoria*. Knoxville, TN: Whittle Direct Books.

Garfinkel, H. 1967. *Studies in Ethnomethodology*. Englewood Cliffs, NJ: Prentice Hall.

Garfinkel, H., and A. W. Rawls. 2002. *Ethnomethodology's Program: Working Out Durkheim's Aphorism*. Lanham, MD: Rowman & Littlefield.

Gibson, D. 2005. "Taking Turns and Talking Ties: Network Structure and Conversation Sequence." *American Journal of Sociology* 110:1561–1597.

Godechot, O. 2001. *Les Traders: Essai de sociologie des marchés financiers*. Paris: La Découverte.

Hennion, A. 1993. *La passion musicale: Une sociologie de la médiation*. Paris: Métailié.

Hertz, E. 1998. *The Trading Crowd: An Ethnography of the Shanghai Stock Market*. Cambridge: Cambridge University Press.

Hull, J., and A. White. 1990. "Pricing Interest-Rate Derivative Securities." *Review of Financial Studies* 3:573–592.

Hull, J. C. 1997. *Options, Futures and Other Derivatives*. Upper Saddle River, NJ: Prentice Hall.

Jakobson, R. 1971. *Fundamentals of Language*. The Hague: Mouton.

Keynes, J. M. 1936. *The General Theory of Employment, Interest and Money*. London: MacMillan.

Knight, F. H. 1936/1971. *Risk, Uncertainty, and Profit*. Chicago: University of Chicago Press.

Knorr Cetina, K., and U. Bruegger. 2002. "Traders Engagement with Markets: A Postsocial Relationship." *Theory, Culture and Society* 19:161–185.

Lancaster, K. 1971. *Consumer Demand: A New Approach*. New York: Columbia University Press.

Latour, B. 1987. *Science in Action: How to Follow Scientists and Engineers through Society*. Cambridge, MA: Harvard University Press.

Latour, B. 2005. *Reassembling the Social: An Introduction to Actor-Network-Theory*. Oxford, New York: Oxford University Press.

Lave, J. 1988. *Cognition in Practice: Mind, Mathematics and Culture in Everyday Life*. Cambridge: Cambridge University Press.

Lave, J. 1990. "Views of the Classroom: Implications for Math and Science Learning Research." In *Toward a Scientific Practice of Science Education*, edited by M. Gardner. Hillsdale, NJ: Erlbaum Associates.

Law, J., and J. Hassard, Eds. 1999. *Actor Network Theory and After*. London: Blackwell.

Leland, H. E. 1980. "Who Should Buy Portfolio Insurance." *Journal of Finance* 35:581–594.

Lépinay, V.-A. 2003. "Les formules du marché. Ethno-économie d'une innovation financière: Les produits à Capital Garanti." PhD diss. Centre de Sociologie de l'Innovation. Paris: ENSMP.

Lépinay, V.-A., and E. Hertz. 2004. "Deception and Its Preconditions: Issues Raised by Financial Markets." In *Exchange, Deception and Self-Deception in Economics*, edited by Caroline Gerschlager. London: Palgrave MacMillan.

Livingston, E. 1986. *The Ethnomethodological Foundations of Mathematics*. London: Routledge & Paul Kegan.

Livingston, E. 1999. "Cultures of Proving." *Social Studies of Science* 29:867–888.

MacKenzie, D. 2003. "An Equation and Its Worlds: Bricolage, Exemplars, Disunity and Performativy in Financial Economics." *Social Studies of Science* 33:831–868.

Metz, T. 1988. *Black Monday: The Catastrophe of October 19, 1987, and Beyond*. New York: Morrow.

Miller, P., and T. O'Leary. 1998. "The Factory as Laboratory." Pp. 120–150 in *Accounting and Science*, edited by Michael Power. Cambridge: Cambridge University Press.

Miller, P., and T. O'Leary. 2002. "Rethinking the Factory: Caterpillar Inc." *Cultural Values* 6:91–117.

Millo, Y. 2003. "Where Do Financial Markets Come From? Historical Sociology of Financial Derivatives Markets." PhD diss. Edinburgh: University of Edinburgh.

Morgan, M. 2000. *Experiments without Material Intervention: Model Experiments, Virtual Experiments and Virtually Experiments*. London: London School of Economics. Centre for Philosophy of Natural & Social Science.

Muniesa, F. 2003. "Des marchés comme algorithmes: Sociologie de la cotation électronique à la Bourse de Paris." PhD diss. Centre de Sociologie de l'Innovation. Paris: Ecole Nationale Supérieure des Mines de Paris.

Ochs, E., S. Jacoby, and P. Gonzales. 1994. "Interpretive Journeys: How Physicists Talk and Travel through Graphic Space." *Configurations* 2:151–171.

Ochs, E., E. A. Schegloff, and S. A. Thompson, Eds. 1996. *Interaction and Grammar*. Cambridge: Cambridge University Press.

Pickering, A., Ed. 1992. *Science as Practice and Culture*. Chicago: University of Chicago Press.

Pickering, A. 1995. *The Mangle of Practice: Time, Agency and Science*. Chicago: University of Chicago Press.

Ricardo, D. 1815/1951. *Works and Correspondence*. Cambridge: University Press for the Royal Economic Society.

Rosental, C. 2003. "Certifying Knowledge: The Sociology of a Logical Theorem in Artificial Intelligence." *American Sociological Review* 68:623–644.

Ross, S. 1976. "Options and Efficiency." *Quarterly Journal of Economics* 90:75–89.

Sacks, H., and G. Jefferson. 1992. *Lectures on Conversation*. Oxford: Blackwell.

Sobel, R. 1968. *Panic on Wall Street: A History of America's Financial Disasters*. New York: Macmillan.

Star, S. L., and J. Griesemer. 1989. "Institutional Ecology, 'Translations' and Boundary Objects: Amateurs and Professionals in Berkeley's Museum of Vertebrate Zoology, 1907–39." *Social Studies of Science* 19:387–420.

Steinherr, A. 2000. *Derivatives. The Wild Beast of Finance: A Path to Effective Globalisation?* Chichester: Wiley.

Tarde, G. 1904. *Psychologie économique*. Paris: Félix Alcan.

Thévenot, L. 1986. "Les investissements de forme." Pp. 21–71 in *Les conventions economiques*. Paris: PUF.

Zuckerman, E. 1999. "The Categorical Imperative: Securities Analysts and the Illegitimacy Discount." *American Journal of Sociology* 104:1398–1438.

Zuckerman, E. 2004. "Structural Incoherence and Stock Market Activity." *American Sociological Review* 69:405–432.

Chapter 5 —————————————————————

How to Do Things with Experimental Economics

FRANCESCO GUALA

In July 2003 two U.S. senators, Ron Wyden and Byron Dorgan, publicly denounced a Pentagon plan to create an online "market for terror."[1] Anonymous buyers and sellers would exchange, on a government Web site, "futures for terrorist attacks," effectively betting on the likelihood that a certain site or prominent individual would become a target of Bin Laden's kamikazes. The project, initially allocated an $8 million budget for two years, was defined as "morally repugnant" and "grotesque" and was quickly withdrawn by the Bush administration following outrage in the news media and public opinion.[2]

The aborted plan wasn't merely an odd combination of army idiocy and market extremism. The market for terrorism was in many ways cutting-edge science. It was inspired by the repeated successful use of electronic markets to forecast uncertain events. The prototype and most famous example, the Iowa Electronic Markets, had been running since the late eighties and had predicted the results of major political events, notably the U.S. presidential elections, with a better margin of errors than the latest polls.

The roots of electronic markets lie in experimental economics, a research program recognized by the 2002 Nobel Prize.[3] The key idea—known as the "Hayek Hypothesis"—is that markets can be extremely efficient mechanisms for the aggregation of information. Indeed they are able to perform the remarkable trick of transforming imperfect individual information into an efficient market outcome, by means of a signal (a price) that incorporates at once all the preferences and expectations of the individuals in the market. The Hayek Hypothesis was a key weapon in the hands of free-market apologists during the so-called socialist calculation debate of the thirties, but for a long time it was little more than a speculation based on fairly abstract philosophical assumptions.[4] General equilibrium models in the Walrasian tradition, moreover, seemed to have cast doubt on the hypothesis by relying heavily on perfect information and other unrealistic assumptions to prove the theoretical existence of efficient equilibria, until, very recently, the

Hayek Hypothesis was corroborated in a series of ingenious laboratory experiments (see, e.g., Davis and Williams 1991; Plott 2000; Smith 1982b). Such experiments were introduced by economists like Vernon Smith and Charles Plott, who since the sixties had devoted their careers to constructing little "flesh and blood" markets (with real human sub-jects) in their university labs. Economists were also quick to exploit the opportunities provided by the Internet revolution, and the Hayek Hypothesis soon took the very concrete form of future markets for events of all sorts—from the results of political elections to the Oscars— and indeed, were it not for the two senators and a hypersensi-tive post-9/11 public opinion, for terrorist attacks.[5]

But these are neither the only nor the most important applications of experimental economics to date. Since the eighties experimental econo-mists have designed mechanisms for the allocation of airport slots (Grether et al. 1989); for the pricing of space stations (Plott and Porter 1996); for the regulation of inland water transportation (Hong and Plott 1982), of the gas industry (Grether and Plott 1984), and of gas trans-portation networks (Plott 1988); for the construction of the new Ari-zona Stock Exchange (Smith and Williams 1992); for the regulation of the market for new physicians and surgeons (Roth and Peranson 1999); and for the allocation of telecom licences (Plott 1997). The list is incom-plete and likely to grow in the next few years. The experimental game theorist Ken Binmore, who codesigned with Paul Klemperer the widely acclaimed 3G mobile phone auctions in the United Kingdom,[6] foresees applications in some key areas of the welfare state. How about a market for hospital beds?

> One way to do that would be to run a computerised market. Not the idiot internal market of Mrs Thatcher. . . . I cannot imagine a more irresponsible experiment . . . a real computerised market so each morning someone from each hospital can update their screen and say what they are willing to buy and sell beds for because you have to have an exchange of real resources for this to work. (Binmore in Atkinson 2000, p. 22)

Given the current political climate, this is not an unlikely prospect. Experimental economics is a relatively rare instance of social science that *works*. I mean "work" in a very broad way: it works sociologically, for after a low-key start it has been generally accepted within the scientific profession, as recognized by the Swedish Academy.[7] It works also scien-tifically, in the sense that it generates replicable results, allows one to make fairly precise predictions, and seems to provide strong insights in the mechanisms that govern market behavior. Experimental economists have even become so arrogant to name their society the "Economic

Science Association." (The subtext regarding the rest of economics is pretty obvious and astonishing—remember that this is not a small club of cranks or heterodox social scientists.)

But most important, as we have seen, experimental economics can be (and has been) used effectively to *intervene*, to change the institutions that regulate and coordinate economic behavior. Which takes me finally to the Austinian title of this chapter. Economists traditionally do things *with* models and field data; these are their basic tools, upon which their persuasive powers crucially rely. In order to do things "with," they do things *to* models and data—they manipulate them, analyze them, and try to show "what would happen if" such and such a policy were to be implemented in such and such circumstances. With experimental economics, in contrast, you can *do things to the economy*. You can manipulate and intervene in the microeconomies you have built in your laboratory, and this activity in turn is instrumental to intervening in real-world, full-size markets.

This view of laboratory experimentation as a tool for shaping and building economic entities emerged slowly and with difficulty over the years, having to struggle against a tradition that sees experiments in quite a different light, as aimed mainly at theory-testing. Actually the struggle is not quite over yet, although the building tradition seems to gain more and more momentum. Part of this chapter is devoted to drawing the contrast between these two traditions. I hope you will excuse my schematic attempt at reconstructing some very recent history of science, for it is eventually aimed at making a point about the core theme of this volume. The builders, I want to claim, are winning because they have understood performativity—or at least they have learned how to use it constructively. The testers have chosen a weak model of social science, according to which performativity is primarily an impediment for scientific research. On the contrary, performativity is a *resource* for the social scientist, and a very powerful one too.

Testers and Builders

That one could do things with experiments was by no means obvious in economics only a couple of decades ago. The relatively quick breakthrough of experimental economics within the current (broadly neoclassical) paradigm, an interesting topic for a historian of science, is a story that still remains to be told. What we have instead is a series of recollections by the main protagonists—published partly for the sake of historical record, partly for propaganda, partly for blatantly self-serving purposes—which have crystallized in a sort of "official" history of experimental economics.[8]

What follows is by no means intended to fill the gap but rather to sketch the minimal historical background, without which the significance of the laboratory revolution in economics is difficult to appreciate.

I'll skip the usual and useless attempts to trace the first prehistoric experiment back in time. Whether it was some betting experiment in the eighteenth century or a laboratory study of consumer theory in the 1930s has little importance, because experimental economics in its present form is entirely a post–World War II phenomenon. The mythology of the discipline customarily identifies three foundational moments. The first is a conference held in Santa Monica in 1952, where the newborn American community of experimental game theorists met shortly after the publication of von Neumann and Morgenstern's *Theory of Games and Economic Behavior* (1944). Many contributions described how real human beings (as opposed to perfectly rational agents) behave in simple social dilemma and bargaining situations. The second foundational event was almost simultaneous: the 1952 conference held in Paris where the earliest empirical counterexamples to von Neumann and Morgenstern's expected utility theory were presented to an audience of distinguished economists and statisticians. Like the Santa Monica conference, the Paris meeting was prompted by the publication of *The Theory of Games*, but it focused specifically on individual decision making. The third event is slightly posterior and significant almost only with hindsight: in 1962 Vernon Smith (later to become Nobel Laureate, in 2002) published his first experimental paper on the equilibrating and efficiency properties of a market governed by a double oral auction institution.[9]

A story based on the foundational myths leads pretty straightforwardly to identify three main currents within contemporary experimental economics: game-theory experiments, decision-theory experiments, and market experiments. This is as accurate a taxonomy as many others, but it turns out to be not very useful for my purposes. To understand what goes on in experimental economics, I believe, identifying *two* distinct approaches, which I call the *theory-testing* (or "testing," for short) and the *institution-building* (or "building") approach, is more useful. This classification cuts not at the level of the theories that drive experimental research but at a deeper level: the purposes of experimentation itself.

Roughly, the testers see experimentation through the spectacles of a philosophy of science textbook of the sixties; the builders, in contrast, are interested in "doing things with experiments." (I shall explain what this means in more detail soon.) This dichotomy maps onto the traditional threefold classification rather straightforwardly. Most of decision theory belongs to the testing approach, and most market experiments fall in the building camp. Game theory experiments are spread across the divide.

It is important to stress that the two groups are not neatly separated, and many researchers work in both traditions. Perhaps it is more accurate to say that testing and building refer to two logics of experimentation rather than two communities or tribes. The building/testing taxonomy helps to understand, to begin with, why experimenters happen to have a mixed reputation in neoclassical economics. On the one hand, experimental results are frequently invoked by the enemies of neoclassicism, as providing the ultimate evidence (what is stronger than experimental evidence, after all?) that the received theory is deeply flawed. On the other, experimental economics is often cited as a source of stunning confirmations of the standard theory; indeed experiments are found at the frontier of some impressive market reforms inspired by neoclassical economics.

Part of the explanation is that testers and builders tend to have very different agendas. Testers are often also dissenters; they look for refutations of the standard theory in the laboratory, and they find plenty. Builders have a more cautious attitude, they work inside the orthodoxy and tend not to make bold claims that might scare their fellow neoclassical economists. They also find lots of anomalies but strategically highlight the discoveries that are broadly consistent with the neoclassical spirit.

The testing approach, moreover, tends to transgress disciplinary barriers. The testers of decision and game theory work in close contact with experimental and cognitive psychologists. They sometimes call themselves "behavioral economists," by way of a contrast with the neoclassical habit of reasoning from models rather than from empirical data. Behavioral economists rely on various sources of empirical evidence, including laboratory experiments. They try to construct alternative models of human decision making that usually depart from the standard assumptions of rational behavior and are more firmly based on the data. In general, they don't get along very well with mainstream economists.[10]

Once upon a time the rhetoric of theory-testing was prevalent. To locate the shift in the balance of power between the testing and the building traditions, examination of the official propaganda of the discipline in methodological articles, presidential addresses, and books (the sort of stuff economists don't normally write, unless there is a very good political reason to do so) is useful. Exactly when the shift took place is difficult to say, but my hunch is that it is fairly recent. Although pioneers like Charles Plott have been writing from a "building" perspectives since the early eighties (see, e.g., Plott 1981), the testing rhetoric is still prevalent in methodological overviews like Smith (1989) or Smith, McCabe, and Rassenti (1991). In the nineties, slowly, titles like "The Economist as Engineer" (Roth 2002) and *Paving Wall Street: Experimental Economics and the Quest for the Perfect Market* (Miller 2002) began to appear more and more frequently.[11] In his post-Nobel writings, Vernon Smith engages in an overt apology of the instrument-building tradition in the natural sciences, from which economists have much to learn, in his view: "I think all sciences are influenced far more by the machines builders than either the theorists or experimentalists" (Smith 2002a, p. 69); "it's the machines that drive the new theories, hypotheses, and testing programs that take you from atoms, to protons, to quarks" (2002b, p. 105).

An Example: Social Dilemma Experiments

What kind of "machines" can be built in an economics lab? Since most people are not familiar with economics experimentation, it is worth illustrating by means of a simple example. Social dilemma experiments are a good case because, like most game theory experiments, they cut across the divide between the testing and building traditions. They are also among the most replicated experiments, and they happen to be widely popular outside of economics. In a social dilemma situation an agent acts under the influence of two considerations pulling in opposite directions. Rational strategic considerations suggest that the individual payoffs are maximized by following one strategy (the "free-rider" strategy), but it is easy to see that the rational strategy leads to a socially inferior (Pareto-inefficient) outcome if universally followed. The simplest and most popular social dilemma situation is the one-shot prisoner's dilemma game (see table 5.1).

The first number in each cell represents the payoff of the row player, the second one of the column player. Here the free-riding strategies are Down for Row and Right for Column, leading to a payoff of 2 units each. The reasoning behind this solution (the Nash solution or Nash equilibrium of the game, from the mathematician John Nash, recently celebrated in the Hollywood movie *A Beautiful Mind*) is simple: whatever Column may do, Row is better off by playing Down; similarly, Column is always better off by playing Right, regardless of what the opponent does. But, somehow paradoxically, both would be better off if they played Up–Left.

The game in the laboratory is usually played simultaneously via computer networks and without the possibility of binding agreements;

Table 5.1

The One-Shot Prisoner's Dilemma Game

	Left	*Right*
Up	5, 5	0, 10
Down	10, 0	2, 2

customarily players are also denied face-to-face interaction and the possibility of communication. I say "customarily" because in three decades
of experimentation almost every possible variation in the setup has been
explored, and it has been discovered that different arrangements have
significant effects on the results.[12] I can't review these results in detail
here, but as is well known in a "standard" social dilemma experiment a
considerable number of subjects play cooperatively (Up–Left, in the
game above), contrary to the prediction of standard economic theory.

What does this mean? Most testers are pretty adamant that this is a
falsification of the standard theory. What ought to be done, surely, is to
reject the theory and replace it by a better one that is able to account for
this and other robust empirical anomalies.[13] Builders have a more sophisticated attitude: they begin by noticing that several subjects cooperate, but many others free ride. Then they ask what can be done to put
them in line—whatever the "line" is. Under what conditions does everybody's behavior converge on the Nash equilibrium? And under what
conditions does it converge to the Pareto optimum? How can we help
people to achieve a desirable distribution of the payoffs (once "desirable" has been defined precisely enough, of course)?

We shall examine some of the tools that builders use for this purpose
later. Here I would like to notice that the testing tradition, despite all the
anomalous evidence it has accumulated, has been ineffective in defeating
the standard theory. Why? A standard answer is that economists are
simply not good scientists, that they are hopelessly influenced by their
ideological commitments, or something along these lines. Another line,
the one that I will follow here, is that in order to be successful you need
to learn to *do things* with experimental economics, and the testers have
not been very successful at that. The builders are way ahead in this
respect, and builders are not interested in refuting the received theory.
They rather want to *use* it, alongside many other tools (such as, crucially, experiments), to perform the economic world.

Performativity as Experimental Bias

The debate on performativity in social science tends to focus on two interrelated issues. The first is a general ontological thesis concerning the nature of social entities. Social properties are extrinsic properties of a special
kind: they depend on the context, and in particular on what other human
beings know, believe, or in a single word *intend* about the entity in question. The queen (the individual Elizabeth Alexandra Mary Windsor) is the
queen only if she is widely recognized as such. Her legitimate claim to the
throne, moreover, depends on the original performance of a series of

actions—including linguistic utterances (think of a crowning ceremony, for example)—which literally brought her social status into being. The contrast here is with natural properties (the structure of the molecule of a given substance, say) that are what they are (and constrain what you can do with them) independently of what people say or think about them. Of course this does not mean that certain natural properties are not created or brought about by human intervention, or that human beliefs do not play a part in the genesis of these properties. But the idea is that natural properties are not "made up" of such beliefs in the same way as social properties are.[14]

The second focal point in the debate concerns the process (or processes) by means of which social entities and phenomena begin, continue, and cease to exist. This being an empirical issue, no entirely general story can probably be told. But for the same reason, this is also where most of the interesting action is, from a sociological point of view. Most empirical studies tend to highlight the positive feedback effects (or "looping" effects, to use Ian Hacking's [1999] expression) of social concepts: if by saying that X has the (social) property Y we induce people to treat X as if it had property Y, then property Y may well come into being. The social sciences, of course, can play an important role in such processes:

> The social sciences seek to refer to referring activities in general; the social sciences are particular instances of referring activities. Accordingly, full independence of knowledge and its referents cannot be hoped for in the social sciences. (Barnes 1983, p. 524)

In one of the best applications to economics so far, for example, Donald MacKenzie analyzed how a "looping effect" of this kind led to the self-referential verification of the Black-Scholes theory of efficient financial markets in the 1970s. The theory, to use Austin's terminology, "performed" the market by helping to create and sustain the entities it postulated. The markets were reformed and reshaped by regulators keeping the theory in mind; and the pricing model of the theory was widely used by market makers when they operated in the market itself. This case study is particularly rich because it also provides examples of destructive or "counterperformative" effects, the 1987 crash and also the bubble created by the LTCM investment fund, which led to its eventual failure in 1998 (see MacKenzie's chapter, and also MacKenzie 2006; MacKenzie and Millo 2003).

Michel Callon (1998) recently proposed extending the feedback story to account for the whole of economics. (Indeed, as Callon emphasizes in his chapter, "economics" is broadly construed to include accounting, marketing, management, and other disciplines customarily considered peripheral to the "hard core" of neoclassical theory.) Callon's project is also based on a series of detailed empirical studies of how economics performs the economy; despite the boldness of the thesis, again, the presumption is that at the micro level there may be no general story to be told here.

A distinctive feature of contemporary work on performativity is its awareness of both its creative (positive) and its destructive (negative) aspects, whereas earlier accounts tended to focus on the negative side only. A classic example is Robert K. Merton's (1957) seminal discussion of the self-fulfilling prophecy. The rumor suddenly spreads that a bank is about to become insolvent. As a consequence, clients begin to withdraw their money from their accounts. Soon, the rumor turns into reality: the bank really *is* insolvent, "merely" because people have become convinced that it is. Similarly, consider the much-discussed problem of predicting the results of an election. A prediction (based on a poll), once made public, may trigger a "bandwagon" or an "underdog" effect that will falsify the prediction itself.

The "Mertonian" approach sees performativity as a threat, both for society—because it may lead to disastrous results such as the failure of a financially sound bank—and for social science—because it blurs the boundary between what scientists say about reality and reality itself, and in many cases seems to be an obstacle to the use of social science for the prediction of future events.[15] Something like the Mertonian approach can be found in experimental economics, too. Performativity worries are typically raised in the theory-testing tradition and take the form of concerns about the representativeness of the sample of subjects. The standard "laboratory rat" in experimental economics is the undergraduate student. And for obvious reasons of access the (self-selected) samples used in most experiments are largely made of *economics* students. The worry then is: do these individuals behave like everybody else? Isn't the fact that they are taught economics theory a source of bias in the experiments aimed at testing the theory itself?

This issue has been famously raised in the context of social dilemma experiments. Two experimental psychologists, Gerald Marwell and Ruth Ames (1981), first presented evidence that economics majors play the cooperative strategy less often than non-economics students in games of this kind. One tempting explanation is that they behave as free riders because economic theory tells them that that's the way in which people generally behave. Furthermore, the theory tells them that that's the *rational* way to behave. *Homo economicus*, if this interpretation is correct, would turn out to be a straightforward effect of economic theory itself. But since not all people have a degree in economics, the Marwell and Ames result opens serious doubts about the generalizability of neoclassical economics models based on the assumption of rational selfish behavior. It also raises the issue of the validity of laboratory experimentation itself: if people are so diverse that they behave in widely different ways depending on their cultural and educational background, how useful can these tests be? Performativity becomes a problem for both the theorist and the experimenter, from a theory-testing perspective.[16]

Is this interpretation of the Marwell and Ames result correct? Successive studies have replicated the significant difference between the behavior of economics and non-economics students. But they have also cast doubt on the performativity interpretation of this phenomenon. The most plausible explanation of the Marwell and Ames result points toward a selection effect: the sort of people who tend to behave more individualistically are also those who tend to do economics degrees.[17] In a recent study Frey and Meier (2003) found that freshmen who are about to start an economics degree are on average less cooperative even *before* they have attended their first economics class. This lower propensity to cooperate remains constant throughout their university career: teaching does not seem to make much difference to the way people behave (although interestingly the propensity to free ride tends to diminish slightly, but significantly, during PhD years).

The prominent game theorist Ariel Rubinstein also argues on the basis of pre- and postclass test results that teaching does not influence the way in which students behave—and fortunately so, he is keen to remark (Rubinstein 1999). Moreover, experimenters' informal experience as well as the systematic analyses of subjects' debriefing interviews suggest that students often *believe* they are following the theory, whereas in fact they are not.[18] Indoctrination, again, seems to have less effect than one may initially have thought. This of course does not provide much relief to neoclassical theory—people after all still behave in various ways that differ widely from the theoretical prediction. But it suggests that those who behave as predicted by economic theory do not do it because they have been taught to do so. Which, in turn, shows two things: (1) in some circumstances making people behave as economists think they should is probably not so easy; and (2) if the performativity hypothesis is true—if economic theory helps shape the economy, as Callon, MacKenzie, and others suggest—it must be in a more subtle way.

To figure out how, we have to look more carefully at the nature of economic models and theories. Economic theory does not merely describe how people behave: it describes how a specific kind of individual behaves *in some highly specific types of environment*. An economic model is a detailed description of the sort of circumstances that must occur for the interaction between agents of a certain kind (individualistic maximizers of their own utility) to produce outcomes of a certain kind (efficient market equilibria, typically). Among experimental economists, the builders have devoted more energies than anyone else to studying the institutional *structures* that govern market trading. The most innovative contribution of experimental economics lies in this area of research rather than in the study of individual decision making. And here performativity takes a rather different, more interesting, and more complicated form.

How to Do Things with Preferences

I have located the origins of the building tradition in the market experiments of Vernon Smith and his colleagues. The distinction between builders and testers, however, applies to the origins of experimental economics only with hindsight, for market experiments initially were presented as attempts to test the theory of competitive equilibrium. But how do you test such a theory? Economic theories are sets of models, and models are notoriously tricky entities. A literal reading of neoclassical models of competitive markets in the Walrasian tradition, for instance, leads to the rather paradoxical conclusion that they cannot describe any economy that does (or even can possibly ever) exist. Economic models are in no way special, from this respect: classical mechanics describes the behavior of dimensionless mass points and perfectly rigid objects, ignoring electromagnetic effects and the influence of other nongravitational forces. Similarly, neoclassical equilibrium theory analyzes the properties of frictionless markets populated by perfectly rational, perfectly informed agents trading homogeneous noncomplementary goods.

The idealization that has attracted most interest in experimental economics lies at the institutional level. Competitive markets in the real world are organized in various ways, in the sense that different systems of (explicit and implicit, formal and informal) rules regulate the interactions between buyers and sellers. If one is interested in issues of general equilibrium—as Walrasians are—it is obviously necessary to simplify and represent these different institutions by means of a single device. Walras introduced for this purpose an ideal auctioneer who collects from buyers and sellers the quantities they would be willing to trade at a given price. The auctioneer then adjusts the proposed price if the quantity offered falls short or exceeds the quantity demanded, until the two quantities coincide. The "equilibrium point" is the price at which trading eventually takes place (the price that makes the market "clear") and under various restrictive conditions can be shown to have the well-known efficiency properties formally defined by Pareto and his followers.

Although a few market institutions are vaguely similar to the Walrasian auctioneer (Walras himself was allegedly inspired by trading at the Paris stock exchange), the latter is largely a fictional entity, because no real market uses *tâtonnement* to determine prices. But the auctioneer has the advantage of being an entity of which the theory's equations are true: if such an institution existed, then Walrasian equilibrium theory would fit it perfectly. Indeed, Walras in the fourth edition of the *Elements of Pure Economics* seems to suggest that the term "*tâtonnement*" refers to the technique of solving a system of simultaneous equations by iteration.[19] The motivation behind the use of *tâtonnement* is probably more mathematical than empirical in character. But then either equilibrium theory is supposed to apply only to markets governed by (something very similar to) the Walrasian auctioneer; or the auctioneer really just "stands for" a whole class of different institutions which are supposed to deliver the same result (efficient equilibria, clearing markets) by means of different rules and procedures.

The first interpretation is pretty uninteresting for a theory aiming at policy relevance (remember that general equilibrium was used unashamedly in concrete political battles like the socialist calculation debate) because the institutions that are very similar to the Walrasian auctioneer are rare. But then is the second interpretation *true*? Are different market institutions equivalent? Economic theory was surprisingly silent on this issue until recently, for a variety of reasons (see Mirowski, forthcoming) including the lack of analytical techniques to deal with it rigorously. In the sixties and seventies game theorists began to construct models of auction systems that seemed to provide some insight in the way different institutions work.[20] But then the same question could be raised again for these game-theoretic models: do they characterize correctly the functioning of *real* markets? Are they empirically adequate?

An obvious way of testing this proposition would be by observing different institutions at work. This sort of empirical testing, however, is difficult in nonlaboratory circumstances. A major problem with field data is that some key variables of economic theory, like agents' preferences, are not directly observable. If you are interested in explaining, say, price variations in a market, in order to derive the demand and supply schedules (two crucial explanatory factors) from the observable data, you have to rely on auxiliary assumptions that are usually as difficult to test as the main research hypothesis itself.

Subjects' preferences and beliefs are directly unobservable in laboratory experiments too, of course, but can be more easily *controlled* therein. The way in which experimental economists try to do that is by *paying* their subjects. The idea of using monetary rewards often generates hilarity among noneconomists ("Hey, these guys pay their subjects to behave like economists would like them to behave!"), whereas the absence of incentives is dismissed by economists equally bluntly ("What can you learn from cheap talk? Put your money where your mouth is!"). Indeed, the presence of "adequate" monetary incentives (we shall see what "adequate" means shortly) has become de facto a prerequisite for publication in economics journals—and, conversely, the lack of incentives is considered a sufficient condition for the rejection of an experimental paper.

Social, cognitive, and economic psychologists tend to apply a less rigid policy. Many experiments in these areas are performed with incentive structures that would be considered inadequate in economics, and often lack monetary incentives altogether.[21] Early economic experiments (even "paradigmatic" ones like Smith 1962, or Allais 1953) also lacked what contemporary experimental economists consider an "adequate incentives structure." The norms regulating financial incentives were codified later, in a series of papers written in the late seventies and early eighties by Vernon Smith (1976, 1982b) and Luis Wilde (1981).[22] The use of incentives is regulated by four of the five so-called *precepts* of experimental economics:

> 1. *Nonsatiation*: the medium of reward is such that of two otherwise equivalent alternatives, subjects will always choose the one yielding more of the reward medium.
> 2. *Saliency*: the rewards are increasing in the good and decreasing in the bad outcomes of the experiment.
> 3. *Dominance*: the rewards dominate any subjective costs associated with participation in the experiment.
> 4. *Privacy*: each subject in an experiment receives information only about her own payoffs.

The fifth precept (*parallelism*, or external validity) is mostly (although not entirely) independent from incentives issues, and I shall ignore it in this chapter.[23] The precepts form the core of so-called Induced Value Theory (Smith 1976), and are to be interpreted as "a *proposed* set of *sufficient* conditions for a valid controlled microeconomic experiment" (Smith 1982b, p. 930, my emphasis). The precepts were proposed as hypothetical conditionals ("if you do this and that, you will achieve control"), and should emphatically not be taken as axioms valid a priori. "The truth of these precepts can only be established empirically" (Smith, 1982b, p. 930, n. 10).

The precepts provide broad guidelines concerning the control of individual preferences, which may be implemented in various ways, and which may require ad hoc adjustments depending on the context and the particular experimental design one is using. In fact, money or financial incentives are never mentioned in the precepts. The principles only state in abstract terms what kind of properties an appropriate reward medium should have; they do not say what the medium should be. Money may be one way of implementing the precepts, but not necessarily the only one. In light of the fairly rigid interpretation that has become prevalent in experimental economics, the Smith-Wilde precepts appear distinctively liberal in their original formulation.

Even more important, the precepts were originally supposed to apply to market experiments only. In his seminal Induced Value Theory article Smith states explicitly that the principles apply "to experiments designed to test price theory propositions conditional on known valuations. Separate experiments can be designed to test propositions in preference theory" (Smith 1976, p. 275). To explain their rationale, Smith couches the precepts in a conceptual framework borrowed largely from the mechanism design theory of the sixties and seventies. A so-called microeconomic system is analyzed into three major components: the environment, the institution, and the outcome. The outcome (the behavior of the agents in the market) is modeled as a function of the environment and the institution. The institution is basically (I'm simplifying here) a set of rules governing behavior by setting incentives, punishments, and their enforcement. The environment is a complex set of factors including the commodities to be exchanged, the agents in the market, their individual endowments, their utility functions, and the technology (costs).

To study empirically the effect of these factors on the outcome (the sort of prices that are generated in a market defined by a certain environment and a certain kind of institution, for example), the ability to control preferences is crucial. By controlling preferences, for example, one can try to systematically vary the supply/demand schedules in a given institution and observe the results of such variations. Alternatively, one can keep the preferences fixed "in the background" and observe the effect of using different institutions in a given environment (cf. Smith 1982b, p. 927).

A typical application works as follows. Suppose you want to induce in your experiment supply and demand schedules like those of figure 5.1. (The "swastikas" are the discrete, experimental counterparts of the perfectly smooth curves of textbook equilibrium theory.) The customary way of achieving this goal is by assigning your subjects some definite roles in the experiment, dividing them in groups of buyers and sellers with well-defined reservation prices. The reservation price of a seller can be interpreted as the cost of production for each unit of the exchange good. The reservation price of a buyer can instead be seen as the price the experimenter is willing to pay each buyer for a unit of the good once the experimental market is closed.

The supply/demand schedules of figure 5.1 can be "induced" by setting reservation prices as in table 5.2 (assuming that each buyer can exchange only one unit of the good during the experiment).

Notice that the prices are expressed in experimental tokens. The key move, according to the precepts of induced value theory, is to make sure

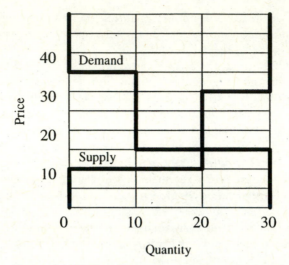

Figure 5.1 "Induced" supply and demand schedules in an economic experiment

that the tokens will be exchanged (privately) at the end of the experiment for some other reward medium, at a rate that satisfies the criteria set out in the precepts themselves. Hence the habit of using real money, in quantities that are likely to dominate all other costs of participating in the experiment.

If this sort of control is effectively achieved, the effect (the outcome) of different institutions can be compared while keeping the preferences (the environment) fixed. To an observer this may seem a big "if", but experience shows that convincing people to try to maximize the experimental payoffs is quite easy. Whether monetary rewards play a crucial role or not (whether role-playing is a key factor, for instance) is obviously

Table 5.2

By setting reservation prices as shown, the supply/demand schedules of figure 5.1 can be "induced" (assuming that each buyer can exchange only one unit of the good during the experiment)

Number of Subjects	Reservation Price
10 sellers	30 tokens
20 sellers	10 tokens
10 buyers	35 tokens
20 buyers	15 tokens

debatable.[24] But here the approach is what matters: market experiments work by creating *homines economici* in the lab, not by questioning their existence.

Explaining Anomalies Away

I would like now to use a typical Sociology of Scientific Knowledge (SSK) trick, and examine a controversy raised by the (mis)application of Induced Value Theory. Induced Value Theory can be seen as a turning point in the history of experimental economics. A rigid implementation of the precepts makes little sense in the context of other (nonmarket) economic experiments, yet the precepts inform standard methodological practice in *all* areas of experimental economics. Of course this causes some friction, and scientific friction is very helpful to bring the tacit commitments of scientists into the open.

One obvious motivation behind the indiscriminate application of the precepts is economists' desire to mark a methodological distinction between what they do and psychologists' experimental practice. But there may be more to be said, here. Theory-testing experiments on social dilemma games, for example, do not fit the straitjacket of the precepts. When the assumptions of rational choice theory are themselves under investigation, the aim is to figure out whether individual preferences (and/or beliefs) have the structure postulated by the standard models. The precepts lose much of their appeal in such a context, because clearly there is little point in trying to induce the behavior one is supposed to be testing in the first place.

Yet, surprisingly, a strict implementation of the precepts is usually advocated in these contexts too. As we have seen, a substantial portion of experimental subjects playing social dilemma games choose to play cooperatively, contrary to the prediction of standard game theory. The straightforward interpretation of these results is that many human beings (fortunately) do not behave as predicted by the theory. But a considerable number of economists reject this interpretation and argue that the problem must lie with incentives. If they don't conform to game theory predictions, people must be put in line. Experimental economics is then turned into the exploration of the conditions of applicability of an economic model.

The first step consists of arguing that the preference rankings of the subjects who play cooperatively in these experiments might be inadequately represented by the numbers in the classic prisoner's dilemma game matrix (see table 5.1).[25] According to the orthodox interpretation of game theory, the numbers represent the (ordinal) structure of agents' preferences. The actual numbers do not even matter, as long as the payoffs are ordered "Down–Left" > "Up–Left" > "Down–Right" > "Up–Right" (from the perspective of the row player; modify accordingly for the column player). Thus, the argument goes, if we observe anomalous behavior in the experiment, it is likely that the initial conditions postulated in the model weren't instantiated in the experiment. Subjects were playing not the prisoner's dilemma game but another game of their choice.

I'm interested here in the general significance of arguments of this kind. For someone working in the testing tradition the standard reaction to the anomalies of cooperation is to conclude that individual agents do not behave as predicted by economic theory. For someone who believes in the control of individual preferences, in contrast, the immediate reaction is to try to make the anomalies disappear by means of a tighter design. The most obvious move is the scaling up of monetary incentives: surely if one is playing for hundreds of dollars (rather than the relatively low payoffs commonly used in experiments with college students), he or she will have better reasons to behave as a proper *homo economicus*. (Increasing the monetary rewards is an attempt to implement the dominance requirement, in other words.)[26] Other similar devices are the strict enforcement of privacy (in order to neutralize other-regarding preferences), the introduction of training sessions at the beginning of the game (in order to make sure that subjects understand what is in their "real" interest, what "ought" to be done rationally, or what "really" to expect from others), and so on.

The effect of these moves is mixed, for norms of fairness and reciprocation seem to be rather robust. But the interesting question is why is so much effort invested in preference control? Suppose we *did* manage to achieve control of subjects' preferences. What would be left to test in a trivial game like the one-shot prisoner's dilemma? The rationality hypothesis (that actions follow from preferences and beliefs) is not really in question in simple games like this. There is little to learn, from a theoretical viewpoint, by making sure that the "right" preferences are instantiated in the experiment.

But imagine you ultimately intend to construct a little machine, a prisoner's dilemma in flesh and blood (and microchips, if the game is played on a PC network). Then these moves make much more sense. Why should one want to construct such a device, though? Social dilemmas epitomize the failure of uncoordinated strategic behavior—a situation to be redressed rather than replicated. True, and in fact you don't do very much with a social dilemma machine.[27] Much higher stakes are placed on the applications of game theory to market design, especially in the area of auction theory. The example of social dilemmas is interesting because it shows how the official methodological apparatus of experimental economics is pretty incomprehensible from a theory-testing perspective. Experimental economics is successful not because it confirms or refutes neoclassical theory, but because it "works." Because you can do things with experiments.

Building Economic Machines

The trajectory of the institution-building tradition in experimental economics intersects with that of the new institutional economics and the theory of mechanism design.[28] Vernon Smith's methodological pronouncements in the late seventies draw explicit links with this theoretical literature. The main idea behind mechanism design theory (or the "[New]^2 Welfare Economics," or "New Institutionalism"—I shall use these labels interchangeably) is to treat institutions as *variables* that affect the allocation of economic goods (see Hurwicz 1972, 1973). Normative (welfare) economics plays a role at the level of defining a set of criteria used to assess market allocations, or in other words the exogenously defined, presumably politically negotiated objectives to be achieved by means of the economic exchange. Then game theory enters the scene: the market institution is represented as a game that rational agents are trying to solve. The "best" institution is the one that leads the agents to satisfy the welfare criteria "as if guided by an invisible hand," by setting the right incentives and by giving them enough information to solve the problem they are facing.

The step from this abstract framework to the creation of an experimental branch of mechanism design is short: all you have to do is replace game-theoretical agents with real human beings playing for real money, and abstract institutions with concrete systems of rules. The result, as Smith points out in several of his papers, is a dramatic increase in the realisticness of the result: "Laboratory microeconomies are real live economic systems, which are certainly richer, behaviorally, than the systems parametrized in our theories" (Smith 1982a, pp. 923–924).

The success of a real-life (laboratory) market depends then on the successful matching of the appropriate kind of agents with the appropriate system of rules. The two are highly interdependent, because rules must be interpreted by agents, and the way in which the agents behave depends in part on the institutional rules.

Consider the assumption of rationality, to begin with. The economic engineer cannot just *assume* that market traders are rational selfish maximizers of the kind postulated in most economic models (including mechanism design theory). One has to *make sure* that this is the case, for the presence of a single "crazy" player may have a devastating impact on the functioning of a market. The mobile phone auctions that have been run in many countries since the early 1990s provide a neat example of the challenges posed by market design. The auctioned goods are licenses for frequencies, owned by the government and sold to private telecom companies. The exact value of each license is unknown, but the general assumption is that potential users (the companies) can make a better estimate of their value than a bureaucrat or politician, because they have better knowledge of the market and the technology. Even the buyers, however, can only estimate—the market is dominated by *uncertainty* about the value of the goods. The value of one license, moreover, is likely to depend in part on the ownership of other (neighboring) licenses, complicating considerably the evaluation of the "optimal" allocation. A popular design to deal with this kind of complexity and uncertainty is the "simultaneous continuous ascending auction," where all the bidders can be active on different markets for different licenses at the same time. The exact rules of the game can be rather complicated (see Klemperer 2004; Milgrom 2004), but Ken Binmore, the experimental game theorist who codesigned the U.K. auction of 2000, simplifies them as follows:

> If a company wants to stay in the bidding it has to either hold the top bid for one of them or overbid a set amount. The price keeps going up and up until there are only five bidders left. . . . The advantage of this design is that it allows the bidders to concentrate on what their valuations for the licences are. After each round what a bidder should do is to say what's my current value for each licence because the events of the last round might change their value for the licence. If you see someone withdrawing from the auction that you didn't expect to see withdraw that's valuable information to you and you might want to change your valuation on that basis, but once you know what your valuation is you then simply ask yourself well what minimum bid would I have to make to become top bidder on a licence. Subtract that bid from your valuation for that licence and that will give you your profit on that licence and then you simply bid to maximise your profit on the assumption that that bid will be the winner. (Binmore in Atkinson 2000, p. 22)

Underlying values, in other words, are not given but constantly updated in light of the moves made by other bidders. This transparency and exchange of information is the main advantage of the simultaneous continuous mechanism compared with other market institutions like sealed-bid auctions. But then of course if other competitors behave irrationally, they may send misleading signals to the market. Game theory assumes common knowledge of rationality: I am rational, you are rational, and I know that you are rational, you know that I am rational, I know that you know that I'm rational, and so on. At a more concrete level, the design of a market institution assumes behavior with certain formal characteristics on the agents' part, but each agent must also be aware of these assumptions and must be confident that the other agents are willing to and capable of fulfilling the mechanism's requirements. But how do you make sure that this is the case in a real market?

The answer is a neat example of performativity. Game theorists are keen to stress the simplicity of their preferred mechanisms and the small demands they impose on bidders: "Anybody can do that. That does not require any great skill and it's no secret"; but, just in case, "All bidders have got a pet game theorist to give them their advice" (Binmore in Atkinson 2000). Economists design the market *and* advise the companies that will compete in that market. The common knowledge problem becomes: I know that you know that I know . . . that you have a game theorist on your team.[29]

But that's not the end of the story. Economic rationality is not like Newton's laws, which are supposed to be at work everywhere in the universe. It is a fragile property that must be carefully preserved by creating a hospitable environment. It is a *capacity* or a *potentiality*, and the goal of experimental market design is to create the "right" circumstances for it to be actualized.

> Designs are motivated by a mechanism (a mathematical model, a body of theory) that is perhaps completely devoid of operational detail. The task is to find a system of institutions—the rules for individual expression, information transmittal, and social choice—a "process" that mirrors the behavioral features of the mechanism. The theory suggests the existence of processes that perform in certain (desirable) ways, and the task is to find them. This is a pure form of institutional engineering. (Plott 1981, p. 134)

A good market must impose a certain amount of *discipline,* in other words (a Foucauldian terminology is very appropriate here), and the precepts of Induced Value Theory help you to do that. The precepts define an artificial situation. It is simply not true that privacy, for example, is in general instantiated in nonlaboratory economic situations. Such a requirement, however, is crucial in the process of applying highly abstract models to concrete cases by helping to build the experimental counterpart of the theoretical restrictions that make demonstrations from economic models possible.

One way to capture the process of market design is to imagine a hierarchical structure. At the most abstract level, we have highly theoretical concepts such as competitive equilibrium. These are embedded in a structure of deductive reasoning from a set of strict assumptions that define the conditions under which such concepts may be deductively demonstrated. But at this stage the description of the causal structure that brings about effects like efficient equilibria is still abstract. The "real-world"

counterparts of theoretical entities like the rational economic people of
our models are instantiated only under further restrictive arrangements.
These arrangements define the bottom level of concreteness for the applicability of economic models.[30]

Economists are guided by experimental and practical, as well as theoretical knowledge in designing their experiments so that these conditions
are satisfied. But the circumstances in which an economic system maintains its own structural properties may be narrow and fragile. Consider
how difficult it is to control information concerning the identity of bidders (and hence privacy) in a real auction. Richard Cramton, an economist who worked as a consultant for the PageNet team in the first U.S.
auctions for telecommunication licences, recalls, for example:

> It was common for a bidder that did not need to bid, because it was the cur-
> rent high bidder, to pretend to place a bid, so as to conceal its identity. These
> pretend bids were not always successful before round 18, because a bidder
> could not ask for written confirmation of the pretend bid. Almost all bidders
> asked for written confirmation for their bids. To get a written confirmation,
> the bid assistant would have to walk across the room in public view. In round
> 18, the FCC announced, "Beginning with this round, you may go into the bid-
> ding booth and request from the bidding assistant a confirmation of your ac-
> tions regardless of whether you bid, exercise a proactive waiver, or do not
> submit a bid." Even this met with limited success, since the sheet on which the
> written confirmation was printed was folded differently depending on
> whether it was a real bid or a fake bid. (Cramton 1995, p. 287, n.23)

Computerized auctions are used extensively to create "appropriate"
market conditions, precisely because they allow controlling tightly the
quality, amount, and flow of information between buyers and sellers.
But a computerized auction system obviously can be used only if we are
absolutely sure that the institution will accomplish its goals—for it permits no tinkering with the rules and no adjustments like those described
by Cramton. "Black boxing" is appropriate only at an advanced stage
of scientific engineering, when most problems and uncertainties have
already been solved.[31]

Until then the fragility or sensitivity of a market mechanism to the details of the material (institutional) arrangements is of great concern to
the economic engineer, whose machines are supposed to work for several
years, in different contexts and without the constant supervision of their
manufacturer. In order to build a successful auction, then, one has to pay
attention to the computational abilities and preferences of its users. One
has to make sure that the tasks the bidders face are not too complicated
or the rules unclear. Bidders' reactions to possible strategic situations
must be analyzed in the light of a realistic view of individual cognitive

capacities. One cannot just presume that buyers behave "as if" they were rational. Bidders must react adequately to new situations and sometimes be creative in devising new strategies, as opposed to just relying on established routines. The economic engineer must design the market mechanism keeping individuals' *real* capacities in mind. On the other hand, it is by designing and implementing an adequate mechanism that the engineer ensures that rational choice models can work. Since it is partly by virtue of the structure of the situation that economic agents behave rationally, a great part of economic engineering is devoted to make sure that the structure is "right" (and experiments are invaluable for that).[32]

The Philosophy, Politics, and Economics of Market Design

Part of the experimental economics and mechanism design revolution consisted in emancipating economics from its obsession with high theory and appreciating the complex relation between abstract and applied work. Paul Klemperer says provocatively that in practice mechanism design requires little more than undergraduate economic theory. The key lesson, in his view, is to "pay more attention to elementary theory, to the wider context of the auctions, and to political pressures—and pay less attention to sophisticated mathematical theory" (Klemperer 2004, p. 125).

> The really bad mistake in running an auction is just to take an auction design off the shelf, as shown by a comparison of the British and subsequent European 3G auctions. Auction design is a matter of "horses for courses," *not* one size fits all; each economic environment requires an auction design that is tailored to its special circumstances. (Binmore and Klemperer 2002, p. C94)

Again, this should come as no surprise to science-studies scholars: several local factors determine the success or failure of a scientific application. Some of these factors are cognitive, some are physical or technological (e.g., the reliability of a piece of software), some are political. A market design, to be successful, must be attractive to its users, to the government, as well as to the private firms who will compete in the newly designed arena. Consider the telecom auctions once again; the nightmare of the governments was to give away the licences for too little or even not sell them at all. The companies' executives, in contrast, had to justify the money spent to their bosses and shareholders; their nightmare was to pay a sum that looked unreasonably or unnecessarily high—by outbidding other firms by too great a margin, for example.

These opposite interests affect the design immensely, for politicians, executives, shareholders, and the public in general do not necessarily see a market mechanism in the same way as an economist would. Consider a sealed-bid auction mechanism where the winners pay the price of their bid. Executives are unlikely to love this mechanism, because justifying the difference between a successful bid and the second-highest bid may be embarrassing—especially if the difference is in the area of hundreds of millions of euros or dollars. An alternative solution is to have a continuous ascending auction where the winner can always monitor the bids of other competitors. But this mechanism is more fragile to collusion or may lead to a collapse in the level of competition if potential buyers drop out too early from the market (if, for example, they are intimidated by a competitor's aggressive bidding at the beginning or even before the auction). A possible solution is to make sure that there are enough *serious* bidders right from the start by imposing high entrance fees that make it very costly to drop out with nothing in hand. But in order to be effective such fees must be very high—indeed, quite close to the final price paid for the licences. And this is scary for the government officials, because setting the entrance fee too high could result in nobody participating in the auctions in the first place.

Solutions to all these problems must be negotiated (see Klemperer 2004, ch. 3–4, for a general discussion); negotiation usually leads to small concessions, sometimes to concessions that seem *politically* small but may be economically high. (A small change like lowering the entrance fees can, for instance, lead to a loss of a few *billions* for the government.) And not all designs are equally robust to political pressure. Mechanism design has taught among other things, that one must be very careful about what happens outside the economic realm. This is big news in economics—a science that has tried to separate itself from the other social sciences most vigorously during the last half-century or so.

Remember where it all started from: Walrasian general equilibrium theory does not (and presumably cannot) pay too much attention to the specific characteristics of single markets. However, at the price of some "heroic" abstraction it delivers an entirely general proof of the invisible hand theorem, one that promises to establish once and for all the superiority of markets with respect to other systems of allocation. Unfortunately nobody has ever seen (or will ever see) a pure Walrasian market at work, and experimentation has demonstrated that "impurities" matter enormously. Somehow paradoxically the highly successful applications of neoclassical theory so far have revealed that markets work in subtly diverse ways, and that a general recipe for market design is a chimera.[33] Adam Smith's invisible hand requires a lot of fine-tuning and tinkering in order reliably and consistently to transform individual greed into social benefits. But this important lesson simply makes economics look much more like "proper" science—like physics or biochemistry, where general laws and theories are applied successfully to specific conditions only after a lot of effort and at the price of several adjustments and compromises.

An interesting question for the historians of the future is why this revolution is occurring now. I can imagine a plausible answer along the following lines: general equilibrium theory—like much economics of the 1960s and 1970s—is "cold war economics" (Mirowski 2002), science devoted first and foremost to winning an ideological game with extremely high stakes. The real limits of applicability of economic theory were too dangerous and tricky an issue to be properly discussed in such a climate. Market design and experimental economics in the building tradition is, in contrast, genuinely "third-way" economics. The market can do great things for you if you learn to use it properly; the difficult task is to find out what "properly" means.

Market design, then, has the political advantage of satisfying everybody's tastes—right to left, from the apologists of free markets to the believers in regulation. Moreover, the difficulty with which the power of markets is unleashed, the need for quite a lot of preliminary intervention, engineering, and control—all this plays into the hands of economists as a profession. Suddenly the "dismal scientists" are empowered by a new kind of expertise. Unlike the Hayekian economist, who gives up on prediction and control, and in the end can engage only in propaganda, the experimental economist and game theorist can sell her expertise as designer and consultant.

This is not unproblematic, of course. There are reasons to be wary of self-appointed experts, especially when considerable profits are at stake. As Phil Mirowski and Edward Nik-Khah highlight (in this volume), the use of game theory has been interwoven with the business interests of the telecommunication companies. For these and other reasons, Mirowski and Nik-Khah see economists' new "market-designing" role as dangerous. Where we differ perhaps is that Mirowski and Nik-Khah have already decided that neoclassical theory is so bankrupt that it can't possibly work as applied science.[34] Here I would advise to follow the spirit of the Edinburgh School and apply the "symmetry principle": *both* science and pseudoscience are carriers of sociopolitical interests, and telling a sociological story does not in principle detract from a discipline's scientific status. Only a *scientific* argument can decide that.[35]

This has important implications about performativity. Consider the ultimate ontological question: do the entities (e.g., the efficient markets) described by economic theory exist? Again, I don't think this is a question I can answer here.[36] But let me try a milder suggestion: *if* the entities described by economic theory exist, they are probably not very common. Economic theory seems to be still a long way off from providing an approximately accurate description of most of the economic world. I'm following here those philosophers and sociologists of science—like Bruno Latour, Nancy Cartwright, and John Dupré—who have insisted that science provides an accurate description of at best only *niches* of the real world.[37] Most of these niches, moreover, are artificially created to give the theory its "best shot," so to speak, by eliminating all the disturbances and the imperfections that normally impede its application to "naturally occurring" circumstances. The story that I have told here and elsewhere about experimental economics can be seen as just an extension of this overall philosophical outlook.

This "localist" position, interestingly, was originally devised in the context of the natural sciences (biology for Latour and Dupré, physics for Cartwright). This suggests an important distinction to be introduced in the discussion of performativity in the social sciences. Economics helps shape the economy in at least two different ways. The first one is indirectly by informing institutional design: economists identify the appropriate initial conditions (to use an old-fashioned philosophical concept) to bring about a certain effect or result. The policy maker then implements the suggestion, for example, by redesigning or by creating a new market that fulfills such requirements. This is not a distinguished form of performativity, however: natural science intervention often works in the same way, and performativity theories attempted, at least originally, to distinguish the peculiar nature of social entities from (an idealized version of) natural reality.[38] This is not to deny that the initial conditions in social science are institutions, rules, informational constraints, and so on, that usually need to be created and maintained by means of performative procedures. The point is rather that the relevant science plays only an indirect role in this process. Other institutions or actors do the main job (the SEC for financial markets, the FCC for telecommunications markets, etc.) by setting the rules, incentives, and punishments that supposedly create the "right" conditions for the result to be obtained. The agents in the market then are just supposed to act as they normally would, regardless of their knowledge of the science in question.

Drawing again on some old-fashioned philosophy of science, notice that to set the "right" initial conditions does not guarantee the success of a scientific application. One must also bet on the correctness of the relevant theories/models, or on the existence of the laws or causal mechanisms that supposedly connect the initial conditions with their effects. In economics this link is largely constituted by the actions or choices of the individuals in the market. Here is where the second role of economics in performing the economy becomes evident: economics not only identifies the "right" conditions for the coordination of (given) individual action, but it can shape (change) the behavior of the individuals who will act in the designed environment. Here is where the performativity thesis has more bite, and where the natural versus social science/world contrast becomes more striking—in the making of *homo economicus*.

This second (more interesting) role of economic theory is perhaps the only one that is worthy of a new technical term—"performativity." Economics can shape behavior because it works in part as a *norm* for the agents in the market, just like the priest's utterance "you are now man and wife" creates powers and obligations for the individuals involved in a wedding ceremony. This special feature (normativity) distinguishes "genuine" performativity from similar phenomena, such as "bandwagon" and "underdog" effects, that are often conflated with it.

This distinction between "Type-1" (spurious) and "Type-2" (genuine) performativity cuts at a different level from MacKenzie's "generic" and "Barnesian" performativities (in this volume). The latter refers to those—perhaps relatively rare—cases where a speech act (utterance, theory) brings about or perpetuates the very entities or phenomena it refers to. It denotes, in other words, a particularly tight self-referential loop triggered by the normative character of a speech act. Whether this special Barnesian case is common in economics is an interesting question but one which may prove to be particularly difficult to answer (it is, after all, a variant of the more general question of the truth of economic theory).[39] That's why I prefer to use performativity in a broader fashion, to include all those cases in which "economics matters," but it does so *by virtue of its normative character*.

This is what distinguishes my Type-1 from Type-2 (genuine) cases of performativity. It also allows highlighting of the peculiar ontological role of social science discourse in changing the social world, by generating new entities and relationships. This take on performativity divides sharply. On the one hand is the tradition of ontological analysis that leads from Austin to Barnes and Searle; on the other is the Actor-Network tradition of Callon and his collaborators. Actor-Network theorists, I suspect, find the first type of performativity more interesting *precisely* for the opposite reason: because it blurs the distinction between natural and social entities.

Market design is a very rich area of investigation, where one can find plausible examples of both types of performativity.[40] In my discussion I have also tried to show how these two procedures are conceptually distinct but in practice tightly interdependent (which probably explains why the distinction is often overlooked). I think this interdependency is due to the simultaneous power and weakness of economics as a science. Economics is *powerful* because, unlike physics, it can in principle directly shape the economy (people's behavior) by virtue of its own authority, with or without the intermediate intervention and support of other institutions (the SEC or the FCC). But it is also *weak*, because it is not capable of doing so always and everywhere. Indeed, one of my claims in this chapter is that the second (direct) form of performativity—without doubt the philosophically more interesting one—can rarely take place without the assistance of performative processes of the first (indirect) kind. The two forms thus go hand in hand and can rarely, if ever, be observed independently from one another.

Notes

1. I would like to thank all participants in the meeting on the "Performativities of Economics" in August 2004 for the lively and interesting discussion during and after the workshop. In particular, Vincent Lépinay, Edward Nik-Khah, Phil Mirowski, and Yuval Millo provided many comments which helped to improve the paper. As usual, I am responsible for all the remaining mistakes.
   2. See Hulse (2003).
   3. Two faculty members of the University of Iowa who ran the first electronic market in 1988 (Robert Forsythe and Forrest Nelson) had worked for many years at the California Institute of Technology, one of the pioneering centers for experimental economics. Forsythe is an experienced experimenter himself, as are other current directors of the Iowa project like Joyce Berg and Thomas Rietz. (I'd like to thank Joyce Berg for this information, in personal communication.)
   4. Which didn't prevent it from winning the argument on the impossibility of a centrally planned efficient economy.
   5. See, for instance, the Austrian Political Stock Market, the Election Stock Market at the University of British Columbia, and the Hollywood Stock Exchange (all Internet addresses are in the references).
   6. The auctions raised £22.5 billion for the government, or approximately 2.5 percent of U.K. GDP; see Binmore and Klemperer (2002), Klemperer (2004).
   7. There is still some resistance, in the form of routine arguments about the absence of laws in the social sciences, the "fact" that human beings are "free to choose," and so on (see, for instance, Economics Focus 1999). But these are by now rear-guard skirmishes in a battle that has been largely won by experimental economists.
   8. Examples can be found in Smith (1991a, 1992), Davis and Holt (1993, ch. 1), Friedman and Sunder (1994, ch. 9), and Kagel and Roth (1995, ch. 1). Leonard (1994) is the only study by a professional historian that I know of, but it focuses on bargaining experiments only. Mirowski (2002) reconstructs the milieu of mid-twentieth-century economics, where the conditions for the birth of experimental economics were created, and devotes a short section to Vernon Smith's experimental research program (pp. 545–551). Two PhD dissertations at Notre Dame are beginning to investigate the origins of experimental economics and of the mechanism design tradition (Lee 2004; Nik-Khah 2005).
   9. The proceedings of the Santa Monica conference are published as Thrall, Coombs and Davis (1954), those of the Paris conference can be found in CNRS (1953). Vernon Smith's first experimental paper is Smith (1962).

10. The history and current practice of experimental economics cannot be fully understood if one does not take the divide between psychology and economics seriously. The builders fought the battle on two fronts: at a purely rhetorical level, as mentioned in the chapter, but also at a more subtle methodological level, by introducing standards of experimental validity that are at the same time more strict, more formalized, and more in line with the usual assumptions of economic theory than those customarily adopted by experimental psychologists (I'll discuss these standards below).

11. See also Plott (1987, 1994), Smith and Williams (1992), Roth (1991), Schotter (1998), Milgrom (2004), Klemperer (2004).

12. The most common format nowadays is probably not the prisoner's dilemma game but the so-called public goods game, where subjects play in groups of several players and have to decide how much money out of a given sum to contribute to a "public project," knowing that the latter will produce some revenue that will be divided equally among the members of the group independently of their individual contributions. See Ledyard (1995) for an introduction and survey of results.

13. For a representative example of this attitude cf., e.g., Kahneman, Tversky, and Thaler (1986) and Dawes and Thaler (1988).

14. Various philosophical analyses of the ontology of the social world follow this line of thought. Barnes (1983) provides one of the earliest and best discussions in my view. Searle (1995) is one of the most recent and popular ones. See also Gilbert (1989), Hacking (1999), and Tuomela (2002).

15. It is interesting to see how this purely negative perspective was superseded in different areas of the social sciences. In economic theory, a simple fixed-point theorem can be used to demonstrate the very possibility of positively self-fulfilling predictions (Grünberg and Modigliani 1954; Simon 1957): a solution is logically possible, therefore the problem has been solved. In sociology, Krishna (1971) first argued that as a matter of fact social reality itself is the result of a massive and extraordinarily complex series of performative acts or self-fulfilling prophecies. The interesting task, then, is to investigate the *robustness* of social entities (rules, norms, institutions) to changes in the beliefs and desires of individuals and groups.

16. This concern for representativeness is quite typical of experimental psychology, whereas economists tend to worry about financial incentives and downplay representativeness (see Loewenstein 1999). We shall come to incentives shortly.

17. They also tend to be male, and boys on average free ride more in social dilemma games.

18. As an amateur experimenter, I remember several conversations with subjects who claimed confidently that they had followed the theory by cooperating in the initial rounds of a finitely repeated social dilemma game and by free riding in the last one. They usually appeared puzzled when I recalled what the theory actually says (that you should free ride right from the start). Apparently backward induction arguments are very difficult to digest.

19. On the Walrasian auctioneer and its various possible interpretations, see de Vroey (1998).

20. See, e.g., Vickrey (1961), Wilson (1977), and Milgrom and Weber (1982).

21. Unsurprisingly, then, the issue of incentives is often couched in terms of "the economics–psychology methodological divide." I don't want to review this more general debate here, but see, e.g., Cox and Isaac (1986), Hogarth and Reder (1986), Smith (1991b), Loewenstein (1999), and Rabin (1998, 2002).

22. The idea of using monetary rewards was borrowed, somewhat ironically, from the work of two psychologists (Fouraker and Siegel 1963).

23. But see Guala (2005, ch. 7–10).

24. See, for example, the debate sparked recently by Hertwig and Ortmann (2001). On behalf of monetary incentives, it must be said that economic experiments have become a real business in some universities, used by students to top up their grants (an attractive alternative to a part-time job at MacDonald's, in other words).

25. There is an interpretation of game theory according to which the preference structure of cooperative subjects is *necessarily* misrepresented by the prisoner's dilemma matrix, because the numbers represent *revealed* preferences or observed choices rather than psychological entities or dispositions. Ken Binmore has been the standard-bearer of this view for a while (Binmore 1994), but since his position suffers from several problems and is probably inconsistent (see, e.g., Guala 2006a; Hausman 2000), I shall ignore it here. The weaker and more reasonable position outlined in the text is defended, for example, by Weibull (2004).

26. High monetary incentives obviously raise the cost of experimenting, which explains why psychologists have traditionally been more flexible in the implementation of this precept. Note one potentially interesting aspect of the use of incentives as an entry barrier to research: economic experiments require research grants, and the competition for grant money introduces a preliminary selection on the research that is done in economics, even before it reaches the publication stage. In a highly "paradigmatic" science like economics (in the Kuhnian sense), this may be functional to achieving more social control of research production.

27. Most recent research focuses on the (symmetric) problem of "pushing" free riders toward the Pareto-optimal solution. See, for instance, Fehr and Gachter (2000) and Burlando and Guala (2005).

28. Lee (2004) and Nik-Khah (2005) investigate these connections.

29. The lineup of Market Design Inc., for example, a company created in 1995 on the wave of success of the first telecommunication auctions, is impressive: Peter Cramton, Lawrence Ausubel, John MacMillan, Preston McAfee, Paul Milgrom, Robert Wilson, Jeremy Bulow, Eric Maskin, and others among the finest U.S. academic economists are among the principals.

30. This way of understanding the relation among models, experiments, and engineering owes a lot to Nancy Cartwright's work. See in particular Cartwright (forthcoming).

31. Muniesa (2000) describes the creation of a computerized stock exchange. On black-boxing and the study of markets (especially finance) see MacKenzie (2005).

32. For the practitioners' view on so-called robustness requirements, see Schotter (1998) and Klemperer (2004).

33. On the recent turn in neoclassical economics away from general equilibrium and toward the details of market mechanisms, see Mirowski (forthcoming).

34. I should also mention that although Mirowski and Nik-Khah's account of
the construction of the FCC auctions overlaps in various ways with mine (in
Guala 2001), I have reservations about several points they make (for example,
I disagree with their interpretation of the role played by experimental economists). See Guala (2006b) for a more detailed discussion of our disagreements.

35. By this I do not mean to suggest that SSK is not scientific. I rather mean
that issues of this kind must be resolved by studying *markets*. This is different
from the standard approach in SSK, which is devoted to studying *scientists*.

36. In Guala (2001) I was much less cautious, however. Callon (1998) also
answers a bold "yes" to this question. MacKenzie (2006, ch.1) includes a good
discussion of the problems involved in testing performativity claims.

37. See, e.g., Latour (1984), Cartwright (1999), and Dupré (2001); see also
Guala (2003).

38. Barnes (1983), Hacking (1999), and Searle (1995) are typical in this respect.

39. This is the use of performativity language that Mirowski and Nik-Khah
(this volume) dislike, because they fear it constitutes a defense of contemporary
economic theory.

40. But one can find other examples in the literature, for instance the influence
of the efficient markets theory in reforming (designing) financial markets versus
the use of the Black-Scholes model directly in calculating the prices of
derivatives; see MacKenzie's chapter in this volume, also MacKenzie (2006) and
MacKenzie and Millo (2003).

References

Allais, M. 1953. "The Foundations of a Positive Theory of Choice Involving
    Risk and a Criticism of the Postulate and Axioms of the American School." In
    The Expected Utility Hypothesis and the Allais Paradox, edited by Maurice
    Allais and Ole Hagen. Dordrecht: Reidel, 1979.
Atkinson, M. 2000. "Auctioneer with a Lot to Sell." *The Guardian*, April 22: 22.
Austrian Political Stock Market. Technische Universität Wien, http://ebweb.
    tuwien.ac.at/apsm/index.html.
Barnes, S. B. 1983. "Social Life as Bootstrapped Induction." *Sociology* 17:
    524–545.
Binmore, K. 1994. *Game Theory and the Social Contract. Vol. 1: Playing Fair.*
    Cambridge, MA: MIT Press.
Binmore, K., and P. Klemperer. 2002. "The Biggest Auction Ever: The Sale of the
    British 3G Telecom Licences." *Economic Journal* 112: C74–C96.
Burlando, R. M., and F. Guala. 2005. "Heterogeneous Agents in Public Goods
    Experiments." *Experimental Economics* 8:35–54.
Callon, M. 1998. "Introduction: The Embeddedness of Economic Markets
    in Economics." Pp. 1–57 in *The Laws of the Markets*, edited by M. Callon.
    Oxford: Blackwell.

Cartwright, N. 1999. *The Dappled World.* Cambridge: Cambridge University Press.

Cartwright, N. Forthcoming. "Abstract and Concrete Knowledge." In *The Rise and Fall of Historical Political Economy,* edited by Emma Rothschild and G. Stedman Jones.

CNRS. 1953. *Econométrie* (Paris, May 12–17 1952). Paris: Colloques Internationaux du Centre National de la Recherche Scientifique.

Cox, J. C., and R. M. Isaac. 1986. "Experimental Economics and Experimental Psychology: Ever the Twain Shall Meet?" In *Economic Psychology: Interactions in Theory and Application,* edited by A. J. MacFadyen and H. W. MacFadyen. New York: North Holland.

Cramton, P. C. 1995. "Money Out of Thin Air: The Nationwide Narrowband PCS Auction." *Journal of Economics and Management Strategy* 4:267–343.

Davis, D. D., and C. H. Holt. 1993. *Experimental Economics.* Princeton, NJ: Princeton University Press.

Davis, D. D., and A. W. Williams. 1991. "The Hayek Hypothesis in Experimental Auctions: Institutional Effects and Market Power." *Economic Inquiry* 29:261–274.

Dawes, R. M., and R. H. Thaler. 1988. "Anomalies: Cooperation," *Journal of Economic Perspectives* 2:187–197.

de Vroey, M. 1998. "Is the Tâtonnement Hypothesis a Good Caricature of Market Forces?" *Journal of Economic Methodology* 5:201–222.

Dupré, J. 2001. "Economics without Mechanism." In *The Economic World View,* edited by U. Mäki. Cambridge: Cambridge University Press.

Economics Focus. 1999. "News from the Lab." *The Economist,* May 8:96.

Election Stock Market. University of British Columbia, http://esm.ubc.ca/.

Fehr, E., and S. Gachter. 2000. "Cooperation and Punishment in Public Goods Experiments." *American Economic Review* 90:980–994.

Fouraker, L. E., and S. Siegel. 1963. *Bargaining Behavior.* New York: McGraw-Hill.

Frey, B., and S. Meier. 2003. "Are Political Economists Selfish and Indoctrinated? Evidence from a Natural Experiment." *Economic Inquiry* 41: 448–462.

Friedman, D., and S. Sunder. 1994. *Experimental Methods: A Primer for Economists.* Cambridge: Cambridge University Press.

Gilbert, M. 1989. *On Social Facts.* London: Routledge.

Grether, D. M., R. M. Isaac, and C. L. Plott. 1989. *The Allocation of Scarce Resources: Experimental Economics and the Problem of Allocating Airport Slots.* San Francisco: Westview.

Grether, D. M., and C. L. Plott. 1984. "The Effect of Market Practices in Oligopolistic Markets: An Experimental Examination of the Ethyl Case." *Economic Inquiry* 22:479–507.

Grünberg, E., and F. Modigliani. 1954. "The Predictability of Social Events." *Journal of Political Economy* 62:465–478.

Guala, F. 2001. "Building Economic Machines: The FCC Auctions." *Studies in History and Philosophy of Science* 32:453–477.

Guala, F. 2003. "Experimental Localism and External Validity." *Philosophy of Science* 70:1195–1205.

Guala, F. 2005. *The Methodology of Experimental Economics*. New York: Cambridge University Press.

Guala, F. 2006a. "Has Game Theory Been Refuted?" *Journal of Philosophy* 103:239–263.

Guala, F. 2006b. "Getting the FCC Auctions Straight: Reply to Nik-Khah." *European Economic Sociology Newsletter* 7:21–28.

Hacking, I. 1999. *The Social Construction of What?* Cambridge, MA: Harvard University Press.

Hausman, D. M. 2000. "Revealed Preference, Belief, and Game Theory." *Economics and Philosophy* 16:99–115.

Hertwig, R., and A. Ortmann. 2001. "Experimental Practices in Economics: A Methodological Challenge for Psychologists?" *Behavioral and Brain Sciences* 24:383–451.

Hogarth, R. M., and M. W. Reder, Eds. 1986. *Rational Choice: The Contrast between Economics and Psychology*. Chicago: University of Chicago Press.

Hollywood Stock Exchange, http://www.hsx.com.

Hong, J. T., and C. L. Plott. 1982. "Rate Filling Policies for Inland Water Transportation: An Experimental Approach." *Bell Journal of Economics* 13:1–19.

Hulse, C. 2003. "Pentagon Prepares a Futures Market on Terror Attacks." *New York Times,* July 29: A1.

Hurwicz, L. 1972. "On Informationally Decentralized Systems." In *Decision and Organization*, edited by R. Radner and C. B. McGuire. Amsterdam: North Holland.

Hurwicz, L. 1973. "The Design of Mechanisms for Resource Allocation." *American Economic Review* (Proceedings) 63:1–30.

Kagel, J. H., and A. E. Roth, Eds. 1995. *The Handbook of Experimental Economics*. Princeton, NJ: Princeton University Press.

Kahneman, D., A. Tversky, and R. Thaler. 1986. "Fairness and the Assumptions of Economics." In *Rational Choice: The Contrast between Economics and Psychology*, edited by Robin M. Hogarth and Melvin W. Reder. Chicago: University of Chicago Press.

Klemperer, P. 2002. "How Not to Run Auctions: The European 3G Telecom Auctions." *European Economic Review* 46:829–845.

Klemperer, P. 2004. *Auctions: Theory and Practice*. Princeton, NJ: Princeton University Press.

Krishna, D. 1971. "The Self-Fulfilling Prophecy and the Nature of Society." *American Sociological Review* 36:1104–1107.

Iowa Electronic Markets. University of Iowa, http://www.biz.uiowa.edu/iem/index.html.

Latour, B. 1984. *Les microbes: Guerre et paix*. Paris: Métailié; Engl. transl. *The Pasteurisation of France*. Cambridge, MA: Harvard University Press, 1988.

Ledyard, J. O. 1995. "Public Goods: A Survey of Experimental Research." In *The Handbook of Experimental Economics*, edited by John H. Kagel and Alvin E. Roth. Princeton, NJ: Princeton University Press.

Lee, K. S. 2004. "Rationality, Minds, and Machines in the Laboratory: A Thematic History of Vernon Smith's Experimental Economics." PhD diss., University of Notre Dame.

Leonard, R. 1994. "Laboratory Strife: Higgling as Experimental Science in Economics and Social Psychology." In *Higgling*, edited by N. B. De Marchi and M. S. Morgan. *HOPE* supplement, Vol. 26. Durham, NC: Duke University Press.

Loewenstein, G. 1999. "Experimental Economics from the Vantage-Point of Behavioral Economics." *Economic Journal* 109:F25–34.

MacKenzie, D. 2005. "Opening the Black Boxes of Global Finance." *Review of International Political Economy* 12:555–576.

MacKenzie, D. 2006. *An Engine, Not a Camera: How Financial Models Shape Markets*. Cambridge, MA: MIT Press.

MacKenzie, D., and Y. Millo. 2003. "Constructing a Market, Performing Theory: The Historical Sociology of a Financial Derivatives Exchange." *American Journal of Sociology* 109:107–145.

Marwell, G., and R. E. Ames. 1981. "Economists Free Ride, Does Anyone Else?" *Journal of Public Economics* 15:295–310.

Merton, R. K. 1957. "The Self-fulfilling Prophecy." In *Social Theory and Social Structure*. London: Free Press.

Milgrom, P. R. 2004. *Putting Auction Theory to Work*. Cambridge: Cambridge University Press.

Milgrom, P. R., and R. J. Weber. 1982. "A Theory of Auctions and Competitive Bidding." *Econometrica* 50:1089–1122.

Miller, R. M. 2002. *Paving Wall Street: Experimental Economics and the Quest for the Perfect Market*. New York: Wiley.

Mirowski, P. 2002. *Machines Dream: Economics Becomes a Cyborg Science*. Cambridge: Cambridge University Press.

Mirowski, P. Forthcoming. "Markets Come to Bits." *Journal of Economic Behavior and Organization*.

Muniesa, F. 2000. "Un robot walrasien: Cotation electronique et justesse de la découverte des prix." *Politix* 52:121–154.

Nik-Khah, E. 2005. "Designs on the Mechanism." PhD diss., University of Notre Dame.

Plott, C. R. 1981. "Experimental Methods in Political Economy: A Tool for Regulatory Research." Pp. 117–43 in *Attacking Regulatory Problems*, edited by A. R. Ferguson. Cambridge, MA: Ballinger.

Plott, C. R. 1987. "Dimensions of Parallelism: Some Policy Applications of Experimental Methods." In *Laboratory Experimentation in Economics: Six Points of View*, edited by A. E. Roth. Cambridge: Cambridge University Press.

Plott, C. R. 1988. "Research on Pricing in a Gas Transportation Network." Office of Economic Policy Technical Report 88-2, Federal Energy Regulatory Commission.

Plott, C. R. 1994. "Experimental Methods in Economics and Political Science: The Design and Testing of Policy Options." *Human Dimensions Quarterly* 1:5–8.

Plott, C. R. 1997 "Laboratory Experimental Testbeds: Application to the PCS Auction." *Journal of Economics and Management Strategy* 6:605–638.

Plott, C. R. 2000. "Markets as Information Gathering Tools." *Southern Economic Journal* 67:1–15.

Plott, C. R., and D. P. Porter. 1996. "Market Architecture and Institutional Testbedding: An Experiment with Space Station Pricing Policies." *Journal of Economic Behavior and Organization* 31:237–272.

Rabin, M. 1998. "Psychology and Economics." *Journal of Economic Literature* 35:11–46.

Rabin, M. 2002. "A Perspective on Psychology and Economics." *European Economic Review* 46:657–85.

Roth, A. E. 1991. "Game Theory as a Part of Empirical Economics." *Economic Journal* 101:107–114.

Roth, A. E. 2002. "The Economist as Engineer: Game Theory, Experimentation, and Computation as Tools for Design Economics." *Econometrica* 70:1341–1378.

Roth, A. E., and E. Peranson. 1999. "The Redesign of the Matching Market for American Physicians: Some Engineering Aspects of Economic Design." *American Economic Review* 89:748–780.

Rubinstein, A. 1999. "Experience from a Course in Game Theory: Pre and Post-class Problem Sets as a Didactic Device." *Games and Economic Behavior* 28:155–170.

Schotter, A. 1998. "A Practical Person's Guide to Mechanism Selection: Some Lessons from Experimental Economics." In *Organization with Incomplete Information*, edited by M. Majumdar. Cambridge: Cambridge University Press.

Searle, J. R. 1995. *The Construction of Social Reality*. London: Penguin.

Simon, H. 1957. "Bandwagon and Underdog Effects of Election Predictions." In *Models of Man*. New York: Wiley.

Smith, V. L. 1962. "An Experimental Study of Competitive Market Behavior." *Journal of Political Economy* 70:111–137.

Smith, V. L. 1976. "Experimental Economics: Induced Value Theory." *American Economic Review* 66:274–277.

Smith, V. L. 1982a. "Microeconomic Systems as an Experimental Science." *American Economic Review* 72:923–955.

Smith, V. L. 1982b. "Markets as Economizers of Information: Experimental Examination of the 'Hayek Hypothesis.'" *Economic Inquiry* 20:165–179.

Smith, V. L. 1989. "Theory, Experiment and Economics." *Journal of Economic Perspectives* 3:151–169.

Smith, V. L. 1991a. *Papers in Experimental Economics*. Cambridge: Cambridge University Press.

Smith, V. L. 1991b. "Rational Choice: The Contrast between Economics and Psychology." *Journal of Political Economy* 99:877–897.

Smith, V. L. 1992. "Game Theory and Experimental Economics: Beginnings and Early Influences." In *Toward a History of Game Theory*, edited by E. Roy Weintraub. HOPE Supplement, Vol. 24. Durham, NC: Duke University Press.

Smith, V. L. 2002a. "Interviews: Vernon Smith." In *Experimental Economics: Fi-*

nancial Markets, Auctions, and Decision Making, edited by Fredrik Anderson and Hakan Holm. Dordrecht: Kluwer.

Smith, V. L. 2002b. "Method in Experiment: Rhetoric and Reality." *Experimental Economics* 5:91–110.

Smith, V. L., K. A. McCabe, and S. J. Rassenti. 1991. "Lakatos and Experimental Economics." In *Appraising Economic Theories*, edited by Neil De Marchi and Mark Blaug. Aldershot: Elgar.

Smith, V. L., and A. W. Williams. 1992. "Experimental Market Economics." *Scientific American,* December:72–77.

Thrall, R. M., C. H. Coombs, and R. L. Davis, Eds. 1954. *Decision Processes.* New York: Wiley.

Tuomela, R. 2002. *The Philosophy of Social Practices.* Cambridge: Cambridge University Press.

Vickrey, W. 1961. "Counterspeculation, Auctions, and Competitive Sealed Tenders." *Journal of Finance* 16:8–37.

von Neumann, J., and O. Morgenstern. 1944. *The Theory of Games and Economic Behavior.* Princeton, NJ: Princeton University Press.

Weibull, J. W. 2004. "Testing Game Theory." In *Advances in Understanding Strategic Behaviour*, edited by S. Huck. New York: Palgrave Macmillan.

Wilde, L. L. 1981. "On the Use of Laboratory Experiments in Economics." In *Philosophy in Economics*, edited by J. C. Pitt. Dordrecht: Reidel.

Wilson, R. B. 1977. "A Bidding Model of Perfect Competition." *Review of Economic Studies* 44:511–518.

Chapter 6 ⸻⸻⸻⸻⸻⸻⸻⸻⸻⸻

Economic Experiments and the Construction of Markets

FABIAN MUNIESA AND MICHEL CALLON

The use of the word "experiment" has become pervasive in contemporary economic life.[1] We hear about firms conducting experiments on new products in order to calibrate their marketability, about financial exchanges launching new tradable derivative contracts in an experimental manner, or about supermarkets experimenting on new display and merchandising devices. In all of these instances, the use of the notion of "experiment"—a notion used by economic actors themselves—is far from being purely metaphorical. Of course, these experimental activities might not always correspond to the paramount site of scientific inquiry—laboratories. But this does not mean that they do not partake of some form of investigation. These experimental activities are research activities in the sense that they aim at observing and representing economic objects, but also—and quite explicitly—in the sense that they seek to intervene on these economic objects: to seize them, to modify and then stabilize them, to produce them in some specific manner. To experiment is to attempt to solve a problem by organizing trials that lead to outcomes that are assessed and taken as starting points for further actions. Experimentation is action and reflection.

Economic experiments perform economic objects, in a quite general sense. What experimenters describe is indeed produced by them in the experimental setting. They account for what they provoke. Experimental objects are both observed and fabricated—fabricated in order to be observed and vice-versa. This is already noticeable if we limit the notion of experiment to the realm of academic science, as in the case of laboratory experimental economics (see Guala's chapter in this volume). But it becomes even more remarkable if we expand the notion of experiment to the multiple research activities that are at work in markets and other economic institutions. Experimental techniques are extensively used in marketing research, financial engineering, and economic policy design.

Marketing research techniques such as consumer tests and focus groups are market experiments that include a performative stance: they are about how to observe attachments between consumers and goods but also about how to enact them (Cochoy 1998). For experiments that use a real economy as their testing ground (as in the case of the release of the test version of a product in a controlled retail area), the performative stance is even clearer. The case of postmarketing surveillance of pharmaceutical drug effects—"pharmacovigilance"—convincingly illustrates how markets can be configured as testing sites (Daemmrich 2004, pp. 116–150). Financial markets provide particularly telling examples of the experimental nature of the construction of new tradable products or the implementation of new pricing techniques (e.g., MacKenzie 2003; MacKenzie and Millo 2003).[2] The fact that a national economy can be used (or even explicitly constructed) to test an economic doctrine should also be regarded as a revealing, sometimes critical example of this performative capacity of economic experiments (Bockman and Eyal 2002; Goswami 2004; Mitchell 1998, 2002; Morgan and Den Butter 2000; Stark 1999; Valdés 1995). Economic experiments are increasingly becoming a constitutive element of the construction of markets—which are increasingly presented as experimental artifacts. And, especially in the case of real-scale experiments, these experimental activities are subject to dispute, which opens ways for economic entities to become political objects.

The purpose of this chapter is to illustrate how economic experiments are engaged in the construction of markets and to propose a framework for coping with the variety of these experimental forms. Considered within this wide context, the boundaries of what an experiment is are fuzzy. Economic experiments are performed by collectives that may vary in size, nature, and scope, collectives that may include professional researchers (social scientists, engineers) but also other kinds of actors (market practitioners, public agencies, and stakeholders of many sorts).[3] The issues at stake are also varied: allocation principles, goods' qualities, pricing strategies, and national productivity all can be tested in different manners. Different forms of experimentation engage in different forms of demonstration, different forms of exploitation of experimental outcomes, and different scales of application.

To shed light on this variety of experimental forms, we focus on three criteria: the sites of such practices (i.e., their material display and location), the nature of the manipulations that are imposed on the object of experimentation (i.e., the operations aiming at provoking some specific forms of behavior), and the forms of demonstration that govern the experimental method (i.e., the ways in which explicitness is constructed). We use these criteria to identify three ideal-typical configurations of economic experiments—the laboratory, the platform, and the in vivo experiment—that we illustrate with some examples.

Location, Manipulation, and Demonstration

One relevant source for the identification of the features of economic experiments is experimental economics. Of course, laboratory experimental economics represents just one particular—rather extreme—instance of market experiments. But, mainly because this discipline is constantly confronting difficult methodological problems, its own insights about how an experiment works can prove to be most useful. In this section, we use some experimentalist claims to point out the relevance of location, manipulation, and demonstration in the construction of an economic experiment.

A Detour through Experimental Economics

Jean-Baptiste Say is one of the first authors to claim that economics is an experimental science; he meant that economics should be devoted to the observation and gathering of facts in order to point to causal regularities (1841, pp. 1–54). This perspective has opened the way to an increasingly influential science, mainly with the assistance of statistics and the birth of econometrics. But Say was not reckless enough to imagine that economics could lock itself into laboratories, as in the case of natural sciences. For him economic facts were produced by economic activities, not by economists. It is Vernon Smith along with other pioneers of experimental economics who dared to take that step and lock up economics inside laboratories. This decision is a severe one: it is about setting oneself apart from the "world out-there"—or at least keeping some distance—and manipulating objects specially devised and configured for the laboratory.

It is not surprising that, since its inception, experimental economics has had to struggle to justify its validity, that is, the "external validity" of its empirical results (see Guala's chapter, also Guala 1999, 2001, 2003, 2005). Although experimental economics has introduced empirical concerns to the heart of a rather formalistic economic science, it has been widely accused of working out "artificial" laboratory conditions, extreme configurations which are not representative of real economic life. How can this form of knowledge claim to apply to the world "out-there," that is, to be externally valid? It is easy to recognize here a classical problem of laboratory practices that has been extensively scrutinized in science studies (Collins 1985; Knorr Cetina 1981; Latour 1987; Latour and Woolgar 1979; Lynch 1985). Experimental economists themselves have provided some clarifications that are quite illuminating in this regard.

One primary aspect of laboratory economic experiments is their location; the soundness of an experiment is, above all, a question of site. To claim that laboratory markets are "artificial"—as if "real" markets were not—makes little sense but to say that they are confined to a specific location does. The theoretical justifications of experimental economics are explicit on that precise point. When defining the conditions for the "external validity" of an economic experiment, Vernon Smith clearly states that "the experimental laboratory *is* a real world, with real people, real institutions, real payoffs and commodities just as real as stock certificates and airline travel vouchers, both of which have utility because of the claim they legally bestow on the bearer" (1989, p. 109). To draw a relation between such a world and another one is, above all, a problem of location. The fact that Smith prefers the notion of "parallelism" to that of "external validity" is particularly relevant in this regard. The relation of applicability of an experimental result is not exactly a jump onto an external, undefined "real" world, but a relation between "one microeconomy (laboratory or field)" and "other microeconomies (laboratory or field)" (Smith 1989, p. 108). The relation between the "interior" and the "exterior" of the laboratory turns, in fact, into a topology of different sites between which connections have to be worked out. The ways to build and stabilize these relations (i.e., making *ceteris paribus* conditions[4] hold together, in economists' terms) are, of course, varied and disputable. But what appears to be somewhat clear, even for experimental economists themselves, is that an experiment works, primarily, in its experimental setting.

A second feature of experimental economics that needs to be born in mind is its manipulative capacity. As Guala notes in his chapter, "Induced Value Theory"—a set of methodological precepts for the design of experimental settings—focuses explicitly on the manipulative character of laboratory experiments (Smith 1979, 1982, 1989). The experimental setting is meant to provoke reality, which is quite different from any attempt at preserving and recording the spontaneity of some sort of "genuine" economic behavior. Any claim accusing experimental economics of constructing unrealistic and aberrant situations—and thus of "making up" its objects of inquiry—misses the very ambition of this discipline: it is all precisely about that. It is common, for instance, in experimental economics conscientiously to train experimental subjects so that they will behave appropriately in the experimental environment. The precepts of Induced Value Theory do not seek to simulate field situations.[5] On the contrary, experimenters operate the experimental setup in order to extract—or, better, to provoke—the purest expression of one particular economic trait, a trait that is most likely not observable as such in ordinary economic life.

This leads to a third important aspect of experimental economics: its object. What does this science look at? Were not experimental economists meant to study economies, that is, human economic behavior?

These are not exactly the right terms. Experimental economics origi-
nated, at least in Vernon Smith's version, as a means to test economic
theories: a way to study the behavior of theories, so to say, not of people.
Although the scope of experimental economics is not limited to an en-
dogenous self-observation of economics, it is important to note that the
experimental setting is meant to mimic economic theories rather than
economic life (Smith 1982, 1994).[6] This is what the notion of "microeconomic system"—the very object of experimental economics—is all
about. A microeconomic system is a sort of a mechanism that operates
in a stabilized environment. Economic agents characterized with utility
functions are part of the environment; human actors—but also computer
programs—may play these economic agents in order to activate the
"microeconomic system" observed in the laboratory. In such conditions,
experimental economics can produce legitimate knowledge without
"parallelism" of any sort: "Insofar as we are only interested in testing
hypotheses derived from theories, we are done" (Smith 1982, p. 935).
Even when the scope moves further, theory can still make a good alibi: to
say that an experiment is unrealistic might turn out to be a criticism
against the tested theory, not against the experimental setup (Smith
1982, p. 937). Of course, the situation becomes more intricate when
experimental economics loses this purely theoretical sight—for instance,
in situations of economic engineering. But this self-declared purpose
gives an important clue about one thing experimental economics does: it
demonstrates abstract theories by way of transforming them into explicit
mechanisms.

Economic Experiments at Large

These three brief considerations about experimental economics are far
from exhaustive. It is not the objective of this chapter to analyze the epistemology of this particular kind of science. Furthermore, Vernon Smith's
version of these research practices cannot be used to understand the
many facets of this scientific field. But these considerations point to three
features that need to be taken seriously. The first is that generalization of
experimental results is not a straightforward operation: experimentalists
are quite aware of the localism of their practice. As Guala (2003) suggests, localism is not an impediment to generalization. Generalization,
however, cannot be but the partial and difficult result of the alignment of
particular sites through metrological networks (O'Connell 1993). The
second feature is that objects are not observed at a distance but produced
inside the experimental setting. They are formed and deformed in order
to put forward some particular economic traits. The manipulations they
undergo are similar to those of any situation of testing (Pinch 1993; Sims

1999). The third feature is their particular demonstrative stake. The objective of a laboratory experiment is often that of turning an elliptic theory into an explicit set of rules and behaviors. This turn toward explicitness was already the central motive of Chamberlin's early experiments (1948). In this respect, experimental economics connects with recent developments in market microstructure theory that aim at putting notions of equilibrium and efficiency to the test of concrete trading protocols (Madhavan 2000).[7]

These three features (location, manipulation, and demonstration) are crucial for the understanding of experimental economics—and of economic experiments at large. They can provide useful criteria to describe the variety of experimental forms that populate markets. Of course, the way in which location, manipulation, and demonstration are handled in laboratory economics will differ thoroughly from the way in which these three features are mobilized in marketing experiments, for instance. But, still, these three characteristics can allow us to highlight (1) the fact that an economic experiment takes place in a located site that might be described as a specific sociotechnical device and characterized by the actors that can access it, (2) the way in which objects of experiments are constructed and tested in order to put forward some specific traits, and (3) the operations of demonstration, verification, testing, and proof that render both problems and solutions explicit.

Experimental sites are material sites. It is important not to take this characteristic in a purely metaphorical sense. Economic experiments in economics usually take place in classrooms. They can also be run on computers, as in the case of computational economics. But a supermarket (or a whole retail catchment area) can also become an experimental site, as much as a trading room, a firm, or a marketplace. Precisely because of their materiality, these spaces can be characterized by such features as their size and their degree of openness. What things and which persons can access an experimental site? Access control is an essential feature of experimental settings, but in some cases this access cannot be but open, at least to a certain degree. This is particularly the case of experiments that need to be based on compromises with the actors at stake (actors at stake as both witnesses and participants) or of experiments that purposefully enlarge, beyond the laboratory, the boundaries of the experimental perimeter.

Manipulative intervention in the experimental site can also embrace many forms, depending on the economic trait that is to be fostered and on the kind of entities that are experimented upon. As in the case of automobile testing, an experiment can end with the destruction of the experimented object. In other cases, experimented objects can be projected into a simulation that saves the costs of engaging into a real-scale experience.

Objects gathered for experimentation can also be more or less recalcitrant. The manipulations imposed on them can stumble over their complexity or their morality. Overall, there are various kinds of trials and various kinds of resistance to trials. The form of these trials will strongly depend on the degree of openness of the experimental device.

Finally, an experiment stages a public demonstration, test, or proof. As brilliantly shown by Claude Rosental (2003) in his analysis of proof in logic, a demonstration is about exhibiting something or, in other words, about rendering some aspects explicit while taking for granted other aspects. But explicitness is not a straightforward operation. Rendering things explicit is producing a public collective for which explicitness works. Consequently, the nature and capacities of the actors engaged in the experiment and, moreover, the associations drawn between them are also at stake in demonstration. What public does the experiment address? Which audience is engaged into the experiment and how? Is the public directly affected by experiments? Are members of the audience also members of the experimental community? Are they also experimental subjects? The responses to these questions will point simultaneously to the degree of public acceptance of demonstrations and to the degree to which the experimental site can become a political site.[8] In other words, these questions determine the extent to which the experiment can become an issue (Barry 2001; Callon 2004).

Laboratories, Platforms, and In Vivo Experiments

In this section, we introduce a schematic distinction between three experimental configurations: the laboratory, the platform, and the in vivo experiment. An experimental configuration combines, in a specific manner, the three features of an experiment: location, manipulation, and demonstration. We propose three typical configurations that we find relevant, but, of course, there might be more than three. These three types are characterized primarily by their degree of openness. The laboratory is a site that is well-known for its confinement. At the opposite end, real-scale experiments (which we can also call "in situ experiments" or "in vivo experiments") abolish this distance between the "inside" and the "outside." Both configurations are also characterized by the nature of trials and the forms of demonstration. The platform is an intermediate configuration, more open to compromises with several kinds of actors than the laboratory. We focus on how location, manipulation, and demonstration are handled in each configuration and we illustrate each of them with some examples: we use an experimental study on willingness to pay to point to some relevant features of the laboratory configuration, we suggest consumer testing and econometric modeling in the electricity market as two kinds of experimental platform, and we describe, finally, an in vivo experiment in a stock exchange.

Laboratories

THE LABORATORY CONFIGURATION

The laboratory is characterized by the rarefaction of actors engaged in experimentation. The fact that these actors are often mainly research professionals provides good evidence of this rarefaction. The collectives that organize experiments are reduced, even if connections between several laboratories (that cooperate or compete) are possible. Access to experimental sites is restricted. The list of actors is defined a priori, as much as the list of objects that enter the laboratory. This is an important condition in achieving the rather high level of control that characterizes laboratory experimental activities.

This confinement incidentally translates into the construction of a strong distance between an "exterior" and an "interior"—a distance that is the very product of the laboratory setting (Latour 1987). In natural sciences, this "exterior" is called "nature," and in social sciences, "society." In experimental economics, the latter can be also termed "the real economy." Once this distance has been set, objects are transported from the "exterior" into the "interior" of the laboratory. But this movement is an operation of transformation and reduction: objects are "purified" in order to make them fit for manipulation and production of controlled information.

Laboratory demonstration is then about exhibiting this information to specific audiences: scientific colleagues and, in some cases, a larger public of decision makers. Demonstration is about linking one or several problems to solutions, actions, and decisions that correspond to the laboratory conditions. For these solutions, actions, and decisions to expand into the "out-there world," concrete directions about how to overcome the distance between the "exterior" and the "interior" need to be proposed, and they usually consist of directions about how to transport the laboratory conditions to other sites.

EXPERIMENTAL CONSTRUCTION OF WILLINGNESS TO PAY

A recent research program conducted in France by a team of experimental economists provides a good example of the *modus operandi* of economic laboratories. This research program centered on the following question: how much are consumers willing to pay for a foodstuff labeled as free from genetically modified organisms (GMOs)? The program, funded by public agencies and actors of the industry, aimed at assessing the possibility of developing a sector labeled "GMO-free" in the French agrofood industry. To calibrate the costs of such an initiative, an estimate of the public's disposition to buy such products was needed. To assess this initiative, a group of economists decided to use experimental methods (Ruffieux and Robin 2001).[9] The purpose of the experimental setting they devised was to generate a robust indication of the disposition to buy such goods for a sample of statistically representative shoppers. The idea was to avoid the biases of opinion surveys by confronting these shoppers—turned into experimental subjects—with a real purchase situation.

But should this experimental purchase situation look like a "natural" purchase situation? The aim of the experiment was to obtain in the laboratory data that were difficult to capture "in the wild": the consumer's willingness to pay. In order to do this, these economists constructed a market device that, far from resembling to a current supermarket situation, plunged the experimental subjects into an extremely artificial situation in order to obtain "purified" willingness-to-pay data. These experiments were not about re-creating a market in order to study, with better precision and control, what happens in a real purchase, but to reveal a parameter—willingness to pay—that was hard to isolate in its pure form in a supermarket situation. This operation of "revelation" was openly constructivist: in order to emerge, willingness-to-pay needed to be provoked.

To conduct their experiment, the economists decided to use an auction, which is a market mechanism that diverges consistently from current retail market environments where prices are posted. Among the wide variety of existing auction mechanisms the experimenters chose a Vickrey auction. Also known as "second-price sealed-bid auction," this mechanism is named after William Vickrey, the economist who modeled it. The protocol is simple: participants submit secret written bids and proposed prices are not known by them during the auction process. Moreover, the auction is won by the participant who posts the highest bid, but she pays only the price proposed at the second-best bid. This form of auction, common in the auction theory literature in economics, is seldom seen elsewhere.[10]

The Vickrey auction is well-known among economists for its "counterspeculative" properties (Vickrey 1961). In theory, this device can frustrate gaming behavior and make participants limit themselves to the expression of their own individual "reserve price." The sealed-bid rule renders superfluous any attempt at taking into account the bidding behavior of other participants. The second-price rule is meant to cancel the utility of taking the risk of overbidding. Participants can effectively maximize their return if they just submit the price they are really ready to pay. Any divergent strategy does not improve the probability of winning but increases the probability of losing. This device turns to be, consequently, a good instrument for revealing the intrinsic preferences of individuals. But this revelation is costly and needs to be carefully constructed. Experimental subjects need some time to learn how to conform to this rule.

One of the most important elements of the experimental setting is the "training period," whose purpose is to teach experimental subjects how to behave appropriately in a Vickrey mechanism (Ruffieux and Robin 2001 pp. 30–33). This part of the experimental protocol is extremely difficult.[11] The experimenters have to face many forms of recalcitrant behavior: participants often try to deploy gaming strategies instead of limiting themselves to the individualistic exercise of submitting directly their reserve price. Experimenters rely on empirical know-how that allows calibration of the way in which the expected behavior is induced. In this case, they used a training game.

During the training period, participants had to get used to the particular rationale of this unusual trading protocol. Apart from hearing pedagogical explanations from the experimenters, participants had to take part in a training game. During this preparatory game, participants had to bid for tokens, using a certain amount of money that was given to them by the experimenters. The value of such tokens was arbitrarily set by the experimenters through a repurchase agreement. Each participant was given a personal "repurchase value" for the token: if a participant had a personal "repurchase value" of 4 euros, this meant the experimenters were ready to buy the token back at a price of 4 euros. If she attempted to obtain the token at a lower price in the auction, she could make a profit. The purpose of the training game, which could last for four or five auction rounds for each experimental group, was to show to the participants that the only winning strategy in the Vickrey auction was to bid exactly at the repurchase value, no more and no less; they had to understand that there was no gaming possibility, since the best strategy was simply to reproduce the given arbitrary repurchase value in the sealed bid.

The purpose of this training was to imprint on the experimental market an essential feature if individual preferences needed to be retrieved: in this market, collective reflexivity needed to be neutralized. In order to purify willingness-to-pay, any gaming effect or mimetic behavior had to be ruled out. The training game was precisely set as a way to force the experimental subjects to conform to such principle: do not look at the others; do not play with price-setting strategies; just tell what is the price you are really willing to pay, and do not cheat, because cheating might cause you to lose money.

After participants had undergone this training process, they entered a series of auctions in which they were asked to bid for a set of cereal bars. These items were first tasted in a blind protocol, auctioned, and then displayed with their original packaging and auctioned again. For the last auction, the experimenters pointed out the labeling of these bars emphasizing the references to GMOs. The consecutive change in bidding behavior was taken as an isolated signal of the willingness to pay for this specific information.

"Individual preferences" are the result of a specific methodological construction: that of the Vickrey protocol. The fact that these data are "constructed" does not mean they are false. The experimental market is a real market, but it is a rarefied market. Its elements are manipulated in a way that renders willingness-to-pay explicit, in a localized valid manner. Extrapolations are also possible, and this research program aimed overtly at suggesting some policy directions (Noussair et al. 2003). But the resources for demonstration are somewhat constrained by the *ceteris paribus* clause. Research results are delivered in a scientific format (mainly through scientific publications) that corresponds to the laboratory setting. They can be taken into account by politicians and stakeholders (if they are convinced) but cannot be applied as such without further tinkering.

Platforms

THE PLATFORM CONFIGURATION

The platform constitutes a second family of devices for experimentation that enlarges the frame imposed by the laboratory and puts at issue the distance (and the distinction) between the "inside" and the "outside." The notion of platform was introduced in the world of firms and technology in order to refer to new forms of organizing research and innovation. It is now a widespread notion and is even used in the social sciences. Keating and Cambrosio (2003) showed how the platform materializes the transformation introduced by biomedical research in the relations among patients, clinics, and R&D.[12] The laboratory becomes a second-line site, and the platform comes to the forefront because of its openness and flexibility. Similarly, Ciborra (1996) uses the notion of platform to refer to flexible organizational forms in where surprise is more a resource than a problem, and Kim and Kogut (1996) explore how platform technologies constitute a resource for strategic innovation.

The platform differs from the laboratory because of its (relative and reasonable) openness to a plurality of actors, often previously well-identified, who are invited to join the experimental collective. The platform is a device conceived to favor hybridization and confrontation of interests, skills, and projects as a way to induce robust compromises. It is thus open to researchers and engineers from various disciplines, but also to other actors (consumers or users, economic actors of many kinds, actors from the political or juridical sphere). In this sense, platforms favor "research in the wild" (Callon and Rabeharisoa 2003). In the case of markets, platforms do not stop at gathering economists and psychologists; they also assemble stakeholders, politicians, and technologists. The material infrastructure of platforms allows for coordination and interaction between these agents without them being asked to abandon their respective identities, skills, or projects. Actors do not hybridize; it is the platform that produces hybridization. Different platforms might cooperate or compete. They are often responsible for the emergence of what cognitive or economic approaches call "epistemic and practice communities" (Amin and Cohendet 2004).

Platforms construct objects and act upon them in different ways than do laboratories. The platform tries (partially) to overcome the distance that an experiment generates between the "inside" and the "outside" of the experimental setting. To achieve that aim, the platform constructs tools, equipments, and procedures to simulate the contexts in which these objects are meant to live. This implies the recognition of the analytical complexity of the objects subjected to experimentation, instead of focusing on reduction and purification. This way of rendering visible the complexity of the object oscillates between two experimental modes: simulation-by-testing (which sometimes requires the destruction of the object itself) and simulation-by-modeling (which preserves the integrity of the object).

Demonstration and verification in a platform are about compromise— about recognizing the diversity of actors and the complexity of objects, and about imagining experimentation that may transform the positions of actors and the qualities of objects. Relations of strength (*rapports de force*) are tied and crystallized in compromises. The problem, then, is to keep these compromises stable in other sites, and this raises the question of the representativeness of actors at stake and of the relevance of the characterization of goods. The design of a platform and the management of its evolution often require the intervention of some kind of social science.

MODELING FRANCE'S ELECTRICITY MARKET

A good illustration of the construction of a platform that operates simulation-by-modeling is provided by Gabrielle Hecht's (1998) remarkable analysis of the history of French civil nuclear program and particularly the breaking point of the 1960s that led to the choice of light-water reactors and, simultaneously, to the reorganization of the electricity market. EDF (Electricité de France, the state electricity company) succeeded in imposing its nuclear (and economic) model against the one defended by the CEA (Commissariat à l'Energie Atomique, the national agency for atomic energy in France). This episode was crystallized into the controversy around the cost of the competitive kilowatt-hour and into the transformation of market structure by which the controversy was closed.

This transformation was made possible through simulation or, more exactly, through simulation-by-modeling. Econometric optimization models were prepared inside the SEEG (Service des Etudes Economiques Générales, EDF's center for economic research) and inside the Commissariat Général du Plan (the state office for economic planning) by a small team of engineers and quantitative economists. The main task of the SEEG (run by the brilliant economist Marcel Boiteux) was "to forecast the nation's electricity demand, to analyze external factors that would influence the cost and pricing of electricity production, and to prepare management and rationalization tools to help 'optimize' the electricity production system" (Hecht 1998, p.102).[13]

The aim was to simulate in order to convince the government and other actors of the necessity of supporting EDF in the reconstruction of the market. The role of models was not that of a simple rhetorical weapon. They enabled EDF not only to make and defend choices, but also to reshape the terms of the nuclear debate. Simulation was made possible by the use of mathematical and computational tools that stood as acceptable substitutes for real-scale industrial experience. Optimization models were capable of drawing (or calculating) compromises that otherwise would have remained unmanageable. At the heart of the simulation was the modeling of the evolution of electricity demand, and, therefore, the possibility of representing electricity consumers. Calculations allowed by these models made it possible to simulate different investment strategies, and especially to compare the costs of alternative industrial trajectories, that is, the relative costs of different technical options. In the end, it was EDF's nuclear plant regime, quite different from the one imagined by the CEA, that imposed itself.

The design and use of these models provided, according to Hecht, "a widely respected method of 'experimentation'" (1998, p. 109). This "experimentation" corresponds to what we call a platform. This market experiment allowed for the introduction of a variety of actors who were previously excluded or not taken into account. Engineers were constrained to discuss and negotiate with economists and econometricians, but also with civil servants from the Commissariat Général du Plan, with subcontractors, and with trade unions. They were required to include in their deliberation the future of consumption, the evolution of financial markets, and the strategies of oil producers. This extension, and the discussion that went along with it, was made possible through models: through the explicitness of alternatives and variables, the rigor of reasoning, and the construction of different scenarios. Modeling put its object—electricity market—in quite demanding conditions (it was scrutinized by several groups and subjected to several criteria and interests) that emphasize its potential complexity and take it apart from the simple and reduced version that the CEA had imposed before (with its quasi laboratories). In the platform configuration, the market is deployed. Models contribute to this deployment. Models also demonstrate to a larger audience the possible options and their consequences. The demonstration aggregated interests, building sociotechnical alliances that are stronger that the ones proposed by the CEA.

The French electricity market was radically reshaped. How was the industry structured before this transformation? We find the CEA, its engineers, the gas-graphite technology, and the plants that produce plutonium and, secondarily, electricity. We find a landscape of hybridization of civil and military policies, of private firms that are in charge of producing entire nuclear plants in the name of a "national champions" kind of policy, with trade unions taken apart, a government that is instrumentalized by engineers, a national market that is incompatible with foreign markets, an investment logic focused on productivity (producing as much plutonium and electricity as possible), and on a physical definition of efficiency (producing the maximum power in the most thermodynamically efficient manner), and low concerns about the evolution of demand for electricity and of the prices of conventional fuel and power. What did the landscape look like after this period of change? We find EDF and its engineers, but also (and above all) its economists, who work closely with the technocrats of the Commissariat Général du Plan and discuss light-water reactors—which disconnect civil from military nuclear industry—with the government, specialized firms, and subcontractors that design and produce specific components for the reactors. We also find trade unions that are deeply implicated in the governance of EDF, and an investment logic that puts forward a more economic concept of efficiency and that takes into account not only the long-term evolution of the energy market but also the fluctuations of interest rates and amortization periods. This move toward more economic definitions of productivity and efficiency is best illustrated by the shift from the notion of *rendement* (producing as much electricity as possible) to that of *rentabilité* (producing the cheapest possible electricity). As shown by Hecht (1998, pp. 102–111), at the center of this shift was the crucial relevance of the cost of the kilowatt-hour. It is not only market structures that have changed. It is the very sociotechnical market device that has been reconfigured in order to include different players, different procedures, but also different technologies.

TESTING FOR A CONSUMERIST MAGAZINE

One well-known advantage of simulation is that it can base demonstrative evidence on forecasting, without performing on the real-scale object at stake (France's electricity in the example above). But models are not the only tools that allow for the simulation of contexts of use and trajectories of evolution. The properties of an economic object can also be deployed through testing. One extreme example of this kind of trial is given by the tests conducted by consumerist associations. The simulation is performed on the real objects; they are purchased, sorted out, and exposed to regular or extreme uses, often ending up with the destruction of the object (as in the case of resistance, security, or composition tests). Alexandre Mallard (2000) has studied the role and functioning of particular experimental actors: French consumerist associations linked to consumerist magazines such as *Que Choisir* and *60 Millions de Consommateurs*. What is at stake in the tests organized by these associations is what we call the "qualification" of the products that are examined: the trials aim at making the product's qualities appear. The particular form of "qualification" (Callon et al. 2002) undertaken by consumer organizations often leads to criticism of producers and sellers.

These tests extend the universe of concerned actors and of the points of view that are taken into account in qualification trials. This extension refers to the definition of the population of products that enter into comparisons as well as to the participation of groups that were not present in qualification trials, which expresses the desire to locate the product in its context of purchasing and use. The experimenters, in their testing platforms, construct an hyperequipped consumer, an autonomous and independent consumer, which faces objects whose qualities are hyperexplicit (it is a journalist-consumer) and which is allowed to deform—literally—a wide selection of products from the same category. This mediating entity, which is fully engineered in the testing platform of the consumerist association, has a leading voice in the magazine published by the association: it is a prescriptive agent (Hatchuel 1995); it informs as well as forming the consumer-reader.

Demonstration is the result of an equipped, metrological, and (to some extent) public observation of tests. The primary audiences are the producers, the engineers, and the journalists in charge of "representing" the point of view of the final consumer. The latter has still to be convinced. Consumerist magazines such as *Que Choisir* deploy an interesting strategy aiming at integrating individual end-consumers as part of the experimental platform. Surveys and calls for witnesses are launched periodically. Car owners, for instance, are asked to report observations on the qualities of a particular model. Demonstration is obtained through an extension of the platform. In some cases, the platform extends to lawyers, as *Que Choisir* decides to engage in lawsuits against manufacturers or distributors. The notion of "demonstration" is closer to a militant one. In this context, demonstrating is often about exposing, about debunking.

In Vivo Experiments

THE IN VIVO CONFIGURATION

The in vivo experiment extends the openness of the platform and abolishes the opposition between an "inside" and an "outside," or between the experimental site and the "out-thereness" of society. Society is "in-there" because the experiment takes place in situ. But the notion of "in vivo" better captures this way of functioning than the notions of "in situ" or "real scale." This kind of experimental configuration is not only about widening the scale of the experimental site. The biomedical metaphor helps to take into account also the fact that this experimental site becomes more uncertain and that different sorts of precautions have to be put forward.

The list of actors involved in this kind of experiment (i.e., the identity and force of the different actors that are to be engaged in the experiment and alter its course) is not defined a priori. To some extent, this list includes all the actors that would have been implied in an experimental platform if this kind of setting had been used. But the starting point is to consider that the exact composition of such a list is not known ex ante. Some actors might be invisible when the experiment starts and might become visible later on; others are engendered—rendered explicit—by the experiment itself and the trials it organizes. The in vivo experiment's main objective is to make these actors appear. The collective that experiments is not only open in the sense that it grants access to the actors that are already there; it also extends the list of actors.

The complexity of the experimented objects is openly considered nonmanageable through analytical reduction (in a laboratory) or through simulation (in a platform): these methods are meant to work with objects that are already quite well delineated. The privileged method, here, is that of "injection," that is, of controlled intervention as a way of observing how the object reacts and deducing its properties and the manners in which it can be transformed. In the case of in vivo economic experiments, a market, for instance, is neither reduced nor deployed. It is maintained as a black box that is exposed to a targeted treatment; the generated reactions, captured with the proper monitoring tools, are then interpreted and taken into account for further action.

In vivo experiments are intended to overflow, and, consequently, one of their objectives is to find the "natural" boundaries within which the effects produced by the experimental injection are contained.

Demonstration aims at rendering visible, analyzable (and eventually calculable) these reactions, initially unexpected, of the collective and the objects subjected to experimentation.[14] Once it has been "updated" by the experiment, the collective must be convinced of the validity of the reactions recorded, of the interpretations provided, and of the transformations proposed. For in vivo experimentation, the power of conviction relies on the fact that it is actors themselves that have played their own roles—delegation is minimal.

EXPERIMENTING IN A STOCK EXCHANGE

The case of innovation in financial markets is particularly appropriate to illustrate this kind of experimental configuration. A stock exchange, for instance, can introduce a modification of its trading protocol in a straightforward manner, without much calibration of the consequences of this innovation. But it can also do it in an experimental manner, testing the robustness of the modification before full-scale implementation. Muniesa (2003, pp. 165–191) documented an episode in which a particular stock exchange, the Paris Bourse, was compelled to use this kind of in vivo experimental configuration to alter its trading mechanism.[15] The episode took place in the early 1990s. The Paris Bourse was already a fully automated marketplace. Buy and sell orders were transmitted, matched, and executed through the CAC (Cotation Assistée en Continu) system, the Parisian version of Toronto Stock Exchange's pioneering technology CATS (Computer-Assisted Trading System). But the system was relatively old (designed in the late 1970s and implemented in Paris in the 1980s) and concerns were raised about the capacity of this system to absorb increasing trading volume. In 1993, the French government announced an important privatization program that was presumably going to cause a growth of trading flow and, perhaps, a collapse of the system.

Individual shareholding was central to the newly devised French economic policy and, at an aggregate level, small investors' orders were expected to cause a quantitative growth of trading volume. But these orders were to be qualitatively problematic too: small investors' orders are small and, from the point of view of CAC's architecture, the size of orders was crucial. The Paris Bourse used board lots. Stocks were not traded one by one, but in lots, typically of 10, 50, or 100 shares. This was a common practice in stock exchanges—a way to economize calculative resources that was inherited from open-outcry practices. But investors were not obliged to make their orders conform to board lots. Therefore, the market had to cope also with "odd lots," orders whose quantity was below the official board lot (or above but not a multiple). The new French individual shareholder was most likely to access the market with orders below the board-lot threshold, which was prohibitively high.[16]

How were odd lots handled at the Paris Bourse? The CAC system admitted only board lots. Stockbrokers had to take care of odd lots, but in compliance with the prices set by CAC for board lots. More precisely, stockbrokers had to stand as counterparties for odd lots transmitted by their clients at the price given by CAC upon reception, and then fill up the missing volume needed in order to constitute a board lot to match it in the central CAC market system. Stockbrokers had to assume the discrepancy between the price given to the client and the price obtained for the execution of the corresponding board lot.

In 1993, a special commission on individual shareholding set by the Paris Bourse issued a report calling for the abolition of board lots. In other words, CAC should allow minimum orders for a single share inside its central order book. On a technical level, this reform was far from straightforward. Would the computational capacities of CAC be a constraint on the flow of orders? The complete upgrade of the system was not to be ready until 1995. In the meanwhile, the Paris Bourse needed to handle the situation, since the first IPOs were already being scheduled. In order to calibrate the appropriate solution to the problem, the Paris Bourse needed reliable information about the quantity of potential odd lots and about their potential impact on the CAC system.

Many of the uncertainties regarding the removal of board lots were linked to the impossibility of knowing, in advance, whether CAC would be able to overcome the flow. The main reason for this was that the Paris Bourse lacked enough data to estimate properly the real flow of odd lots. The processing of odd lots was heterogeneous and distributed, as were the data regarding them. The reaction to an increase of flow without board lots was tested at the Paris Bourse. But this simulation was conducted during nontrading hours using synthetic data. The data regarding the real quantity and nature of odd lots held at the stockbrokers' level was unknown. It was, at least, possible to have slight indications of the average percentage of odd lot orders reaching the brokerage houses. But crucial information was missing: the amount of "true" odd lots (i.e., lots whose quantity was below the board lot) and of "false" odd lots (i.e., bigger than the board lot, but nonmultiples). False board lots had to be split into several orders to be handled. But how? Stockbrokers would not provide this information, possibly because of some distrust of the Paris Bourse, but also because the management of odd lots was often a matter of tinkering that was difficult to quantify.

An "experiment on some stocks," to use the terms of the Paris Bourse's officials (Muniesa 2003, p. 185), was the only possible way to obtain reliable data.

The engineers in charge of the experiment decided to start working at low doses, removing board lots for only a small set of the lesser liquid stocks. The results of the experiment were encouraging: the flow increase was less significant than expected. But these results also made visible some crucial information about true and false odd lots. The rise in flow due to the presence of odd lots in the CAC system was compensated for by the disappearance of the problem of dividing nonmultiple lots (false odd lots). In other words, the fact that false odd lots did not have to be divided any more balanced the increase due to new incoming true odd-lot orders. This statistical behavior of the market could emerge only by way of an in vivo experiment, which was the only way of making explicit the presence of small orders in the market.[17] In other words, the only way for the Paris Bourse to gather data about the potential impact of individual shareholders in a single statistical space was to draw them into the physical space of the CAC system.

To some extent, the purpose of this experiment was to reveal the composition of the market. Enmeshed in computational technicalities lay the central issue of privatization. Was the Paris Bourse able to absorb the burst of individual shareholding? Of course, this short account of the board-lots episode does not illustrate the full complexity of the situation. But it shows the crucial role of the in vivo experimental strategy in gaining knowledge and control over the gathering of the market collective. Exchange engineers, brokers, bankers, listed companies, and investors were literally put to the test of the market architecture in a context in which no straightforward information about the potential statistical behavior of the market existed beforehand.

Other examples can illustrate this kind of procedure, even if their experimental nature is not always fully assumed. Donald MacKenzie and Yuval Millo studied the interesting episode of the introduction of the Black and Scholes pricing formula in Chicago financial derivatives markets (see MacKenzie's chapter, also MacKenzie and Millo 2003). In some measure, this situation can also be considered as of an experimental nature, since it was in part about testing the performance of the formula in the market. But the outcome of the test was far from straightforward. The appearance and performance of one particular kind of actor—arbitrageurs—was particularly crucial to the process. The action of arbitrageurs was not an ex ante certainty but a property of the market that was engendered through the in vivo trial, that is, by the "injection" of the Black and Scholes formula into the real-scale market. The process of tinkering and composition that this innovation called for was far from meeting the requirements of laboratory conditions, and also far from permitting the degree of analysis and simulation that characterizes an experimental platform. Accordingly, the degree of engagement of the parties at stake was maximal: the distinction between "experimenters," "witnesses," and "experimental subjects" was blurred in the extreme.

Concluding Comments and Remarks

To talk of markets as "laboratories" becomes more and more tempting, given the increasing role of calculative technologies and of expert knowledge in the construction of contemporary economies (Callon and Muniesa 2005). The typology presented here is an attempt to go beyond this metaphorical temptation. It is worthwhile to consider laboratories in a literal sense, but in that case the analysis of the ways in which specific forms of research—especially experimental research—study markets and intervene in them has to be handled with care. Of course, it is possible to say that markets have always partaken of some form of research. One can even claim that when we explore the bakeries in a new neighborhood we are conducting an experiment in baguette purchasing. But this loose usage would lead us to ignore the quite demanding material conditions of experimental location, manipulation, and demonstration.[18] The distinction among laboratories, platforms, and in vivo experiments brings out the various ways in which these three features matter.

Laboratories, platforms, and in vivo experiments are ideal types. These modalities of experimentation are not mutually exclusive. Laboratories can be linked to platforms, and platforms to in vivo experiments. It would be empirically more accurate to talk about networks of experimental sites, with all that this implies in terms of network dynamics and coordination (Callon et al. 1999). Platforms play a crucial role in these networks of experimental sites. A hypothesis might be put forward about the increasing role of platforms within such networks and about their capacity to generate locked-in phenomena and to become obligatory passage points in the dynamic of experimental "validity." Platforms may be in a good position both to request laboratory purification on demand and to collect evidence in vivo in order to close a demonstration.

We think that the combination of several experimental configurations (including the three configurations highlighted here) is a crucial element of the enlargement of performative chains in the economy. Many contemporary market innovations connect, at some point, laboratories to platforms to in vivo experiments. The case of the design of spectrum auctions in the United States documented by Guala in his chapter and in Guala (2001), and by Mirowski and Nik-Khah in their chapter, constitutes for us an excellent example of performation—it provides an interesting yet idiosyncratic example of such combinations. Guala, Mirowski, and Nik-Khah analyze the intervention of game theorists and experimental economists in the design and adjustment of the new allocation mechanisms implemented by the FCC (Federal Communications Commission) in 1994. As these authors show, this intervention was far from corresponding to a situation where laboratory results were produced and demonstrated by scientists, then circulated among decision makers who, once convinced, decided to use them as guidance for the construction of a real-scale market—but, in our view, one does not need a scenario as simple as that in order to be able to argue that economics is performative (see Callon's chapter). Rather, what the spectrum auctions seem to show is a situation of cross-alliances between economists and practitioners in which the actors at stake engaged in a purposeful displacement of the laboratory conditions to the in vivo situation. It was not the laboratory result that circulated; it was the laboratory setting itself. Even economists themselves had to circulate, literally: some were hired as professional bidders to perform for bidding companies. Moreover, this movement was the result of intensive compromise and political tinkering in which actors of various kinds, starting with telecommunication companies, engaged in the construction of the experimental market device (the fact that industrial interests were at work in this episode is clear). Matters of laboratory validity were at stake, but demonstration turned also into an exercise of political communication and corporate strategy. This experimental space was not reducible to the sole features of the laboratory. It constituted, in our view, an experimental platform.

Our threefold typology allows for quite a measured understanding of the variable degree of openness of experimental sites and the variable strength of experimental outcomes. In other words, it helps to follow the shifting nature of the circuits of performation. From one type of site to another, the equilibrium between "framing" and "overflowing" (Callon 1998) is managed differently, with different partitions between the "inside" and the "outside." In the laboratory, a rather rigorous framing imposes a tight inside/outside boundary. Overflowing is repressed or ignored. The advantage of the laboratory is clear: the object is proper (appropriate and appropriated) and the manipulative capacities are high. Difficulties arise, however, at the demonstration stage, beyond the laboratory workers. The solution (necessarily brutal) is the transposition of the laboratory itself. With the platform, framing is suppler. The experimental setting takes into account the more acknowledged and probable risks of overflowing. Still, demonstration might fail because some entities have been poorly taken into account, or not taken into account at all. But the transposition is easier than in the case of the laboratory because a negotiation process has been initiated. The experimental device might not be totally open, but it is a shared device. In the case of in vivo experiments, framing is large and wobbly: all the attention is focused on the overflowing. In order to reduce the scope and variety of overflowing, one important strategy consists of limiting intervention as a way of minimizing the effects produced (even if this proportionality cannot be taken for granted). Demonstration is more straightforward because the experimenters are at stake in what is being experimented.

The boundaries between these three types of experimental instances are fuzzy. For instance, a situation in which a laboratory configuration is deeply engaged in "institution building" (see Guala's chapter) can easily be considered as a platform configuration. However, the framing of actors can provide a nuance in differentiating laboratories from platforms. In a platform, actors engaged in the experimentation are typically at stake, that is, they are part of the public to be convinced and play a role in discussing the research outcomes. In a laboratory, recalcitrant voices are framed in a more thorough way; for instance, experimental subjects are disposable after the experiment. In in vivo experiments, issues of public concern are intensified. To some extent, the swing between "matters of fact" and "matters of concern" (Latour 2004) can be found at work in the movements between these three kinds of research configurations.

The performative perspective is a complex one and the study of economic experiments can help to elucidate it. Experiments are a particular instance of performativity. The experimenter performs, in a quite basic sense. She brings things into being by assembling them in a particular manner (in a particular site, through particular trials, and for a particular audience). While the idea of "performativity" often brings about the problem of distance (the distance between a claim and its object), the practice of experimentation explicitly addresses the instruments of convergence—the means of holding things together. An experiment is a crucible in which theories, discourses, practices, interests, and materials can be gathered together and elaborated. Experimental performativity is not exactly about transporting things outside the laboratory, but more about constructing different experimental sites that go beyond the pure laboratory conditions and that redefine (or even abolish) the boundaries between the "inside" and the "outside." This consideration opens ways of analyzing the politics of experimental objects. What are the conditions for these objects to remain open issues or, conversely, to turn into closed facts? Contemporary economies seem to provide a particularly fertile ground to tackle this question. The disputability of economic experiments cannot anymore be restricted (if they ever were) just to the perimeters of epistemological debates or scientific expertise.

Notes

1. Preliminary versions of this chapter have been discussed at the following meetings: EGOS Conference (Ljubljana, 2004), Inside and Outside Markets Workshop (Paris, 2004), Workshop on "The Performativities of Economics" (Paris, 2004), and 4S-EASST Conference (Paris, 2004). We thank discussants and commentators for their valuable suggestions.

2. See Soros (2003) for a remarkable account of a purposefully performative real-scale financial experiment.

3. Economic regulation can be analyzed as an experimental activity to a large extent, as pointed out by Millo and Lezaun (2006).

4. See Boumans and Morgan (2001).

5. These precepts include instructions on how to make clear to experimental subjects that they should try to maximize their reward, that this reward is distinctively dependent on their behavior, and that they should not take into account the behavior of other experimental subjects, unless requested by the experimenter. See Guala's chapter.

6. On the "theory testing" dimension of experimental economics, see Guala (this volume).

7. Interestingly enough, researchers in market microstructure are starting to use the notion of "natural experiment" to refer to situations in where real-scale market events can be monitored as laboratory experiments (control on data and *ceteris paribus*). Specific market architectures, such as electronic order-driven markets, are among the best candidates to provide the conditions for such monitoring.

8. For a remarkable analysis of the diplomacy of early experimental psychology, see Despret (2004).

9. These experiments were innovative in the field and generated a number of contributions to the literature (e.g., Noussair et al. 2002, 2003, 2004).

10. The Vickrey auction is rare, but it is not a pure product of economics. Contrary to a widespread belief, the Vickrey auction format was not invented by Vickrey. Recent research (Lucking-Reiley 2000) has shown that this form of auction has been widely used in philatelic exchanges since the nineteenth century, and that it is not difficult to find among auctioneers the same reasoning as in Vickrey's own demonstration.

11. See Teil and Muniesa (2005) for an account of these experiments based on participant observation.

12. See also Cambrosio et al. (2004) for a network analysis of this kind of configuration.

13. On this episode and on the role of economists in the history of EDF, see also Picard et al. (1985).

14. "Demos" are a particularly relevant form of demonstration in these situations. Rosental (2002) considers "demos" precisely as devices that aim at gathering information from an audience and analyzing its reactions.

15. These kinds of in vivo experiments are common in an environment like the Paris Bourse. See Muniesa (2003, pp. 301–328, 377–392) for other examples and Muniesa (2005) for an account of the early automation of the Paris Bourse in the 1980s.

16. The presence of odd lots in a market is often taken by economists, precisely, as a sign of the presence of small investors in a market place.

17. A second unforeseen effect of the removal of board-lot restrictions was also made visible: a large portion of new incoming orders (former odd lots) were indeed "market orders" (as opposed to "limit orders"), that is, orders without a price limit that were executed immediately against the best available counterparty. This results in a lower congestion of the system, as those orders do not need to be stored in the system's memory.

18. A marketing agency conducting focus groups on bread consumers, a consumerist association performing tests on the composition, prices, and taste of a representative sample of Parisian baguettes, or a retail distributor introducing a new kind of bread in a retail catchment area in order to record consumers' response are more convenient instances of economic experiments, in the sense presented in this chapter.

References

Amin, A., and P. Cohendet. 2004. *Architectures of Knowledge: Firms, Capabilities, and Communities*. Oxford: Oxford University Press.

Barry, A. 2001. *Political Machines: Governing a Technological Society*. London: Athlone Press.

Bockman, J., and G. Eyal. 2002. "Eastern Europe as a Laboratory for Economic Knowledge: The Transnational Roots of Neoliberalism." *American Journal of Sociology* 108(2):310–352.

Boumans, M., and M. S. Morgan. 2001. "*Ceteris Paribus* Conditions: Materiality and the Application of Economic Theories." *Journal of Economic Methodology* 8(1):11–26.

Callon, M. 1998. "An Essay on Framing and Overflowing: Economic Externalities Revisited by Sociology." Pp. 244–269 in *The Laws of the Markets*, edited by M. Callon. Oxford: Blackwell.

Callon, M. 2004. "Europe Wrestling with Technology." *Economy and Society* 33(1):121–134.

Callon, M., P. Cohendet, N. Curien, J.-M. Dalle, F. Eymard-Duvernay, D. Foray, and E. Schenk, Eds. 1999. *Réseau et coordination*. Paris: Economica.

Callon, M., C. Méadel, and V. Rabeharisoa. 2002. "The Economy of Qualities." *Economy and Society* 31(2):194–217.

Callon, M., and F. Muniesa. 2005. "Economic Markets as Calculative Collective Devices." *Organization Studies* 26(8):1229–1250.

Callon, M., and V. Rabeharisoa. 2003. "Research 'in the Wild' and the Shaping of New Social Identities." *Technology in Society* 25(2):193–204.

Cambrosio, A., P. Keating, and A. Mogoutov. 2004. "Mapping Collaborative Work and Innovation in Biomedicine: A Computer-Assisted Analysis of Antibody Reagent Workshops." *Social Studies of Science* 34(3):325–364.

Chamberlin, E. H. 1948. "An Imperfect Experimental Market." *Journal of Political Economy* 56(2):95–108.

Ciborra, C. U. 1996. "The Platform Organization: Recombining Strategies, Structures, and Surprises." *Organization Science* 7(2):103–118.

Cochoy, F. 1998. "Another Discipline for the Market Economy: Marketing as a Performative Knowledge and Know-How for Capitalism." Pp. 194–221 in *The Laws of the Markets*, edited by M. Callon. Oxford: Blackwell.

Collins, H. M. 1985. *Changing Order: Replication and Induction in Scientific Practice*. London: Sage.

Daemmrich, A. A. 2004. *Pharmacopolitics: Drug Regulation in the United States and Germany*. Chapel Hill, NC: University of North Carolina Press.

Despret, V. 2004. *Hans, le cheval qui savait compter*. Paris: Les Empêcheurs de Penser en Rond.

Goswami, M. 2004. *Producing India: From Colonial Economy to National Space*. Chicago: University of Chicago Press.

Guala, F. 1999. "The Problem of External Validity (or "Parallelism") in Experimental Economics." *Social Science Information* 38(4):555–573.

Guala, F. 2001. "Building Economic Machines: The FCC Auctions." *Studies in History and Philosophy of Science* 32(3):453–477.

Guala, F. 2003. "Experimental Localism and External Validity." *Philosophy of Science* 70(5):1195–1205.

Guala, F. 2005. *The Methodology of Experimental Economics*. Cambridge: Cambridge University Press.

Hatchuel, A. 1995. "Les marchés à prescripteurs." Pp. 203–224 in *L'inscription sociale du marché*, edited by A. Jacob and H. Vérin. Paris: L'Harmattan.

Hecht, G. 1998. *The Radiance of France: Nuclear Power and National Identity after World War II*. Cambridge, MA: MIT Press.

Keating, P., and A. Cambrosio. 2003. *Biomedical Platforms: Realigning the Normal and the Pathological in Late-Twentieth-Century Medicine*. Cambridge, MA: MIT Press.

Kim, D.-J., and B. Kogut. 1996. "Technological Platforms and Diversification." *Organization Science* 7(3):283–301.

Knorr Cetina, K. 1981. *The Manufacture of Knowledge: An Essay on the Constructivist and Contextual Nature of Science*. Oxford: Pergamon.

Latour, B. 1987. *Science in Action: How to Follow Scientists and Engineers through Society*. Cambridge, MA: Harvard University Press.

Latour, B. 2004. "Why Has Critique Run Out of Steam? From Matters of Fact to Matters of Concern." *Critical Inquiry* 30(2):225–248.

Latour, B., and S. Woolgar. 1979. *Laboratory Life: The Social Construction of Scientific Facts*, London: Sage.

Lucking-Reiley, D. 2000. "Vickrey Auctions in Practice: From Nineteenth-Century Philately to Twenty-First Century e-Commerce." *Journal of Economic Perspectives* 14(3):183–192.

Lynch, M. 1985. *Art and Artifact in Laboratory Science: A Study of Shop Work and Shop Talk in a Research Laboratory*. London: Routledge.

MacKenzie, D. 2003. "An Equation and Its Worlds: Bricolage, Exemplars, Disunity and Performativity in Financial Economics." *Social Studies of Science* 33(6):831–868.

MacKenzie, D., and Y. Millo. 2003 "Constructing a Market, Performing Theory: The Historical Sociology of a Financial Derivatives Exchange." *American Journal of Sociology* 109(1):107–145.

Madhavan, A. 2000. "Market Microstructure: A Survey.", *Journal of Financial Markets* 3(3):205–258.

Mallard, A. 2000. "La presse de consommation et le marché: Enquête sur le tiers consumériste." *Sociologie du Travail* 42(3):391–409.

Millo, Y., and J. Lezaun. 2006. "Regulatory Experiments: Genetically Modified Crops and Financial Derivatives on Trial." *Science and Public Policy* 33(3):179–190.

Mitchell, T. 1998 "Fixing the Economy." *Cultural Studies* 12(1):82–101.

Mitchell, T. 2002. *Rule of Experts: Egypt, Techno-politics, Modernity*. Berkeley, CA: University of California Press.

Morgan, M. S., and F. Den Butter, Eds. 2000. *Empirical Models and Policy Making: Interaction and Institutions*. London: Routledge.

Muniesa, F. 2003. "Des marchés comme algorithmes: Sociologie de la cotation électronique à la Bourse de Paris." PhD diss. Paris: Ecole Nationale Supérieure des Mines de Paris.

Muniesa, F. 2005. "Contenir le marché: La transition de la criée à la cotation électronique à la Bourse de Paris." *Sociologie du Travail* 47(4):485–501.

Noussair, C., S. Robin, and B. Ruffieux. 2002. "Do Consumers Not Care about Biotech Foods or Do They Just Not Read the Labels?" *Economics Letters* 75(1):47–53.

Noussair, C., S. Robin, and B. Ruffieux. 2003. "De l'opinion publique aux comportement des consommateurs: Faut-il une filière sans OGM?" *Revue Economique* 54(1):47–70.

Noussair, C., S. Robin, and B. Ruffieux. 2004. "Do Consumers Really Refuse to Buy Genetically Modified Food?" *Economic Journal* 114(492):102–120.

O'Connell, J. 1993. "Metrology: The Creation of Universality by the Circulation of Particulars." *Social Studies of Science* 23(1):129–173.

Picard, J.-F., A. Beltran, and M. Bungener. 1985. *Histoire(s) de l'EDF: Comment se sont prises les décisions de 1946 à nos jours*. Paris: Dunod.

Pinch, T. 1993. " 'Testing—One, Two, Three . . . Testing!' Towards a Sociology of Testing." *Science, Technology & Human Values* 18(1):25–41.

Rosental, C. 2002. "De la démo-cratie en Amérique: Formes actuelles de la démonstration en intelligence artificielle." *Actes de la Recherche en Sciences Sociales* 141–142:110–120.

Rosental, C. 2003. *La trame de l'évidence: Sociologie de la démonstration en logique*. Paris: PUF.

Ruffieux, B., and S. Robin. 2001. "Analyse économique de la propension des consommateurs à acheter des produits garantis 'sans OGM' et choix du signal distinctif pertinent." Research report. Paris: INRA-FNSEA.

Say, J.-B. 1841. *Traité d'économie politique, ou simple exposition de la manière dont se forment, se distribuent et se consomment les richesses*. Paris: Guillaumin.

Sims, B. 1999. "Concrete Practices: Testing in an Earthquake-Engineering Laboratory." *Social Studies of Science* 29(4):483–518.

Smith, V. L. 1979. "Experimental Economics: Induced Value Theory." *American Economic Review* 66(2):274–279.

Smith, V. L. 1982. "Microeconomic Systems as an Experimental Science." *American Economic Review* 72(5):923–955.

Smith, V. L. 1989. "Experimental Methods in Economics." Pp. 94–111 in *The New Palgrave: Allocation, Information, and Markets.* edited by J. Eatwell, M. Milgate and P. Newman. London: MacMillan.

Smith, V. L. 1994. "Economics in the Laboratory." *Journal of Economic Perspectives* 8(1):113–131.

Soros, G. 2003. *The Alchemy of Finance.* New Work: Wiley.

Stark, D. 1999. "Heterarchy: Distributing Authority and Organizing Diversity." Pp. 153–179 in *The Biology of Business: Decoding the Natural Laws of Enterprise,* edited by J. H. Clippinger III. San Francisco: Jossey-Bass.

Teil, G., and F. Muniesa. 2005. "Donner un prix: Observations à partir d'un dispositif d'économie expérimentale." Working paper. CSI Working Papers Series 002.

Valdés, J. G. 1995. *Pinochet's Economists: The Chicago School in Chile.* Cambridge: Cambridge University Press.

Vickrey, W. 1961. "Counterspeculation, Auctions, and Competitive Sealed Tenders." *Journal of Finance* 16(1):8–37.

Chapter 7 —————————————————————————

Markets Made Flesh

PERFORMATIVITY, AND A PROBLEM IN SCIENCE STUDIES, AUGMENTED WITH CONSIDERATION OF THE FCC AUCTIONS

PHILIP MIROWSKI AND EDWARD NIK-KHAH

> There are two positions we have to abandon. The first is the idea of
> critique of hard economists, which is intended to show them that
> they are wrong. And the second position is to describe markets just
> to say that they are more complicated than economists or political
> decision makers believe. . . . Let us stop criticizing the economists.
> We recognize the right of economists to contribute to performing
> markets, but at the same time we claim our own right to do the
> same but from a different perspective.
>   (Michel Callon in Barry and Slater 2003, p. 301).

We suspect that the academic formation known as "Science and Technology Studies" (STS) stands poised at a rather crucial crossroads nowadays.
This is not to suggest that STS has ever enjoyed the status of a gaggle of
complacent academics flying in elegant formation, chorusing a shared
agenda and sweet consensus over fundamental issues; nor do we discount
the rather furious controversies that have broken out over the last
decade, ranging from disputes between theoretical perspectives from
within (Pickering 1992) to withering criticism from without (e.g., the late
"Science Wars"). However difficult these contretemps may have seemed
to those who had the misfortune to weather them, we expect they will
pale by comparison to the impending turbulence we think we see looming
just over the horizon. In this chapter, we want to suggest that the future
of STS as envisioned by the Paris School, and lately expressed by their
primary spokespersons Michel Callon and Bruno Latour, if followed to
their logical conclusions, would lead to the eventual dissolution of the
project of STS. It has occurred to us *de temps en temps* that Latour, at
least, might actually have come to welcome such an eventuality,[1] so that
we feel that our assertion need not be regarded as hyperbolic, ominous,
or unwarranted.

   This chapter starts with a local controversy over what has come to be
called the "performativity" of the economy by economists, first broached
by Michel Callon (1998), endorsed by Latour in his most recent book
(2004b, p. 272, n.11), and of late given qualified endorsement by
MacKenzie (see MacKenzie's chapter in this volume; also MacKenzie
and Millo 2003). Far from being a minor development in the sociology
of science, we believe these writings signal the outlines of the prospective
future envisioned by these authors for the role of science studies within
the ecology of the post–Cold War regime of scientific research. In short,
after a long period of silence, STS now has decided it wants to say something about economics. Our complaint about this literature concerns the
content of what is being said about economics. We argue that the crux of
this dispute derives from a systemic intellectual problem STS has had
with the social sciences almost since its inception, one exacerbated by
modern structural changes occurring in the social organization of scientific research in the direction conventionally called "commercialization."
We believe these two phenomena have become juxtaposed in a rather
curious way to produce Callon's version of "performativity," which
turns out (among other things) to be an overture to a prospective
alliance to be struck with neoclassical economists, as illustrated by the
quote that starts this chapter. This version of STS has finally committed
to a particular version of social theory, and we doubt it resembles anything most science studies scholars would find auspicious, once they
come to understand it.
   We fear that this proposed pact with neoclassical economics would
be a prescription for disaster for the field of STS. However, in this
chapter we elect not to argue against the pact on pragmatic grounds;[2]
rather, we propose to first explore what sorts of considerations might
have led such prominent spokesmen for the version of STS formerly
known as "Actor-Network Theory" (ANT)[3] to such a precipitous pass,
and then to subject what seems to be one of their exemplary empirical
instances of "performativity"—the American institution of a certain
specific type of auction to allocate the communications spectrum under
the auspices of the FCC (see Muniesa and Callon's chapter in this
volume; Callon's chapter in this volume; and MacKenzie 2002)—to a
skeptical audit. The net result of this exercise is to begin to reveal just
how little solid in the way of usable analysis can be expected to come
out of the performativity thesis. Therefore, it is a poor argument for a
rapprochement with neoclassical economics, allowing science studies to
get on with its business, although the nature of that business remains
more than a little vague: Is it to "not say anything positive on any state
of affairs" (Latour 2004, p. 42)? Is it to learn humility and passivity, in
that "as social scientists, our duty is not to put some order into the

world" (Latour in Barron 2003, p. 81)? Or is it to capture a slice of the consulting pie (Fuller in Barron 2003, p. 87)? Or perhaps is it merely to secure a niche in the newly commercialized university in the immanent era of globalized privatized science?

The Nagging Inconveniences of the "Social" for STS

Science studies as an academic formation has long harbored a number of reasons to be uncomfortable with the social sciences, and economics in particular.[4] Right off the bat, there are its largely unacknowledged roots in the Marxist "Social Relations of Science" movement of the 1930s (McGuckin 1984). And then there is the underappreciated fact that the British branch of the movement tended to be constituted in opposition to most of what passed for the "sociology of knowledge" in the immediate postwar period, be it Mannheim or Merton or Zilsel. But also significant is the fact that many of its earliest protagonists were recruits from the natural sciences, with little or no formal background in the social sciences. This had the salutary effect of warding off the attacks of the most virulent of initial opponents to science studies, adamant that absent formal training in the natural sciences, outsiders had no business saying anything whatsoever about content, much less the operation, of the modern *Naturwissenschaften*. But it also had the unintended consequence that it left the leaders of the nascent field of research with more than a little ambivalence about the intellectual and professional commitments of the social science disciplines, even those to which they sometimes became formally attached within the hierarchical postwar university, since it was rare that STS achieved the status of a freestanding academic department.

Maybe this seems a little harsh, but we detect a vestige of the knee-jerk disdain of the twentieth-century natural scientist for the human sciences lodged in the interstices of the writings of the science studies community. Possibly much of this skepticism had its legitimate justifications; this is not something that we could begin to parse in this context. Nevertheless, it did have some immediate fallout that is relevant to our present argument. One decay product of the radiant disdain was a tendency to avoid explicit resort to the social sciences for much of any sort of "theoretical" underpinnings for their nominally "sociological" or "anthropological" empirical exercises which constituted the bulk of the work of early STS.[5] The greater the degree to which analysts of science would testify allegiance to an existing orthodoxy in some contemporary social science or other, the lesser the degree of influence they would tend to exercise within STS. A second, more important byproduct stood as corollary: a demonstrated unwillingness to focus on the human sciences as suitable grist for

the STS mill. It would still appear to be the case that the more esoteric
and tough-minded the branch of natural science subjected to STS
scrutiny, the broader the appeal it bore for a generalist STS audience. For
some, this peculiar bias seems to be so obvious that it does not require
any explanation, much less provoke a second thought. As Ian Hacking
wrote, no one would bat an eyelash at a book entitled *The
Social Construction of the Federal Reserve Bank*, but most people would
still get flustered when confronted with a book about the social construction of, say, the quark.

Hence the Groucho-Marxist quality that has pervaded the postwar
history of STS persists: it was never quite content to join any academic
club that would have it as a member. This neurosis goes some distance to
explain some of the more curious episodes in the history of STS, such as
the intense but short-lived fascination with the problem of reflexivity
(Ashmore 1989; Woolgar 1988): why should we believe in the "Social
Construction of X" when you won't apply it to STS? Yet, more to the
point, we are convinced that the disproportionate impact of Bruno Latour's
Science in Action (1987) upon science studies and the subsequent fame
of the Paris School has been very much predicated upon the derivative
hostility expressed within their precincts to the very idea of a "social
explanation" of science, and indeed, social theory *tout court*. Latour, in
his own jocular style, now pleads guilty to removing the word "Social"
from the title of the second edition of *Laboratory Life*, "like faces of
Trotsky deleted from pictures of Red Square parades" (in Ihde and
Selinger 2003, p. 27). Yet the insistence upon the essential illegitimacy of
social science explanation has made its appearance in various ANT man-
ifestos for something approaching two decades now. Some of his texts
are more disparaging than others; our own personal favorite source is
"A Prologue in the Form of a Dialogue between a Student and His
(somewhat) Socratic Professor."[6] A *menu dégustation*: "I have no patience for context"; "I have no patience for interpretative sociologies";
"We are in the business of descriptions. Everyone else is trading on
clichés"; "Organization Studies, Science and Technology Studies, Business Studies, Information studies, Sociology, Geography, Anthropology,
whatever the field, they cannot rely, by definition [of ANT], on any
structuralist explanation"; "So an actor for you is some fully determined
agent, plus a place-holder for a function, plus a bit of perturbation, plus
some consciousness provided to them by enlightened social scientists?
Horrible, simply horrible." The following quotation reiterates a position
that has now become hardened into boilerplate:

> The word "social" . . . does not designate a "kind of stuff" by comparison
> with other types of materials. . . . Are the facts discovered by sociologists and

economists so much stronger than the ones constructed by chemists, physicists and geologists? How unlikely. The *explanandum* does not match the
explananda. More importantly, how could the homogeneous stuff of almighty
"society" account for the bewildering variety of science and technology?
Constructivism, at least in our little field of science and technology, led to a
completely different program than the one repeated *ad nauseam* by critical sociology. Far from trying to explain the hard facts of science with the soft facts of
social science, the goal became to understand how science and technology were
providing some of the ingredients necessary to account for the very making and
the very stability of society. (Latour in Ihde and Selinger 2003, pp. 28–30)

It is imperative to understand the ambitions of the research program
formerly known as "Actor-Network Theory" in order to begin to comprehend its present impasse, and then to grasp further the significance of
the recent initiative by Michel Callon concerning "performativity." Most
would agree that since its inception in the Callon-Latour paper of 1981,
ANT sought to transcend what it regarded as a raft of problematic
dichotomies: nature/society, agency/structure, normative/descriptive, doing/
knowing, and so forth. We agree with Zammito (2004, p. 184) that
Latour aspires to a "first philosophy" which will resolve some basic
problems in science through the promotion of a novel metaphysics; ANT
was his (now superseded?) attempt to insist "the social possesses the
bizarre property of not being made of agency and structure at all, but
rather of being a circulating entity" (Latour 1999, p. 17).

That someone would even attempt such a quest from a position outside philosophy proper is of course incongruous in the extreme, but further comprehension of this is a "social" question that we leave for
another time and place.[7] What is relevant to our current argument is
that ANT has been promoted as a Theory of Everything (in the way that
physicists commonly use the term) that would permit a view from
nowhere, validated, it would seem, entirely on ontological grounds.
Somehow explanation would proceed from neither Nature nor Society,
but would originate neither with agents nor with structure; it would
instead emanate from that vast blank no-man's-land situated between
those portentous dichotomies. The ANT analyst would therefore be
doing social theory without being a social scientist; she would discuss a
generic "Science" without becoming committed to a generic "scientific
method"; she would "follow scientists around" without ever becoming
subject to the disciplinary codes (and pecuniary accounts) regimenting
the scientists. And most paradoxically, although ANT in the conventional sense appears to have no "protagonists" (here we nod toward the
notorious attribution of symmetry between agents and things, given its
strongest statement by Callon), we find ourselves enmeshed in a situation

of unmitigated and incessant aggression and war. "The similarity between the proof race and the arms race is not a metaphor. It is literally the mutual problem of *winning*. . . . It is only now that the reader can understand why I have been using so many expressions that have military connotations. . . . I have used these terms because, by and large, technoscience is part of a war machine and should be studied as such" (Latour 1987, p. 172).[8]

It would take us more space than we have here to demonstrate that there is very little new under the sun, particularly when it comes to social sciences that seek to deny their own status as social sciences in the post–World War II era. In particular, we should like to suggest that many of the philosophical moves of ANT were in fact pioneered within a novel discipline forged in the battles of World War II, which later became the source and inspiration of many of the academic postwar social sciences, from decision theory to artificial intelligence, from management science to computational theory, from logical positivism to American neoclassical economics. That ur-discipline was dubbed "operations research," or OR.[9] While one of the present authors has written extensively on the history of OR elsewhere, all we wish to suggest here is that many of the ambitions and attributes of ANT can be found in relatively developed form in OR, a field which preceded ANT by four decades. This turns out to be pivotal for our understanding the appeal of "performativity."

The hallmark of OR is that it was indeed promoted as a Theory of Everything, which evinced a distinct interest in blurring most conventional ontological boundaries between the Natural and the Social, between agency and structure. It accomplished this in the first instance by projecting physical models onto agglomerations of men and machines or, as proponents of ANT prefer to call it, technoscience, in order to develop a science of war. Crucially, the first operations researchers proudly bore their own contempt for the social sciences, feeling that their training in a natural science endowed them with a portable competence in the "scientific method," which would sanction their pronouncements on any and all mobilizations of men and materiel to achieve specific ends. Furthermore, OR officers managed to "consult" on the conduct of war without having to be responsible for the commands given or even to become subordinate to the military command structure. They were given special dispensations to "follow the colonels around." Some of the earliest use of formal network theory was conducted under the rubric of OR; but more to the point, OR modeled all interactions as trials of strength in the face of duplicitous, propagandistic, and unscrupulous opponents. OR served as the incubator for game theory, which has become the mathematical model of choice in many of the contemporary social and biological sciences, but especially within American neoclassical economics.

Little imagination is needed to detect the family resemblances of OR and ANT. "Actor network theory, and for that matter almost every other approach in STS, portrays science as rational in a means-ends sense" (Sismondo 2004, p. 70). In this, it merely conforms to the usual format of discourse in almost all postwar Western social theory. But as one of Latour's interlocutors has insisted, "Your theory defines the types of actants who define their own worlds in specific ways. You focus on antagonisms and goal-oriented rationality metaphorics" (in Ihde and Selinger 2003, p. 23). This description fits OR at least as well as it captures ANT. As one of the major ANT authors, John Law, has admitted, the experience of working on military aircraft research and development jolted him into realizing that "the terms used by those working on, in and around the project, were more or less the same that I was using to analyze it. . . . [It tended] to make similar analytical and lived assumptions about the proper and perhaps the necessary ways of practicing technology" (2003, p. 6). "Actor-network theory may actually be reinforcing the standard account of science, where science is bounded, separated and superior" (Erickson, 2005, p. 85). It was the operations researchers who pioneered the practice of agnosticism about "defining the actors of the world in advance," as well as intervening to bring about the realities their theories describe, not Monsieur Latour & Cie. Indeed, as one modern game theorist (Binmore 2004, p. 481) testified:

> Cyborgs use an individualistic methodology, because we can thereby construct coherent models that are reasonably tractable. We don't care at what level of organization an individual is defined, provided that its actions are sufficiently consistent that they can be described in terms of maximizing the expected value of a utility function. We know that individual human beings are sometimes irrational, and so don't always behave with the consistency that our theories require of a player. But experiments in the field and in the laboratory confirm that human beings are sufficiently consistent in some contexts that our theories work like clockwork. How else would it be possible for us to use game theory to design the big telecom auctions that recently amazed the world by generating billions of dollars in revenue apparently from nowhere?

So perhaps ANT, along with its proponents Latour and Callon, are not quite so radical or avant garde or as "amodern" as they first appear to those innocent of the proliferation of science/society hybrids incubated within the military in our recent past. Moreover, this brief glimpse of history suggests that there might be closer consanguinal relationships with certain social sciences—and here, we point the finger at *economics*—than might have been suspected, given the self-denying ordinance that ANT has promulgated with regard to the social sciences. Indeed, we think ANT has tended to walk and talk more and more like the stick

figure *homo economicus* from neoclassical economics for quite some
time now. Parenthetically, we are not the first to broach this suggestion;
see McClellan (1996) and Hands (2001, pp. 208–211). Latour has more
recently admitted that his replacement program for ANT, which has
been promoted under a banner that now reads "political ecology," might
appear to outsiders to resemble economics (although not in all
respects).[10] Latour has also echoed Callon's plea quoted at the outset of
this chapter to just stop sniping at the economists:

> There has surely been enough complaining about the economizers' hardness
> of heart. . . . Dangerous as infrastructure, economics becomes indispensable as
> documentation and calculation, as secretion of a paper trail, as modelization.
> (Latour 2004b, pp. 152–153)

Thus the exhortation to "stop worrying and learn to love the Nash
equilibrium" turns out to have been percolating deep within the ANThill
for some time now. The "performativity thesis" merely brings it more
explicitly out into the open. But most convenient for our present argument, we note that *both* advocates of performativity and the modern
economist point to the very same set of events—the FCC spectrum auctions in the US and their European imitators—to provide what they consider to be some of the best evidence supporting their ontological claims.
Game theory, writes MacKenzie, "was no longer an external description
of the auction, but had become—as Callon would have predicted—a
constitutive, performative part of the process" (2002, p. 22).
  Could this provide important clues to the real significance of the doctrine of "performativity"?

Callon on Performativity and Economics

Donald MacKenzie has called Callon's performativity thesis "the most
challenging recent theoretical contribution to economic sociology"
(MacKenzie and Millo 2003, p. 107); yet there persists a fair amount
of dissent and confusion as to its provenance and significance.[11]
MacKenzie himself once sought to situate it within the tradition of British
Austinian ordinary language philosophy, whereas the progenitors themselves have insisted upon its roots in semiotics and, in particular, the
work of Greimas (Latour 2004b, p. 264, n.26; Callon's chapter in this
volume). Unfortunately, neither genealogy seems to do much to clarify this
case; moreover, as has been trenchantly observed by MacKenzie and Millo
(2003, p. 108), neither do the "case studies" that accompanied the initial
enunciation of the thesis in Callon (1998). In that book, Callon asserts
that "the economy is embedded not in society but in economics" (1998,

p. 30), rejecting the assertion that "the market is socially constructed." Later on, he proposes,

> By ridding ourselves of the cumbersome distinction between economics (as a discipline) and the economy (as a thing) and showing the role of the former in the formatting of markets, we find ourselves free from a positivist, or worse still, a constructivist conception of law. Market laws are neither in the nature of humans and societies . . . nor are they the constructions or artifacts invented by social sciences. (1998, p. 46)

From our previous section, we can appreciate that any doctrine which so insistently eschews the very existence of a category called "society" can readily emit such denials; the problem begins with what Callon and the research program previously known as ANT understand as constituting "economics." We believe the reader of *The Laws of the Markets* cannot come away from the experience without the conviction that the authors therein persistently and willfully confuse and conflate "economics" with the activities of accounting and marketing. Indeed, one of our complaints below will be that Callon and his comrades do not look closely enough at the details of what does and does not count as legitimate "economics" among the agents.

Now, partly this may be a cross-cultural phenomenon (although one wonders if the protagonists would even allow such a notion: French academic economics has been the most insistent late twentieth century holdout in the globalization of neoclassical economics as *lingua franca* of the world of commerce and politics); and we are not interested in engaging here in academic "boundary work" between artificially distinguished academic disciplines. Rather, we simply point out that if any pecuniary or catallactic social discourse whatsoever is deemed a manifestation of "economics," and any arbitrary utterance is not to be treated as ontologically distinct from any action falling into the same category, then the performativity thesis becomes trivially true and therefore utterly uninteresting. We might suggest that Callon's chapter in this book skirts very close to this tautology.

We would hope that the research program formerly known as ANT (henceforth, to avoid this phrase, we replace it with the neologism REPFLIKANT) would not want to be caught trafficking in bootless tautologies, and therefore it becomes imperative to try and understand just what is being asserted about "economics" by REPFLIKANTs. We think we can discern four related though distinct propositions in the writings of Callon:

> A. *Markets are a set of diverse, imperfectly linked calculative entities, conceived of sometimes using computer metaphors, and sometimes using Darwinian metaphors.*

Callon insists upon "the prime importance of the existence and hence the formatting of calculative agencies. . . . Several types of organized market exist, depending in particular on the nature of the calculations of the calculative agencies . . . the market is a process in which the calculative agencies compete and/or co-operate with one another" (Callon 1998, p. 32). "Markets evolve and, like species, become differentiated and diversified. But this evolution is grounded in no pre-established logic" (Callon et al. 2002, p. 194).

B. Once A is acknowledged, then there is nothing standing in the way of treating actual existing markets as technoscientific phenomena, in much the same way REPFLIKANT has been treating speed bumps, scallops, and microbes for years now.

"Instead of considering 'laboratory' markets, like those studied in experimental economics, as caricatures of real markets, we can explore how a particular calculative element is simulated in a particular way, and how the relationship between a market simulation in a laboratory and the actual 'scale one' market is constructed" (Callon and Muniesa 2003. pp. 197–198). "The natural and life sciences, along with the social sciences, contribute toward enacting the realities that they describe. The concept of performativity affords a way out of the apparent paradox of this statement" (Callon's chapter in this volume).

C. Once B is acknowledged, then in this instance the "scientists" whom science studies should be "following around" are the certified economists, who in turn have been known to claim that they pursue their prognostications in a space outside the "economy," but in fact by their activities (help) produce it. (Professions that do openly profess to construct economic life, like accountants, lawyers, marketers, government regulators, and corporate managers, would appear not to be suitable targets for this activity, thus they are treated as secondary.) This, it seems, is the effective content of the "performativity" thesis.

"Homo economicus really does exist. . . . He is formatted, framed and equipped with the prostheses which help him in his calculations and which are, for the most part, produced by economics" (Callon 1998, p. 51). "Without economics the market would not exist . . . economics in the wild is not pure economics; it is mixed with engineering, life sciences and management science" (Callon's chapter in this volume).

D. Once C is acknowledged, then it follows that REPFLIKANTs can't go around challenging the legitimacy and efficacy of the economists, any more than they should challenge the legitimacy and efficacy of the natural scientists they formerly shadowed. This means that economic models are to be approached as "true," although with the caveat inserted that it is the economists and their allied actants who make it so. Conveniently, this implies that REPFLIKANTs can go wherever the economists go, forge many of the same alliances, and be engaged by the same client groups that support the economists.

> "Professional economists no longer have the direct or indirect monopoly (assuming they did ever have it) on authorized and legitimate discourse" (Callon et al. 2002, p. 195). "Economists have succeeded in creating alliances with technocrats . . . we can imagine economic sociologists co-operating with actors who are interested in thinking about ways of organizing markets in order to counter the role of the mainstream economists. What is very important is to abandon the critical position, and to stop denouncing economists and capitalists and so on" (Callon in Barry and Slater 2003, p. 301). "I would be reluctant to use this programme to co-operate with governments for the purposes of public administration" (p. 306).

Rather than discussing performativity in a vague way, we believe our restatement sharpens the issue and renders the production of case studies themselves more pointed and apt. In the rest of the chapter, we shall settle on the case identified by Callon, Muniesa, and MacKenzie as one illustration of the program of performativity, the FCC spectrum auctions. Contrary to their intuitions, we shall interpret the case as supporting proposition *A* above, but calling propositions *B, C,* and *D* into question. Foreshadowing, study of the events in question reveals that the evidence does not support the widespread impression, apparently shared by both the economics and science studies communities (Guala 2001; MacKenzie 2002; Parkin 1998), that economists' game-theoretic accounts of auction theory dictated the format of the auctions adopted, and therefore rendered the economists' theories "true" by construction. The auctions as they finally materialized were a curious amalgam of technical achievement and crude politics, but this does not imply that a flat ontology of "actants" and networks would help us understand how they came about. Indeed, in our opinion, so far it has only served to obscure the actual causes of events—in the same manner that the economists themselves have misrepresented the causes. Finally, if science studies scholars do become actively involved in these events, as we hope and advocate, it will be almost impossible not to be put in the position of challenging and criticizing the neoclassical economists. Perhaps they will even find themselves trying to forge alliances with the "public administrators"!

The FCC Auctions

In 1994, the U.S. Federal Communications Commission (FCC) commenced for the first time the practice of auctioning spectrum licenses to the highest bidder. The process of determining the best method of selling off rights to control certain frequencies of the electromagnetic spectrum was marked by another innovation: the heavy involvement of academic game theorists, practitioners of one of the most abstract mathematical fields of economics, often thought to exist at a remove from practical problems. Once the first set of auctions was complete, and the dollar tally came in, those economists gleefully took credit for what was initially perceived as a highly successful performance.[12] Within economics the episode has become the textbook exemplar of the practical relevance of game theory, and it was directly responsible for the choice of at least one Nobel Prize recipient. One of the most interesting uses of the FCC auction results has been to bolster claims concerning successes ensured by the participation of economists themselves in producing the given exercise.

In depicting the FCC auctions as the outcome of an instance of performativity, Callon, Muniesa, and MacKenzie follow the work of Francesco Guala, who has developed an account of the FCC auctions as "a tour de force from [the] preliminary identification of the target to the final product" (2001, p. 455). The US Congress established the "target," which was an auction that would meet several organizational, distributional, and macroeconomic goals. Guala (2001, p. 457) then writes:

> Rational choice theory is an extremely valuable analytical tool in this enterprise. Once the environment (agents' preferences) is defined, it is possible to think of institutional rules as defining a game, which the agents are facing and trying to solve rationally. Ideally, it should be possible to predict exactly what outcome will be achieved by a given mechanism in a given environment by means of equilibrium analysis.

The "final product" was, in Guala's terminology, an "economic machine" which was representative of "our best science and technology" and ultimately judged by Guala to have been a "success" (2001, pp. 473–474). Guala comes closest to the "performativity thesis" in the following quote:

> The real FCC auctions included professional game theorists hired by firms in order to maximize their chances of putting together a profitable aggregation. This way, the classical game-theoretic assumptions of rationality and common knowledge . . . were most likely to be satisfied. . . . The institution assumes behavior with certain formal characteristics on the agents' part, but each agent must also know these assumptions, and must be confident that the other agents are willing and capable of fulfilling the mechanism's requirements. (2001, pp. 474–475).

In his chapter in this volume, Guala qualifies his endorsement of the notion of performativity in ways we cannot consider in detail here.

However, it does seem to us that he still subscribes to the thesis that the auctions were "successful" in ways seconded by Callon—a thesis we do call into question in this chapter.

The "economic machine" account works by focusing on a stylized notion of techniques used in product research and development[13] and derives its evidence almost exclusively from a few published accounts of the major game theory participants. From this vantage point, an R&D process takes place not only in the "abstract realm of theory," but also in the "university lab" (Guala 2001, p. 475), the different locations corresponding to different stages in the systematic process of developing a fully functioning "machine." It is concerned with "building economic machines" (Guala 2001), and with the methods economists use to help accomplish the task. The machine R&D narrative regards itself as following the economists around as they overcome difficulties and obstacles in the development process, some involving the "aims to be pursued" (Guala 2001, p. 455), and others arising from the "peculiar features" of the licenses themselves (p. 458). We do not think it out of place to point out that neither Guala nor Callon has actually followed any economists around in this instance; what they followed instead is a subset of the economists' own self-serving accounts published after the fact, or as related in interviews. Nevertheless, Callon has cited those accounts with approval, preferring only to substitute the neologism "calculative collective device" for "economic machine," and to interpret the R&D process (as he and Muniesa do in their chapter in this volume) as the construction of a "relationship between a market simulation in a laboratory and the actual 'scale one' market" (Callon and Muniesa 2003, p. 198).[14]

This REPFLIKANT account tends to obscure the process of determination of the goals, the methods by which the economists were recruited by interested parties, and the *social* maneuvers used to deal with the presence of incompatible aims. As Callon puts it in the final chapter of this book, "It is not the environment that decides and selects the statements that will survive; it is the statements that determine the environments required for their survival." In good REPFLIKANT fashion, the economic setting deliquesces into a gauzy spider's web of networks, hazy and indistinct. Guala is more concrete but more abstracted, somewhat abrupt in his dismissal of political considerations, equating "political success" with satisfying Al Gore (2001, p. 473 n.30) and referring to the diverse aims of the auctions as "constraints," which evokes the orthodox economists' preferred description of the process: a hint of a maximization program pursued by the disinterested expert that makes everyone better off.

REPFLIKANT accounts tend to foster the impression that they situate conflict over goals, trials of strength over the creation of concepts, and struggles over the recalcitrance of phenomena at the very center of the analysis; as Latour has asserted, it opens up the "black box" shut by the victors. We think that their track record does not support this belief; if everything is an "actant", then it is hard to fill in the dance card with identifiable protagonists. In this particular instance an awareness of the different objectives pursued by the carefully differentiated participants is indispensable to understanding the FCC auctions. In our suggested counternarrative, we identify four salient participant groups: the government (represented by the FCC), a handful of large telecommunications firms, and two groups of economists (game theorists and experimentalists), each possessed of a distinct set of objectives. A blend of theoretical, pecuniary, and political motivations resulted in an auction that did not meet any of the originally stipulated objectives, and yet eventually managed to promulgate the impression that it was, nevertheless, a "success."

Accounts of the FCC auctions frequently begin with a discussion of the stipulation of several goals for the auctions by the U.S. Congress. This is a particularly important feature of the REPFLIKANT narrative, because it gives the impression that the goals for the auctions were propounded independent of the process, before it began. In fact, Congress charged the FCC with:

1. The development and rapid deployment of new technologies, products, and services for the benefit of the public, including those residing in rural areas, without administrative or judicial delays;

2. Promoting economic opportunity and competition and ensuring that new and innovative technologies are readily accessible to the American people by avoiding excessive concentration of licenses and by disseminating licenses among a wide variety of applicants, including small businesses, rural telephone companies, and businesses owned by members of minority groups and women;

3. Recovery for the public of a portion of the value of the public spectrum made available for commercial use and avoidance of unjust enrichment through the methods employed to award uses of that resource; and

4. Efficient and intensive use of the electromagnetic spectrum.

The list represents the outcome of a prolonged debate over the aims of telecommunications policy and the role of the government in promoting access, innovation, and competition. The FCC, however, would eventually take the position that all these complicated considerations involving industrial organization, macroeconomics, and distributional equity should ultimately be reduced to the narrower "economic efficiency," and that the most appropriate goal to pursue should be to award licenses to their highest valued users (FCC 1993, ¶34; 1994, ¶70). One participating economist noted that while the drastic collapse of multiform intentions to drab uniformity elicited some controversy, the decision represented the

adoption of an economist's criterion (Milgrom 2004, p. 4). Our first observation is that the criterion adopted was certainly not universally respected by economists across the board but was broadly consistent with
the preferred understanding of game theorists.

By replacing the goals of Congress with their preferred "efficiency"
criterion, the FCC staff economists were able to ground their policy
analysis in game theory, the true significance of which was not, as has
been commonly asserted, the substitution of political with scientific considerations (McMillan 1994; Milgrom 2004) but rather the enrollment
of a specific group of academic game theorists into the FCC's policy-
making process. Academic game theorists were first invited to participate following the FCC's release of a *Notice of Proposed Rulemaking*
(NPRM) for Personal Communications Services licensing. In every
rulemaking process, the FCC is required to ask for comments from
"interested parties"—broadcasters, telephone companies, equipment
manufacturers, industry groups, government agencies, and to a far less
extent consumer groups—that would be affected by changes in administrative rules. This particular set of rule changes would be met with
heated debate, as Congress punted the most contentious political issues
to the FCC (Galambos and Abrahamson 2002, pp. 163–164). In
response, FCC Chairman Reed Hundt hit upon the idea of calling for the
involvement of game theorists. The appearance in the NPRM of a call
for game-theoretic analysis of auction policy was unprecedented, and it
gave certain interested parties—mostly "Baby Bells"—the idea of hiring
academic game theorists to further their objectives.[15]

Those hoping to ground controversial public policy in uncontentious
science would soon be disappointed, as the enlistment of an increasing
number of game theorists would result in a remarkably diverse array of
inconsistent recommendations concerning auction specifications, and
ultimately a failure to produce any clear-cut recommendation. One plan
for the auction of licenses called for a sequence of English auctions
(Weber 1993a, b), a second called for a sequence of Japanese auctions
(Nalebuff and Bulow 1993a, b), and a third called for simultaneous sales
of all licenses (McAfee 1993a, b; Milgrom and Wilson 1993a, b). (An English auction is one for which prices increase, with the bidder placing the
highest bid winning the item. A Japanese auction is similar to an English
auction, but all participants are considered active bidders until they drop
out. Studies of the formal properties of ascending auctions frequently
substitute the Japanese auction for the English auction.) Some proposals
insisted on admitting bids for bundles of geographically linked licenses
whereas others favored restricting bids to individual licenses only.

The sticking point was that game theory supplied no global discipline
with regard to the type of recommendations tendered: a game theorist

could legitimately support any of an array of auction forms by stressing one set of information properties over others. Game theory is not and has never been a unified theoretical tradition (Mirowski 2002). Game theorists recruited by the FCC did display a penchant to conceptualize an auction as a Bayesian learning game; this tended to focus attention on the release of information during the auction that would better promote knowledge of the licenses' true value, hence promoting efficiency. Generally, the version of game theory favored by the economics orthodoxy dealt with a single good and assumed knowledge of the "true value" of this good to be distributed stochastically among participants; the state of play is conceptualized as information being released during the conduct of an auction, which will promote the participants learning the true value of the good. There was, however, no conventionally accepted standard for determining the precise value of the information provided by a given auction, much less the "true" value of any good, which constituted a problem for attempts to generalize existing results to an environment with multiple heterogeneous goods. Game theorists therefore supported their recommendations not with their own conventionally accepted standards of mathematical proof, but with loose analogy and piecemeal analysis, mired in seemingly clear but frequently contradictory catchphrases such as "the more open, the better," or "make sure participants get quality information," or "avoid free-rider problems."

Participants in the runup to the spectrum auctions have acknowledged that game theory was unable to provide a knock-down argument for the optimality of a specific auction form (McAfee and McMillan 1996, p. 171; McMillan et al. 1997, p. 429). A REPFLIKANT account (following, for example, Muniesa and Callon's chapter in this volume) might attribute the lack of a determinate recommendation to the essential inadequacy of "abstract theoretical reflection" for the development of a working product, but faulting arid abstraction does not begin to get to the heart of the matter. The lack of a determinate recommendation was less a disagreement over the significance of various learning effects than it was a disagreement over the *aims* for the auction. For example, while most economists recognized the potential for a combinatorial auction favorably to assist bidders seeking more than one license, that led some to characterize such assistance as "bias," whereas others deemed it "efficient." While there was ample room for disagreement over the efficiency properties of the auction proposals, firms' narrowly constituted interests clearly played a major role in the policymaking process:

> The business world was fully aware of [the strategic significance of] the rule-making process and had engaged many groups of consultants to help them position themselves. Businesses understood that the rules and form of the auction

could influence who acquired what and how much was paid. The rules of the auction could be used to provide advantages to themselves or to their competitors. Thus, a mixture of self-interest and fear motivated many different and competing architectures for the auctions as different businesses promoted different rules. (Plott 1997, p. 606)

Several firms (TDS, Bell Atlantic and MCI) favored sequential (as opposed to simultaneous) auctions. TDS seemed to favor sequential auctions because they felt it would favor their strategy of acquiring smaller license [sic] surrounding the large markets such as Chicago. They wanted to be sure who would be the licensee in the "hubs" before they bid on the "spokes." Bell Atlantic (BA) and MCI seemed to favor sequential (or a mixed system in the case of BA) auctions largely because they believed that it would be administratively less complex and therefore more likely for the FCC to be able to implement quickly . . . MCI also supported a variant of the Commission's initial proposal to provide for sealed bids for a nationwide combination of PCS licenses, presumably because MCI thought this would facilitate their plan to acquire a nationwide spectrum block. (Kwerel and Rosston 2000, p. 263)

Still others have focused on the interests commonly shared by all prospective bidders:

The gain from efficiency and revenue from allowing package bidding appears to come at some expense to bidders' surplus . . . if the surplus attained is all that is important to the potential participants in an auction, and if efficiency is allowed to take a back seat to self-interest, then bidders should be expected to argue for the simultaneous auction, while the seller should be expected to argue for the inclusion of package bidding. (Ledyard et al. 1997, pp. 656–660).[16]

The most prominent "consultants" used by businesses to "position themselves"—for example, in promoting sequential auctions on behalf of TDS and a mixed system of sequential and simultaneous auctions on behalf of BA, and in arguing against package bidding on behalf of several large telecoms—were the academic game theorists. For this reason, tracing the lack of consensus over the architecture of the auction to conflicting goals established by Congress, or the complicated characteristics of the licenses themselves, or the essential poverty of abstract theorization is insufficient. The main lesson we can take from these observations is that the conflict over architecture mirrors the conflicting interests of those looking to participate.

In an ironic twist, the task of determining the public version of what academic game theory ultimately dictated fell to the FCC. The multiplicity of aims and proposals forced the FCC to display some creativity in conjuring a "consensus" recommendation for the auction form—the simultaneous–multiple round–independent (SMRI) auction—given that this was the one that most economists opposed.[17] Experimental economists appeared to demonstrate that the combinatorial auction was more effective than the SMRI auction. But the SMRI auction did possess the virtue of being broadly consistent with the concerns of a distinct group of large telecoms that were united by their fear of being leapfrogged by MCI, which would assume a commanding position if it acquired a nationwide license.

Working out the details of the never-before-implemented SMRI turned out to require more elaborate competencies and redoubled efforts beyond those deployed in the initial rounds of the public policy-making process. Consequently, experimental economists were recruited to participate in the design of the auction. There persists a widely shared impression that the work of experimental economists was limited to corroboration of theorists' conjectures and determining the relative importance of the various contradictory effects postulated by the game theorists (e.g., McMillan 1994; Milgrom 1995). In actuality, it was the adoption of a seemingly innocuous proposal of some game theorists to computerize the auction that unwittingly endowed experimentalists with their most important role and put the process on track to build some real machines. Though the FCC initially regarded computerization as unnecessarily adding complication to the auctions, the members were ultimately persuaded by an experimental auction demonstration at the California Institute of Technology (Cal Tech) that the provision of auction software would be a relatively straightforward matter. The FCC would soon discover otherwise, as attempts to produce a prototype auction failed.[18] The FCC was thereby induced to seek help from the experimental economists responsible for the original Cal Tech demonstration, and it devolved to them to accept major responsibility for coding the auction. Thus computerization—and not the pesky abstractness of the theory—prompted the inclusion of experimental economists.

What had started off as a mere sideshow rapidly managed to become the main arena of the contest. The decision to computerize the auction would have several unintended consequences; one among them was to effect a change in the criteria pursued. This point requires careful development because every single account until now of the FCC auctions has failed to take note of it. Experimentalists did not view themselves primarily as software engineers or troubleshooters or *bricoleurs*, but rather as a distinct professional group in possession of their own ideas about how to design markets.[19] Because their ideas concerning markets would come to influence the goals pursued for the auctions, it is necessary to review how experimentalists differed from game theorists. For our present purposes, it is possible to reduce the differences between game theorists and experimentalists to three primary areas of disagreement:[20]

1. *Whereas game theorists tended to represent markets as Bayes-Nash games, experimentalists represent them as combinatorial optimization procedures.* Experimentalist market theory has roots in Walrasian general equilibrium theory, and particularly in efforts searching for determinate, Pareto-optimal, price-adjustment processes. They were particularly concerned with the existence of a competitive equilibrium in the presence of complementarities, and they noted that complementarity produces a nonconvexity in the consumption set, which, if serious enough, rules out the existence of a competitive equilibrium (Banks et al. 1989, pp. 2–3). In the absence of a competitive equilibrium prices no longer suffice to coordinate agents to optimal allocations (Ledyard et al. 1997, p. 656). The attainment of competitive equilibrium is generally not a concern for game theorists.[21] What absorbs their attention, rather, is the putative mendacity of participants, who are the ultimate sources of information about the economy. For game theorists all the action happens in the mind of the participant, modeled as an inductive machine assumed to "learn" through Bayesian inference; for experimentalists most of the action happens in the price-adjustment process, conceived as a price-discovery device.

2. *Game theorists want to improve the "price system" by increasing the amount of information it provides, whereas experimentalists seek improvements in its capacity for information processing.* Game theorists focus on methods for discovering and publicizing the information that they assume to be already dispersed in the minds of participants. While experimentalists are undeniably interested in the same information, they focus their efforts mostly on finding procedures that will make the best use of this increased access to information. This focus on construction of a tractable optimization program (a difficulty for integer-programming problems because they are computationally burdensome) encourages experimentalists to treat the market rules as an algorithm. There is no such equivalent imperative for game theorists, who provide only the most stylized descriptions of markets; they conceive of their machines abiding inside peoples' heads. While experimentalists tend to "black box" the mind to study features of the exchange process, game theorists black box the exchange process to focus on treating the mind as an inference engine.[22] As a consequence, it has been the experimentalists who have tended to foster appreciation of the importance of the sheer diversity of market forms.[23]

3. *Whereas game theorists generally judge the success of a market by how it assists learning, experimentalists tend to judge it by the reliability of the successful execution of trades.* This is reflected in the different criteria used by the two groups (see Table 7.1). Game theorists pursue the criterion of *ex post* Pareto optimality (the bidder who would create the most value from owning the license wins it); experimentalists pursue *ex ante* Pareto optimality (the

Table 7.1

Rival Approaches to Market Design

	Game Theory	*Experimental Economics*
Market	Bayes-Nash auction game	Combinatorial optimization problem
Solution	Increase information	Improve information processing
Welfare criterion	*Ex post* Pareto optimality	*Ex ante* Pareto optimality

bidder who values the license highest at the outset acquires it). These differences in criteria are responsible for different styles of arriving at a "solution": the experimentalists' prescription is frequently described as the product of a balancing act between "full central processing" of information, which relies on the processing algorithm to use the information, and "decentralization," which relies more on participants to use information. Because game theorists are concerned only with the "processing" that takes place in the heads of the participants, they are concerned only with producing a form that maximizes the amount of information given to the participants.

The controversy that erupted over the combinatorial auction during the intermediate phase provides perspective from which to observe the rival approaches at work. Both game theorists and experimentalists were concerned with the presence of interdependent values of different geographic spectrum allocations, but they understood the problem they posed in a radically different way. Experimentalists argued that the only sort of market algorithm that could be counted on to produce a dependably "optimal" allocation of licenses (by arriving at a competitive equilibrium price vector) required a method for collecting information on the value of *packages*, or combinations of licenses, in addition to the value of individual licenses. They recommended package bidding, and they devoted much of their efforts to finding what they considered the best method of processing the information to ensure convergence of prices to the competitive equilibrium under such a regime. By contrast, the game theorists who opposed the combinatorial auction argued that merely asking for information on package values would actually *reduce* the amount of information collected.[24] While citing what they believed were the informational advantages of their preferred auctions (in the sense of reducing probabilistic uncertainty), the game theorists did not feel compelled to discuss what would be done with this increased information, preferring instead to leave it up to participants to decide how to benefit from this information.

The experimentalists ultimately failed to convince the FCC to resort to the combinatorial auction, but when charged with the computerization of the auction, they took over responsibility for determining the criteria the algorithms would meet. Banished were concerns with issues of learning, and the criterion of *ex post* Pareto optimality came to be trumped by "technical" issues of computation and practical imposition of coordination and the criterion of *ex ante* Pareto optimality. But while the participation of experimentalists would significantly diminish game theorists' effective participation in the process of "putting flesh on the markets," the experimentalists actually promoted the success claims of game theorists. In coding and testing the market, experimentalists encountered and resolved nagging inconsistencies and ambiguities of the SMRI. This work looked very much like the "bugchecking" that characterizes the manufacture of all computer programs—a practical activity directed at the development of an operational product—but actually freighted in a theoretical element as well. A good example of "theory patching" by experimentalists is a feature of the auctions commonly attributed to the game theorists Paul Milgrom and Robert Wilson, the so-called activity rule that speeds the close of the auction by progressively lowering a firm's eligibility for licenses until it is exactly equal to the bundle the firm intends to purchase. Although the concept of speeding up a game has no exact analogue in game theory, the acceleration of convergence corresponds much more directly to the "stability of equilibrium" problem in general equilibrium theory. The activity rule as finally built into the auction, then, was a response to a perceived instability problem, and a relatively crude response at that. More generally, because they conceived themselves as theorizing the core institutional features of "who should communicate with whom and how, as well as who should take various actions and when" (Ledyard 1995, p. 116), experimentalists were prepared to offer responses to other questions:

> Can one wave and bid at the same time? What happens if you withdraw at the end of the auction: should the auction remain open so the withdrawal can be cleared? How shall a withdrawal be priced? How is eligibility of everyone influenced by withdrawals? Should it go up so anyone can buy the item released to the market? How is eligibility influenced by increments: should eligibility be lost if increments are reduced because of lack of bids? (Plott 1997, p. 629)

From a game-theoretic perspective, the issues raised by such questions might seem to touch only on software engineering (Milgrom and Wilson 1993a, p. 21), but experimentalists understood methods of restricting communication and action (i.e., under what circumstances should one be able to bid?) as the proper object of theory.

To review our inordinately telegraphed summary, the performativity narrative informs us that the FCC sets the goals for the economists to attempt to achieve, subject to congressional constraints. The economists imagine a world, and then set about to make their words and equations flesh. As Callon puts it in his chapter in this book: "To make a formula or auction system work, one has to have tools, equipment, metrological systems, procedures, and so on. . . . A host of professions, competencies, and nonhumans are necessary for academic economics to be successful. . . . They are engaged in the construction of a world described and performed by statements and models that we readily agree belong to the world of economics, in the strict sense of the word." Well, no: we don't all agree. Our narrative finds fault with such an account for its portrayal of the economists, telecoms, and government officials as a single undifferentiated team united in pursuit of the pragmatic operability of a "machine." REPFLIKANTs have misunderstood what economics was, as well as how societies do and do not work. The FCC thought the economists might help them exert some control over the process of the allocation of spectra, but maybe they were a bit naive. Game theorists and experimentalists were not necessarily "on the same page," seeking to bridge the inevitable gap between pure science and its applied contexts. Until very late in the game, nobody was really sure about where the machine would even be situated (Between the ears? On the silicon chip? In the patented algorithm? At the corporate merger specialist's office?), much less about what it accomplished. Everyone was busily trying to recruit everyone else, although some "actants"—the telecoms—were unequivocally "more equal" than everyone else. Once the diversity of aims and understandings has been accounted for, we are left with a story in which some economists managed to redefine the goals for the government to achieve, subject to the telecoms' veto, while letting a different set of economists bask in the limelight and take the credit. Is this an instance of "performativity," or is it rather another instance of bigger forces determining the economic outcomes while masking their activities with a fog of learned disputation and superfluous mathematics, a hoary old chestnut that Latour professes to despise? Or, more disturbingly, is the thesis of "performativity" yet another way to help mask those very same forces?

Perhaps, though, by focusing so insistently upon the narrative structure of the REPFLIKANT account, we have missed out on the REPFLIKANTs' true aims. Callon and Muniesa point out "the increasing role of R&D and experiments in the conception of markets or in the regulation of interventions on their modes of functioning," and suggest it is part and parcel of economics becoming a "truly experimental science" (Callon and Muniesa 2003, pp. 226–227; see their chapter in this book). But this message was surely not intended purely as a contribution to the methodology of the social sciences. Experimental economics has already found a secure niche within the economics profession and certainly has no need of science studies to provide it with some convenient rationale. (No one harps on "science" more than experimental economists, as Guala emphasizes in his chapter.) Rather, Callon is actually more interested in engaging in "R&D," largely because he wants to argue "the role of the sociology and anthropology of economics is precisely to design tools and to provide actors with such tools" in order to "influence or structure institutions" (Callon in Barry and Slater 2002, p. 300). What Callon seems to be doing is arguing for creation of a space for his preferred disciplinary reference groups to participate in "social engineering." But why should we expect that science studies scholars would prove any more nimble than the game theorists, or any less naive than the FCC?

It should be clear from our account that much redirection of goals takes place in the process of social engineering, but only by those who have something to offer in the way of vision and resources to the interested parties. Who, then, will sponsor the REPFLIKANTs' performance? And what exactly do they bring to the table? Game theorists brought to the table more than expertise in game theory, and on occasion became involved in the auction process very directly. One participating game theorist reported:

> On the eve of the FCC PCS spectrum auction #4, the author made a television appearance on behalf of Pacific Bell telephone, announcing a commitment to win the Los Angeles telephone license, and successfully discouraging most potential competitors from even trying to bid for that license. (Milgrom 2004, p. 23 n.23)

The lesson has sunk in: game theorists have gleefully noted *The Economist*'s conclusion that "for the firms that want to get their hands on a sliver of the airwaves, their best bet is to go out first and hire themselves a good game theorist" (1994, p. 70; quoted in McAfee and McMillan 1996, p. 159).

Game theorists have been loudly trumpeting the success of the FCC auctions for over a decade now, leading directly to the explosion of the subfield of "auction theory." And their claims have gone more or less unchallenged despite considerable evidence piling up in the interim to the contrary. The original congressional mandates have of course gone by the board, conveniently forgotten. Many businesses buying licenses defaulted on their down payments (Murray 2002, pp. 274–275), leading to considerable "administrative delay" in reawarding licenses.[25] The lion's share of licenses won by "small" and "entrepreneurial" businesses went to entities bankrolled by large telecoms, representing a failure to get licenses into the hands of a "wide variety of applicants."[26] The auctions have not lived up to their promise to promote "rapid deployment [in] rural areas," as both large telecoms and smaller firms have tended to concentrate their effort on large metropolitan areas (Copps 2004; Meister 1999, pp. 76–77). Overall, the allocation of licenses produced by the auctions proved to be unstable, as the industry has gone through a spate of mergers and acquisitions and telecom failures, ultimately leading to a high degree of license concentration (Murray 2002, pp. 289–291). True, the auctions did capture a tidy sum for the government coffers, but perhaps they did so at the expense of any solid foundations for the economic health of the industry over the medium term.

Indeed, there might be an altogether different way of coming to grips with the "performativity" thesis, one that seems not to have been intended by the REPFLIKANTs. The operant question is not "How did economists come to make their theories 'true' through their active interventions in the economy?" The better question might be "How is it that the game theorists continue to make their characterization of the 'successes' of the FCC auctions stick, given the mounting evidence to the contrary?" Isn't all this attention trained on the fine points of the auction setup just missing the forest for the trees?

Only a mind disposed to conspiratorial thinking, though, will believe that the "success of the FCC auctions" story is held together entirely by the mesmerizing words and numbing mathematics (no matter how loudly trumpeted) of a few game theorists. (REPFLIKANTs are loathe to discuss "beliefs.") Rather, the story lives on because the FCC policy-making process resulted in a compromise among differently constituted parties—not among different governmentally generated goals, as some would have it—whose interests developed over the course of the auctions. Not every group got everything they wanted, but the compromise did leave all groups thinking they were better off.

Observers have tended to frame the SMRI auctions as a victory over the lobbying power of large companies, but they have failed to grasp the reasons why certain large telecommunications firms would voluntarily extol the FCC's "highest valued user" criterion, so long as it was interpreted as "willingness and ability to pay the most" and they were not required to pay as much as they were willing and able. Where the interests of large firms were opposed to one another there were winners and losers: for instance, the rejection of the combinatorial auction would disappoint some of the Baby Bells. In a struggle that pitted large telecoms against one another, the Baby Bells succeeded in knocking MCI out of the auction, a direct result of the rejection of the combinatorial auction (Thelen 1995).[27] Plans to bring small companies and entrepreneurs into the industry came to grief as the vast majority of spectrum licenses fell to large telecoms. But lacking any significant advocacy machinery (one artifact of pledging troth to the Magic of the Market), the concerns of the smaller telecoms went mostly unheard.[28]

Game theorists discovered early in the process that "it will be possible to label the license auction a 'success' no matter what happens" (Weber 1994). It certainly was, as one participant noted, "a huge success for the auction theorists involved" (Cramton 2002, p. 3). There were professional benefits: before the auctions "the status of game theory within economics was a hotly debated topic," but six years later, "the US National Science Foundation . . . featured the success of the US spectrum auctions to justify its support for fundamental research in subjects like game theory" (Milgrom 2004, p. 1). A decade later, there is still residual skepticism about the "applicability" of game theory (Rubinstein 2001). The many game theorists who disagreed with Milgrom and Wilson nevertheless found it to their advantage to close ranks to make sure that the lesson became standard curriculum: game theory can deliver to clients a valuable service. One of the most interesting upshots of the spectrum auctions was the development of companies—with many of the key participant game theorists taken on as partners—devoted to the construction of markets.[29]

Experimentalists muted the extent of the rivalry inherent in their approach and accepted their public role as theory testers and technical experts.[30] Experimentalists, too, represented a field that had only recently attained respectability in economics (which most would date from the 1990s), and they appreciated the wisdom of gaining support through cultivation of their own set of client groups. But in the case of the spectrum auctions they were limited by the client groups that had hired them—the NTIA (National Telecommunications and Information Administration, the U.S. federal agency responsible for managing government spectrum use) and the FCC (to whom they initially tried to sell a combinatorial auction). Though their clientele had permitted them the freedom to propose market forms that otherwise would not have been admissible, they were not the 500-pound gorillas that the telecoms were, and therefore the experimentalists were not perceived as ultimately having a substantial input into the auctions. By acquiescing in this version of events they were able, eventually, to incorporate themselves into later design processes and maintain their assertion of a separate tradition of market design (Roth 2002).

The government, too, enjoyed short-term benefits from the auctions. Tens of billion of dollars went into the treasury without the need to perturb the taxpayer. The wall of the FCC chairman's office displays a fake check in the amount of $7,736,020,384 made from "The Personal Communications Services Industry" to "The American Taxpayer," while a trophy case exhibits a note from Al Gore, clearly spelling out the importance of auction revenues: "For the FCC Auction Team—Thanks for creating hundreds of millions of dollars—out of thin air—for the federal government!" (Day and Tran 1997, p. 81). The strangest aspect of the efforts spent trumpeting the revenues of the auctions was that revenue maximization was the only goal that Congress explicitly originally ruled out as a basis for telecom policy. Furthermore, revenue was not really "maximized." Prior to the auction, large bidders—with the approval of the FCC—maneuvered to reduce competition by forming "mega-alliances" (Galambos and Abrahamson 2002, p. 170). During the auction, bidders were able to exploit the openness of the SMRI auction to limit competition for licenses (Cramton and Schwartz 2000; Weber 1997). Perhaps one of the biggest advantages from the vantage point of the FCC was the appearance of putting the screws to the industry it was charged to regulate in the public interest, all the while bringing congressionally mandated policy changes back in line with their wishes and intentions. It was, as they say in business schools, a win-win situation.

Bringing "Society" Back In

The time has come to try to make sense of all the talk about construction and performativity, specifically with regard to the relationship of science studies to economics. It should be obvious by now that we find ourselves unable to agree with Latour that "political ecology [his current neologism for REPFLIKANT] alone is finally bringing the intrinsically political quality of the natural order into the foreground" (2004b, pp. 27–28). The fact that Natural Order is dragooned to political purposes is old news, at least as old as Leviticus (Douglas 1984, 1986). The fact that order, natural or otherwise, is made, not found, is equally unprepossessing. What bothers us is that REPFLIKANTs seem uninterested in the details of how order is wrought. It seems to us that for the bulk of the history of the neoclassical orthodoxy in economics, the comparison of the price system to a natural mechanism existed precisely in order to repress both these inconvenient facts (Mirowski 1989). In the neoclassical tradition, Markets were Natural, pitched somewhere beyond the bounds of the social. The sea change, if indeed one can speak in such terms, has come about only recently, when neoclassical economists have conceived of the ambition to *fabricate* markets, and not simply treat them as States of Nature. This has created all sorts of tensions and barely acknowledged contradictions in their projects and self-image (Mirowski forthcoming). It appears that the REPFLIKANTs, and Callon in particular, view this as a golden opportunity to bring the economists round to their own program, by getting them to see the attractions of a "constructivist" approach. The alliance is made all the more plausible by the very real family resemblances between REPFLIKANT and modern neoclassicism, due to the fact both share a consanguinal ancestry with operations research, and both nurture a jaundiced opinion of society, as indicated above. REPFLIKANTs apparently believe that once the economists are brought to a more refined level of appreciation for the nature of science, and acknowledge that their theories are powerful because they make them so, then they will graciously make room for science studies to have its say.

Two or three things are wrong with this glorious vision of the radiant future. The first is that the neoclassical story is so persistently flawed that it cannot be made to "work" for much longer than it takes to come up with another (possibly contradictory) story to take its place. Over the course of the twentieth century alone the neoclassical orthodoxy with regard to its core price theory has "flipped" at least three times (Marshallian supply & demand/ Walrasian general equilibrium/Nash non-cooperative equilibrium), not to mention a host of further slapdash alternatives. The spectacle has been, if anything, far less dignified than Neurath's Boat. The second is that the neoclassical school has nonetheless maintained its appearance of monolithic continuity and placid confidence not due to anything particularly conceptual that the economists have said or done; it is rather more directly attributable to more durable structures like the nation-state, the corporation, and the military. We have seen from our retelling of the saga of the FCC spectrum auctions that only when you leave out the government and the telecoms on the one hand, and that notorious shape-shifter the computer on the other, can you conceive of the auctions as the result of the free play and creative tinkering on the part of the economists, even folding into the account a little help from their friends. It is that despised entity Society and its doppelganger Nature that lend rigidity and structure to what otherwise might seem a fluid and circulating ether. We stress *this is not at all isomorphic to the performativity thesis,* at least as we have attempted here to render it precise.

But if Society may not so easily be banished, then perhaps it follows that the REPFLIKANTs are not quite so free themselves to forge alliances and pursue their constructivist programs as they wish. For instance, the very idea that neoclassical economists would consort openly with the REPFLIKANTs, much less be willing to share their sources of support with them, appears to us risible. American-trained economists are notoriously allergic to self-reflection and deign to learn anything about the other social sciences only as a prelude to moving in as an occupying power. Science studies scholars are kidding themselves if they ever think that the present orthodoxy in economics would ever consent to treat them as equals, much less permit REPFLIKANTs to horn in on their resources. At best they will end up as indentured apprentices to the real apologists.

Therefore, returning to our quadripartite characterization of REPFLIKANT, we agree with proposition *A* that much of economic theory is predicated on computer metaphors and tends to approach markets as calculative devices (Mirowski forthcoming). However, recourse to scientific metaphors does not dictate that (*B*) economic theory can be approached in the same way that other technoscientific phenomena have been framed within science studies. Too much concentration on machinic metaphors tends to distract critical attention from some of the most important social processes going on underneath, as we argued with respect to the FCC auctions. Furthermore, isolating the economists as the key protagonists to "follow around" (*C*) again tends to distract attention from those who may be the major players involved in the construction and shoring up of the "economy." In the case of the FCC auctions, it led both Callon and Guala to ignore the pivotal role of the telecoms in orchestrating the outcome, not to mention slighting the actual intellectual history of game theory and the sad saga of the cooptation of the FCC. We thus conclude that the economists were hardly the "immobile mobiles" that Callon makes them out to be. Finally, it seems that prescription *D*—that science studies make a pact with the neoclassical economists—is at least as potentially disastrous as the alliance that the FCC thought it was forging with the game theorists. Helping promote the fiction of *homo economicus* might have all sorts of blowback for science studies, which needs to be thought through much more carefully. It might turn out to be Foucauldian, as Guala suggests in his chapter in this volume. In our view, it might even end up as prettified neoliberalism decked out in new rags. When actants begin to believe their own spin, then they are ripe for exploitation.

Notes

1. See, for instance, Latour (2004a, 2002). However, one does not get that impression from Latour (2004b).

2. Although one of us has done something similar for the modern predicament of the philosophy of science (see Mirowski 2004). To prosecute the argument on a purely philosophical level, as has been the wont of Latour for more than a decade now, would actually clash with one of our reasons for rejecting ANT in the first place, as we argue below in the conclusion.

3. For Latour's (tongue-in-cheek?) repudiation of this label, see his 1999 and 2002 papers. Callon in his 2003 interview also seems unwilling to resort to this designation. Nevertheless, it still rates an entire chapter under that heading in a recent STS textbook (Sismondo 2004).

4. Here we wish to register our gratitude to Steve Fuller, who has been one of the few science studies scholars to insist that this stands as one of the endemic problems within STS (see Fuller 2000a, b; Barron 2003).

5. We wish to insert two qualifiers to what may seem an inflammatory assertion. First, we wish to acknowledge we are aware of some important counterexamples to the generalization—David Bloor's use of Durkheim and Mary Douglas; Michael Lynch's use of Garfinkel's ethnomethodology—and possibly a few others. Nevertheless, we insist this assertion will elicit assent in most cases. Second, we are also aware that major disciplinary journals in sociology and anthropology published many important STS papers—but the reasons behind this phenomenon would themselves be an interesting subject for sociological investigation.

6. The quotations are from Latour (2002) and a slightly altered published version (2004c).

7. Latour, as usual, is candid on this issue: "Although I teach sociology, I have always considered myself as a philosopher at heart" (in Ihde and Selinger 2003, p. 15).

8. The current attempt unilaterally to "declare peace" by peremptorily swapping "democratic" for military metaphors in (Latour 2004b) deserves its own consideration but would take us too far afield from our current concerns.

9. The argument linking the history of OR to the above social sciences can be found in Mirowski (1999, 2002, 2004).

10. "To all appearances, however, [economics] deals with all the topics we have evoked up to now under the name of political ecology. It too bears on groupings of humans and nonhumans . . . it too seeks to take into account the elements that it has to internalize in its calculations; it too wants to establish a hierarchy of solutions, in order to discover the optimum in the allocation of resources; it too speaks of autonomy and freedom. . . . Apparently, then, the collective that we have deployed does no more than rediscover the good sense of political economics" (Latour 2004b, p. 132). Latour then goes on to denounce aspects of what he understands as modern economics because of its naturalism, which he believes he has escaped.

11. See, for instance, Slater (2002), Miller (2002), Fine (2003), and the contributions to this volume.

12. Many aspects of this sequence of events will be related in only the most cursory manner in this chapter. However, they are covered in the detail one has come to expect from science studies in Nik-Khah (2005). This doctoral dissertation relies on the FCC's notices, reports, and orders and the unpublished affidavits, reports, and responses of the other principals to construct an unexpurgated account of the circumstances surrounding the participation of academic economists in the FCC auctions.

13. For instance, Guala conflates the way a Walrasian theorist uses the terminology of "mechanisms" with the way it is used by philosophers of science such as Nancy Cartwright and John Dupré. The terminological conflation is not harmless, we might suggest. A better history of postwar mechanism design in economics can be found in Lee (2004) and Nik-Khah (2005).

14. It should be mentioned that Guala appears to have different aims than the REPFLIKANTs. Guala believes that "interpretations of a scientific theory (in the natural and the social sciences) should take applied science as their point of departure" (2001, p. 453), and uses that method to provide a philosophically motivated intervention to the debate over rational choice theory. His argument is that

rational choice theory can be made to work with an understanding of its "real capacities." Guala (in his chapter in this volume) also distances himself from the REPFLIKANT account in various other respects, which would lead us too far afield in the present context.

15. Here we would like to register a demurrer with Guala's chapter in this volume. He makes it seem as though the telecoms hired the economists merely to help them "bid properly" or reconfigure their corporate representatives into a better *homo economicus*. We, by contrast, insist the telecoms recognized that the *entire process of defining a "market solution" was up for grabs*, and that game theorists might be useful in helping skew the whole process in their direction. The narrower perspective is more characteristic of the economists' own versions of events.

16. It is important to note that while some firms did favor limited use of package bidding, or a limited combinatorial auction, no firm favored the type tested by Ledyard, Porter, and Rangel. Only the NTIA, a governmental agency, supported their proposal.

17. While Guala reflects current beliefs in stating that only a "minority of economists favour the combinatorial one over the simultaneous ascending one" (2001, p. 465 n.20), at the time most participating economists were in favor of some form of combinatorial auction. The reader interested in a detailed discussion of the FCC's decision-making process is referred to Nik-Khah (2005).

18. The extent of this failure is on vivid display in the experimentalists' report to the FCC of their tests of the auction software (Ledyard et al.1994).

19. There is a relationship between this observation and the point made by Galison (1997) that experimentalists as a group have conceptual traditions themselves not determined by the beliefs of theorists. The route of the experimentalists to market design through Walrasian mechanism design (and not game theory) is discussed by Lee (2004).

20. The full contrast is provided by Nik-Khah (2005). Guala (2001, p. 466) inadequately attempts to reconcile the opposed approaches under the rubric of "personality robustness" versus "environmental robustness."

21. There has been considerable misunderstanding of this point. For example, Guala tends to conflate Nash game theory with Walrasian general equilibrium theory: "Complementarities are one of economists' nightmares, because models of competitive markets with goods of this kind in general do not have a unique equilibrium and are unstable. No theorem in auction theory tells you what kind of institution will achieve an efficient outcome" (2001, p. 458). The ramifications of complementarity for uniqueness and stability have no place in auction theory, only in general equilibrium theory. However, one should admit that textbooks often elide this distinction to foster the impression of the unity of microeconomics.

22. Game theorists displayed no appreciation of the computational features of the market. The ways in which experimentalists tend to neutralize the vagaries of the minds of their subjects are discussed in Mirowski and Lee (2003).

23. This case is made with greater specificity by Mirowski (forthcoming).

24. The argument propounded by game theorists is in the form of an analogy with the well-known "free-rider" problem. There was considerable dispute

among economists whether this was a general problem of combinatorial auctions (McMillan 1994, p. 156) or the artifact of a particular representation (Chakravorti et al. 1995, p. 364).

25. The process of reauctioning finally concluded in February 2005—a full decade after the auctions commenced.

26. Commenting on the success of large companies in displacing and coopting small and entrepreneurial firms, one anonymous FCC official candidly observed that "this certainly does make us look like a bunch of idiots" (Labaton and Romero 2001).

27. MCI decided instead to partner with Nextel in a plan considered by many to offer the best chance for forming a nationwide network. However, the deal eventually fell through.

28. The lack of the small telecoms' voice became apparent with a well-publicized rift within the Cellular Telecommunications and Internet Association (CTIA), the major industry group for wireless telecommunications (Carlson 2000).

29. Market Design Incorporated (http://www.market-design.com/) "offers consulting services in the design of auction markets." Criterion Auctions (http://www.criterionauctions.com/) "provides strategic advice to governments who design auctions or firms who participate in those auctions." And Spectrum Exchange (http://www.spectrum-exchange.com/) boasts it is "creating value through the efficient exchange of spectrum."

30. A prime example of such playing down is found in the words of the experimentalist Charles Plott, who did not fault game theorists for their inability to account for "the complex ways in which the rules interact, and the presence of ambiguities," but did find fault with the "language of lawyers and those writing policy," noting that it "is not precise from the point of view of game theorists" (1997, pp. 627–628). He could just as easily have replaced "lawyers and those writing policy" with "game theorists" and "game theorists" with "market designers."

References

Anon. 1994. "Revenge of the Nerds." *The Economist*, July 23, p. 70.

Ashmore, M. 1989. *The Reflexive Thesis*. Chicago: University of Chicago Press.

Banks, J., J. Ledyard, and D. Porter. 1989. "Allocating Uncertain and Unresponsive Resources: An Experimental Approach." *RAND Journal of Economics* 20:1–25.

Barron, C. 2003. "A Strong Distinction between Humans and Non-humans Is No Longer Required for Research Purposes: A Debate between Bruno Latour and Steve Fuller." *History of the Human Sciences* 16:77–99.

Barry, A., and D. Slater. 2003. "Technology, Politics and the Market: An Interview with Michel Callon." *Economy and Society* 31:285–306.

Binmore, K. 2004. "A Review of Philip Mirowski's *Machine Dreams*." *Journal of Economic Methodology* 11:477–483.

Callon, M., Ed. 1998. *The Laws of the Markets*. Oxford: Blackwell.

Callon, M., and B. Latour. 1981. "Unscrewing the Big Leviathan." Pp. 277–303 in *Advances in Social Theory and Methodology*, edited by K. Knorr-Cetina and A. Cicourel. London: Routledge & Kegan Paul.

Callon, M., C. Méadel, and V. Rabeharisoa. 2002. "The Economy of Qualities." *Economy and Society* 31:194–217.

Callon, M., and F. Muniesa. 2003. "Les marchés économiques comme dispositifs collectifs de calcul." *Réseaux* 122:189–233. Translated version available at http://www.coi.columbia.edu/pdf/callon-muniesa.pdf. Accessed October 12, 2006.

Carlson, C. 2000. "Small Carrier Members Disgruntled with CTIA." *Wireless Week*. Available at http://www.wirelessweek.com/article/CA3066?spacedesc=&stt=001. Accessed October 12, 2006.

Chakravorti, B., W. Sharkey, Y. Spiegel, and S. Wilkie. 1995. "Auctioning the Airwaves: The Contest for Broadband PCS Spectrum." *Journal of Economics and Management Strategy* 4:345–373.

Copps, M. 2004. "Statement of Commissioner Michael J. Copps." *Report and Order and Further Notice of Proposed Rulemaking*. FCC Docket No. 04–166.

Cramton, P. 2002. "Introduction to Chapter." In *Game Theory in the Tradition of Bob Wilson*, edited by B. Holmstrom, P. Milgrom, and A. Roth. Berkeley, CA: Bepress. Available at http://www.bepress.com/wilson/. Accessed October 12, 2006.

Cramton, P., and J. Schwartz. 2000. "Collusive Bidding: Lessons from the FCC Spectrum Auctions." *Journal of Regulatory Economics* 17:229–252.

Day, F., and H. Tran. 1997. *Regulation of Wireless Communications Systems*. Rockville, MD: Government Institutes.

Douglas, M. 1984. *Purity and Danger*. London: Ark.

Douglas, M. 1986. *How Institutions Think*. Syracuse: Syracuse University Press.

Erickson, M. 2005. *Science, Culture and Society*. Cambridge: Polity.

FCC (Federal Communications Commission). 1993. *Notice of Proposed Rulemaking* (NPRM). FCC Docket No. 93–455.

FCC (Federal Communications Commission). 1994. *Second Report and Order*. FCC Docket No. 94-61.

Fine, B. 2003. "Callonistics: A Disentanglement." *Economy and Society* 32: 478–484.

Fuller, S. 2000a. *Thomas Kuhn: A Philosophical History for Our Time*. Chicago: University of Chicago Press.

Fuller, S. 2000b. "Why Science Studies Has Never Been Critical of Science." *Philosophy of the Social Sciences* 30:5–32.

Galambos, L., and E. Abrahamson. 2002. *Anytime, Anywhere: Entrepreneurship and the Creation of a Wireless World*. New York: Cambridge University Press.

Galison, P. 1997. *Image and Logic*. Chicago: University of Chicago Press.

Guala, F. 2001. "Building Economic Machines: The FCC Auctions." *Studies in History and Philosophy of Science* 32:453–477.

Hands, D. W. 2001. *Reflection without Rules: Economic Methodology and Contemporary Science Theory*. New York: Cambridge University Press.

Ihde, D., and E. Selinger, Eds. 2003. *Chasing Technoscience*. Bloomington, IN: Indiana University Press.

Kwerel, E., and G. Rosston. 2000. "An Insider's View of the FCC Spectrum Auctions." *Journal of Regulatory Economics* 17:253–289.

Labaton, S., and S. Romero. 2001. "Wireless Giants Won F.C.C. Auction Unfairly, Critics Say," *The New York Times*, February 12.

Latour, B. 1987. *Science in Action*. Cambridge, MA: Harvard University Press.

Latour, B. 1999. "On Recalling ANT." Pp. 15–25 in *Actor Network Theory and After*, edited by J. Law and J. Hassard. Oxford: Blackwell.

Latour, B. 2002. "A Prologue in the Form of a Dialogue between a Student and His (somewhat) Socratic Professor." Available at http://www.ensmp.fr/~latour/articles/article/090.html. Accessed October 12, 2006.

Latour, B. 2004a. "Why Has Critique Run Out of Steam? From Matters of Fact to Matters of Concern." *Critical Inquiry* 30:225–248.

Latour, B. 2004b. *The Politics of Nature*. Cambridge, MA: Harvard University Press.

Latour, B. 2004c. "On Using ANT for Studying Information Systems: A (Somewhat) Socratic Dialogue." Pp. 62–76 in *The Social Study of Information and Communication Technology*, edited by C. Avgerou, C. Ciborra, and F. Land. New York: Oxford University Press.

Law, J. 2003. "Networks, Relations, Cyborgs: On the Social Study of Technology." Centre for Science Studies, Lancaster University. Available at http://www.lancs.ac.uk/fss/sociology/papers/law-networks-relations-cyborgs.pdf. Accessed October 12, 2006.

Ledyard, J. 1995. "Public Goods: A Survey of Experimental Research." Pp.111–194 in *The Handbook of Experimental Economics*, edited by J. Kagel and A. Roth. Princeton, NJ: Princeton University Press.

Ledyard, J., C. Plott, and D. Porter. 1994. "A Report to the Federal Communications Commission and to Tradewinds International, Inc.: Experimental Tests of Auction Software, Supporting Systems and Organization." PP Docket No. 94-12.

Ledyard, J., D. Porter, and A. Rangel. 1997. "Experiments Testing Multiobject Allocation Mechanisms." *Journal of Economics and Management Strategy* 6:639–675.

Lee, K.-S. 2004. "Laboratory Markets as Information Systems: Vernon Smith Designs Some Mechanisms." Paper presented to HES conference, Toronto.

MacKenzie, D. 2002. "The Imagined Market." *London Review of Books*, October 21, Pp. 22–24.

MacKenzie, D., and Y. Millo. 2003. "Constructing a Market, Performing Theory: The Historical Sociology of a Financial Derivatives Exchange." *American Journal of Sociology* 109:107–145.

McAfee, R. P. 1993a. "Auction Design for Personal Communications Services." *Comments of PacTel*. PP Docket No. 93–253.

McAfee, R. P. 1993b. "Auction Design for Personal Communications Services: Reply Comments." *PacTel Reply Comments*. PP Docket No. 93–253.

McAfee, R. P., and J. McMillan. 1996. "Analyzing the Airwaves Auction." *Journal of Economic Perspectives* 10:159–175.

McClellan, C. 1996. "The Economic Consequences of Bruno Latour." *Social Epistemology* 10:193–208.

McGuckin, W. 1984. *Scientists, Society and the State.* Columbus, OH: Ohio State University Press.

McMillan, J. 1994. "Selling Spectrum Rights." *Journal of Economic Perspectives* 8:145–162.

McMillan, J., M. Rothschild, and R. Wilson. 1997. "Introduction." *Journal of Economics and Management Strategy* 6:425–430.

Meister, A. 1999. *Evaluating the Performance of the Spectrum Auctions: A Case Study of the PCS Auctions.* PhD diss. University of California, Irvine.

Milgrom, P. 1995. "Auctioning the Radio Spectrum." Available at http://www.market-design.com/files/milgrom-auctioning-the-radio-spectrum.pdf. Accessed October 12, 2006.

Milgrom, P. 2004. *Putting Auction Theory to Work.* New York: Cambridge University Press.

Milgrom, P., and R. Weber. 1982. "A Theory of Auctions and Competitive Bidding." *Econometrica* 50:1089–1122.

Milgrom, P., and R. Wilson. 1993a. "Affidavit of Paul R. Milgrom and Robert B. Wilson." *Comments of PacBell.* PP Docket No. 93-253.

Milgrom, P., and R. Wilson. 1993b. "Replies to Comments on PCS Auction Design." *Reply Comments of PacBell.* PP Docket No. 93-253.

Miller, D. 2002. "Turning Callon the Right Way Up." *Economy and Society* 31:218–233.

Mirowski, P. 1989. *More Heat than Light.* New York: Cambridge University Press.

Mirowski, P. 1999. "Cyborg Agonistes." *Social Studies of Science* 29:685–718.

Mirowski, P. 2002. *Machine Dreams: Economics Becomes a Cyborg Science.* New York: Cambridge University Press.

Mirowski, P. 2004. "The Scientific Dimensions of Social Knowledge and Their Distant Echoes in 20th-Century American Philosophy of Science." *Studies in the History and Philosophy of Science A* 35:283–326.

Mirowski, P. Forthcoming. "Markets Come to Bits." *Journal of Economic Behavior and Organization.*

Mirowski, P., and K.-S. Lee. 2003. "The Purest Form of Rationality Is That Which Is Imposed." Notre Dame working paper.

Murray, J. 2002. *Wireless Nation.* Cambridge: Perseus.

Nalebuff, B., and J. Bulow. 1993a. "Designing the PCS Auction." *Comments of Bell Atlantic.* PP Docket No. 93-253.

Nalebuff, B., and J. Bulow. 1993b. "Response to PCS Auction Design Proposals." *Reply Comments of Bell Atlantic.* PP Docket No. 93-253.

Nik-Khah, E. 2005. *Designs on the Mechanism.* PhD diss. University of Notre Dame.

Parkin, M. 1998. *Economics,* 4th ed. Reading, MA: Addison-Wesley.

Pickering, A., Ed. 1992. *Science as Practice and Culture.* Chicago: University of Chicago Press.

Plott, C. 1997. "Laboratory Experimental Testbeds: Application to the PCS Auction." *Journal of Economics and Management Strategy* 6:605–638.

Roth, A. 2002. "The Economist as Engineer: Game Theory, Experimentation, and Computation as Tools for Design Economics." *Econometrica* 70: 1341–1378.

Rubinstein, A. 2001. *Economics and Language.* Cambridge: Cambridge University Press.

Sismondo, S. 2004. *An Introduction to Science and Technology Studies.* Malden, MA: Blackwell.

Slater, D. 2002. "From Calculation to Alienation: Disentangling Economic Abstractions." *Economy and Society* 31:234–249.

Thelen, J. 1995 "Milgrom's Progress." *The Recorder*, May, p.S5.

Weber, R. 1993a. "Comments on FCC 93-455." *Comments of TDS.* PP Docket No. 93-253.

Weber, R. 1993b. "Reply to Comments on FCC 93-455." *Reply Comments of TDS.* PP Docket No. 93-253.

Weber, R. 1994. Letter to John McMillan. PP Docket No. 93-253.

Weber, R. 1997. "Making More from Less: Strategic Demand Reduction in the FCC Spectrum Auctions." *Journal of Economics and Management Strategy* 6:529–548.

Woolgar, S., Ed. 1988. *Knowledge and Reflexivity.* London: Sage.

Zammito, J. 2004. *A Nice Derangement of Epistemes.* Chicago: University of Chicago Press.

Chapter 8

Which Way Is Up on Callon?

PETTER HOLM

How are markets built up and stabilized?[1] How are entities, material and nonmaterial, human and nonhuman, transformed into commodities? How is it possible for actors in markets to calculate the consequences of their actions? What is the role of economists and economic theory for the functioning of markets and the economy?

Michel Callon has posed such questions in work stretching from *The Laws of the Markets* (1998b) to his contributions to this book. His answers—which can be summarized under the heading of "performativity of economics"—draw on and contribute to Actor-Network Theory (ANT). ANT is controversial and has often been targeted for heavy criticism (Amsterdamska 1990; Bloor 1999a; Collins and Yearley 1992; Schaffer 1991). The performativity version of ANT seems posed to continue in that tradition, and Callon's ventures into economics have already occasioned serious attacks (such as Fine 2003; Mirowski and Nik-Khah's chapter in this book). One of the sharpest is Daniel Miller's essay "Turning Callon the Right Way Up" (2002).

As already noted, the subject of this aspect of Callon's work is markets and economics. To understand Miller's interest in and rejection of Callon's approach, we must note that this subject is one that Miller also holds dear. Miller's understanding of markets and economics is not the same as Callon's. As it happens, Callon's 1998 book came out in the same year as a book coedited by Miller entitled *Virtualism: A New Political Economy* (Carrier and Miller 1998). These two books overlap a great deal. Both are interested in market models and in market behavior. Both ask what role economists and economic theory have for the way markets are organized and how economies function. But of course, as is obvious from the very first sentence of Miller's review, he and Callon do not come to the same conclusion. We have, in other words, a classical confrontation: between two books; between two authors; between two different interpretations of the same phenomenon.

This chapter describes these two approaches and tries to explain why they clash. The structure of the chapter is as follows. First, I outline Miller's reading—or misreading—of Callon. Next, I turn the tables and give, from an ANT perspective, a diagnosis of the problems with virtualism. In the third section I lay out Callon the right way up, that is, I try to explain Callon's position as plainly as possible. Finally, I illustrate some of the most interesting differences between ANT and virtualism by way of individual transferable quotas (ITQs).

Miller on Callon

As I have already said, Miller and Callon are interested in the same issues, which they approach in similar ways. They ask how we can understand the market and market behavior. They are both preoccupied with the role of economic models in economic practices. Both reject the understanding of economists themselves, that economists simply study economies; that economic models are accurate representations of an underlying reality of economic phenomena. Instead, Miller and Callon agree that there are important causal arrows going the other way around, from economic models to economic behavior. For Miller, a key proposition is that economists have managed—somehow—to project their abstract models onto economies. While economic man, say, at the outset is a purely abstract invention of economics, it gradually becomes true because powerful actors manage to reconstitute the world in its image. In very much the same way, Callon rejects the idea that economics—the theoretical abstractions of economists—can be separated out radically from the practical workings of the economy. Instead, he insists that economists are active partners in economic activity. Economists do not study the economy; they perform it.

But here the agreement between Miller and Callon ends. While Miller concurs with Callon that economists do not study the economy but reconstruct it, he does not think that Callon follows up on that premise. Instead, he says, Callon ends up "treating the economic model of the market as though it were core to actual economies rather than a projection of economists" (Miller 2002, p. 219). Instead of offering an alternative to, and a critique of, the standard economic perspective, as Callon promises, he ends up in defense of the economists' view of the market, and with a rejection of how anthropologists and sociologists understand things. Callon, in Miller's eyes, has betrayed the good people who struggle against capitalists and dehumanizing market forces; he is in cahoots with the economists, the World Bank, Reagan, and the powers that be.

As I shall suggest, Miller's criticism is not quite on target. But it is an interesting criticism, not least because it echoes a charge that has fairly often been directed against ANT. Harry Collins and Steven Yearley, two important figures within science and technology studies (STS), have, for instance, blamed ANT, represented by Latour and Callon, for betraying the sociological position within that field.[2] Collins and Yearley's dissatisfaction with Latour and Callon is about their refusal to see scientific knowledge as embedded in and reducible to social relations and culture. Instead, ANT takes scientists seriously and accepts that scientific practices actually achieve results that cannot be referred back in any meaningful way to societal factors. Say Latour and Callon: society, or nature for that matter, does not determine what happens in laboratories. Society and nature emerge from—are produced in—laboratories.

For Collins and Yearley ANT's rejection of the standard sociological explanation can only be a betrayal, a reactionary move back to a time when the sociologist of science took a reverential attitude toward the great white-coated geniuses of science. If Latour and Callon do not agree with us, the sociologists, Collins and Yearley feel, this can only mean that they side with the scientists and hence can do no better than reproduce a variety of the scientists' insider view of things. In much the same way, Callon's refusal to accept the standard sociological view of the market as embedded in cultural and moral relationships means for Miller that he sides with the opposition, the economists. In Miller's words: "Callon follows the economists in mistaking a representation of economic life for its practice" (Miller 2002, p. 219).

For Miller, Callon's mistake is that he, along with the economists, accepts the reality and importance of markets, as portrayed by market models. Callon does not believe, as Miller would prefer, that the economists' market is an abstraction, and as such ultimately a distortion of human relationships. For Callon, these markets really exist and make a difference in the world. This does not mean, however, that Miller is correct in claiming that Callon is indistinguishable from an economist. Callon does not believe in economic man, that perfect, maximizing rationalist, as naturally given and universal. Instead, he insists that markets sometimes can be formatted in such a way that real people achieve some powers of calculation and rationality. In the same way, Callon does not believe that commodities, those items traded in markets, just exist, *in natura*, as detached objects ready to be exchanged in markets. Instead, he insists, objects can sometimes be disentangled from the numerous relationships in which they are embedded in such a way that market exchanges become possible.

As these formulations already suggest, there are aspects of Callon's viewpoint that you would not expect from the average economist. Dismissing him as another economist doesn't seem quite right. But Miller does have a point when he blames Callon for saying, along with the economists, that the economists' markets are important; they actually do something to commodities; they really have an impact on who people are and what they can do. Just like the economists, Callon insists that these markets are in the real world and make a difference there.

This brings us to back to Miller's understanding of markets. What is it in Miller's view that makes Callon's perspective so provocative to him? As already suggested, a starting point here is that standard sociological notion of seeing things that at first brush look natural, rational, or technical as fundamentally socially shaped and culturally constituted. Are gender and sexuality objective and given by nature? "Of course not," the sociologist will reply. Brotherhood, then? Nope. Illness and dying? Socially constituted through and through. And even if we think up the really hard cases, like scientific facts, the laws of physics, mathematics, or even reality itself, the sociologist will show us how they all can be— must be—explained and ultimately reduced to social factors, interests, values, moral precepts, culture. What we think of as hard, detached, objective, "thinglike", turn out, in the sociologists' able hands, to be subphenomena of what we usually think of as soft and insubstantial, namely, social relationships. For the sociologist, society is hard, basic, and can do the explaining. Nature is soft, superficial, and needs to be explained.

Where do markets fit into this picture? This depends on what we mean by markets: the theoretical abstraction in economic textbooks or real-life economic practices. The economic models, the abstractions invented by economists, are in Miller's picture not real, not part of basic reality. They are ideological representations, moral and cognitive superstructures employed to patch over and protect the established order of things. While economists postulate perfect markets, economic man, and rational behavior as objectively real, naturally occurring phenomena, they have no liking for actual economic entities and behavior. The economy itself, real market behavior, is something else altogether. Real markets are not constituted by thin rationalities, by disentangled commodities and calculative agencies. On the contrary, real market behavior is hot, moral, value-laden, politicized, and entangled. While the economic models, the abstractions, do not exist in reality, they are—increasingly— projected onto real-life economic behavior with such force that people take them as objective, natural, thinglike, and outside society, in much the same way as they think of gender, illness, death, and the laws of physics. But the sociologist knows better: economists' market models are superficial abstractions, ideological representations that do not describe real-life economic behavior, but shield from view its true nature as embedded in social relationships and culture (Carrier 1997; Carrier and Miller 1998).

Take as an illustration a market transaction concerning a motor car (an example used by both Callon and Miller). For Callon, such a transaction is possible only because rigorous framing has been performed:

> This framing has reduced the market transaction to three distinct components: the buyer, the producer-seller, and the car. The buyer and the seller are identified without ambiguity, so that property rights can be exchanged. As for the car, it is because it is free from any ties with other objects of human agents that it can exchange ownership. (Callon 1998a, p. 18)

For Callon, the market transaction, that the property rights to an automobile can change hands, is possible only because the entities involved have been—as a result of hard and sustained work—disentangled, decontextualized, alienated from all kinds of relationships and overflows.

For Miller, in contrast, such disentanglement is impossible. In his rendering of the automobile transaction, he underlines all the externalities, the social ties, the extra meaning and values that abound in the act of car buying. Look only at all those unaccounted-for externalities of car ownership and use: pollution and global warming; the cost of road building and maintenance; the profusion of human pain and misery resulting from automobile accidents. He also emphasizes all those complex considerations that enter into the buying of a car, from practical and economical ones, to the less tangible, how environmentally friendly it is or is considered to be, the car as a fashion statement, the social status it projects etc, and so on (Miller 2002, pp. 224–227). Contrary to Callon's position that a successful market transaction is possible only on the condition of radical disentanglement, Miller insist that this is never possible. No amount of framing can manage to reduce all the entanglements—the technical, practical, cultural, moral, and esthetic factors that enter into the car transaction—to the thin, abstracted, disentangled objects and rationalistic actors portrayed by Callon and the economists. While Callon believes that markets, in order to work, must become practical enactments of the economists' models, Miller believes that markets forever are entangled in social complexities, and hence that market models are false abstractions.

Now we perhaps begin to see how deep is the split between Callon and Miller. Callon believes that the economists' market models are real and perform work; he asks how economic models format the economy. For Miller, in contrast, such fusion—confusion—of economics and economy, of abstraction and reality, is a mistake of the worst kind. What is needed is "to radically separate out the market as a ritual and ideological system constructed by economists" on the one hand and "the actual practice of the market" on the other (Miller 2002, p. 224). For Miller, economists have no real leverage on reality. Instead, they are merely ideologues. They are the high priests of capitalism; their role is to preach the inevitability and morality of their own market fables (Miller 2002, p. 223).

We can understand why Miller claims that Callon's version is upside-down. For Miller, Callon takes market transactions as modeled by economists as basic and real when in reality they are abstract representations and ideology. He has confused base and superstructure.[3] Instead of fighting the good fight, revealing the economists' dangerous ideology for what it is, he has joined their ranks and contributes to the materialization of that ideology. Callon is upside down. He is the quintessential economist, since he takes the abstraction—economic theory—for the real thing: embedded social practices.

ANT on Virtualism

Miller's paper is a review. As a review, we expect, as a start, a presentation of the object in question: Callon's book *The Laws of the Markets*. But Miller does not make much of an attempt to explain to the reader what Callon's overall intellectual project is about—unlike, for example, Mirowski and Nik-Khah in their chapter, however harsh their critique may seem.[4] Instead, Miller jumps right to his conclusion, that since Callon has not adopted the socioculturalist perspective on markets, he is with the economists. To substantiate this conclusion, Miller must take a few questionable turns. First, he dissociates Callon, the editor, from the other contributors to the book, claiming the substantial chapters for his own cause. This done, he goes on to construct Callon as a kind of economist. To make that charge stick, however, he must disregard a number of Callon's points. That is, Miller is attentive when Callon speaks about disentanglement and successful framing but somehow misses out when Callon in the next paragraph turns to the other half of the equation, talking about the great effort this requires, which can never be finished and will never be completely successful—that there are always entanglements and overflows; that entanglement and disentanglement, framing and overflow, are two sides of the same process. It seems like Miller decided, at the outset, that Callon is an economist and excludes as irrelevant the parts of the text that do not fit his theory. In the same way, Miller's counterexamples to Callon, the Indian Jajmani system and car buying, can serve as counterexamples only if Callon had claimed that the embeddedness of economic practices and the entanglement of objects were irrelevant and could be disregarded. This is not Callon's position, however, but stems instead from Miller's reading of Callon.

The key concept in Miller's analytical repertoire is "virtualism." Let me first try to explain what this means. As said already, an idea common

to Callon and Miller is that there are interesting interactions between
market models and marketplaces; between economics, the discipline,
and the economy, the practice. Now, it is a commonplace that there are
flows going from the economy to economics; that economics is the *study*
of the economy, so that economic models *reflect* actual economic practices. As already noted, however, the idea that Callon and Miller have in
common is that causation also goes in the opposite direction and market
models influence and cause changes in market practices.[5]

For Callon, this point is made by refusing to accept the distinction
between market models and market practices (1998a, p. 2). He wants to
give up the notion of market models as abstractions; that there are two
radically different things in the world, market models here and market
practices way over there, so that the former can be taken to be detached
representations of the latter. Instead, market models for Callon form
crucial parts of markets; they are among the items that make markets
tick. I shall have more to say about this in a little while. I mention it now
because this is a point that Miller does not take on board. For him, to
uphold the distinction between the market model, the abstraction, and
practical market activity is crucial. This distinction is at the heart of the
notion of virtualism. Virtualism happens when the market model, seen
as pure abstraction, is mistaken for reality and forms the basis for organizing practical market exchanges. Says Miller of the key argument in his
book on virtualism: "What needed to be emphasized was the degree to
which economics and other abstract models were managing to accrue
such power that they were able to transform actual economic practices,
making them accord more with these same models" (2002, p. 229).
Thus in virtualism too a causal arrow goes from the market model to
market practice. But even as the market model is enacted in practice and
people are forced to follow the economists' prescriptions, the model remains detached from reality, forced upon it, as an ideological foil and
false consciousness. When market models are taken from economics
textbooks and turned into reality, then, this cannot be real reality; it is
virtual reality. It might look real, but it isn't; it's all illusion and superstition, and it can be sustained only because of the massive amounts of
power and ideological work that is constantly employed to force it down
over people's heads.

Let me say at once that I think that the concept virtualism is not fertile.
Virtualism does not, in my view, allow much leverage for explaining why
market models have such a strong hold on people. Since such models, according to the virtualist, are abstractions, understood as illusions that do
not connect to real markets, they cannot draw their power from what
they do. The first move the virtualist makes here is to deny the claim
made by economists that their markets actually work. For the virtualist,

this cannot be, since the markets then wouldn't be virtual any more. But this creates a problem for him or her: how to explain the great power economic models have on events in the world. In the virtualist perspective, this cannot be explained endogenously, from effects emerging in markets, since it then would be impossible to deny that market models actually make a difference. The only solution to this dilemma is to introduce some external power, a power so potent that it can maintain general faith in this grandest of modern illusions, the most globalized of Western superstitions, and produce the economists as the mightiest of social scientists, despite the fact, as the virtualist knows, that they don't understand how reality works.

What is this power? Where does it come from? What are its sources? We know the general answer to these questions. For the virtualist, the only possible source of such power—any power—is the sociocultural context, people embedded in hot and entangled social relationships. But since this is the only thing the virtualist accepts as real anyway, it doesn't help solve the problem. If one part of the embedded social world gains power over another part of that world, how can we explain it? Since the virtualist denies reality to market models, or any other such thing, because they are abstractions and can only be explained but never do the explaining, little is left to work with here. So what can Miller do? Well, he revives Hegel and Marx, suggesting that everything falls into place in a grand narrative of dialectical style. While he of course knows about the troubling homogenizing and westernizing tendencies in such metahistorical glosses, he isn't particularly shy about this suggestion, instead maintaining that it is ironic that "this tradition is being attacked at the very moment when history itself is coming into line with its own story" (Miller 1998, p. 189). The reason he thinks that history now is in line with its own story is this:

> I wish to suggest that today, rather more than at the time Hegel lived, there exist forces of such power and global reach that certain trends have become ubiquitous, and hence that we can talk meaningfully, perhaps for the first time, about history having a direction. (Miller 1998, p.189)

Miller thus is allowed to tell metanarratives because there now are metapowers in the world. Great forces mandate great stories. Although this sounds right, we are again left without the source of the power in question: Where does it come from? Miller's answer here is an updated version of Marx. First there was capital, which robbed the workers of the fruits of their labor. Unfortunately, Marx was wrong in his prediction of the next turn of the dialectical story. But no matter, says Miller, since, "if he were to be consistent" with his own theory, the one thing Marx wouldn't have been if he was alive today is a Marxist (Miller 1998, pp. 189–190). Instead of a communist revolution, as he foresaw, what really happened—according to Miller—was that the workers took their labor back by becoming avid consumers. They reembedded the alienated fruits of their work in meaning and cultural contexts, bringing the commodities back as entangled objects within their hot and value-laden social worlds. This is the point in history where we are now. Reassuringly, as everyone now realizes, the next dialectical move will give it all back to the Consumers, or whatever label that, at the next stage, might fit the character filling the role of the oppressed and virtuous in this majestic pas de deux of good and evil.

I don't think virtualism delivers what Miller promises it will. Instead of an account of the source of a power great enough to reorder history and give it purpose and direction for the first time, we are offered a story of history so flexible that it can accommodate any scenario and contain any future and any past whatsoever. This is of course greatly disappointing, since we were promised a glimpse of that tremendous, world-ordering power that virtualism postulates and requires. That power, however, is little but illusion, a theoretical entity that is needed by virtualists in order for their model to avoid immediate implosion. It would seem, then, that it is the virtualists, not Callon or the economists, who live by abstraction and have mistaken reality for their own false model of it. Callon is up. Miller is upside-down.

The Right Way Up on Callon

To say that Callon is up—that it is he, not Miller, who has the better grasp on economics and the economy—is one thing. If virtualism is as weak as I have made it out to be, after all, not much is needed to beat it. But to explain exactly *which way* is up on Callon, that is, to give a precise and understandable presentation of Callon's perspective, is another thing.

Now, the trouble for the virtualists, as I have suggested, is that they start out insisting that economics makes a difference only in the virtual world, not the real one, so that explaining the great influence economic models and economists do have, which is plain to see for everyone, is very difficult for them. Since such influence and power, for the virtualists, by default cannot be explained endogenously from the effects market models produce by reformatting the economy, they must introduce some mysterious, external power source, reaching down to us from an eternal Hegelian heaven. Instead of such mysticism, Callon starts with a simple hypothesis: market models work. If they are popular and have legitimacy, at least with those who count, it is because they make a difference. When they, as often is the case, are immensely illegitimate and highly contested, but still manage to hang on, it is because they produce so much profit, so much power—for some groups—that they can take the beating.

Notice, now, that even if Callon accepts that market models work, this does not mean that he makes the economists right in everything they say. Take that typical economist's position that the market is the realization of innate human capacities for calculation and utility maximization. Even though Callon rejects the virtualists' attempt to reduce economic behavior to social relationships and cultural scripts (Callon 1998a, pp. 5–6), he also rejects the economists' mirror-image attempt to reduce it to natural endowments and universal human nature. For Callon, both these essentialisms, or purifications as ANT would call them, are untenable. While Callon refuses to be a sociologist, that does not mean he must be an economist. Instead, Callon is interested in how those items that are typically posited in market models, like calculating agencies, commodities, and property rights, are constructed and put to work. At this point, Callon is in full agreement with Miller that actors and objects—at the outset—are enmeshed in social networks and obligations, are buried under layers and layers of social meaning, are deeply entangled in sticky cultural contexts. It is exactly because this is the case that framing and overflows, disentanglement and reentanglement, become so crucial. In order for market actors to calculate the probable outcomes of their choices, buyer and seller must be produced as fairly separate and autonomous agencies. The object to be traded must be constructed as reasonably stable and thinglike. A minimum of agreement as to the nature and limits of property rights and how they can change hands must be negotiated. These things do not lie in wait, ready to spring forth from universal human nature, but need to be constructed, often with tremendous amounts of hard work. More precisely, standards must be defined, measuring systems constructed, systems for surveillance and enforcement invented and put in place. It is these devices that allow framing and disentanglement, and they are built into organizations, routines and regulations, physical structures and machines. The more institutionalized, naturalized, technological, material, and thinglike they become, the better they will work in dis-embedding agents and objects from their social, cultural, and technological contexts, setting them free to realize—put into reality—the market model invented by the economist.

In this picture, market models are blueprints for real markets. But this formulation still doesn't go far enough, since it suggests the existence of a map way over here, which is used as a model to construct a real market all the way over there. While such a use is also included in Callon's picture, he has in mind a much tighter traffic between theory and practice, between economics and the economy. Market models are also implicated in the practical management of the market, in the definition of its standards, in the management of the identity of its agents, in the definition of property rights, in the surveillance of exchange processes, in the constant adjustments, refinements, and reconstructions that are required to keep the exchanges flowing. The market model is not so much like a preconceived construction plan, which can be put away in a drawer when the building project in question is finished, but more like a production schedule, a practical device used for measuring, adjusting, and coordinating the complexities of actual market transactions. For Callon, then, the distinction between representation and reality, between market model and market practice, dissolves. Market models are constituent parts of market practices; they belong with the devices that make markets run.

Individual Transferable Quotas

Enough theory. Let's look at an example: the introduction of individual transferable quotas (ITQs) in the fisheries. The ITQ model is an invention of neoclassical economics. It was first developed as a fishery management model by Christy (1973) and Moloney and Pearse (1979) on the basis of the earlier work of Gordon (1954) and Scott (1955) (cited in Squires et al. 1995). The starting point for the model is the total allowable catch (TAC) (Gissurason 2000). A TAC is an intervention mechanism designed to regulate fishing on the basis of scientific fish counts. By making the TAC binding on the fishery, a cap is put on the biomass taken out of the stock. This should achieve—on the assumptions that the TAC is adhered to and also fixed according best scientific practice—one fundamental management objective, namely, optimal biological utilization of the biological resource. There is a hich, however. The simplest way to implement the TAC is to allow free access and competitive fishing until the total quota is taken, and then to close the fishery. This system, known as "Olympic fishing," may solve one major problem, biological overexploitation. It creates a new one, however, fleet overcapacity. In the race for fish, investment in bigger vessels and better gear creates an excess of fish-killing power. From the standpoint of society as a whole (or the "taxpayer," as the economists so elegantly phrase it), this is a waste. From a more restricted management perspective it is also problematic, since overcapacity (together with the negative profitability it produces) invites cheating and also generates political pressure to set TACs above what the scientists recommend.

This is where ITQs come in. Instead of the Olympic model, the manager can split up the TAC in small packages and allocate them (as gifts or by auction) to fishermen as individual quota rights.[6] There are two advantages here, one on top of the other. The first is realized when you go from capacity-generating Olympic competition to individual vessel quotas (IVQs). Under an IVQ system, the fishermen can, instead of engaging in a headless race for fish, take their time, and they can minimize costs and maximize fish quality. They can fish when prices are good, avoid bad weather, and so on. In the long run, they can invest in vessels that maximize their profit from the given quota. Instead of the technical overcapacity as produced by Olympic competition, individual quotas will produce, in sum, a better fit between harvest capacity and resource base.

Promising stuff, but it gets even better. The second advantage comes if you allow the fishermen to buy and sell quotas among themselves. Now, the fisherman, being a quota owner (and rational lest you forget) must consider this: will I make more money by fishing myself, or selling the quota to someone else? If the market works according to theory—and why wouldn't it?—the quota will flow to the most efficient fisherman, since he, everything else equal, will be able to pay the best price (Arnason 2000; Neher et al. 1989; Scott 2000).

ITQs were invented by neoclassical economists in an attempt to make their pet model, the competitive market, the basis for solving the perennial problems of overcapacity, high management costs, and rampant politicization within fisheries. The economists promised that ITQs will transform fisheries from an overgrown, inefficient, irrational, unmanageable sector full of hot-headed cheaters who will overfish the resources they depend on, if given half a chance, into a small, efficient, modern, rational, and predictable money-making machine whose members—the new class of fisherman-owners—will be intensely preoccupied with the health of the resource, since the return on their investments depends on it. In this picture, then, ITQs have transformative powers of considerable proportions; they are an instrument which, if let loose on the fisheries, will change almost everything. Fishermen will turn into owners and investors. The fish itself, that elusive creature of the sea, transforms into private property. The overfishing problem shapeshifts into an issue of capital management. The fisheries of the past, that hot, politicized sector tied up in sticky traditions and coastal culture, turns into a cool and rational sector for the future, free to enter the stock market and the elegant business offices of the City.

I'm sure you'll agree that the ITQ model, in all its clean-cut parsimony, is powerful and attractive as well as terrifying and repulsive. Just think of the brutal processes of alienation and disentanglement ITQs require and reproduce. The fish, which previously was regarded as a common heritage of the coastal people, is expropriated, without compensation, and given, free of charge, as private property to a small elite (Helgason and

Pálsson 1998). These fisherman-owners now get to decide whether to fish the quota or to sell it, without the communities that depend on such decisions for their survival having any say in the matter (Pálsson and Petursdottir 1997). Compared to such radical acts of dispossession, it would seem a minor point that ITQs also leave the crew—the fishermen that didn't get lucky in lottery of ownership rights—radically separated from the fish, which now has become the exclusive property of the owner-manager (Pálsson 1998). But it is not unimportant here that this new distinction at the microlevel of the vessel also has a parallel at the mesolevel of fishermen's organizations, which are split right down the middle, with the fisherman-owners joining ranks on the one hand, sharply divided from the newly formed class of fishermen-workers on the other. In this way, ITQs reconstruct the interest structure and shift around political resources within the fishing industry.[7]

Fascinating as the ITQ model is in itself, we need to return to the quarrel between ANT and virtualism. For the virtualist, the ITQ model is a dry economist's dream, which must be forced down over people's heads if it ever is going to make it into reality. For this to happen, however, great acts of violence must be performed on coastal people's conceptions, morality, and way of life. This will provoke so much resistance that the ITQ model can be sustained only by external, top-down exertion of pure oppression and intense propaganda. In the end, hopes the virtualist, coastal people will take back their birthright, standing up to their oppressors, so that everything can return to the happier situation of yesteryear (Helgason and Pálsson 1998, pp. 129–131).

Unfortunately, at least for those who think that ITQs are bad, they slip into reality with much greater ease and consequence than the virtualist imagines. That is because they work. Even though they may not perform with the cool elegance portrayed by the economists, they still have tremendous reorganizing effects in the real world. With the aid of property rights, fish quotas start shifting around, elevating some to quota barons, leaving others—and the communities they live in—out of the loop. Fishermen are transformed; some become owner-managers and profiteers, but most end up dispossessed even down to the hope of one day becoming skipper on a vessel of their own. ITQs have the capacity to rearrange political structures; to cut the sector lose from coastal traditions and reinsert it in the midst of corporate culture. ITQs even have the capacity to change the nature of the fish. Before ITQs it is fishermen who go hunting for the fattest fish. With ITQs, the fish goes hunting for the best owners.[8] The really terrifying thing with the ITQ model is not that such transformations must be imposed from the outside, but that it actually produces and reproduces them from raw materials on the coast, be it human agencies or material nature. When ITQs are deployed, new cultures and societies emerge; new actor-types are created, new politics are defined, new natures are constructed. The virtualist believes— hopes—that ITQs are abstract missiles launched from the economists' think tank, which may explode but cannot really inflict any deeper harm on the impervious, age-old rock of coastal culture. It is much worse, in ANT's view, since the ITQ model comes complete with its own culture; since it is capable of making fishermen betray their roots; since it rede- fines nature to fit its image.

The Cyborg Fish

This leaves us with only one problem. Even if ITQs, once in place, can re- produce the social and natural conditions that sustain them, how can we explain the first move, that first precarious leap from economic textbook into practice? This is a not a slight problem, since, before ITQs can go to work, a great deal of preparatory work is required. Property rights have to be defined; distribution of quota shares agreed on; mechanisms of transferability and their limitations decided. But not only that: those who stand to be dispossessed must be silenced or suppressed and those who hold veto power must be persuaded or paid off. The introduction of ITQs is likely to be a hot political issue and must be handled with care if it is going to carry the day. The problem here is not only that ITQs require so much violence to established practices, but that such violence must be sanctioned in an arena where the defenders of the old order hold senior positions, while those who stand to gain from the new order still are in diapers. In all likelihood, then, the defenders of established ways will have all kinds of opportunities to sabotage the ITQ proposal; to squash it in its infancy, long before it has had time to dig in and go to work.

For the virtualist, this seems easy to explain. All that is required is one single, great burst of external, top-down oppression. But while this ex- planation may carry some truth, it still exaggerates the power of formal offices and abstract models. It also requires an "X-files"-like frame of mind, embracing conspiracy and paranoia, which has its attractions but is basically unsound.

Callon's notion of performativity offers an escape from that unpleas- ant world. A great deal, in fact almost all of the preparatory work needed to pull off the highly conspicuous ITQ revolution has already been carried out under the cover of the slow, deliberate, mundane, and almost invisible processes that turned resource management into the overriding concern in the fisheries. At the center of this "invisible revolu- tion" (Holm 2001) we find the reconstruction of the fish, from a wild creature of the sea into a complex, cyborglike, scaled, and modeled entity—a resource fit for management. You may be excused here if you here think I am referring simply to the invention of mathematical models of the behavior of exploited fish stocks. But such models are only the tip of the iceberg, drawing attention away from the much more basic work of setting up measurement procedures, sampling standards, and networks of data collection and refinement that allow the variables in the models to be filled with realistic-looking numbers. It is by way of such complex networks of measurement systems, as much as by the abstract models they tie into, that the fish can be captured and transported into computers and made to produce scenarios for times to come. And when the fish finally has made its way up to this iceberg-tip of abstract modeling, it starts working its way back down again, now in the form of quota propositions, from negotiation table to negotiation table, becoming increasingly harder, more enforceable, and more subdivided, until it ends up as a catch allowance or quota for a particular fishing vessel.

This complicated and long-winded story, if I had the space to tell it in full, would be about the construction and stabilization of a heterogeneous network, tying the fish in with fishermen, echo integrators, log books, legislation, computers, bureaucracies, mathematical formulas, and surveillance procedures. It is within such a network that the fish-as-fit-for-management springs to life, as a true cyborg: part nature, part text, part computer, part symbol, part human, part political machine. It would be a story about entities with variable ontologies, about actors that become what they are as their relationships with other actors stabilize. It would be a story about performation, about theories of fish and fishermen that make the leap from flat paper surfaces into reality.

When the cyborg fish is installed, when the invisible revolution has been completed, almost all the preparatory work required for introducing ITQs has already been accomplished. Now fish can easily be divided into individual quotas and there is no particular problem attaching property rights to them. When the cyborg fish is in place, the most violent acts of dispossession against coastal communities have already been undertaken; the fisheries commons have already been closed; the heritage of the coastal people has already been parceled and laid out, ready for the auction. With the successful introduction of fisheries resource management, most of the organizational and institutional apparatus that could have served as a power base for those who want to resist ITQs has already been squashed. Since all this violence has been successfully grounded in nature and is seen as required in the name of eternal fish stocks, as objectively known by science, this revolution, this great political upheaval and transformation in the fisheries, has been rendered invisible. The cyborg fish has changed everything, but it is as if nothing has happened.

Here's my proposal then: the visible ITQ revolution, dramatic and conspicuous as it is, becomes possible because it has been prepared by decades after decades of slow, deliberate, invisible work. The virtualists are wrong when they hope that it cannot succeed, that the ITQ model is merely an abstraction that will be destroyed when it collides with the century-old cultural bastions of coastal culture. They are wrong because these bastions already have been smothered by the cyborg fish and the invisible revolution. This is also why the introduction of ITQs, as is about to happen in Norway, can occur without an explicit ITQ reform. Even if the explicit proposal to sanction ITQs as a policy model gets beaten in the political arena, we get ITQs at the level of practical action anyway, set into circulation by the fishermen themselves.

Performing Performativity

How can I conclude otherwise than saying that Callon is up and Miller is down? How can I avoid saying that when Miller goes after ANT, it is virtualism that ends up defeated, because it is too weak; it is built on a dream; because it is an abstraction and lacks the power.

Of course I must conclude this way. But this is not all. This chapter has not only been *about* Callon and Miller, virtualism, ANT, ITQs, and the cyborg fish. It has at the same time been a performance of Callon's perspective. While I have talked about and theorized framing and entanglement, I have also performed an exercise in framing and entanglement. For instance, I have, particularly for this text, constructed a forceful author position, resourceful and reckless enough to dispose of Miller and virtualism. I have done all sorts of maneuvers to tie this figure in with Callon, performativity, ANT, and the cyborg fish, setting this assemblage up against a contrasting network of Miller, virtualism, and sociology, which—need I really say it?—was also constructed for the occasion.

As I'm writing this text, of course, it is still confined to the flat surface of the computer screen. Although the text I'm constructing, and the creatures that live in it, are layered and refer to many kinds of entities in a less flat, perhaps more "real" world outside of it, the dominant movement is still representational, from the outside in. For this text to be what I claim for it, an exemplar of performation, there needs to be some transport the other way around, from the text into the world.

In principle, only one kind of actor can make this happen, and that is the reader of the text. If this text is going to be performative, it has to be transported into reality by its readers. Hopefully, then, the actants constructed in this text—be it performativity, virtualism, the right-way-up Callon or the head-over-heels Miller—will rise up from the flat landscape of the text, bulk up, and venture into the world. Typically, the first step here would be that the readers replicate elements of this text onto other flat surfaces, in the form of citations and quotes in other academic texts. But if enough readers do that, actants in the text may gradually take on more substantial form, for instance, if the version of performativity proposed here is put into circulation and starts informing performativity as a research practice. In this way, the theory of performation, as proposed in this text, may get to be translated into a practice of performation.

At least all this will come to pass if I made a good job of it—that is, if I, through the previous pages, managed to dissociate Callon from the economists, turn him back right-side-up, and tie him together with the cyborg fish into a neatly packaged and easily transferable commodity in the academic marketplace under the trademark of performativity.

Notes

1. This chapter is a polite version of Holm (2003).
2. Collins and Yearley (1992). See Callon and Latour (1992) for a reply. For other examples of this type of criticism of ANT, see Amsterdamska (1990), Schaffer (1991), and the recent exhange between David Bloor (1999a, b) and Bruno Latour (1999).
3. See also Barry and Slater (2002, p. 185).
4. Miller's reference list does not contain a single ANT item, except, of course, the book he is reviewing.
5. In Miller's words: "I entirely concur with [Callon's] initial warning that economists tend not to study economies, but rather attempt to project their models onto economies" (2002, pp. 218–219).
6. In the fisheries where ITQs have been deployed, about 98–99 percent of people fishing actually are men. The gendered term "fishermen" displays that reality. Consequently, I choose to use "fishermen" instead of neutral terms like "fisher" or "fisher people."
7. Brox (1997). See also Holm, Raanes, and Hersoug (1998).
8. Perhaps "hunting" is not the right word here. Nevertheless, the market mechanism will ensure that the fish quotas—and thereby the fish—are redistributed in favor of the most efficient actors. The result is a quota distribution that looks as if it was produced by fish hunting for the best owner.

References

Amsterdamska, O. 1990. "Science in Action—Latour, B." *Science Technology & Human Values* 15(4):495–504.

Arnason, R. 2000. "Property Rights as a Means of Economic Organization." Pp. 14–25 in *Use of Property Rights in Fisheries Management. FAO Fisheries Technical Paper 404/1*, edited by R. Shotton. Rome: FAO.

Barry, A., and D. Slater. 2002. "Introduction: The Technological Economy." *Economy and Society* 31(2):175–193.

Bloor, D. 1999a. "Anti-Latour." *Studies in History and Philosophy of Science A* 30(1):81–112.

Bloor, D. 1999b. "Reply to Bruno Latour." *Studies in History and Philosophy of Science A* 30(1):131–136.

Brox, O. 1997. "Academic Rationality, Economic Interests and the Making of Public Opinion: How the ITQ Revolution Is Being Implemented in the Norwegian Fishing Industry." Pp. 51–59 in *Social Implications of Quota Systems in Fisheries. TemaNord 1997:593*, edited by G. Pálsson and G. Petursdottir. Copenhagen: Nordic Council of Ministers.

Callon, M. 1998a. "Introduction: The Embeddedness of Economic Markets in Economics." Pp. 1–57 in *The Laws of the Markets*, edited by M. Callon. Oxford: Blackwell.

Callon, M., Ed. 1998b. *The Laws of the Markets*. Oxford: Blackwell.

Callon, M., and B. Latour. 1992. "Don't Throw the Baby Out with the Bath School!" Pp. 343–368 in *Science as Practice and Culture*, edited by A. Pickering. Chicago: University of Chicago Press.

Carrier, J. G., Ed. 1997. *Meanings of the Market: The Free Market in Western Culture*. Oxford: Berg.

Carrier, J. G., and D. Miller, Eds. 1998. *Virtualism: A New Political Economy*. Oxford: Berg.

Christy, F. 1973. *Fishermen's Catch Quotas. Occasional Paper 19*. Kingston, RI: Law of the Sea Institute.

Collins, H. M., and S. Yearley. 1992. "Epistemological Chicken." Pp. 301–326 in *Science as Practice and Culture*, edited by Andrew Pickering. Chicago: University of Chicago Press.

Fine, B. 2003. "Callonistics: A Disentanglement." *Economy and Society* 32(3): 478–484.

Gissurason H. H. 2000. "The Politics of Enclosures with Special Reference to the Icelandic ITQ System." Pp. 1–16 in *Use of Property Rights in Fisheries Management. FAO Fisheries Technical Paper 404/2*, edited by R Shotton. Rome: FAO.

Helgason, A., and G. Pálsson. 1998. "Cash for Quotas: Disputes over the Legitimacy of an Economic Model of Fishing in Iceland." Pp. 187–213 in *Virtualism: A New Political Economy*, edited by J. G. Carrier and D. Miller. Oxford: Berg.

Hersoug, B. 2002. *Unfinished Business: New Zealand's Experience with Rights-Based Fisheries Management*. Delft: Eburon.

Holm, P. 2001. "The Invisible Revolution: The Construction of Institutional Change in the Fisheries." PhD diss. Norwegian College of Fishery Science, University of Tromso, Tromso.

Holm, P. 2003. "Which Way Is Up on Callon? A Review of a Review: Daniel Miller's 'Turning Callon the Right Way Up.' On Michel Callon: The Laws of the Markets." *Sosiologisk årbok* 1(8.1):125–156.

Holm, P., S. A. Raanes, and B. Hersoug. 1998. "Political Attributes of Rights-Based Management Systems: The Case of Individual Vessel Quotas in the

Norwegian Coastal Cod Fishery." Pp. 113–126 in *Property Rights and Regulatory Systems in the Fisheries*, edited by D. Symes. Oxford: Fishing News Books.

Jentoft, S., P. Otnes, and G. Pálsson. 2002. "Instilling fra komite for bedømmelse av Petter Holms avhandling." Tromsø: Det samfunnsvitenskapelige fakultet.

Latour, B. 1999. "For David Bloor . . . and Beyond: A Reply to David Bloor's 'Anti- Latour.'" *Studies in History and Philosophy of Science A* 30(1):113–129.

Miller, D. 1998. "Conclusion: A Theory of Virtualism." Pp. 187–215 in *Virtualism: A New Political Economy*, edited by J. G. Carrier and D. Miller. Oxford: Berg.

Miller, D. 2002. "Turning Callon the Right Way Up." *Economy and Society* 31(2):218–233.

Moloney D., and P. Pearse, 1979. "Quantitative Rights as an Instrument in Regulating Commercial Fisheries." *Journal of the Fisheries Research Board of Canada* 36:859–866.

Neher, P. A., R. Arnason, and N. Mollett, Eds. 1989. *Rights Based Fishing*. Dordrecht: Kluwer.

Pálsson, G. 1998. "The Virtual Aquarium: Commodity Fiction and Cod Fishing." *Ecological Economics* 24(2–3):275–288.

Pálsson, G., and G. Petursdottir, Eds. 1997. *Social Implications of Quota Systems in Fisheries*. TemaNord 1997:593. Copenhagen: Nordic Council of Ministers.

Schaffer, S. 1991. "The Eighteenth Brumaire of Bruno Latour." *Studies in History and Philosophy of Science* 22(1):174–192.

Scott, A. 2000. "Introducing Property Rights in Fishery Management." Pp. 1–13 in *Use of Property Rights in Fisheries Management. FAO Fisheries Technical Paper 404/1*, edited by R. Shotton. Rome: FAO.

Squires, D., J. Kirkley, and C. A. Tisdell. 1995. "Individual Transferable Quotas as a Fisheries Management Tool." *Reviews in Fisheries Science* 32:141–69.

The Properties of Markets

TIMOTHY MITCHELL

The sociological criticism of neoclassical economics accuses it of misrepresentation. In reducing the complexities of social life to the outcomes of the calculations of rational agents responding to incentives in ways that maximize their interests, it is said, economics leaves out of the picture any account of how agencies are constituted, interests are formed, incentives are managed, or resources are initially distributed. This criticism has plenty of force, but also a clear weakness: it assumes that the work of social science is to represent a material world external to itself.

What if we think of economics differently, as Michel Callon (1998) suggests? Suppose it operates from within the sociotechnical world, not from some place outside it. Suppose it provides a set of instruments of calculation and other technical devices, whose strength lies not in their representation of an external reality but in their usefulness for organizing sociotechnical practices, such as markets. The narrowness of neoclassical economics then serves a purpose. Among other things, it helps perform the operations that Callon calls "framing" or "disentangling." Markets would not work if people were not allowed to exclude things, to leave certain costs or claims out of the calculation, and to deny responsibility for certain consequences. Economic analysis helps organize these exclusions. It helps distinguish what can count in the act of exchange from what cannot, and what must be paid for and what should not. From this perspective, economics should be analyzed not in terms of the reality it represents (or fails to represent), but in terms of the arrangements and exclusions it helps to produce.

Critics of Callon's argument about the performativity of economics often agree with him that one should examine economics at work in the economy, but assume that economic knowledge should still be thought of simply as a set of representations. They read the argument as a version of Ian Hacking's notion of looping: that social-scientific classifications may interact with the actions of those who adapt their way of life to the way they are classified (Hacking 1995, 1999). Seen in this way, if the economic representations taken up by economic actors fail, then one can return to the original critique. For example, if game-theoretic models are used to design an actual market, and the market does not work, one can use this experimental failure as further evidence of the representational inadequacy of economic theory. The failure must be due to more powerful forces—political interests, corporate power, cultural beliefs—that the models of economics were too simple to take into account. Neoclassical economics can once again be dismissed as something inadequate, or at best as a screen for disguising what is actually going on.

To understand the performativity of economics, it is not enough to look for economics at work in the economy; one must also stop understanding it simply as (mis)representation. The effectiveness of economics rests on what it does, not on what it says. It does not work alone. It operates together with other techniques, sets of information, arrangements, and agencies, with different strengths and resources. Enframing a market does not happen only by employing the methods of classification or calculation that economics may provide. The exclusions on which market transactions depend take a variety of forms and acquire different degrees of force and effectiveness.

Another, interrelated set of arrangements is the law. Contracts must be calculable, but also enforceable. Goods must be "qualified" (in other words, their characteristics must be identified and rendered explicit), but goods also must be transferable and open to being forfeited or reclaimed. Employees must be put to work, or may be locked out or fired. Businesses may be taken over, or shut down. The performation of markets involves a mixture of technologies, calculative devices, methods of control, and trials of strength.

Where do these arrangements acquire the forms of compulsion they require? In the first place, from what is called the rule of law. Markets depend on a form of politics in which relations among agents are governed by rules of property and contract. These are among the distinctive technologies of power and obligation in market societies, generating a variety of micro sovereignties, disciplinary regimes, and coercive forces.

Property arrangements are often relatively stable, but they are never static. Forms of property proliferate. Many of the chapters in this book explore the ways technosciences develop new objects, interests, and agents, for example, with the radio spectrum (Mirowski and Nik-Khah), new financial formulas (Lépinay; MacKenzie), or the transformation of the fish in the oceans into cyborgs (Holm; Holm and Nielsen 2004), to which claims of ownership can be attached and then traded. As these chapters illustrate, the very nature of property is continually up for renegotiation, requiring new forms of enframing and disentangling, and the management of new frontiers. The promise of a performative approach is to open up these sociotechnical processes to explication, and at the same time to alternative political possibilities.

But property relations have another kind of limit. While the airwaves or the oceans can be rearranged into new forms of property, and thus transformed into markets, other sites have known property relations for decades or generations yet have kept the rules of the market at arm's length. In fact, most people in most of the world live lives in many ways protected against the rules of private property and the market. They may live in self-built housing on plots they do not formally own, or farm agricultural land that is protected against outside purchase, or produce food intended largely for household consumption. Local systems of marriage or inheritance may operate to ensure that land, livestock, or other goods are not lost to the market through the turnover of generations.

Formal rules of property help determine what is legal and illegal and what is public and private. Such distinctions define the market but also create ways to survive outside it or in the pathways and spaces that these distinctions open up. People may produce and trade illicit goods, such as hemp or opium, in which no legal property rights are available. Their main asset might be the public space of an urban street, as in the wealthier neighborhoods of car-choked third-world cities, where people establish a territory and earn a living as informal parking attendants, or the corridors of a government office, where the difficulty of obtaining legal permits and approvals enables informal expediters to thrive.[1]

These kinds of informal or nonmarket practices used to be thought of as something residual, representing pockets of resistance to the market or transitional regions occupying some intermediate space. But as examples such as informal urban housing suggest, many of these arrangements are constantly expanding, possibly faster than formal market arrangements. Although they are thought to exist outside the market, and outside the laws of property, they are far from lawless. Even when relatively new, such as the squatter settlements in Calcutta described by Partha Chatterjee (2004), they are characterized by complex moral claims, social rights, and political obligations. As Elyachar (2005) shows, they can embody alternative modes of economic success and offer some of the most vibrant forms of economic life. As Lawrence Liang's account of "porous legalities" (Liang 2005) suggests, they also can penetrate the pathways of the law, seeping into the more closely governed arrangements of property and the market.

Despite the porosity of such arrangements, the idea persists that the market, indeed capitalism in general, has a boundary. The boundary is thought to separate the market from the large areas of material activity and resources that seem to exist beyond its limit. For countries outside the West, the idea of a boundary provides a common way not just to think about these places but to diagnose their problems and design appropriate remedies. Such remedies are increasingly popular. Older ways of approaching non-Western development typically referred to different sectors of the economy, such as the traditional and the modern, the rural and the urban, or the agrarian and the industrial. These sectors had moving and sometimes overlapping boundaries. Development could be planned as a series of transitions, in which people and resources were to be moved from one sector to another, or in which the expansion of the market transformed different parts of the economy at different moments. Since the changes occurred over time, the difference between the nonmarket and the market, or the noncapitalist and the capitalist, represented as much a temporal transition as a territorial one.

Today those sorts of temporal-spatial understandings often appear to have been displaced by a much simpler set of proposals: the capitalist economy is surrounded by a boundary, outside which stands the noncapitalist, nonmarket world. The task of development economics is to help extend the rules of the market into these other spaces. The popularity of such proposals can be gauged by the success of the work of Hernando de Soto, a Peruvian entrepreneur and economist, whose two books, *The Other Path* (1989) and *The Mystery of Capital* (2000), have become the most widely cited studies of non-Western economic development in a generation. The Institute for Liberty and Democracy (ILD) in Peru, which carried out the research presented in these books, has been called the second most influential think tank in the world (*The Economist*, 1991). Both books describe the forms of wealth and material activity that exist outside the capitalist economy, diagnose the nature of the barrier that keeps them out, and propose techniques for bringing them in. The ILD works in several countries in Asia, Africa, and Latin America devising procedures to enable what is trapped outside capitalism to be brought in. The sociotechnical design and implementation of these mechanisms has become one of the most popular solutions to the problem of economic development in the global south.

This chapter investigates this conception of the market and its limits. It proposes a different way of understanding the boundary of the market and the status of the difference between capitalism and the noncapitalist. It focuses in some detail on the ILD's project and the mechanisms it has helped to design. The chapter proposes the following:

> **1.** The distinction between market and nonmarket or capitalist and noncapitalist should be considered not as a thin line but as a broad terrain, in fact a frontier region that covers the entire territory of what is called capitalism. The region is the scene of political battles, in which new moral claims, arguments about justice, and forms of entitlement are forged.

2. When economics helps to devise technical mechanisms to move people and assets across a line from outside to inside the market, it plays a part in this politics. Such mechanisms do not move things across a fixed line, but they do rearrange the control and distribution of assets. The line is something created by these mechanisms, as part of the battle over redistribution and control.

3. For economics this involves what might be called a work of misrepresentation, for the outside must be constituted in terms of its relation to the market—that is, in terms of its deficiencies, as the nonmarket, as something defective or dead. Yet it is inadequate just to call this a misrepresentation, for it implies the possibility of an adequate representation of the nonmarket from within capitalocentric discourse. It is more useful to consider what kind of world the (mis)representation helps to organize.

4. Technologies of representation claim a double role in these arrangements. First, economic analysis tries to help reorganize sociotechnical life by representing a world outside the market, as part of the process of seeming to bring it inside. Second, in describing what this nonmarket world lacks, economics tends to diagnose its defects as an absence of techniques of representation. Things are stuck outside the market because they are not properly represented—by property records, prices, or other systems of reference. What economics does, however, is not to represent what was previously unrepresented, but to try to reorganize the circulation and control of representations.

5. To argue that the power of economics is performative is not to argue that its power necessarily lies in getting people to adopt its (mis)representations; rather, in helping to constitute the apparent border between the market and the nonmarket, economics contributes to the work of sociotechnical mechanisms that reorganize how people live, the political claims they can make, and the assets they can control. Its particular role, I argue, is in formatting a form of exclusion-inclusion.

A Very Great Book

Presenting the findings from research in five countries, *The Mystery of Capital* argues that the main reason most countries outside the West have failed to emulate the West's economic development is that a large amount of their wealth lies outside the formal economy (de Soto 2000, pp. 5–6). It is trapped in forms that cannot enter the market, and therefore cannot be invested to create further wealth. Described as "dead capital," this wealth consists principally of land and housing. Most people in non-Western countries live in housing whose ownership is not formally registered with the state, and thus lack proper title to their property. These people, says de Soto, "are outside the global economy, are in fact outside the market economy, are certainly outside the capitalist economy" (2001). Because their assets are outside the economy, they are unable to use them as collateral to borrow funds. The assets are locked in the material form of their houses and cannot be transformed into cash or credit. Credit is "live" capital that can be accumulated, invested in business ventures, and turned into further income.

Live capital, according to de Soto, is created by devising techniques of representation. Representations of material assets transform their value into abstract forms, which can live an "invisible, parallel life" alongside their physical existence. The West has invented procedures to create these invisible forms. Individuals in the West can unlock the assets accumulated in physical property, transforming material wealth into abstract capital. Using a house as collateral for loans, says de Soto, is an important source of credit for launching small businesses, providing a large reserve of funds to stimulate economic growth. The most important difference between successful capitalist economies and the rest of the world lies not in the wealth they possess, he argues, but in how that wealth is held. The rest of the world holds its assets in "defective forms." The absence of property title and the mechanism of credit it enables are the principal reasons for the failure of capitalist development outside the West (de Soto 2000, pp. 5–6).

The solution to global poverty, it follows, is to construct in every country a simple apparatus of representation that will transform dead capital into live assets. The machinery consists of neighborhood-based programs to enable people to register ownership of their property and simplified rules for using the property as collateral for loans.

De Soto organized wide support for these proposals. In 1994, he persuaded the government of Peru to launch a property titling program under the ILD's direction that by 2002 gave formal title to 1.2 million urban households.[2] Numerous other countries subsequently recruited the ILD as consultants, to measure the extent of their countries' untitled assets and devise mechanisms for moving them into the market. De Soto's researchers found their most impressive results in Egypt. They estimated that as much as 92 percent of the country's housing was held in defective forms, representing $248 billion in underused assets. In one of their most widely repeated statistics, they said this dead capital represents more than fifty-five times the amount of all the direct foreign investment ever recorded in modern Egypt, including digging the Suez Canal in the nineteenth century and building the Aswan High Dam in the twentieth (de Soto 2000, p. 5).

Some of the reasons for the appeal of these programs are easy to see. Compared to other diagnoses of the problems of development, de Soto offers a much more positive account of the resources and potential of the majority of the people of the global south. His earlier book, *The Other*

Path, a study of the informal economic sector in Peru, argued that un-regulated economic activity is more dynamic and more efficient than the overregulated formal economy. The size of the informal sector is not an indication of backwardness but a rational response to excessive bureaucratic regulation of formal economic activities (de Soto 1989). *The Mystery of Capital* showed that the poor possess not just entrepreneurial skills but also assets. The failure fully to develop these assets is not the fault of those who own them and therefore cannot be blamed on the backward or traditional culture of the poor. It is the fault of the formal sector. Governments in the global south have failed to introduce the legal arrangements and financial mechanisms that are the unnoticed secret, de Soto argues, of the success of capitalist development in the West. The development of modern property rights during the previous two centuries was so successful that the West now takes this apparatus for granted and fails to notice its absence or incompleteness in most countries outside the West.

These arguments were useful alternatives to popular ideas about the poor as people incapacitated by their own traditions or culture. They presented the poor as competent economic agents who need to acquire only the proper technical equipment to be brought into the market. But the success of de Soto's arguments was due to something more. They provided a way to bring the poor into the arguments and programs of neoliberalism.

De Soto's proposals were developed and circulated within the network of political agencies and financial resources of the Euro-American neoliberal movement. From its beginnings in the late 1940s as a small association of conservative economists and political theorists supported by corporate benefactors, the neoliberal movement grew over the following decades into a transatlantic network of think tanks, academic economists, and policy makers, funded by private foundations and corporations, that came to play an influential role in the shaping of government policy in the West (Plehwe 2006).

In 1981, Antony Fisher, a leading organizer and benefactor of the movement, established the Atlas Foundation for Economic Research, based near Washington D.C., to coordinate the growing network of think tanks and launch "a concerted effort," in the words of a letter of support from Friedrich Hayek (1980), "to create similar institutes all over the world." Hayek wrote the letter after returning from a trip to Peru, where he spoke at a conference funded by German neoliberals and organized by Hernando de Soto (Bromley 1990). At Hayek's urging, the Atlas Foundation helped de Soto set up the Institute for Liberty and Democracy. Atlas provided financial support and trained de Soto and his collaborators in the economic ideas of neoliberalism and the techniques it had developed for political organization and advocacy (Mitchell 2005).

The support from Hayek and the neoliberal movement enabled the ILD to carry out its research into property rights and the poor, published in *The Other Path* and *The Mystery of Capital*, and to introduce its first property titling programs in Peru. The property titling programs failed to have any effect on household poverty. As I showed in another paper (Mitchell 2005), other benefits that were supposed to compensate for this failure were equally illusory. Yet the failures did not prove an obstacle to de Soto's success. Neoliberal writers and organizations reviewed his books favorably and recognized the author and his organization with well-publicized awards. *The Other Path* carried endorsements from two former U.S. presidents and received a prize from the Atlas Foundation. *The Mystery of Capital* received endorsements from Margaret Thatcher, Jeane Kirkpatrick, Thomas Friedman, Francis Fukuyama, and William F. Buckley Jr.[3] De Soto received the Milton Friedman Prize for Advancing Liberty from the Cato Institute, the Compass Award for Strategic Direction from Forbes Magazine, the Adam Smith Award, the Goldwater Award, and several other prizes.[4] At the same time, the populist tone of his arguments on behalf of the poor persuaded others to see him as a progressive. The ILD reported on its Web site that even the left-of-center British journal *The New Statesman* had written that de Soto's work "has put him in the pantheon of great progressive intellectuals of our age." Although this was not what the journal wrote, de Soto managed to claim supporters well beyond the limits of the neoliberal movement.[5]

The ILD's work also benefited from the neoliberal networks connecting it to academic economics. De Soto was more a practitioner than a scholar, producing research in a think tank rather than a university. Academic economists praised his work not as a contribution to academic theory but as a practical demonstration of neoclassical truths about property rights. Two Nobel laureates in economics, Ronald Coase and Milton Friedman, endorsed *The Mystery of Capital*. It is "a very great book," wrote Coase, "powerful and completely convincing."[6] This positive reception enabled its arguments to flow back into academic economics. De Soto's work became the basis for further university research and provided the subject matter for teaching materials in economics, endorsed by economists such as Friedman, again, and Douglass North (Mitchell 2005).

Despite the continuing absence of reliable evidence that his ideas worked, de Soto came to be described as one of the world's leading experts on development. The World Bank funded the ILD titling program in Peru, the International Monetary Fund promoted its ideas, the United States Agency for International Development provided the think tank with continuous funding for its overseas operations, and the International Labor Organization appointed de Soto to its World Commission on Globalization (World Bank 2004). In September 2005, the United Nations Development Program supported the establishing of the High Level Commission on the Legal Empowerment of the Poor, cochaired by de Soto and Madeleine Albright, the former U.S. Secretary of State, with the goal of generating further international support for de Soto's political program.[7]

The success of *The Mystery of Capital* and its author's recognition, manufactured by de Soto's public relations efforts with the help of the Euro-American neoliberal movement, enabled the ILD to transform its own activities into a form of property. In marketing his property-rights program to governments around the world, de Soto's method was to bypass government ministries and local development agencies and seek authorization and support directly from a country's head of state. This enabled the ILD to win exclusive government consulting contracts, typically awarded without the normal request for competitive bids from rival consulting firms.

In Tanzania, for example, de Soto met the country's president when both of them were appointed to the World Commission on Globalization. He used this connection to obtain a no-bid government contract, even though other development agencies had been working on the reform of Tanzanian property rights for many years. The ILD justified its exclusive contract on the grounds that its method of ending global poverty, explained in *The Mystery of Capital*, was unique and could not be combined with existing programs. Signed in November 2004, the contract included a requirement that the Tanzanian government "respect ILD's intellectual property rights over the methodology and techniques it provides."[8] Explaining why other development agencies had not been allowed to bid for the contract, the executive director of the ILD, Manuel Mayorga, said that "in this particular area, we invented the wheel. Understanding the gap between the formal legal and extralegal sectors, analyzing how these two parallel sectors operate, evaluating their problems . . . quantifying their economic effects, and how they might be integrated under one rule of law creating a modern, productive economy is the area that the ILD has pioneered."[9] Thus de Soto's claim to ownership of knowledge about markets became a means to the accumulation of capital—through protecting his own activities from competition in the market.

In Egypt, the ILD gained the backing of Gamal Mubarak, the son of the country's president and the wealthiest and most powerful of a younger faction among large Egyptian entrepreneurs seeking to strengthen the powers of private property as a means of undoing an earlier generation of social reforms. This group used de Soto's arguments to help push through parliament new economic measures, including a mortgage law, a property titling program, and new rules for licensing small businesses. The ILD helped draft the laws and assisted in a public relations campaign to win political support.[10] As in Peru, the outcome of the legislation was disappointing, but the publicity campaign was an immediate success. *Forbes Magazine* published a story in February 2004 predicting that the country's new property laws would "dramatically transform its economy into a wealth-creating, wealth-distributing dynamo that will lead millions of Egyptians into a vibrant, increasingly democratic middle class." The country was poised to become "an economic miracle rivaling Ireland or Hong Kong," the magazine's editor wrote—adding that in doing so "Egypt will deal a devastating blow to global terrorism" (Forbes 2004).

Since Egypt provides the most dramatic instance of the defects that de Soto diagnoses, and overcoming these defects has been said to promise an economic miracle, it seems worth looking at the evidence from Egypt. What can it tell us about the performativity of de Soto's arguments? How are these ideas, despite the lack of evidence to support them, actually put to work?

Outside the Market

The first thing to note is that so-called informal property arrangements have not arisen because people in places like Egypt are ignorant of private property or because the West overlooked the need to export its property system abroad. In the nineteenth century, Ottoman and European rulers in Cairo launched a series of attempts to transform property arrangements into systems based on an absolute right of private ownership.[11] The difference was that in Egypt farmers were able to prevent the complete destruction of livelihoods that absolute property rights entailed. Unlike the victims of property formalization in Europe, where enclosure and other powers of ownership forced millions of people off the land, rural populations in Egypt were able to delay, divert, or limit the introduction of absolute powers of ownership. Unlike the states of western Europe and North America, Egypt controlled no overseas colonies or Indian territories to which to ship a dispossessed rural population, so could not afford the rates of dispossession that private ownership produced. In the course of the twentieth century, popular mobilization forced the Egyptian government to introduce a series of measures protecting small owners and tenants against eviction and placing limits on the amount of land a household could own.[12] Similar protections against eviction were later extended to residents of urban property. So the position of ordinary Egyptians "outside" the mechanisms of private property ownership was the outcome of a long, often violent, but ultimately relatively successful objection to undergoing the dispossession inflicted on the rural populations of Europe or the complete marginalization or elimination of native populations in parts of the world where settler colonialism was carried through.

To describe the outcome of these events as the existence of a world outside the market is curious. For the ILD this outside is a place shaped by ignorance and lack of access. It is a place to which the benefits of formal arrangements were never extended. To think of the outcome as a frontier would be more instructive. People have seen formal property arrangements advance, recede, and advance again. They have sometimes evaded them and sometimes been overtaken by them. They have worked against them from the inside, and sometimes turned them to local advantage. The frontier has been a battleground. It is not a thin line marking the barrier between market and nonmarket or formal and informal. It is a terrain of warfare spread across the entire space of the market, the entire length of what is called the history of capitalism. If it is an outside, then it is an outside found everywhere, a scene of battle that seems to define every point at which the formal or the capitalist can be identified. It is therefore a zone of "inclusive exclusion," since what is declared to be outside the market already plays a role within it, through the declaration of exclusion and the continuous battles over its inclusion.[13]

The proposals for transforming the global south through property titling envision three distinct steps for including what is declared to be excluded: turning property into collateral, collateral into credit, and credit into increased income (Woodruff 2001). What is the evidence that property titling unlocks credit and that the newly available credit has this set of consequences? What is the mechanism that turns assets "outside" the market into financial prosperity within?

The Mystery of Capital has little to say on this question. The main argument presented in the book is a passing reference to the idea that in the United States many people launch small businesses by borrowing funds using their homes as collateral. How significant is this source of credit? De Soto cites no evidence for the claim, and the data available on small-business credit in the United States does not offer much support. Among very small businesses, 40 percent borrow no funds at all and the most common source of loans for those that do is a personal credit card.[14]

One reason why mortgaging one's home may play a less significant role in financing business investments than the ILD believes is that in the West most people do not have homes to mortgage. Although home ownership rates range from 40 percent in Germany and Sweden to 54 percent in France and as high as 68 percent in the United States and Great Britain, these figures include homes that are mortgaged and not yet paid for, including those whose occupants owe more than the value of the house.[15] For a majority of households in the West, using one's home as collateral for a business loan is not an option available.

In the global south, rates of home ownership are often much higher, above 80 percent in India and Mexico, for example (Proxenos 2002). Because of the minimal role of housing credit in these countries, most of these homes are owned outright. *The Mystery of Capital* argues that low-income home owners in the south possess assets that, if they lived in the north, they would transform into live capital. In fact they possess assets that, if they lived in the north, in most cases they would not own.

De Soto describes the informal property systems of the global south as a defective form of capital. The figures on comparative home ownership rates suggest that they might instead be seen as a significant achievement. They enable millions of households to occupy their own dwellings, free of mortgage debt and the threat of foreclosure, even though their incomes are a fraction of those of households in the West, where far fewer can afford to own property.

The advantages of informal housing have been recognized since at least the 1940s, when people like the Egyptian architect Hassan Fathy promoted vernacular housing as an alternative to the plans of postwar governments to pay commercial contractors to build inhospitable and relatively expensive blocks of concrete apartments.[16] By the 1970s, it was widely accepted among development practitioners (but not by governments with ties to large contractors) that informal housing had significant advantages, especially if measures were taken to overcome some of the drawbacks of informality. These drawbacks might include inadequate services, poor site layout, and insecure tenure—but not an inability to use the property as collateral.

Evidence drawn from observations of a village in southern Egypt in 2004 can illustrate how its advantages still operate today.[17] First, informal housing is often self-built. In the village, houses range from simple huts built of palm stalks plastered with mud, occupied by a few of the poorest households, to substantial houses made of mud brick (adobe), to four- and five-story structures built with reinforced concrete frames and fired brick, sometimes accommodating a separate household of the same extended family on each floor. Many households build their own dwellings, often with the help of male relatives. Others hire a builder, who may be a relative or neighbor and usually employs help from the household. Expenses are also reduced by using building materials available locally, sometimes at no cost. Bricks are made from earth, concrete from local sand, and ceiling joists and laths from the trunks and branches of date palms (usually the male trees, which do not produce fruit).[18] Windows, doors, and furniture are made by local carpenters, while cheaper furniture is assembled from palm stalks by the men who trim the trees. Recycled oil cans are hammered together to make doors for the simplest houses. To install electrical and plumbing systems some households employ electricians and plumbers, but most are able to install these systems themselves or with the help of a relative. This mixture of self-building, the services of relatives, and local crafts and trades keeps housing affordable while also supporting a significant local construction industry.

Other advantages of informal, largely self-built housing include the option to build incrementally, adding rooms, floors, or fixtures as needs develop and income arrives, or even to rebuild the entire dwelling later in more durable materials; the use of locally appropriate methods and building supplies; and the ability to design the layout of the house to suit the occupants' needs and to alter it as those needs change—converting a front room into a small store, for example, or a rear yard into a workshop.

The success of self-built rural housing depends on the fact that it seldom requires the purchase of land, which would be beyond the reach of most families. Space for new housing is found by pulling down older, less substantial structures or those in need of renewal, by adding to existing houses, often by reducing the land previously used for domestic animals, or by filling the gaps between dwellings. Those who own no land on which to build look for small plots of vacant land. Some find patches of higher, uncultivable ground, where the government recognizes squatter housing and charges a small rent. Others find the unused margin of their own or a relative's plot of agricultural land, typically along the edges of canals and roads or at the border where the cultivation meets the desert. The completion of the Aswan High Dam in 1971 made it possible to build on agricultural land, much of which was previously protected from building by the annual flooding of the fields for irrigation. A law passed in 1983 to ban construction on agricultural land, reinforced by a military order of 1996, reduced the loss of farmland but failed to eliminate the practice.[19] Most new construction takes place within existing village boundaries or on unused land. However, the shortage of unused plots and the inability of the government to facilitate self-build projects along the desert margin and on military property and other underutilized land exacerbates the problem of access to suitable land.[20]

The housing built in this way may be legal, semilegal (infringing building regulations, for example), or illegal (such as housing built on agricultural land). All owners would prefer their homes to be legal, but not because they plan to use them as collateral. Legal housing does not carry the expense of the frequent summonses and fines imposed on unlawful construction, and it may be easier to connect to the water and electricity supply. The latter has been less of a problem since 1998, when the government decreed that houses built in violation of the 1983 ruling banning construction on agricultural land were nevertheless eligible for connection to utilities.[21]

Legality, however, also has drawbacks. The main problem is that it makes land unaffordable. In 2004, agricultural land in the village sold for about E£1,000 per qirat.[22] Occasionally the Ministry of Agriculture would remove a plot of land from the cultivated area (the "zimam") of the village, for example, because it was surrounded by buildings and no longer received enough sunlight for cultivation. This made it legal to build on the plot. Legalization increased the value of land by a factor of at least ten, to more than E£10,000 per qirat. In more valuable locations, such as agricultural land on the edge of a major town, legalization could increase the value by a factor of thirty or forty.

Urban housing differs from rural in several obvious ways, yet many of the same principles apply. In Egypt, the rebuilding of the city of Ismailiyya following the withdrawal of the Israeli army from the Suez Canal zone after the 1967–1974 occupation included a successful project to demonstrate the advantages of "site and service" programs to facilitate self-building while avoiding the problems of inadequate services, poor site layout, and insecure tenure.[23] The self-funding project made available development sites laid out with building tracts and services, along with small loans and supplies of low-cost building materials. The recipients of the plots were given long periods to repay the value of the unimproved land. Provisions requiring immediate construction, owner occupancy, and delayed acquisition of title discouraged speculators. The project recognized that offering formal title to the land can hamper the provision of low-cost housing, as it encourages property speculators to bid up the price of housing.

Boundaries of Property

The ILD acknowledges many of the advantages of informal housing. Yet its proposals insist that formalization through property titling is the only route to economic development. The insistence is based on an argument not about the relative benefits of the informal but about access to collateral and credit. Only a formal property system, it is claimed, can release the dead capital held in informal housing. It is time to turn more specifically to this argument.

Once again the case of rural Egypt provides evidence with which to begin. Although the proposals the ILD drew up for Egypt were focused on the formalization of urban housing, over the preceding decade some of the reforms they advocated had already been carried out in the countryside. The reforms (actually, the undoing of earlier reforms that had set limits on the agrarian property market) included measures allowing farmers to use their land as collateral for loans from the Agricultural Development Bank and a gradual lifting of rent controls on agricultural land, culminating in the abolition of all security of tenure in 2002. After that date, landowners were free to renegotiate rents or even evict their tenants—households that in most cases had been farming the land at nominal rents since before the land reform of 1952. Taken together the two reforms seemed to promise exactly what *The Mystery of Capital* described, enabling owners to free up the capital locked in their land, either by pledging it as collateral for loans or renting it at increased levels of income.

There is insufficient evidence to draw any general conclusions about the impact of the reforms, in part because circumstances vary greatly from one village to another. In some parts of the country, for instance, entire hamlets farmed land rented from a single owner. In these cases the abolition of security of tenure in 2002 transformed the whole community from effective possessors of the land into landless farmers, who either lost access to the land or were forced to rent at much higher rates. In the village about which I have been writing, the rental plots were much more widely dispersed. This tended to favor the tenants. One group of three households, headed by three brothers, together farmed four acres of land, three acres of which they owned and one they rented. The owners of the rented acre lived in a neighboring hamlet of the same village but were the second-generation heirs of the original owner and had no idea of the exact location of their land. It lay somewhere in the middle of the other three acres, but since individual plots in Egypt have no hedgerows or other permanent boundary markers there was no way to establish its position. The original rental contract specified its position in relation to other plots of land, but these were also unmarked. Even if the owners had managed to locate their plot, they would not have been able to bring irrigation water to it. They had established no rights to use the ditches that carry water across neighbors' fields, and no separate ditch supplied their acre. The owner demanded an increase in annual rent from E£300 (about US$50) to E£1200. The brothers refused, and eventually agreed to pay E£600. If the owners had not been from a nearby hamlet, the brothers would have paid even less.

This case, one of several similar cases that came to light, illustrates some useful points. First, to the extent that the new law increased the rights of property owners, its effect was not to turn dead capital into live. The owners increased their rent, but the increase came from the tenant farmers, whose income declined by E£300 a year. This marked a shift in wealth from the productive labor of farmers to the unproductive labor of a rentier. Second, this transfer of income was limited by the weakness of property records. The inability of the owners of the rented acre to establish fully their claim to the land enabled the tenant farmers to pay a lower rent. The local knowledge of those who farmed the land was more powerful than the incomplete "abstract" knowledge of property entitlement that de Soto sees as the secret to capitalist development. The incompleteness of such knowledge was a means of limiting the diversion of income away from those who worked and knew the land into the hands of relative strangers. Formal property systems undermine this local knowledge by linking ownership into what are called more abstract, certainly more distant, forms, which can be accumulated, managed, and made sources of rent by outsiders. Preventing the transfer of this kind of knowledge into the hands of outsiders or property registers was a resource for protecting local income.

This case was not isolated but one of numerous similar cases in the village. Together, they are corroborated by all the evidence we have about the accumulation of property and the creation of inequality. The creation of formal legal title and property registration becomes a machinery for transferring property from small owners and concentrating it into larger and larger hands. We have already noted the operation of this machinery in Egypt between the mid-nineteenth and mid-twentieth century, and the measures the government was forced to adopt to limit its effectiveness. Evidence from a land titling program in rural Paraguay suggests that gains go only to relatively wealthy producers.[24] Further evidence comes from the impact on the village of the other part of the new agrarian laws—the new powers of the Agricultural Development Bank to take land as collateral for loans and to seize the land if the borrower defaults. Within a few years several farmers lost their land by this mechanism, in every case the defaulters were small owners. The only people in a position to buy land that became available this way were the handful of large owners, no more than a dozen households out of several thousand. Other studies show other adverse consequences of using land as collateral. When households use their land as collateral they have to add to their calculations relatively inefficient insurance measures that help them deal with poor harvests or other unexpected shocks, by keeping to low-risk, low return crops—sugar cane in this region of Egypt (Deininger and Binswanger 1999, p. 253). Given these drawbacks, building up and drawing on forms of credit whose loss is less catastrophic to the household, such as producing and storing grain and raising animals, is more efficient.

A further problem with using property as collateral for credit is that the poor are seldom able to recover from asset losses. They are often forced to sell property at low prices (during a recession or after a bad harvest), when there is little effective demand, and have to buy back in normal times, when prices are higher (Deininger and Binswanger 1999a, p. 253 citing Bidinger et al. 1991). Historically such distress sales play an important role in the concentration of property ownership and are connected with the loss of local ways of managing risk.[25]

What about the alleged benefits of being able to use property as collateral for loans? The evidence available shows there is little or no positive impact. If those with informal property seek title, they do so not to risk it in taking out loans. The titling program the ILD itself devised and managed in Peru, the largest to date, demonstrated this clearly. Four separate studies of the program found that it had no discernible effect on the supply of business credit (Cockburn 1998; Field and Torero 2002; Kagawa 2001; Torero 1999).[26] As one study concluded, "Loan acceptance rates of both standard commercial banks and informal lenders are unaffected by residential ownership status" (Field and Torero 2002). A large property titling program in Thailand was also found to have no effect on the likelihood of receiving bank loans (Feder et al. 1988).[27] Other studies of rural titling programs have found that "the title might make it easier for large producers to access credit but would not make small landowners creditworthy, a situation that would deepen preexisting inequalities" (Deininger and Binswanger 1999a, p. 260). Titling programs can have adverse consequences in other ways as well. Women may lose claims they have under an informal property system, in situations where men deal with the formal system. Titling on demand "has often had disastrous consequences for the poor because individuals with good political connections can often bypass the land rights of indigenous people, women, or other vulnerable groups" (Deininger and Binswanger 1999, p. 266, citing Bruce 1988 and Plateau 1996). Research, publications, and conferences organized by development economists at the World Bank brought together the evidence from dozens of case studies indicating that the ILD's proposals would not work (World Bank 1999, week 1).

We are no longer dealing here with a simple image of dead capital lying outside the market, beyond the boundary of the formal economy. We have a different picture, in which this boundary turns into a terrain of negotiations, the claiming of rights, relations of power, attempts at encroachment and exclusion. Rather than a problem of transferring assets from outside to inside the boundary, rearrangements of power, inequality, and poverty are at stake.

Having to Lose

It is time to consider, not the mystery of capital, but the mystery of *The Mystery of Capital*. Its arguments appear to exist in defective form, ignoring historical experience and unsupported by any of the available contemporary evidence. What is the mysterious process that transforms such defective analysis into live political projects?

There appears to be no evidence to support the ILD's argument for property titling as the key to unlocking the problem of capitalist development outside the West. A large amount of evidence does indicate that this will do nothing to improve the situation, and a strong case can be made that for the majority of the population it will make things worse. These studies provide the kind of detailed evaluations of the success and failure of particular projects that is entirely missing from the ILD's sweeping proposals for global transformation. Given this evidence, where do such arguments acquire their power? How do they come to circulate so widely?

The marketing of de Soto's project through the political networks of neoliberalism, described earlier, provides part of the answer, as does de Soto's claim to proprietary techniques for solving the mystery of capitalism. But these alone do not explain the rapid adoption of the particular program de Soto advocates, which is one of several kinds of neoliberal political reform. The reports of the World Bank, USAID, and other agencies that have funded De Soto's program suggest that what distinguishes the program from other neoliberal reforms is that it appears to be extraordinarily cost-effective (World Bank 2004). It seems to offer something for almost nothing. The problem of the global south, we are told, is that people are poor. The ILD offers them not riches, but a means of realizing wealth that no one knew they had. How is this effect achieved?

The possibility of getting something for nothing rests on the notion that the market has an "outside." The proposal that money can be created out of what presently counts as nothing would make no sense without arrangements whereby things can be said to exist outside the economy. Money is to be created out of nothing by the action of seeming to move resources from the outside to the inside. The production of a place outside the market creates the possibility of assets whose value is both existent and nonexistent. The assets exist as material wealth, but not as capital. The act of bringing this defective wealth inside the economy transforms it from something inert into something active, from death to life.

The power of this account of a boundary between an outside and an inside does not arise from the accuracy of its description of socioeconomic relations. It comes from the tools and arguments that are made available for establishing this inclusive exclusion and performing the transfer of assets. The ILD helps organize the data on unrecorded assets, the identification of obstacles to their movement, and the specification of legal and financial mechanisms needed for this transfer. Its work helps pull together particular alliances of local politicians, international financial institutions, property developers, and even spokespersons for the poor, to carry out the transfer. At the same time, it attempts to silence other kinds of claims and other forms of politics.

Let us consider more closely how the action of moving assets from "outside" the economy to the inside brings capital into being. When owners of irregular housing or land acquire formal title, the value of the property tends to increase. In the village, as noted above, making land legal for building increases in value by a factor of ten. Where informal housing is already built, the increase in value that comes with legalization is less, but still significant. In Brazil, a property titling program led to a doubling in the value of land (Alston et al. 1996 cited in Woodruff 2001, p. 1221). Another study found an increase of 25 percent, and other estimates fell between these two figures (Woodruff 2001, p. 1221). These increases are to be expected. As a World Bank study explained in relation to the titling of agricultural land, "The value of the ability to use unmortgaged land as collateral would be capitalized into land prices" (Deininger and Binswanger 1999, p. 252).

In principle, all owners of irregular property benefit from this increase in value. But very few can sell their properties, since that would leave them homeless. In any case, the need to purchase another property would eliminate any gain. Only those holding property not for their own needs but for speculation would benefit. Likewise, for reasons already discussed, only wealthy owners could take the risk of using their dwelling as collateral for a loan and turning its increased value into credit for investments. Over time, titling leads to the concentration of property in the hands of those able to purchase it at the higher values it now commands, and it creates speculators, who also benefit from the opportunities for income from the rent that such property now offers.

The increase in property value comes from two sources, neither of which represents "dead" capital brought to life. In the short term, it comes from speculative investment. Such investment simply draws existing capital away from more productive ventures, exacerbating broader problems caused by the lack of investment in activities that create employment. But the bulk of any increase in property value is realized only in the longer term, when future householders seek housing. The rising cost of land makes future housing more expensive. It now carries the premium of paying the income of speculators and rentiers. So those saving in the present for a house they hope to build in the future must work harder and longer and save more funds.

The outcome is an intertemporal transfer of wealth. Large owners and speculators gain immediately from the increased value of property. Small owners of property see no benefit from increased values. The gains of large owners and speculators are paid for by future owners, who face the prospect of paying increasing amounts for housing.

How is it possible to reorganize this transfer of wealth from the poor to the rich so that it appears as free money, as a simple act of turning dead capital into live? An important means of achieving this feat is to begin with the assumption that there is a "mystery" to capitalism, a secret that is not visible until it is represented in de Soto's text. Even before the secret is revealed and argued over, the promise that there is such a mystery disarms the reader of the text, or the recipient of the ILD's policy proposals. Capitalism is said to have a hidden key or principle. The multiple forms of expropriation, claim, violence, organization, and resistance whose diversity and motility we have been discussing are imagined to express an underlying principle, whose name is capitalism. Beneath the diversity and violence, we are told, lies some rule or law, whose hidden existence makes every historical case an expression of the same mysterious essential form. The mystery of de Soto's success begins with the notion that there is a mystery.

The persuasiveness of de Soto's arguments can also be connected to crisis in the formal property system in Egypt, Peru, and many other countries that had experienced neoliberal economic restructuring programs in the 1990s. In Cairo, measures to stabilize the currency, reduce government spending, privatize state-owned enterprises, and stimulate private investment had been praised by the IMF for achieving a "remarkable turnaround in Egypt's macroeconomic fortunes" (Subramanian 1997).[28] In the same period, the government and the courts began to alter the laws protecting commercial and residential tenants, freeing property developers from the constraint of rent controls (Moustafa 2003). The investment funds stimulated by the reforms flowed primarily into real estate, as speculators threw up large luxury and middle-income developments, and into exclusive concessions to provide services, such as cell phones or McDonald's restaurants, or to supply imports of electronics, cars, and other luxury goods. In other words, capital was transformed wherever possible into sources of rent rather than into productive activity. The share of manufacturing in the economy declined, non-oil exports fell, and no significant efforts were made to increase large-scale employment.[29]

The boom in property speculation and in luxury imports and services ended in a deep recession by the year 2000. The price of luxury apartments dropped by more than half, and property developers found themselves with tens of thousands of unsold apartments. A solution to these difficulties seemed to lie in the ILD's proposal for a mortgage law.

In 2001, parliament passed the law, as mentioned earlier, following draft legislation and implementation proposals drawn up for the Ministry of the Economy by the ILD and its local partner, the Egyptian Center for Economic Studies (ECES 2005 accessed). A further two years was needed to set up a body to regulate the new industry and to establish the

264 CHAPTER 9

first mortgage company, a subsidiary of the state-owned Housing and Development Bank. The bank also established a company to survey and register informal property, co-owned with the government survey authority (Loza 2004).[30] By 2005, only two mortgage companies had been established and the number of transactions remained very limited (Economist Intelligence Unit 2005).[31] The reasons for the delays and for the failure to establish additional mortgage companies are instructive. First, there was a problem in raising funds. The plan was to capitalize the industry by selling securities (mortgage bonds) on the Egyptian stock market. But neither the procedures nor the investors were available to do this. If the ILD's arguments were valid, this obstacle would not make sense. Property titling and a mortgage law were supposed to create funds by unlocking the dead capital of irregular real estate. In reality, there was no dead capital to unlock. Instead the new mortgage system attempted to draw existing capital into real estate, to bail out the speculators. Little capital was available, so the reforms stalled.

The second and more important obstacle, and a reason for the lack of enthusiasm from investors, was said to be a fear that the government would not enforce new provisions giving mortgage companies the power of foreclosure (Hasan 2004, p. 16; Ingraham 2004).

De Soto had acknowledged that the new property system was about making property owners less secure. People of the global south remain "trapped in the grubby basement of the precapitalist world" not because they have no property, he claimed, but "because they have no property to lose" (de Soto 2000, p. 56). Without the power to evict borrowers who fell into default, the entire project of releasing wealth from dead capital would fail. But a long history of struggle against the powers of foreclosure in the colonial period had made the use of any powers of eviction difficult. One of the main achievements of the 1952 revolution in Egypt had been to consolidate the protection of tenants' rights. Numerous local struggles over the ensuing decades had reinforced a widespread political claim that the state should not be involved in making people homeless.[32] Nothing in the ILD's proposals explains how this claim was to be overcome, how the new forms of coercion were to be put in place and made effective.

An Invisible Parallel Life

In place of an account of the relations of forces involved, de Soto offers a much simpler picture of the procedures required to turn unregistered assets into live capital. He describes the process as one of representation, a concept that plays a central role in his account. Representation is the operation that moves the assets of the poor into the market.

If the poor hold their assets in defective form, the defect is that they are not visible—not visible, that is, to the economy. In the West, de Soto explains, property ownership is represented in a document, which is "the visible sign of a vast hidden process that connects all these assets to the rest of the economy." Thanks to this process of representation, "assets can lead an invisible, parallel life alongside their material existence." Other countries do not have this representational process, and this explains why people have not been able to produce sufficient capital to make capitalism work. Only the West possesses the "conversion process" needed to decode the capital that material assets invisibly harbor. "This is the mystery of capital" (de Soto 2000, pp. 6–7).

How does representation achieve this conversion? The answer is that unlike physical assets, representations of assets are set free from material restraints and therefore can be easily moved around, combined, divided, and used to launch business ventures. By uncoupling the economic value of an asset from its physical form, a representation makes the asset fungible (de Soto 2000, p. 56).

We should note first that this description of the process of representation in the West is misleading. In many Western property systems, including those of the United States and Britain, there was no title document of the sort de Soto advocates. Historically the use of such a document was avoided, because it could be outdated or might be deliberately altered and was therefore an invitation to fraud. Representations can be dangerous things, as their use cannot always be controlled. What distinguishes different techniques of representation, as I argue below, is not their abstractness but the degree of their control. In the United States and Britain, property claims were established through the use of title deeds. A deed is not a representation of property ownership, but its performance. It is a legal instrument used to perform the transfer—not of an object (property), but of a right (ownership). To be legally valid, it had to include a term such as "hereby" indicating that the deed is a performative instrument. And it had to be physically performed, by handing the instrument from the previous owner to the new owner in the presence of a witness. Property titles in Britain and the United States consisted of an accumulation of deeds, marking the successive acts of transfer of rights from one owner to the next.[33]

Even today, attempts to introduce property registers in the way de Soto advocates have been unsuccessful in the United States. Most U.S. states use a system of private title insurance, combined with public registration of transactions. These methods tend to be expensive, as they are open to price fixing and the capture of legislative regulation by private interests. But attempts to replace them with property recordation, in which the state records the ownership and transfer of all property, were unpopular because of the long delays these procedures introduced.[34]

Moreover, the suggestion that informal systems of property lack complex systems of representation is also misleading. We can return briefly to the village discussed earlier. The extent to which villagers are constantly moving resources into and out of a variety of assets is remarkable. The most common instance is the raising of domestic animals. Almost every household is involved in raising small animals (chickens, ducks, geese, rabbits, and pigeons), many have sheep and goats, and more than half own a cow or a water buffalo.[35] These investments are productive, providing food for the table and making their own offspring. But when a need for cash arises, a sheep, some chickens, or a calf can be sold. When surplus income arrives, it can be converted into more secure assets, typically domestic animals (but also gold, stored in the form of jewelry). Households also organize rotating credit unions to raise funds for large purchases, such as a new stove or a water buffalo. Selling a large animal can help pay for a small business venture, such as acquiring a sewing machine to take in dressmaking work, or setting up a kiosk to sell cigarettes or household items (sugar, soap, light bulbs) to neighbors.

Such saving and investment has several advantages over using land and housing as collateral for credit. First, it draws savings into productive activity rather than real-estate investment. Second, it is typically controlled by women, who are more likely then men to direct income toward the basic needs of children and the household. Third, assets are fungible, but not too fungible. Resources held in the form of domestic animals can be converted to cash when urgent needs arise, but they are solid enough not to drip away on casual purchases.

What is the difference between these methods of accumulating and circulating assets and those that de Soto sees as the secret to the mystery of capital? The difference does not lie in the presence or absence of representations, or their degree of abstraction. De Soto may be correct that certain forms of wealth, or certain ways of representing assets, become more mobile, travel longer distances, and are more easily combined and accumulated. However, this mobility does not derive from the degree of abstraction. It derives from establishing techniques of control, which make it possible to manage assets at a distance and accumulate them in larger quantities.

In the village, most household wealth is held in assets controlled by direct supervision. The wealth is accumulated in domestic animals, the fields outside the house, an irrigation pump adjacent to a relative's house across the fields, or a plot of land in the next hamlet. All this is relatively easy to manage. Large landowners face much greater challenges of supervision. They hire guards to protect stores of grain, use client families to operate irrigation pumps in different areas of landholding, and rely on labor contractors to supply gangs of workers for harvesting. The much larger estates built up in the nineteenth and early twentieth century, dismantled after 1952, were possible only after innovations in methods of monitoring and disciplining large labor forces, based on purpose-built worker housing units in which workers could be locked at night and kept under continuous supervision (Mitchell 2002, pp. 66–70). The largest properties possessed "a veritable brigade of employees whose sole occupation was to supervise the workers, continuously and in the closest and most rigorous fashion" (Nahas 1901, p. 141). The powers of supervision, including the new courts, bailiffs, prisons, and armed police forces, were all essential to the accumulation of "representations" of wealth on a new scale.

The accumulation of wealth that de Soto has in mind depends, as I have noted, on the reintroduction of powers of foreclosure and eviction that were abrogated, in the face of popular protest and economic dislocation, in the course of the twentieth century. In other words, rather than a question of creating something more abstract, it is if anything a question of something more physical—more extensive powers of eviction and control. The delay in establishing mortgage banks, despite the appropriate legislation and regulatory body, the setting up of loan companies, and a property titling system, comes down to the failure to secure the most physical of powers.

De Soto's plans envisage a vast creation of wealth by the transformation of so-called dead capital into live capital. In practice, the evidence suggests that this will produce not live capital out of dead, but a transfer of wealth from the less affluent to the more secure, and in particular serve to enrich the more prosperous among the present generation at the expense of the future poor. This is not to be accomplished by moving what is outside the market to the inside, but by deploying this boundary mechanism in new ways. It is not to be accomplished by representing what is currently invisible, but by altering the circulation and management of representations. It is to occur through a reorganization of forces among a variety of parties. And it requires the creation of mechanisms of compulsion.

Inclusive Exclusion

I have argued that the unrecorded and less closely governed forms of socioeconomic life that are described by neoliberal economic reform programs as lying outside the economy are not in fact outside, yet they are not simply inside. They can be understood as a frontier or border, a status that is neither exterior nor interior to the market. They are partially outside, because these assets cannot be priced by the market, just

as the labor of those who control them is not easily available for capitalist enterprise. Economics helps to manage this border, by producing and
validating rules and procedures that demarcate certain forms of life as
informal or nonmarket. Yet those forms of life are in some ways inside,
because the arrangements taken by what is called "capitalism" or "the
market," such as the ways of earning rent that are the principal means
for an elite to reproduce its wealth, are the outcome of a long and continuing interaction with this so-called outside.

De Soto's program, now to be further promoted by bodies like the
United Nations Development Program's High Level Commission on
Legal Empowerment of the Poor, involves the movement of assets from
the outside to the inside. This reordering offers a means to create wealth.
But the wealth is not produced by the method de Soto's account implies.
The process of property titling and the use of property as collateral bring
into being opportunities for speculation, for the concentrating of wealth,
and for the accumulation of rents. The existing assets of the poor are not
the material source of this new wealth. Rather, they are the objects of an
inclusive exclusion. Through schemes such as de Soto's they are turned
into the apparatus through which this reorganization and accumulation
is carried out. The poor remain "outside" this process, for the outcome
of a process of property titling and the mortgaging of property is that
land and housing become even less affordable to the poor. They are further excluded from opportunities for the accumulation of capital. Yet at
the same time they are "inside" the process. Their houses and their lives
must be transformed in order to carry out the production of this wealth.
The starting point of this transformation is to render these ways of life
defective, almost dead, by grasping them in terms of the economic
rationality and forms of representation they are said to lack. Since their
defectiveness is what makes the accumulation possible, it is an outside
on which the so-called inside depends.

A conventional critique of de Soto's proposals would expose the neoliberal fallacies on which they rely for their plausibility and popularity.
It would draw attention to the history of battles over property rights
that de Soto's writings ignore and his inability to account for the moral
claims, financial protections, practical flexibility, and affordability offered, whatever their defects, by alternative property arrangements.
Having dismissed his writings as no more than the latest vulgate of the
neoliberal canon, one could then reveal the real interests for which his
ideas are such a flimsy screen.

The work of neoliberalism, however, does not lie behind a screen. If
the fallacies of de Soto's arguments seem surprisingly easy to expose,
that is because their effectiveness does not rest on the precision with
which they capture the workings of particular property arrangements.

The performative power of economics does not rest on the accuracy or inaccuracy of its representations. De Soto's writings form part of the equipment for neoliberal projects. They provide a means of mobilizing certain facts of neoclassical economics in alliance with the planning of development agencies, the resources of property developers, and the political powers of local regimes. They form part of the novel apparatus by which speculators are to be rescued, the poor made to give up their houses, and new forms of wealth created.

Notes

1. The car parking example is discussed, along with several others, in Bayat (1997).

2. The Institute for Liberty and Democracy created a pilot property registry program and ran it on behalf of the government from 1992 to 1994. In 1996, the government replaced it with the Commission for the Formalization of Informal Property, which was run by the government and staffed by existing and former ILD personnel, with funding from the World Bank. See World Bank (2004).

3. These endorsements are carried inside the front cover of the paperback edition of *The Mystery of Capital*, alongside favorable quotations from reviews in more than a dozen leading U.S. and British journals.

4. For a list of awards see ILD (2005b).

5. John Leonard actually wrote in his review that de Soto's book "has already led the cognoscenti to put him in the pantheon of great progressive intellectuals of our age" (*New Statesman*, September 4, 2000 in ILD 2005a). Nevertheless, Leonard's review reported great enthusiasm for de Soto among advisers to the British Prime Minister Tony Blair. Several other commentators from the center-left of British and American politics were equally enthusiastic.

6. Quoted inside the front cover of the paperback edition of *The Mystery of Capital*.

7. See High Level Commission on Legal Empowerment of the Poor (2005). The commission was supported and funded by the governments of Canada, Denmark, Finland, Iceland, Norway, Sweden, and the United Kingdom. The commission "will approach the issue of global poverty from a unique perspective: the link between poverty and the inability of the poor to access acceptable, legal structures to protect economic assets and support economic activities."

8. *Development Today* (2005).

9. *Development Today* (2005).

10. ILD worked with a local partner, the Egyptian Center for Economic Studies. See ECES (2005).

11. For details of what happened, and the comparison with what occurred in Europe and the United States, see Mitchell (2002, pp. 54–79) and an earlier paper on which the present chapter draws (Mitchell 2003).

12. Pomeranz (2001) provides an important account of the role of colonization in the rapid industrialization of the West, not so much as a source of

"primitive accumulation" but as a means of overcoming the land constraint that previously made it difficult to devote large amounts of land and labor to industrialization, that is, to the production of cotton and other industrial fibers instead of food.

13. The term "inclusive exclusion" is borrowed from the discussion of the topologies (and powers of property) implicit in the logic of sovereignty in Agamben (1998), although my use of the term here owes more to Derrida than Agamben.

14. Figures from a 1998 survey by the U.S. Small Business Administration show that among businesses in the United States with sales under $25,000 a year, 40 percent borrow no funds at all. Only about a quarter of businesses take traditional loans, either from banks and other financial institutions or from family and friends. Twice as many businesses, almost 50 percent, use nontraditional credit. This consists largely of funds borrowed on credit cards, in some cases business credit cards but in most cases personal cards. See U.S. Small Business Administration (1998).

15. U.K. Office on National Statistics, Housing Statistics (2005); U.N. Economic Commission for Europe (2000); Proxenos (2002).

16. See Fathy (1969). Other early discussions include Turner (1968). For subsequent critiques see Ward (1982) and, for the limits of Fathy's vision, Mitchell (2002, pp. 184–195).

17. The observations are based on the study of eight house-building projects in 2004 and additional information on numerous other cases gathered over the previous decade. For more details on the village see Mitchell (2002, pp. 249–266).

18. Pollen from the male date palm is brought to fertilize the female tree by hand, so only one male is needed for every fifteen or twenty females. The other males can be felled for use in building.

19. Law No. 116 of 1983 established penalties ranging from E£10,000 to E£50,000 for unauthorized building on agricultural land. The Prime Minister's Military Order No. 1 of 1996, passed under emergency regulations promulgated in 1981, gave the government powers to destroy such buildings. One estimate suggests that 600,000 acres of agricultural land were lost to construction in the two decades that followed the 1983 law. See Essam El-Din (2003) and El-Diwany and Kamel (2001a).

20. The problem of building on agricultural land is much more serous around large cities and in the Nile Delta north of Cairo, where most land is a long way from the desert margin.

21. The decree (No. 3594 of 1998, amended by Decree No. 261 of 1999) applied only to buildings constructed before the Prime Minister's Military Order No. 1 of 1996; but in practice it was often difficult for the authorities to determine the date of construction (El-Diwany and Kamel 2001b, p. 7).

22. One qirat is 1/24 of an Egyptian acre (or feddan), or 175 square meters. E£ indicates Egyptian pounds. In spring 2004, E£1,000 was equal to about U.S.$160 (U.S.$1= E£ 6.20).

23. See Arab Republic of Egypt, Ministry of Housing and Reconstruction, Advisory Committee for Reconstruction, and United Kingdom, Ministry of Overseas Development (1978).

24. Carter and Olinto (2000), cited by Woodruff (2001, p. 1218 n. 5). For other evidence that land titling tends to benefit disproportionately the better off see Deininger and Binswanger (1999, p. 250) and the online conference hosted by the World Bank Group's Land and Real Estate Initiative (1999, week 1).

25. Deininger and Binswanger (1999, p. 254) citing Kranton and Swamy (1997). Mitchell (2002, pp. 54–79) discusses the role of distress sales in the concentration of land ownership in nineteenth-century Egypt.

26. All four are cited in Field (2003). See also Mitchell (2005).

27. The only effect was that those with title received somewhat larger loans.

28. For an account of the reforms and their outcome see Mitchell (2002, pp. 272–303).

29. See figures, including number of workers employed, in *Business Today Egypt* (2005).

30. Law No. 148 of 2001. The regulatory body was the General Authority for Real Estate Finance.

31. In 2004 the International Financial Corporation (the arm of the World Bank that lends to the private sector) and the German Investment and Development Company put up funds to launch Egypt's first private mortgage company, the Egyptian Housing Finance Company, with an authorized capital of E£100 million. The other share owners were the Egyptian American Bank, holding 40 percent of shares, the Bank of Alexandria, and the Indian-owned Housing Development Finance Corporation.

32. In February 2004 the local authorities in Luxor in southern Egypt began to carry out plans to demolish recently constructed housing on the Nile embankment opposite the town, which was illegal and ruined the dramatic panorama of the Theban hills, a UNESCO world heritage site. The bulldozers moved in but demolished only the unoccupied buildings. The local authorities were unwilling to demolish occupied houses. But at the same time, these concerns do not always protect informal housing against demolition by the government. Cases of demolition are documented by the Egyptian Centre for Housing Rights.

33. Pottage (1994, 1995) describes the "practical art" of forming property titles in England prior to the introduction of property registration procedures in the first third of the twentieth century. He further shows how the new registration procedures transformed property not into a material object that might be transparently represented, but into a bureaucratic artifact.

34. For a discussion of these issues see World Bank online conference (1999, week 2). In England and Wales, the 2002 Land Registration Act, which came into effect in October 2003, attempted to make the existing, voluntary Land Registry a more complete compendium of property claims by increasing the number of events that trigger compulsory registration. But the act also abolished land certificates, which the Registry had previously issued, as (incomplete) evidence of title to a property. The Registry would now keep only an electronic record of deeds and charges, and planned to destroy earlier paper documents and issue on paper only a "title information document." See Land Registry (2005).

35. Even in the cities, domestic animals are a significant source of food security for low-income households. In Cairo, it is estimated that 16 percent of

households raise domestic animals, usually chicken or other small animals raised on the roof of an apartment building or in a rear yard. See Gertel and Samir (2002).

References

Agamben, G. 1998. *Homer Sacer: Sovereign Power and Bare Life*. Stanford: Stanford University Press.

Alston, L., G. Libecap, and R. Schneider. 1996. "The Determinants and Impact of Property Rights: Land Titles on the Brazilian Frontier." *Journal of Law, Economics, and Organization* 12(1):1569–1614.

Arab Republic of Egypt, Ministry of Housing and Reconstruction, Advisory Committee for Reconstruction, and United Kingdom, Ministry of Overseas Development. 1978. *Ismailiya Demonstration Projects*. Cairo: Ministry of Housing and Reconstruction.

Bayat, A. 1997. "Uncivil Society: The Politics of the 'Informal People.'" *Third World Quarterly* 18(1):53–72.

Bidinger, P. D., T. S. Walker, B. Sarkar, A. R. Murty, and P. Babu. 1991. "Consequences of Mid-1980s Drought: Longitudinal Evidence from Mahbubnagar." *Economic and Political Weekly* 26:A105–114.

Bromley, R. 1990. "A New Path to Development? The Significance and Impact of Hernando De Soto's Ideas on Underdevelopment, Production, and Reproduction." In "Production and Reproduction in Latin American Cities: Concepts, Linkages, and Empirical Trends," Special issue, *Economic Geography* 66(4):328–348.

Bruce, J. W. 1988. "A Perspective on Indigenous Land Tenure Systems and Land Concentration." In *Land and Society in Contemporary Africa*, edited by R. W. Downs and S. P. Reyna. Hanover, NH: University Press of New England.

Business Today Egypt. 2005 (accessed). 'Top 100' Companies. Available at http://www.businesstodayegypt.com.

Callon, M., Ed. 1998. *The Laws of the Markets*. London: Blackwell.

Carter, M. R., and P. Olinto. 2000. "Getting Institutions Right for Whom? Credit Constraints and the Impact of Property Rights on the Quantity and Composition of Investment." University of Wisconsin–Madison, Agricultural and Applied Economics Staff Paper 433.

Chatterjee, P. 2004. *The Politics of the Governed: Reflections on Popular Politics in Most of the World*. New York: Columbia University Press.

Cockburn, J. C. 1998. "Regularisation of Urban Land in Peru." *Land Lines*, May. (Cambridge, MA:Lincoln Institute of Land Policy).

Deininger, K., and H. Binswanger. 1999. "The Evolution of the World Bank's Land Policy: Principles, Experience, and Future Challenges." *World Bank Research Observer* 14 (August):247–276.

De Soto, H. 1989. *The Other Path: The Invisible Revolution in the Third World*. New York: HarperCollins; 2nd ed., retitled *The Other Path: The Economic Answer to Terrorism*. New York: Basic Books, 2002.

De Soto, H. 2000. *The Mystery of Capital: Why Capitalism Triumphs in the West and Fails Everywhere Else*. New York: Basic Books.

De Soto, H. 2001. Interview on "The Law Report" with Damien Carrick. December 11, 2001. Transcript available at http://www.abc.net.au/rn/talks/8.30/lawrpt/stories/s437315.htm.

Development Today (Norway). 2005. "Norway and Hernando de Soto. Bankrolling the Presidents' Man," no. 10–11 (July 18). Available at http://www.DeSotoWatch.net.

The Economist. 1991. "The Good Think Tank Guide," October 21.

Economist Intelligence Unit. 2005. "Egypt Regulations: Mortgage Law to Be Amended." *EIU ViewsWire*, January 19.

Egyptian Center for Economic Studies (ECES). 2005. (accessed). "Formalization Action Plan." Available at http://www.eces.org.eg/Research/Index3.asp?l1=2&l2=1&l3=1.

Egyptian Centre for Housing Rights. Available at http://www.hshr.org/housingevictionstorture.htm.

El-Diwany, S., and M. Kamel. 2001a. "Egyptian Laws Governing Real Property and the Use of Land for Building Purposes." Working Paper, Arab Republic of Egypt, Ministry of Planning, and Federal Republic of Germany, German Technical Cooperation, Participatory Urban Management Programme, Cairo, March. Available at http://www.egypt-urban.net.

El-Diwany, S., and M. Kamel. 2001b. "Policies, Procedures, and Channels of Access to Land that May Lead to Informality." Working Paper, Arab Republic of Egypt, Ministry of Planning, and Federal Republic of Germany, German Technical Cooperation, Participatory Urban Management Programme, Cairo, March. Available at http://www.egypt-urban.net.

Elyachar, J. 2005. *Markets of Dispossession: NGOs, Economic Development, and the State in Cairo*. Durham, NC: Duke University Press.

Essam El-Din, G. 2003. "Opposition Wants Deeper Reforms." *Al-Ahram Weekly*, 9 October. Available at http://weekly.ahram.org.eg/2003/659/eg4.htm.

Fathy, H. 1969. *Gurna: A Tale of Two Villages*. Cairo: Ministry of Culture; reprinted as *Architecture for the Poor*. Chicago: University of Chicago Press, 1973.

Feder, G., T. Onchan, Y. Chalamwong, and C. Hongladarom. 1988. *Land Policies and Farm Productivity in Thailand*. Baltimore, MD: Johns Hopkins University Press.

Field, E., 2003. "Entitled to Work: Urban Property Rights and Labor Supply in Peru." Available at http://rwj.harvard.edu/scholarsbio/field/field.htm.

Field, E., and M. Torero. 2002. "Do Property Titles Increase Credit Access among the Urban Poor? Evidence from Peru." Research Program in Development Studies Working Paper No. 223, Princeton University.

Forbes, S. 2004. "Mideast Miracle?" Available at http://www.forbes.com/business/free_forbes/2004/0216/027.html.

Gertel, J., and S. Samir. 2002. "Cairo: Urban Agriculture and Visions for a Modern' City." In *Growing Cities, Growing Food: Urban Agriculture on the Policy Agenda: A Reader on Urban Agriculture*, edited by N. Bakker, M. Dubbeling, S. Guendel, U. Sabel-Koschella, and H. de Zeeuw, RUAF. Available at http://www.ruaf.org/ruafpublications_fr.html.

Hacking, I. 1995 "The Looping Effects of Human Kinds." In *Causal Cognition: A Multidisciplinary Approach*, edited by D. Sperber, D. Premack, and A. J. Premack. Oxford: Clarendon Press.

Hacking, I. 1999 *The Social Construction of What?* Cambridge, MA: Harvard University Press.

Hasan, M. 2004. "Al-tamwil al 'aqari: hal yakhdum mahdudi' hamza l-dakhl?" *Al-Ahram*, March 28, p. 16.

Hayek, F. 1980. Letter to Antony Fisher, January 1, 1980. Available at http://www.atlasusa.org/pdf/2004yearinreview.pdf.

Holm, P., and K. N. Nielsen. 2004. "The Cyborg Fish and the Invisible Hand: Making Market Models Work in the Fisheries." Paper presented at the workshop on "The Performativities of Economics," Ecole des Mines de Paris, August 29–30.

High Level Commission on Legal Empowerment of the Poor. 2005. "Frequently Asked Questions." Available at http://legalempowerment.undp.org/html/faq.html.

Ingraham, J. 2004. "Make or Break Year?" *Business Today Egypt*, February. Available at http://www.businesstodayegypt.com/0402/default.asp.

Institute for Liberty and Democracy. 2005a. "Press and Academic Reviews." Available at http://www.ild.org.pe/eng/reviews.htm.

Institute for Liberty and Democracy. 2005b. "ILD awards." Available at http://www.ild.org.pe/eng/criticism3.htm.

Kagawa, A. 2001. "Policy Effects and Tenure Security Perceptions of Peruvian Urban Land Tenure Regularisation Policy in the 1990s." Workshop Paper, ESF/N-AERUS International Workshop, Leuven and Brussels, Belgium, May 23–26.

Kranton, R. E., and A. V. Swamy. 1997. "The Hazards of Piecemeal Reform: British Civil Courts and the Credit Market in Colonial India." World Bank, Development Research Group, Washington, D.C.

Land Registry. 2005. "Land Registration Act 2002." Available at http://www.landregistry.gov.uk/legislation/.

Liang, L. 2005. "Porous Legalities and Avenues of Participation." In *Sarai Reader 05: Bare Acts*, edited by M. Narula, S. Sengupta, J. Bagchi, and G. Lovink; guest editor L. Liang. Delhi: The Sarai Program, Centre for the Study of Developing Societies, Febuary, 6–17.

Loza, P. 2004. "The Not-So-Real Estate Company." *Al-Ahram Weekly*, March 4–10. Available at http://weekly.ahram.org.eg/2004/680/ec2.htm.

Mitchell, T. 2002. *Rule of Experts: Egypt, Techno-Politics, Modernity*. Berkeley: University of California Press.

Mitchell, T. 2003. "The Properties of Markets: Informal Housing and Capitalism's Mystery." Institute for Advanced Studies in Social and Management Sciences, University of Lancaster, Cultural Political Economy Working Paper No. 2. Available at http://www.lancs.ac.uk/ias/polecon/index.htm.

Mitchell, T. 2005. "The Work of Economics: How a Discipline Makes Its World." *European Journal of Sociology* 47(2):297–320.

Moustafa, T. 2003. "Law Versus the State: the Judicialization of Politics in Egypt." *Law and Social Inquiry* 28(4):883–931.

Nahas, J. F. 1901. *Situation économique et sociale du fellah égyptien*. Paris: Arthur Rousseau.

Plateau, J.-P. 1996. "The Evolutionary Theory of Land Rights as Applied to Sub-Saharan Africa: A Critical Assessment." *Development and Change* 27:29–86.

Plehwe, D. 2006. *Neoliberal Hegemony: A Global Critique*. New York: Routledge.

Pomeranz, K. 2001. *The Great Divergence: China, Europe, and the Making of the Modern World Economy*. Princeton: Princeton University Press.

Pottage, A. 1994. "The Measure of Land." *Modern Law Review* 57(3):361–384.

Pottage, A. 1995. "The Originality of Registration." *Oxford Journal of Legal Studies* 15(3):371–401.

Proxenos, S. 2002. "Home Ownership Rates: A Global Perspective." *Housing Finance International* 17:3–7.

Subramanian, A. 1997. "The Egyptian Stabilization Experience: An Analytical Retrospective." *Working Papers of the International Monetary Fund*, WP/97/105, International Monetary Fund (IMF), Middle Eastern Department, September.

Torero, M. 1999. "Estudio de la Oferta, Demanda y Fuentes de Crédito Informal." Documento Suplementario del Estudio: Perfil de la Demanda y Oferta del Crédito Formal y Informal. Paper prepared for the COFOPRI office, Grupo de Análisis para el Desarollo, November.

Turner, J.F.C. 1968. "The Squatter Settlement: Architecture that Works." *Architectural Design* 38:355–360.

U.N. Economic Commission for Europe. 2000. *Annual Bulletin of Housing and Building Statistics for Europe and North America 2000*. Available at http://www.unece.org/env/hs/bulletin/cnt2_e98.htm.

U.K. Office on National Statistics, Housing Statistics. 2005. Available at http://www.statistics.gov.uk.

U.S. Small Business Administration. 1998. Survey available at http://www.sba.gov/advo/research/banking.html.

Ward, P. M. 1982. *Self-Help Housing: A Critique*. London: Mansell.

Woodruff, C. 2001. "Review of de Soto's *The Mystery of Capital*." *Journal of Economic Literature* 39:1215–1223.

World Bank. 2004. "Implementation Completion Report (SCL-43840) On a Loan in the Amount of US$36.12 Million to the Republic of Peru for an Urban Property Rights Project." Washington DC: World Bank.

World Bank Group's Land and Real Estate Initiative. 1999. Conference "Land, Real Estate, and the Economy," November. Summary of week 1 available at http://www2.worldbank.org/hm/landecon/Week1.doc; summary of week 2 available at http://www2.worldbank.org/hm/landecon/Week2.doc.

Chapter 10 _____

Do Statistics "Perform" the Economy?

EMMANUEL DIDIER

As demonstrated in the other chapters in this book, economics does not simply come down to the observation of economic facts. Quite the opposite, in fact: often it has an effect on the latter; it is the theory itself that produces them. How does this frequently observed effect operate? Many authors have given it a name, imported from the pragmatic, Anglo-Saxon theory of language: performativity. Whereas theory is supposed to simply account for the object, it is said to "perform" it.

The seduction obviously exerted by this vocabulary however, seems to me to be equaled by the problems it raises. While we have indeed been given many examples of that "performativity," still in all, there is something reminiscent of magic about the idea that a *theory* is able to influence *the facts* it supposedly simply describes or explains. To imagine that we can describe or explain something and transform it at the same time is truly difficult. Moreover, everyday experience teaches us that no matter what we say about an object set before our eyes, even if we yell, whisper, wheedle, or give orders, that object will not change by mere dint of our utterances—that would be pure magic. Although that "performative" link between theory and facts has often been observed, we still can barely get a clear conception of it.

Conversely, short of this mysterious performing, we find plenty of other intermediaries making the link between theory and its objects. For example, we find sheets of paper containing prices (as seen, for example, in MacKenzie's chapter), or experimental settings, laboratories and platforms (as seen in Muniesa and Callon's chapter), or even cyborg fish and quotas (Holm's chapter). And, in the middle of this crowd of intermediaries is one that economists use very often, although they paradoxically pay little attention to it, and that is *statistics*. Indeed, the concrete form in which the economy itself enters theory is often a statistical series, and, similarly, when we want to measure any particular effect (including the effect of theory) on the economy, we often use statistics. Whereas these are by far not always the best mediation between theory and facts, they often are. So before wondering whether the relations between theory and facts take the form of performing, we may look at the role of statistics in that relationship. In this case, the question turns into: can it be economic statistics that perform their object? Perhaps it is the descriptor (statistics) of that other descriptor (that is, theory) which performs its object? The hypothesis is worth testing.[1]

To do so, we will take the example of the first economic surveys that made use of statistics.[2] These were the agricultural statistics produced by the government of the United States during the first half of the twentieth century. They are the ancestors of present-day random surveys and polls. What makes this example interesting is, clearly, its resistance: if statistics can have effects on fields and crops, that is on *nature*, through observation, then the argument will be even more convincing than if it had been applied to human beings, who are far more easily influenced than wheat or corn. Furthermore, there is the idea that by looking at one of the earliest instances, the conclusions drawn will remain valid for the later developments in the method, that is, for just about all contemporary economic surveys. Our question, then, is as follows: did the first statistics aimed at describing the agricultural markets "perform" those markets?

To Have Effects Is Not to Perform

In the period between the two world wars, a villain lurked in the United States. He hardly did any harm in the cities, but he preyed constantly on farmers, who were isolated in the middle of their fields and swallowed his line: "You know, mister farmer," he said, "yields have been fantastic this year. I just got back from nearby Oklahoma, and I can tell you that I never saw as much corn in the fields. And in fact, prices have dropped catastrophically. But since I'm on your side, I'll buy yours one cent above the going rate, which is 12 cents a bushel this year." And they clinched the deal, to the satisfaction of both parties. Until the day when the farmer went to town or had a visit from a city cousin, who said to him: "Well, I guess things are going well this year, with corn at 25 cents a bushel."[3]

That loathed character was the *speculator*, who not only misled farmers and got rich by lying, but committed a much worse offense, according to the U.S. government: he distorted the whole *market*. By playing on the asymmetric information caused by farmers' isolation and his own connections, he made it *imperfect* (on the point of building "perfect" markets, see Garcia's chapter in this volume).

That is why the government decided to intervene. The potion it developed to destroy the disease of speculation was statistics. First it began to determine the total yield of the main cereals, expressed in bushels, for the year, then to predict the amounts of farm produce that would be on sale at a given date t, and at the end of the harvest period. Later, those series were enriched and accompanied by increasing amounts of data.[4] To combat what it viewed as the ravages of speculation, the government produced more and more statistics.

To achieve this end, an agency was set up and put in charge of the job. Called the Bureau of Agricultural Economics, it is now the National Agricultural Statistical Service (NASS). Within this agency, one division was specially in charge of statistics, but I am hard put to say which one, simply because it changed names frequently. In 1917 it was called the Bureau of Crop Estimates; in 1921 it became the Division of Crop Estimates; in 1922 it was called the Division of Markets and Crop Estimates; at the end of the period we are studying, it was called the Division of Crop and Livestock Estimates (Taylor and Taylor 1952). To avoid this litany, we will call it "the Division" from now on. The statistics we will be looking at were produced by the Division.

How was this remedy supposed to work? According to Leon M. Estabrook (1915, p. 8), who was a very important head of the Division during World War I and for several years after because of all the technical and technological innovations that took place under his mandate, "The disinterested reports of the Government tend to prevent the circulation of false or misleading reports by speculators who are interested in controlling or manipulating prices." By making public an *objective* measurement of farm produce, the administration enormously complicated the job of speculators, who might perhaps be able to continue manipulating demand (which mostly depended on them) but had much more trouble manipulating supply. The administration felt that the most effective weapon against distortion of the markets would be *objectivity*. Informing the public of the *true figures* for national agricultural production would be the most efficient way of purifying and perfecting the markets.

But is the relationship between objective figures and pure markets as mechanical as all that? Would objectivity automatically frighten speculators, would it be enough to make them recoil and run away? That was not what the administration, or the farmers themselves, thought. For the government's action to be effective it would have to be continued by the work of other actors. Let us see how the figures took part in economic relations.

First, here is how the figures would be useful to farmers, according to the Division:

> Farmers are benefited by the Government crop reports both directly and indirectly; directly by being kept informed of crop prospects and prices outside of their own immediate districts, and indirectly, because the disinterested

reports of the Government tend to prevent the circulation of false or misleading reports by speculators who are interested in controlling or manipulating
prices. (Estabrook 1915, p. 9)

The figures allowed the farmers to keep informed on crop prospects
and prices. How could farmers have possibly not known that information before? "Prices in [the farmers'] own local market are influenced, as
a rule, more by the condition of the whole crop throughout the State or
the United States, and even in foreign countries, than they are by local
conditions" (Estabrook 1915, p. 10). Since prices depended on overall
production rather than local conditions, farmers might be too isolated to
be informed of those factors. The Division then served as a "center of
calculation," centralizing large amounts of scattered data and transforming them into relevant information for each farmer. Estabrook adds:
"In a sense the Bureau of Crop Estimates is a form of farmers' cooperation" (1915, p. 9). The figures therefore kept farmers informed of the
overall state of crops.

But that information served, if we dare say, only to keep farmers informed. Indeed, it did not seem to affect speculation directly. The figures
combated these misdeeds only indirectly. How? According to the Division,
because the figures made it difficult to circulate other figures, or "false information" published by speculators in order to distort the market; "Such
information as interested speculators and dealers might choose to publish
in the newspapers, which might or might not be correct" (Estabrook
1915, p. 11). The speculators were more organized than the farmers, and
above all, they were in a position to "take advantage of fluctuations in
market prices," so that they could publish false figures to manipulate
prices. But inasmuch as the Division published "disinterested" figures, it
put an end to, or at least prevented the circulation of those fallacious reports.[5] The opponents that the administration's figures were fighting, then,
were not men but other figures. But how did they battle? How, concretely,
did farmers use the Division's reports?

Figures alone did not seem able to market farm produce any better, in
the sense that they were not directly useful to farmers when they sold
their produce, because of the complexity of the distribution circuit. The
crops were taken from the farm by a haulage contractor, who brought
them to a cooperative (the shipper) which did the selling. It was the cooperative, then, that used the government figures, but not necessarily to
bargain with purchasers, since market prices were set, leaving no choice
but to accept them. The only thing the cooperative could choose was the
date on which it would sell, and that was where statistics were useful,
for the market price depended on the season (in winter supply is low,
so prices are high, whereas in summer, after harvesting, the supply is

plentiful, so prices are low) and on expectations as to crop size (prices were higher when large crops were expected and lower in the opposite case).

> To do a good selling at the right time, the shipper needs a full range of information as to the present and prospective supply situation. This does not cost much money because most of this information can be obtained free from governmental sources. But it does take time. It is a full-time job for any man to digest, analyze and interpret this information. A farmer who did this job well would have no time left for any other work. (Miller and Shepherd 1933, pp. 76–77)

The figures therefore served to furnish indications to the cooperatives, the only ones with time enough to process the information so as to decide when was the best time to sell. This was how the administration's objective figures cut speculation short and purified the market.

Does this mean they "performed" the economy? They definitely had an *effect* on the economy, and in particular on speculators, who had a harder time circulating their "false reports," and on the cooperatives when they sold farm produce. Through these two intermediaries, statistics then contributed to shaping crop prices (which were then more favorable to producers) and, over and beyond that, although I have not uncovered any indication of this, they probably also influenced farmers' decisions as to how much of each crop to plant (when they saw that a crop had good chances of bringing in a high price they must have been tempted to grow more of it). So statistics certainly did have effects on farming.

But is that any reason to talk about "performativity"? Of course, MacKenzie would argue, because it is exactly a case of what he calls "effective performativity," so long as statistics have changed something in the course of farming; and it may even be a case of "Barnesian performativity" (but one must admit that this remains to be demonstrated), to the extent that figures were aimed at building a purified market and, indeed, purified the market. But it seems to me that to do so either weakens the term or portrays a rather classical process in an unnecessarily complex fashion. The process we have witnessed here, thanks to a few statisticians, is simply a long causal chain, starting at one point (farming) and acting, step by step, until it finally returns to its point of departure. If statistics did influence farming, it is first, because they described it, in the most conventional way, without changing anything, and second, because the description acted on all the other actors, in this case the cooperatives and the speculators, who in turn acted on other actors, and so on until the action returned to its starting point, farming. What we witness here is neither a previously unknown relationship between a means of description and the object described, nor anything truly surprising. The surprise

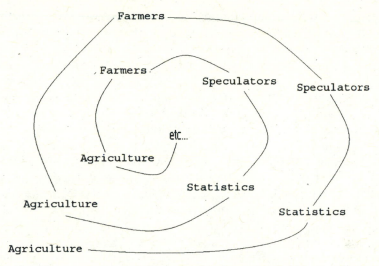

Figure 10.1 The process of statistics is simply a long causal chain, starting at one point (farming) and acting, step by step, until it finally returns to its point of departure. However, farming described on date t changes only at date $t+1$, at the following harvest, once farmers are able to observe the effects on the market and to react to them. Description, as such, therefore does not change what it describes.

is simply due to the fact that we were able to follow its effects long enough to see how they end up returning to their origin in farming. And even so, we say "their origin in farming" but that is not exactly true, since, if Figure 10.1 is correct, farming described on date t changes only at date $t+1$, at the following harvest, once farmers were able to observe the effects on the market and to react to them. Description, as such, therefore does not change what it describes since it is not that which was described, strictly speaking, that changed. What changes something, *in fine*, is the long detour. In this case "effective performativity" is a name given to a classical causal chain that ends up acting on a specific object (which was initially described) but does not designate any singular process, any specific mechanism.

To put it another way, in the words "effective performativity," the important one is not "performativity" but, indeed, "effective." What we have discovered is only that statistical description can have an effect on the realities that it is describing. Statistics are an actor, among thousands of others, in the world of agriculture. They do not have this lightness, this "in the air" characteristic that they may have claim to have. Statistics have, like farmers, mud on their boots, and they act on the state of the farms. This is the great discovery that the word "performativity" has allowed us to make. But why call this effect "performative" rather than simply "having an effect"? It seems to me that, at this point, the argument is not clear.

Nevertheless, if we are to build on this notion, it seems to me that we must keep in mind this most crucial and important idea of performativity: it points to cases where *describing is a specific process, a specific kind of transformation* of the object described. Once we have noticed the similarities between descriptions and facts that allow them both equally to act one on the other, we must go one step further and try to find the ways in which description and theories may regain a new specificity, a new specific way of acting on facts, a sense where the very meaning of "acting," and conversely of "describing," would be intertwined and renewed. Statistics do not act like any other entity; they do act, but in a specific way, and this is what we must now find. If "performing" is to be anything more than a simple shortcut in a classical causal chain, we should be able to see the specificity of statistics in the act of changing something at the same time as they describe it. So we are going to dig deeper into the surveys done by the U.S. agricultural statisticians in the interwar period, to scrutinize the way they go about describing, and consider whether that description itself might be called a "performance" of its object.

What Is the Action of Describing? Three Examples of Statistical Surveys

Agricultural surveys in the United State during the interwar period were huge machines that had to centralize, in Washington, D.C., data coming from places as distant as arctic Alaska and tropical Florida, transmitted by actors thousands of miles apart and living in different time zones. All those data had to converge on the capital as of a set deadline, and in a form allowing comparison between them. It took an enormous amount of energy, then, to collect such information, scattered over such a huge area, within a limited period of time.

The organization designed to accomplish this was state-based. In each state there was a government worker,[6] who we will call the Statistician, whose job was to extract the information from the fields and to put it into a form compatible with the demands made by Washington, where the findings from the different states were aggregated. We have no room here for a complete description of the long statistical chain reaching from a small Arizona ranch painfully growing a few tomatoes down to the publication of the final results for the entire country, put together in the capital. Although every link in that long chain was absolutely necessary to the final aggregation, the whole would be much too long. We will therefore confine ourselves to three zooms, on three points exemplifying the operation of collecting and formulating information, which will enable us to determine whether they simultaneously occasioned a transformation of farming.

Birth of a Survey

In the late 1920s, Verne H. Church, then Michigan's Statistician, noticed that one crop, overlooked in his agency's surveys, actually was very important in his state. That crop was . . . pickles. True, the very name of the vegetable made it laughable; true, it is not a particularly noble food, but still and all, is that any reason to ignore it? Were the poor pickles so ridiculous that they weren't even worth counting? That was what the Division suggested, since it never mentioned them, but Michigan's farmers seemed to disagree, since they went on growing them. Church ended up siding with the farmers and resolved to give them numerical recognition. Listen to him telling how a creature gains statistical existence:

> During my early travels I also noted the large number of towns and villages, particularly in the central and northern parts of the state, that had a pickle-station. I began making inquiries of managers of plants which maintained one or more offices within the state. Some of them supplied me with acreage and production data on cucumbers for pickles; others referred me to their head offices in other states. I wrote to a few of the larger ones and obtained the data I asked for, but there were many lesser companies and I needed a circular letter and questionnaires, for which I had no printing facilities. Michigan produces the bulk of the nation's salt requirements, and I happened to meet a salesman for one of the salt companies in the course of my travels who supplied me with a complete list of pickle manufacturers.
>
> I prepared a circular letter together with the questions concerning needed data, sent them to Washington, and asked that 50 or 60 copies be mimeographed. The reply I received from Washington was to the effect that the crop was considered too minor to bother with. This embarrassed me considerably as I had promised the firms contacted that I would supply them with a report of my findings. I immediately wrote to Washington again, outlined what I had done, the promises I had made, and stated that I had already collected 25,000 acres. I pointed out that, unless the survey was completed, I had wasted considerable time; and I dropped the hint that I would like to know how many acres were required to give a crop recognition. I then concluded the letter with: "Please forward the letters and blanks as previously requested."
>
> They arrived within a few days and within a short time the survey was completed. I showed that the state raised 40,000 acres for pickles that year, more than any other state, more than all other states combined, as determined the

following year from a Nation-wide survey instituted by the Washington office. (Church 1943, p. 12)

Church begins by emphasizing the fact that a Statistician's job is to go out in the field to pick up information. During his travels he noticed that pickles seemed to be a major crop, although the Division took no notice of them. He then sought to obtain legitimacy for a new creature, the countable pickle; he wanted to prove that that entity was worth existing. The demonstration went through three phases: first he made a preliminary investigation, then he turned to Washington, and last, he did the actual survey.

During the preliminary investigation described in the first paragraph he contacted his state's pickles in every possible fashion: by observing towns and villages, writing letters to plant managers, making an unexpected acquaintance (his travels enabled him to make providential encounters; luck, or something of the sort, therefore seemed to play a major role in his work). Each of his contacts reflected some "pickleness" in one form or another: "acreage and production data," "complete list of pickle manufacturers," and so on. This showed that there was something worth investigating, but that thing showed up in very dissimilar forms, making it impossible to count.

During that period, Michigan hardly existed at all. Since Church was looking for people who could send him pickles in any form, he sought out definite locations, factories, salt salesmen—anything that concentrated information about pickles. Consequently, he hardly cared whether the informers were in his state or not. As soon as they mentioned pickles he was interested. Michigan did subsist, however, since Church continued to see "towns and villages . . . of the state," to look for managers who maintained "one or more offices within the state," and when the "head office [was] in other states," that was worth mentioning, negatively that is, for Michigan's borders were still a reference. We do not hear much about the state of Michigan, because Church was simply collecting worthy informers, but it existed as the borders of a whole that did or did not contain those points. This account drew a geographical picture of a set containing objects whose nature varied enormously.

The second part of Church's investigation is recounted in the second paragraph. It contains, for one thing, the points mentioned above, especially the "companies," and for another, Washington. What goes on in Washington? Why turn to that particular place? Because there was a mimeographing machine there. Now, the words "printing facilities" are followed by the words "crop," "survey," and "acres," in particular. The fact of being able to produce identical questionnaires led to a change of vocabulary, moving from the diversity of fieldwork to statistics and their stable categories. In Washington, questionnaires could be printed, all identical and in large numbers, making it possible to establish statistics. Identical reproduction was therefore the first step, so to speak, after which we may speak of statistics.

But Washington and the Statistician disagreed. Church and Washington clashed over the issue of costs. According to Washington, mimeographing cost too much and was not worthwhile, whereas Church pointed out that it would be even more costly not to complete the job. To solve the conflict, Church showed that he could already do some counting, using the set drawn above, and this gave him arguments to advance in the conflict, by stating that he had "already 25,000 acres" of pickles in Michigan and that the crop was therefore an important one. He therefore needed the mimeographed copies so as to be more than approximate, to "complete the survey," which is to say to erase the "already" in the expression "already 25,000 acres." Washington, then, was the place where surveys were *standardized*, in the simplest of ways, thanks to the mimeograph machine. But that standardization had a price, and it took some bargaining to show that the advantages were greater than the cost, that is, for the state to appear. The state (of Michigan) came on the scene, then, only inasmuch as it was worthy of attention, and this evaluation caused a dispute.

The last step, which brought countable pickles into the public eye was a brief one, for Church then did the actual survey. Since this was the first survey, the various pieces of information, all different in size and shape, had to be put into stable and standardized responses on questionnaires. This brought the state as such into the limelight, since it planted 40,000 acres of pickles.

My quotation from Church shows the genealogy of an agricultural survey, that is, how a crop was definitively transformed into statistics. Three phases may be seen. The first involved travels, which sorted out the important and unimportant elements; the second involved expertise, in this case a discussion with Washington leading to standardization; and the third, the concrete achievement of the survey, of which little is said here. During these three phases, innumerable entities, including pickle producers, letters, a list of manufacturers, the mimeographing machine in Washington, and so on, were put together in that peculiar way described by Church, which consists of *listing informers so that they will all fill in a same questionnaire*. One feels how every word in this sentence was the outcome of an inventive effort. For Church, "to list" is evocative of the chance encounter with the right person in a train, "informer" suggests contacting people in distant places and winning their trust, "questionnaire" has to do with writing that introductory letter and developing relevant questions, "the same" refers to the discussion with Washington, and so on. The building of this new statistical object therefore means isolating *repetitions* (listings, questionnaires, etc.) in what appeared initially as immensely diverse.

The way he constructed a whole out of these elements enabled him to ooze out, to *give birth to a new kind of pickle*, the Michigan Pickle, which is a countable plant with a spatial location, as opposed to other pickles, which have many attributes, but not those. The survey itself therefore did not leave agriculture totally unchanged, but gave the initial pickle an additional quality, that of being repeatable, in other words, countable. But to understand how it did that, we must go into greater detail about the part Church describes least, the survey itself, and the interactions between the Statistician and the respondents.

Questioning

One of the first difficulties encountered by pre–World War II agricultural surveys resided in the reluctance of most farmers to give information to investigators, for they rarely understood why federal agents should be allowed to interfere in their business. This reluctance was so strong that the Division decided to get around it by drawing up a list of people who would serve as informers, the same from one survey to another. That way people would have to be persuaded only once and for all of the need to respond, after which they would entertain a stable, trusting relationship with the Division. They received the questionnaires by mail, filled them in, and sent them back to their state Statistician before the deadline. To thank them for their efforts, they received a monthly newsletter entitled *Crops and Markets*, which informed them on the prospects for the farm market, as well as Christmas greetings—in short, they were the Division's darlings. We will refer to them as the Correspondents, rather than respondents (a rather anachronistic designation, in point of fact), to emphasize the lasting relation between the bureau of statistics and its informers, as well as the fact that the ties between them were essentially postal.

To understand how the Division questioned its Correspondents, let us take a look at the broader case of crop surveys, the only ones extant at first, which have remained the largest (and most strategic) surveys. All of the questionnaires certainly did not fall into that group, for there were also surveys on cattle raising and homestead finances. But for the sake of clarity, I prefer to concentrate on one emblematic case rather than dealing with numerous different examples. In the crop surveys, then, the questions put to correspondents pertained to the *acreage cultivated* and the *yield per acre*. By multiplying one by the other, the volume of production could be calculated (if the yield per acre, expressed in volume, is multiplied by the number of acres cultivated, we have the volume produced).

The question was how to formulate the questions so that they would be properly understood by Correspondents.

To estimate the acreage cultivated, the Division first encountered what we would venture to call an anthropological difficulty. Indeed, according to a number of studies it claimed to have conducted on people in general, it had reached the conclusion that making estimates in absolute figures is difficult, whereas giving percentages is easier (Becker 1928). In other words, when asked to say how many acres of wheat he had planted (the acre being the current farming unit at the time), the Correspondent tended to give an imprecise answer, whereas when asked to compare his observations to others, he was more precise. This led the Division to ask its Correspondents what *percentage* of the acreage they had planted with a given cereal the previous year had been devoted to the same crop this year. For example, the Correspondent was supposed to say things like: 80 percent of the land planted in wheat last year was planted in wheat this year. So by the very formulation of its questions, the Division helped its correspondents to be objective, to give the best possible responses. This of course demanded that it find a method for transforming those percentages of variation into absolute figures (which it did, using the census). But this system enabled it to obtain a good estimate of the acreage devoted to each crop each year.

What about the yield per acre? How did the Division go about estimating it? It used a variable we would find surprising nowadays, called the *condition of growth* of plants, which functioned as an indicator of per-acre productivity. For example, if the weather had been very fair throughout the growing season and farmers had sufficient reserves to be able to water their crops properly, an acre may be said to have produced under favorable conditions and to have given a full yield. In the opposite case its condition was bad and so was the yield. The *condition* therefore indicated the productivity of the land.

Like the acre, and in accordance with the above-mentioned studies, the condition, too, had to be expressed as a percentage of variation, but as opposed to acreage, the condition of the present year was not compared to the past year. The condition was defined as a percentage of the *normal condition* of growth of a crop. This notion of a "normal condition" was highly problematic and elicited numerous justifications, explanations, and criticisms, although it actually was in use. Let us dwell for a moment on its definition, as found on the questionnaires sent to the Correspondents:

  1. The condition of the crops on the date indicated for mailing the schedule is not a comparison with a condition at any former period, but with a normal condition of growth and vitality that would be expected at this time

in a crop starting out under favorable condition and not subjected afterward to unfavorable weather, insects pests, or other injurious agencies. If condition is asked for any crop that has already been harvested, give condition at time of harvest.

2. In estimating condition of crops in comparison with a normal condition of growth and vitality giving promise of full yield per acre, 100 is the basis; if nine-tenths of a (normal) yield per acre are indicated by the present condition, the answer should be filled in as 90; if one-tenth, or 10 percent, more than a normal yield per acre is indicated, the answer should be reported as 110, etc.[7]

The normal condition, then, was the condition of growth of a plant that had not been affected by any unfavorable external factor; it was the condition of growth in which it had not been subjected to any insect pests, in which the weather had been good and the farmer had given it the best possible care, so that it had reached its full yield. If the Correspondents observed such conditions, that is, if the plants had not suffered any aggression, they were to report a condition of 100 percent. The normal condition, then, was one in which the plant had developed without encountering any particular fortune or misfortune.

As opposed to acreage, the condition of growth was not compared to the past but to some timeless norm. This represented an additional difficulty, since Correspondents had to be persuaded to resist the reflex consisting of considering exceptional years as the norm (as they tended to do, since their exceptional nature made them memorable), but it had the advantage of simplifying the work of the Division for the transition from percentage to absolute value (which, again, was done using the last census, and a method called the "par"). Be this as it may, questions about condition and acreage differed as to the type of norm to which Correspondents were asked to compare them, but they shared the fact of being formulated in terms of percentages. This type of questioning thereby enabled the Division and its informers to produce high-quality estimates. The information sent by the Correspondents to the Division contained two percentages: one for the acreage planted as compared to the past year's acreage, and the other the condition of growth compared to the normal condition (see figure 10.2).

In conclusion, I would stress the fact that both of these pieces of information are the outcome of a great many composite elements. What elements? There is, for instance, the "theory" according to which Correspondents estimate percentages more accurately than absolute figures; the mountains of letters of thanks to which the Division maintained a trusting relationship with its Correspondents; the strange norm known as the

Figure 10.2 A Correspondent filling in a questionnaire. The picture shows us that this activity demands that the farmer sit down at a clean and orderly living room table, put on his reading glasses, and concentrate on what he is doing.

"normal condition" of growth of crops. Before the survey, all of those elements were separate, with no necessary relationship between them. Thanks to the survey, the list of Correspondents was drawn up, the Division wrote its instructions and sent them the questionnaire; the Correspondent did his own investigation and translated his findings into figures. Finally, all of these elements, taken together, were transformed into a single little percentage, and put on the questionnaire. The survey collected all of these elements and *composed* them into a single little figure written by the Correspondent in the proper box. That figure therefore summarized and contained that multitude of elements, statistically. Thus surveying is not only a problem of isolating repetitions, as we have seen previously, but also of *composing* a great number of diverse elements. But in itself, the percentage in a box was still only a tiny element, applying to a ridiculously small piece of land. It then had to be made available for aggregation at a higher level, and that is why the Correspondents had to mail their questionnaires to their state Statistician, who received a number of them. Let us see what the latter did with them.

Adding Up

The state Statistician's job had at least two complementary aspects. First, he had to pace up and down his state, as we have already seen Church do—that is to travel around it and measure it. In his travels he might discover new crops (a very rare occurrence), but above all he had to meet farmers to try to put them on the list of Correspondents, and at the same time build up his own intimate, personal knowledge of farming in his state. Before harnessing himself to the second part of his job, which entailed processing the questionnaires so as to send the main information to Washington, that intimate expertise enabled him to assess the quality of the answers he was processing and if necessary to "rectify" any answers that seemed absolutely improbable. Following that rectification, he calculated averages for each county and district, then sent them to Washington.

We will now zoom in on that part of the statistician's work that may seem the least interesting, the most mechanical: the calculation of averages. A priori, there is nothing more mechanical than an average; all one has to do is add up the findings and divide the sum by their number.[8] Everyone knows that. But concretely, is it so easy to do? Has the reader already tried to take a hundred or so loose sheets of paper (which is just about how many questionnaires the Statistician received for each farm district), retain only one of the many columns on each, and add up the figures in that column without ever repeating or overlooking any entry? Well, it is not that easy. It was in fact so difficult that the Statisticians originally had the habit of *copying* the columns of figures onto a single sheet before adding them up. But there again, what a waste of time, and above all, what a source of errors! Nothing puts you to sleep more easily than copying a hundred or so whole numbers, most of which are between 70 and 110; nothing is easier than to forget one, or to put one down twice, not to speak of some other less foreseeable risks such as an office door opened unexpectedly, causing a tremendous breeze that sends a whole pile of questionnaires flying, so you have to start all over again. Even if the equation is simple, calculating the average for a good hundred questionnaires is anything but self-evident, concretely speaking.

For that reason, a very ingenious technique was developed to solve all those problems. As Church tells us:

> I quickly learned that the unusual arrangement of the questions and spaces for answers at the bottom was to facilitate the "shingling" for adding. . . . The schedules were sorted by crop-reporting districts and "shingled," one district at a time, without reference to counties within the districts. . . . A blank schedule was placed at the bottom on which the number of reports, sums and averages for each item were entered.(Church 1943, p. 6)

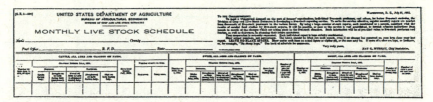

Figure 10.3 A sample questionnaire. This one has to do with livestock, but the form is exactly the same as for cereals. Note that the boxes to be filled in form a strip all along the bottom of the questionnaire.

The aggregation of answers into an average began with the *material* sorting of questionnaires ("schedules") by districts. The statistician began not by adding, but by organizing the questionnaires by means of the invention called "shingling." To understand shingling, it must be said that most questionnaires had a strange shape. They were long and narrow, like a strip of paper, and the boxes in which correspondents had to write their data were at the very bottom, all lined up, with the questions just above the little boxes for the answers (see figure 10.3).

Shingling consisted of taking all of the questionnaires from a district and having them overlap, shinglelike, horizontally, so that only the figures were visible. A blank schedule was placed below the last questionnaire. Then, using a long wooden ruler that looked something like a skirt hanger (except that it was more than 30 inches long), the Statistician solidly pegged all the schedules together. Thanks to this shingling device, a large number of questionnaires could be held together in a very stable fashion (see figure 10.4). The calculations could then be done directly, without having to copy the schedules, and with no risk of overlooking or repeating any items.[9] The sums and the number of Correspondents having answered the question were recorded directly in the boxes of the blank questionnaire placed under the others. It was very easy, then, to calculate the average: one had just to divide one figure by the other.

The first step in calculating, then, involved putting the questionnaires in order, concretely. They had first to be grouped by geographic units, then placed along a stick which arranged them in that very peculiar way, after which the calculation simply finished the aggregation by replacing that cumbersome bunch of schedules by a single figure, and the Statistician was assured that it definitely contained each and every questionnaire, once and only once for each of them. Calculating the average, then, was an operation consisting, first, of *stabilizing* scattered elements, finding a certain lasting relationship between them, and, on the basis of that relationship, evincing a new feature for the initial elements. Before

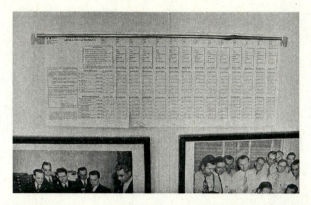

Figure 10.4 The "peg strip," as shown in the office of Richard Allen, former director of agricultural statistics. The questionnaires did not necessarily have the letter format seen here. They tended to be long and narrow. They were then hung by their short side and the addition was done by holding the stick vertically in front of the operator, as is generally done for additions. (National Agricultural Statistical Service, 2004.)

shingling, the questionnaires spoke about their vicinity; once they were all put together in that special shingling relationship they began—and long continued—speaking about their district (the average for their district). Thus, slowly but surely, some elements of the state were jelling, so to speak. By then, shingling had already produced districts.

Conclusion: Statistics Characterize as They Describe

We just followed three phases by which the survey *describes* agriculture: how the survey is born, how Correspondents are questioned, and how averages are calculated. In themselves, these three steps are far from sufficient to produce the ultimate figures. We have left a great deal of the Statisticians' work unmentioned, and above all, we have not said a word about what goes on in the central offices in Washington, which would require a whole chapter in itself. Yet all of those phases, those about which we have said nothing as well as those we have described, are equally necessary to produce figures that are valid for U.S. agriculture as a whole. Overall figures are produced by a multitude of small steps, all as spectacular (or as unspectacular) as those we just studied.

These three steps have at least shown us that description does not leave its object unchanged. In the first example the statistician began by collecting information of all sorts on pickles: here addresses of manufacturers, there figures on crop acreage, elsewhere yields per acre. By dint of a hard-fought struggle he managed to add another item to the list: a mimeographed questionnaire. From then on a definite relationship was established between all of those elements (they were all information needed to fill in the questionnaire), thanks to which a new characteristic appeared: the total amount of pickles in Michigan on date t. The initial elements had been fitted together in a singular fashion, and from that peculiar set a *new feature of the pickle* was extracted: the "sameness" of all the—initially—different pickles, which equates to the fact that it could be exhaustively counted. Without the statistician's descriptive activity pickles would not have had that property. It truly was description that evinced it, and therefore changed pickles, to some extent.

Let us skip the second example, to which we will return shortly, and go on to the third, when the Statistician returned to his office and found himself with a collection of questionnaires and a stick. The schedules were then pegged together (that was their specific relation during this phase), so that the questionnaire not only was now linked to the vicinity of the particular Correspondent who had filled it in, but came to be definitely linked to the entire county from which it was taken. Once attached to all the other questionnaires in the specific way described above, its "part of a county" attribute was actualized, whereas until then it was simply a "piece of information about a district," which is not the same thing. Before pegging, the Statistician had no proper way of moving from a particular area to a whole county; after pegging, the sum could be calculated, making the shift possible. The original elements were therefore articulated in a peculiar way, and *through that articulation, which is nothing but a description, a new property of the whole comes into being, appears.*

It seems to me that these examples clearly show that the tool normally used to *describe* reality does have an *effect* on that reality, *in fine.* The three slightly different actions of extracting repetitions, composing elements, and stabilizing compositions can be summarized in a single one: the *production of new properties* such as the "Michigan pickle," the normal condition, or the county average. Rather than observing its object from afar, the way an astronaut observes Earth, statistics takes hold of it and transforms it, produces it afresh, to grasp it according to a process that definitely resembles the mechanism discovered by Austin: when the mayor of a town says "I pronounce you man and wife" to a solemnly clad couple he is *not describing* the situation as much as *accomplishing an act* by which the attribution "married couple" is produced.

The statistical transformations described here seem rather minute, especially in comparison with a commitment such as marriage. Is it as important for pickles to be countable as it is for a couple of lovebirds to be married? Does having a norm really change something for the condition?

Does belonging to a county really affect questionnaires? Apparently not; they are apparently only *small* differences. But these transformations are not isolated: they are part of a series of articulations occurring all along the statistical survey, which, we must remember, was much more extensive than the three examples we have discussed. Throughout the survey that brought Arizona dust to the federal buildings in Washington, those little changes were aggregated, and that was what ended up making one big transformation. This is best illustrated by the fact that before farming statistics, the only complete counting process extant in the United States was the census, such a tremendous operation that it could be conducted only once every five years.[10] The statistics we are studying here, on the other hand, produced a country that could be totally counted (the total production of the main cereal crops and the main livestock bred) more than once a year. This change of pace, with its essential economic consequences, is far from negligible. Statistics transformed *all of U.S. agriculture*, making it countable several times a year, which was not the case previously. In my opinion a transformation affecting the whole of that gigantic nation is important, perhaps as important as the thousands of marriages celebrated there every year. So farming was no longer the same once it had been "formulated" by statistics (we should say "counted" by statistics), and in that sense, statistical description might seem to be "performative." But is this formulation the best? Does it hold?

Performing or Expressing?

One advantage devolves from the notion of "performativity". It enables us to reverse the usual view according to which statistical description is a simple elaboration based on facts, a consequence of them, showing us that, to the contrary, it may also affect the facts which it supposedly simply reports, according to the usual viewpoint. Statistics may be constructed explicitly to change the economy in which they participate, and they also have that more unnoticed property of characterizing the objects they seize. But having confirmed this refreshing, exciting virtue, shouldn't we stop for a moment to take another look at its meaning and further consequences? For it is a fact that the notion of "performativity" also carries other implicit meanings that must be brought to light so that we will not be disappointed before reaching our goal. Having tickled our palate with the most exquisite game, is performativity serving us some poison for dessert? Has it slipped some rotten ingredient into the dish?

In addition to the effects of the descriptor, performativity raises two related problems, in particular. The first has to do with the role played by language. Indeed, the notion of performativity comes from studies focusing primarily on language. Now, while statistics are also language, the examples given above clearly show that they are definitely *not only* language, and no doubt *not primarily* language. Doesn't the fact of applying an essentially language-related notion to an activity of a different nature entail some difficulties? The second problem has to do with its relation to pure *creation* of reality, comparable to the near-magic effect of baptism or marriage, where it is the words "I baptize you" or "I pronounce you man and wife" that create a new status for the individuals involved (even if those words need a set of "conditions of felicity" to be effective, as already said at length previously, for example, in MacKenzie's chapter, it is still the words, and not the conditions, that create a new situation). Thus, the question is: can that creative power of language be extended to statistics? Following a discussion of these two problems, we will take stock, so to speak, of performativity and draw up a list of elements on the debit and credit sides. If the former win out, we will have to wonder whether another concept would not be more appropriate than performativity for elucidating the effects of statistics.

Is Language the Only Factor at Work in Statistical Descriptions?

According to Austin, performativity is an effect of language on the reality it describes. When sociologists of science extended the notion to their objects, the parallel was acceptable inasmuch as theory replaced language, and the economy stood in the stead of any reality. The *language of theory* was thus supposed to act on *economic facts*. But are we sure that theory is clearly language and language only? Further, while language is definitely a constituent part of it to say the least, is it, or something else, the active component? This is a real question, for if it is not language that acts within theory, then we would have to go back to wondering whether the term "performativity" appropriately designates the effects of theory.

We will not venture to answer the question of whether the theoretical language of economics is capable of shaping economic facts themselves, on its own strength, but let's first state the obvious: what we certainly do know is that the *language of statistics*, all by itself, is unable to control the *objective facts* it is supposed to report. For example, the instructions on the questionnaire pertaining to the growing condition and the normal condition, all by themselves, hardly enabled statisticians to prevent rain from falling, to make the sun shine, or to stop pests from attacking wheat in the fields. In no case could the "condition" such as described in the questionnaire control the real conditions of growth of plants—in other words, have effects on the sun or the rain! We would commit the same error as those poor early twentieth-century statisticians who were so ignorant about and scornful of witch doctors, if we imagined them with the same hypothetical powers! No, no, it is impossible. Language, all by it-self, cannot have given them control over the facts it describes, and above all, not over the weather, or else it is purely and simply doing magic.

Advocates of performativity, no doubt noting the oddities that the op-posite position would entail, have refined the arguments, limiting the list of facts susceptible of being changed by theoretical language to some much less "physical" and "external" elements than insect pests, rain, or fair weather. They restrict it to "social" facts sufficiently close to humans and their consciousness for language to affect them directly. Some objects susceptible of being performed were, for instance, the "legitimacy" of an actor, an instrument, or a commodity, or the way an item is priced.[11] The mechanism involved might be that by dint of theorization, those things had finally been universally acknowledged, meaning that the arguments advanced by economic theory had ended up changing the *legitimacy* of the derivative products because they were able to change the actors' *percep-tion* of them. This kind of argument seems more acceptable than the previ-ous one. It is easier to show that language affects "humanoid" facts (if the reader pardons the expression), that is, close to human-made things and to human consciousness, than other, completely "natural" facts.

The same is true in statistics. For instance, the instructions on the ques-tionnaire, explaining what a "normal condition" is, certainly affected the way Correspondents *reported* them. That was in fact why they were writ-ten and continued to be put on the questionnaires: their aim was to clarify the difference between an optimal condition and a normal condition (which is less good), and they really did increase the percentages reported by Correspondents. As a rule, instructions represent another archetype of "illocutionary" acts as identified by Austin. In statistics, as elsewhere, the simple fact of formulating them has effects on human behavior (regardless of whether people follow them or try to take their distances from them).

The problem raised by restricting the effects of performing to human representations alone is that it tends to transform the latter too easily into lies and sly tricks. And this is exactly the furrow that Daniel Miller—who attacked Callon when the latter came up with his *Laws of the Markets*, and who is so caustically criticized by Holm in his chapter in this volume—has ploughed.[12] Miller writes in his paper concluding his discussion with Callon: "The premise of my paper on virtualism is that we live in a period of history where we can see the increasing ability of certain powerful dis-courses, including that of economists, to realize themselves as models in the world through their increasing control over that world. That is their increasing ability to be performative" (Miller 2005, p. 4). This citation shows clearly that Miller is *not* against "performativity" in itself, quite on the contrary. Why? Because he can understand it as a motto for his "priest" model (later in his paper, Miller compares economists to priests), which can be summarized like this: "powerful discourses" of economists and economics can "control the world" (at this point, "the world" is reduced to its representations) and "realize" themselves in the "world" (which, this time, is the real and material one). These discourses are initially lies, but they have the power of coming to be true, by manipulating and controlling the action of people. In other words, once he asserts first that language will never change things themselves and second that it may, on the other hand, influence the way people relate to those things (the way they report, describe, or comment on them—Miller speaks about "faith"), he almost unavoidably concludes that representations can be manipulated, initially betraying things which remain stable and then, through faith, make people change the world according to this lie. Consequently, statistics (if Miller had taken them into account), through the influence they exert, would be accused of creating a deceitful hiatus between humans and things and then changing the world according to their models. Performativity, then, would be almost necessarily fraudulent, which is certainly terribly restrictive for a theory of the production of knowledge.

This critique of a fundamental *lie* of statistics comes not only from scholars; actors themselves, too, may formulate it (and the actors who formulate it are not always the poor or the orphans). For example, speculators accused the statisticians of asking their questions in terms of the "normal condition" rather than the "optimal condition," since that formulation would tend to have them underestimate the crop condition, which is to say to have them underestimate the final output, which is good for growers (again: lower production means higher prices). The charge, then, was that the formulation of the question put a bias on the figures in the sole interest of one of the parties involved, independently of the amounts really produced.

Yet when our statisticians wrote up their instructions, they were not so much intent on manipulating their Correspondents as in having them participate, in turn, in the production of "normalcy" itself, that new property of the condition. If the questionnaire influenced the Correspondents, it was to get them to participate to the best of their ability, and with the whole statistical apparatus, in the production of that important *entity*, the norm, with which erratic conditions might be compared. The statistical survey did not confine itself to influencing the Correspondents; it *also acted on the condition itself*. It was the condition itself that acquired a new attribute, not the behavior of Correspondents. However, it did so through two procedures, which differ from the model of the witch doctor, or of the priest (according to Miller).

First, instead of trying to control the condition, the statistic characterized it, which is very different. It made no attempt to have more or less rain fall; it showed that there definitely was a characteristic of the condition which was the "normal condition." These two activities, controlling and characterizing, were so different that the characteristic uncovered by the statistic actually had the property of *not being controllable*. The best proof of this is that Correspondents might mistakenly report their condition, and that the Statistician, before doing any calculations, had to "edit" the answers; that is, he had to rectify or eliminate those that were insufficiently consistent with the intimate knowledge of the area he had gleaned during his travels. If Correspondents could make mistakes, then the normal condition did not depend on their say, on their answer alone. To the contrary, in order for the characteristic "normal condition" to be *properly* produced, it had to have the opposite property of *resisting* the possible errors of Correspondents. The language of the instructions, in statistics, therefore performed some behavior in respondents, so as to have them participate in the production of the characteristics studied, which is different from controlling them.

One of the main differences between controlling and characterizing is that Statisticians *did not know in advance* what the outcome of this characterization would be—in other words, it escaped them. A good example of this is the average condition, calculated by the Statistician. Before doing all the operations, he did not know what that average would be, since he had to calculate it. He discovered it only at the end of his efforts. He therefore did not control what that average would be since he had to calculate it to make it exist. Yet by calculating it he definitely characterized it, since he was able to say something like "this month the condition was 78 percent of the normal condition," which is certainly a characterization. Statisticians were often surprised by the things they characterized, and this prevented them from *controlling* them.

Second, although it seemed clear that the instructions (and therefore language) were *necessary* to the evincing of that absolutely essential characteristic of the "normal condition" of growth, it was just as obvious that they were not *sufficient*. Indeed, the normal condition was a characteristic of the condition, which, like every other variable, appeared only at the end of a process comparable to the one narrated by Church for his pickles. That is, all sorts of information had to be gathered about the condition, then a questionnaire, ultimately mimeographed, had to be constructed, after which all of the information contained in the questionnaire had to be assembled, and so on. Next, to construct the condition and the normal condition, averages had to be calculated, first for counties, then for states. As we have seen, this phase demanded some very special questionnaires, with empty boxes for the answers on the bottom, under the designation of the crop involved, and it also required the famous shingling stick thanks to which the figures could be added up.

In short, we need not list them all, clearly a great many things—and not only language—are needed to make that normal condition appear, and to give it consistency. For although instructions clearly are language, it is harder to say that about the little boxes at the bottom of a piece of paper, and harder still for a simple stick, paper, or a mimeographing machine. To give body to the normal condition, which is one characteristic of the growing condition of plants, language was needed, but necessarily attended by all sorts of other statistical tools which, taken together, uncovered the characteristics of the objects they described. Language is therefore by far not the only element acting on the object of the description. Many other elements participate, and that is in fact what gives the condition and the normal condition their solid, natural, "objective" quality. Statistical objects are characterized by a *set of elements*, within which language has a place, but which is not by any means the only component.

We therefore view performativity as one effect of statistics, primarily because statistics work with *instructions*, which are archetypal illocutionary acts. However, this effect itself seems to be only one element in the much broader whole through which statistics characterize their objects. Performativity is only one contributive element in characterization. Now, to take the part for the whole, metonymically, seems out of place here because the problem of the manipulation of actors would inevitably arise then. Indeed, by saying that statistics "perform," there is a risk that we infer that they are a language controlling actors rather than things, which would make them deceitful and, moreover, would not conform with what we have observed. As soon as you say "performativity," you can be sure that a Miller will come out, even though you would prefer him not to, because of the linguistic ancestry of the notion. The role of language in the effects of statistics therefore raises this problem, which makes a first dent in the idea that statistics may "perform" their object. We shall now see that performativity raises a second problem for statistics.

Is Statistical Description a Creation?

Another error to which the use of "performativity" gives rise is less apparent in this book than in earlier work on the notion. The notion of "performativity" pushes authors wrongly to take what is a mere transformation for a pure creation. For example, speaking about economic performativity, and explaining the position of Callon, MacKenzie wrote with Millo: "Economics does not describe an existing external 'economy,' but brings that economy into being: economics performs the economy, creating the phenomena it describes" (2003, p. 108). According to MacKenzie and Millo, theory clearly comes first, as if it were coming out of thin air, and creates the economy, which supposedly was simply elucidated by theory. In this way of thinking, theory would come first detached from any reality, and by its action could confer existence on those facts it finds admissible. Again, I will not ask whether this implicit assumption is true for economics, but will ask whether it is true for statistics. While the latter do produce some characteristics of the object to which they are applied, can we go as far as saying that, as suggested by discussions such as MacKenzie and Millo (2003) of the performativity of economics, it *creates* those objects?

As such, the idea seems quite improbable. One can hardly see how statistics, by waving some magic wand, would suddenly turn the world topsy-turvy and create it in their image. The examples given above look much more like ongoing processes, gradual developments rather than sudden creations. I have never witnessed that kind of wand-waving magic in statistics nor in economics, actually. As described in all the papers of this book, the mechanism is in fact much more subtle; it progresses much less suddenly, and the creation of facts is *diluted over time* so that the writers resort to expressions such as "little by little," "gradually," "as it goes along" to describe performing. Here is another quotation from MacKenzie and Millo (2003, p. 137):

> Black, Scholes, and Merton's model did not describe an already existing world: when first formulated, its assumptions were quite unrealistic, and empirical prices differed systematically from the model. Gradually, though, the financial markets changed in a way that fitted the model.

The authors seem to have difficulty asserting that the theory or the model, when "first formulated," could suddenly transform financial markets. The idea that a mere theory, all by itself and all of a sudden, could move such huge mountains as the interests of banks, the goods exchanged on the stock markets, or the practices of brokers would sound terribly implausible. Rome cannot be changed in a day. That is why the process is diluted over time, and the theory is said to act only *gradually*. So the world does not arise, like Athena, fully armed and shouting cries of victory; rather, it came, *little by little*, to conform to economic theories. Being less sudden, the phenomenon becomes more plausible. MacKenzie and Millo seem to be saying: all right, the whole financial market was not drastically changed overnight by the new theory, but, rather, changes occurred slowly but surely, as they usually do.

What goes on during that period of time? The question is worth asking, since there is a possibility that what took place during it was not exactly a creation, but simply a gradual transformation of the facts, which would look much more like the statistical transformations observed by us.

This is where we have to separate the two MacKenzies. There is the one who stands here in his chapter in this book, which explains very plausibly how changes occur; but there was a previous one, who is far from standing alone,[13] who deserves the attack that follows.

For this latter group of writers, who we might call the *soft constructivists*, what goes on in the process at work during the timespan they grant to performing is that the actors, one after the other, become *convinced* of the interest of Black, Scholes, and Merton's new theory (note that at the beginning the theory is false, as emphasized by MacKenzie and Millo themselves; one wonders, then, why the actors still find it interesting). The actors then begin to act in accordance with it, *as if* the world corresponded to the assumptions of the theory (wrongly so, at the outset, remember). But when a sufficient number of actors are convinced, their efforts are finally successful and they make the world itself conform, in turn, to what was initially a simple ideal and has become a theory (here again, we are not far from Miller's reasoning). For the theory of Black, Scholes, and Merton to function, a great many actors had to model their behavior after that theory, and their number had to transform the world, which ended up adopting the theory as its own rule of conduct. Now it takes time to convert the masses: it takes a whole lot of individual conversions, which necessarily proceed slowly, over time. And that is where the "little by little" designates a series of conversions, each of which is immediate (and in fact equally difficult to understand; why and how each individual is persuaded is never explained) but spread over time.

That "gradually," then, is by no means a *slow* transformation of the state of *things*, but it is, according to the soft constructivists, a series of *mental* conversions, all equally *sudden*, leading to another sudden break, at which point, all of a sudden, the world itself begins to correspond to the prerequisites of the theory. Now, for one thing, MacKenzie and Millo's need to transit by the awareness of actors to account for the creation of an economy raises a serious problem for performativity. It means that it is not just theory that performs, but to the contrary, in the most classical fashion, it is people who, through their work, transform the world (aside from the specific fact that one does not see what their motives are here). This would mean that there is no great need to introduce the term "performativity." But second, if performativity were the outcome of a series of conversions, it does not say anything about the *transformation* of things. It continues to point to radical *conversions* (the actors are or are not convinced by the theory; there is no other alternative); it designates an *aggregation* of those breaks, but each one is still a long way from the *processes* observed in the case of statistics.

In fact, the statistical operations we have tracked down are never creations of that sort. First, each one demands a number of prerequisites, elements which exist prior to the description—maybe those prerequisites are the "conditions of felicity" whose sociological analysis Bourdieu used to criticize Austin, and which MacKenzie presents in his chapter in this volume. When we see Church counting pickles, we first see him collecting information about his object. When the farmer fills in his questionnaire, he too has already done his own observing. Finally, when we see the Statistician calculate the average, his very first act is to assemble the questionnaires and the shingling stick. A number of elements of farming are put together *before* the statistical operation, then.

Next, statistical description involves handling those elements so as to discover the relations between them which were sufficiently stressed above: there is a particular way of attaching the questionnaires together, of expressing the observed condition as a percentage of the normal condition, and so on. The relationship obtained is original, usually peculiar to statistics, but it is nothing more (but nothing less, either) than a relationship *between prerequisite elements*. Those elements unquestionably preceded statistics and were its precondition: there can be no statistics without elements of farming to measure statistically.

Of course, if statistical manipulations presuppose the existence of several objects prior to their description, at the same time they transform those objects by establishing relations between them, thereby actualizing some of their previously nonexistent characteristics. This is why the word "preconditions" does not fit perfectly for our argument: the problem is not only one of a stable mold (the conditions) that would shape the iron in fusion (the theory, the model, or the statistics); but the problem is in fact which elements will be used by the statistician, how precisely he or she will use these resources, and what specific relations he or she will find between them. That things exist prior to their description is unquestionable, but those things look much more like a set of resources for action than like an unchanging and determining condition.

Whence I conclude that "performativity" is either very demanding or very lazy. It is very demanding since it contends that the facts performed are *created* out of thin air. But, although how a pure creation is possible in general is unclear, it is entirely clear that this is not what is observed in the case of statistics. Statistical descriptions in no way *create* the farming elements they describe; they *transform* them. In the first instance we have a series of sudden, quite unaccountable mental conversions, and in the second, an ongoing process with gradual, small modifications of the relations between things. From another viewpoint, "performativity" might be seen as very lazy since it requires only conditions, and nothing more, the transformations under scrutiny taking place sort of automatically once the conditions are there. So if statistics have the property of acting on the object they describe, the way they go about it does not make for full-fledged "performing." This remark therefore makes a second dent in the idea that statistics perform. If so, is there any reason to retain the term? Do its defects exceed its advantages?

Rather than "Perform," Let Us Say "Express"

The two main reasons why the descriptive activity of statistics may be said to "perform" are, first, because they transform the object of the description as they describe it; and, second, because they act on Correspondents through the use of language in their many instructions. But these shared points do not eliminate its incompatitibilities: first, "performativity" does not specify, at all, the kind of action that theory or description might exert on its objects; second, whereas statistics transform their object, they do not create it; and, third, statistical description does not act through language alone, but by means of thousands of other kinds of intermediaries. These three arguments lead us to the conclusion that "performativity" is not the most appropriate word. It remains a simple stopgap.

Instead, I would argue that the process that gives existence to some unsuspected characteristics corresponds to what has often been called *expressing*. This word is to be understood here neither in its day-to-day sense, when we say that a person who gives free rein to his instincts or to his unconscious is "expressing himself," nor in the sense when something is there, hidden inside something else, and comes to be *expressed* in the outside, that is, simply revealed or communicated (both may nonetheless be peculiar, extremely restrictive instances subsumed in the meaning that I elaborate below).

The way in which I use the term "express" draws on a long philosophical tradition, in which one encounters Leibniz, and in which Spinoza played a crucial role, as shown by Deleuze (1968), who I follow here. According to Deleuze's modern reading of Spinoza, "expressing" takes place when various elements (at least two) are gathered in a particular way, and this particular relation evinces a new feature of the whole composed by that coming together. The best way of illustrating this is to return to the earlier example of the shingling process: when the Statistician returns to his office, he finds a collection of questionnaires and a stick. The schedules are then pegged together, so that the questionnaire is now not only linked to the vicinity of the particular Correspondent who filled it in, but comes to be linked to the entire county of which it is a part. Once attached to all the other questionnaires in the specific way described above, its "part of a county" attribute is expressed, whereas until then it was simply a "piece of information about a district," which is not the same thing. Before pegging, the Statistician had no proper way of moving from a particular area to a whole county; after pegging, the sum could be calculated, making the shift possible. The original elements were therefore articulated in a peculiar way, and through that articulation, which is nothing but a description, a new property of the whole comes into being. Similarly, the countable pickle is the *expression* of the set of elements collected by Church to bring it into being; the percentage written on a questionnaire is the *expression* of the investigations conducted by the Correspondent. At each step, statistics express some characteristics of the elements initially involved in it. Each time, the expression gives birth to a characteristic that becomes existent.

Expression, in this strong sense, can also be illustrated by an enological comparison, in which the types of vine stocks and the qualities of the soil express themselves together in the wine. For example, the peculiar, singular relation developed by a mixture of Tannat and Cabernet vines in an encounter with the turbulent soils of the foothills of the Hautes-Pyrénées is expressed in the countrified, robust taste of Madiran wines. That taste was not present in those particular vine stocks, or in those foothills, but it is the specific encounter that brought that new, delicious characteristic into the state of existence. In statistics, we would say that expression is at work in each of the many phases which gradually, taken together, lead to the construction of a figure about the whole of U.S. agriculture. The word "expression" thus enables us to give a very adequate account of the type of transformation operated by statistics on their objects: *statistics express certain characteristics of their objects.*

Thus expression is definitely an action exerted on the elements participating in the process, since the characteristics brought to light *were not* in those elements before they were expressed statistically. Before Church championed pickles, *they were not exhaustively counted*; in other words, that property had not been expressed. And that expression is far from just happening, as Church constantly reminds us in his emphasis on the difficulties he encountered along the way. To come to count pickles, he had to have that first piece of luck by which he met the right person on a train, then he had to get the main producers to support him and agree to answer his questions, to convince Washington that the effort was worthwhile, and so on. Expression means *doing something, making* some previously nonexistent properties *stand out*, and the important word here is *doing/making*, for expression *does* something to, *makes* something of the objects expressed.

But if expression is an *action*, that does not make it a *creation*. When speaking of expression we are not referring to a process in which an entity (statistics, for example) would have the demiurgic power to bring another entity, such as the agricultural economy, into existence all by itself, by dint of its own strength and resources. No, the notion of "expression" emphasizes the fact that this revitalization comes from an *arrangement of* at least two elements and that it is this arrangement, constituting what is expressed, which is new and surprising. Expression is what oozes from at least two elements when we find a way to put them together, rather than a sudden occurrence following an explosion produced by the waving of some magic wand.

In other words, one advantage of the former over the latter is that it is ternary where the other is simply binary. For the fact is that creation only links the creature to the creator, and performation tends to simplify the relation to theory and practice alone, whereas expression requires initial elements (at least two), to begin with, then a way of putting them together, and then the outcome of that arrangement. Church did not "create" the countable pickle; he put together a number of elements (the list of which ended only when he received the mimeographed questionnaire), he assembled all those elements (in this case he had respondents fill in the appropriate boxes on the questionnaire), and the result of the arrangement was the pickle's new characteristic: it was countable. It is inasmuch as expression is *the outcome* of the unprecedented *arrangement* of *initial elements* that we may say that it is not creation, but is nonetheless a transformation and a revitalization.[14]

With "meaningful articulation," Latour (1999, p. 187) proposed a concept very close to our "expression." In effect, one might say that Church articulated pickles, lists of salt producers, and many other entities to produce a countable pickle. But the advantage of "expression" over "articulation" is twofold. First, the former notion has a history in aesthetics; therefore, when we say that statistics "express" something, we clearly hear the creative (not creationist) aspect of the activity, we hear that it invents something. Second, when we say that statistics "express" something, we not only say that it is a game of Meccano, of putting pieces together, but we also say that the pieces are slightly changed, slightly different at the end of the story from at the beginning. Those points are so clear that when Latour explains what he means by "articulation," he himself cannot avoid using the notion of "expression." He says that articulation is "also *a change in the very matter of expression*" (emphasis in original). It is in general very difficult to speak about the type of action here under scrutiny without referring to the idea of "expression."

One reason for this may be that the notion of "expression" is tolerant: it is not very particular about the nature of the elements that may be expressed. More specifically, it does not care whether or not those elements are linguistic, any more than whether or not it is human beings who express themselves. The series of examples discussed above certainly constitute adequate proof of that: the elements involved in the process of expression ranged from wine to the wheat field and included the Correspondents themselves, the instructions, and shingling sticks. Since expression is primarily an assemblage, there is in fact no need for either language or human beings to be central to it. They definitely tend to partake of it, since there are few totally nonlinguistic moments, and those that are outside human grasp are of little interest to us, but language and speaking beings do not occupy any preeminent place.

To complete my argument, I have to say what is so specific with statistical expression. My answer is that statistics do not express just any characteristic, in fact, but usually *reproducible* elements.[15] One thinks, for instance, of the questionnaires or introductory letters which may be easily mimeographed (what is expressed then is the similarity of the receivers), the little identical boxes at the bottom of the questionnaires (if we look at the line of boxes, it is the resemblance of observations about different crops that is expressed; if we look at the columns of boxes, during the shingling operation, it is the similarity of farms within the County that is expressed), or, again, the names written identically one under the other in a list, a roll of Correspondents. Rather often, the objects in the statistical chain are expressed as *reproducible characteristics*. The advantage for statistics is that being able to add similar units together facilitates counting. Statistical expression therefore tends to produce distinct but identical items; it produces, with some difficulty, similarity within diversity.

We must be wary of generalizing too rapidly, however. In many cases statistical expression seems to be singular—qualitative, if I dare say so. This is so, for instance, of the "normal condition," which cannot be reiterated (there is one and only one normal condition). It is also true of the pickle, which cannot exist if it does not receive one exclusive definition. The reproducibility of statistical expressions is therefore reduced to a mere resemblance between these inasmuch as there are many exceptions. How can replicable elements be articulated with singular ones? Let me answer by stressing the fact that the nonreplicable elements are expressed by statistics in view of the reproducible elements. Statistics does seem always to need repetition, but sometimes it cannot obtain this without a detour, without the intermediary of singular, unique elements that enable it to uncover reproducible elements. *Thus statistics seems to express, sometimes in unexpected ways, the replicable characteristics of the objects it studies.*

It seems to me, then, that the vocabulary of expression definitely indicates a certain type of action exerted by statistics on its objects, but does not suggest—and it would be an error to do so—that such action may be a pure and simple creation, or that it is primarily linguistic. For this reason I suggest saying, for example, that statistics *expresses* U.S. farming or, again, that the United States as a whole is *one expression* of statistics, rather than asserting that statistics perform the United States or that the United States as a whole have been performed by statistics.

Conclusion: Statistics Have Effects on or Express the Economy but Do Not Perform It

What conclusion can we draw, *in fine*? Having traveled this long path that took us back into the 1920s, made us pace Michigan up and down to see pickles grow, enter farmhouses to watch Correspondents fill out their questionnaires, follow those questionnaires to the capitals of every state of the Union to see how they were aggregated with all the others. In short, having tracked down statistics in the making, can we answer our first question: do statistics perform the economy they describe? I think I have a response, a two-part one.

For one thing, it is clear, as "performativity" claims, that statistics have effects on the world in which they are established. First of all, the farming statistics we examined here were actually explicitly created for precisely that purpose—that is, to help the administration purify the markets. But there is no difference between this effect of statistics and any other effect. Statistics are produced, and, like any other solid entity, they have effects on their surroundings. It just so happens that these effects are so powerful that they manage to return to their starting point. That is, having influenced a number of actors, they gradually end up influencing farmers themselves and their crops. This is certainly a surprising, amusing circular effect, but it is not very original as a process, and therefore need not be given any special name. There is no reason all of a sudden to claim that "statistics perform . . ." instead of the more natural, classical: "statistics have effects . . ." or "statistics influence . . . ," or, again, "statistics make, or do" . . . .

Moreover, statistics also have direct effects on the object they describe. The relation of statistics to what they describe is also peculiar and is also a certain type of action that is worth analyzing, even though it seems to escape the scope of what is usually called "performation." At the very moment they do their describing, they also transform what they describe. How do they do that? My answer is that they *characterize the repetitive modalities of their object.*

First, they *characterize* what is described; in other words, by arranging a series of elements taken in farming in a singular fashion, they bring out characteristics of those elements that they did not have previously. Statistics produce certain properties of the objects they study. But second, this production is far from being purely linguistic, even if language definitely plays a role here. To the contrary, many material objects, as well as weather conditions, all of which are both physical and constituent of statistics, are a part of this process of production. In other words, language is not the only way in which statistics characterize their objects. Third and last, this production is not a creation but a transformation, a recycling.

Statistics seize hold of already-constituted elements and take possession of them, but they do not create them out of thin air.

Statistics transform their object as they describe it, then. Does this mean we may speak of "performing"? We should refrain from doing so, for the concept suggests that the process is purely linguistic and hints at a pure and simple creation of the object of the description; both of these features are contradicted in the case of statistics. For this reason I prefer the notion of *expression*, which accounts perfectly for the three properties we have identified. Rather than saying "statistics perform their object" we would designate the special effect described here by saying "statistics express the United States" or "U.S. farming is expressed by statistics."

So statistics certainly do transform the world, but regardless of the direction taken by these transformations, independently of whether we look at the effects of well-established statistical figures or at the processes by which those figures are produced, I do not think we have identified any true "performing." The transformations generated by statistics do not represent performativity. Consequently, if economic theory "performs" the economy, it is certainly not through statistics, which nonetheless represent the intermediary par excellence between those two entities. But, then, are we so sure we must call the effects of economic theory "performative"?

Notes

1. For a broader insight into social studies of statistics and especially into their role as social actors, see, for example, Desrosières (1998), Gigerenzer et al. (1989), or Porter (1995).

2. This example is drawn from my forthcoming book, to be published in French (Didier 2006), where I show the whole array of interrelations between, on the one hand, the theories of statistical sampling and, on the other hand, agricultural practices and unemployment, two seminal objects of statistical surveys.

3. One bushel = 35.3 liters. It is a measure of capacity for solids. The American bushel differs from the British bushel, of course.

4. In 1933 the Division prided itself on publishing 65,000 estimates and forecasts yearly (U.S.D.A. 1933, p. 12).

5. The speculator is a character who has a story of his own. Cronon (1991, p. 127) even dates the existence of speculators back to around 1850. According to him, they appear at the same time as "cornering," a technique that developed during the nineteenth century in the Chicago grain market. To corner a market is to purchase future contracts on a particular crop and at the same time to buy the entire crop that is actually put on the market. So that to fulfill his own engagement, the person who has sell the futures is obliged to buy some grain, virtually at any price, from the same man who has tricked him into the deal.

6. In the smaller East Coast states, a single statistician was in charge of several states. There were therefore 41 Statisticians in all.

7. RG 83, entry 75, December 1923 schedule, U.S. National Archives.

8. Take n individuals i who each report the figure Y_i. The average of these reported figures is $M = \frac{1}{n}\sum_{i=1}^{n} Y_i$.

9. I was shown the thing by Richard Allen, who is now Deputy Administrator for Programs and Products at the NASS, today's name of the Division. His office contains not only some rare archives, but also a little museum of the most inventive objects in the history of agricultural statistics.

10. The population census was done every ten years, but from 1920 on there was an additional agricultural census at the midpoint (Anderson 1988).

11. These two examples are taken from MacKenzie and Millo (2003, pp. 107–137).

12. For a brief presentation of Miller's position on performativity, see Miller (1998, 2005).

13. In particular, in France, the historians of polling deserve exactly the same criticism as the one I address to MacKenzie. Champagne (1990) and Blondiaux (1998) both argue that polling *creates* public opinion, because people believe more and more in polls and, one after another, act according to their (expensive) advice.

14. Expression does not eliminate any conceivable creation, however; it becomes a threshold in the extent to which a particular arrangement triggers surprise and possible further developments. See for example Massumi (2001).

15. This point comes from Tarde (1890/2001).

References

Anderson, M. J. 1988. *The American Census*. New Haven: Yale University Press.

Austin, J. L. 1962 *How to Do Things with Words*. Oxford: Clarendon Press.

Becker, J. A. 1928. "Analysis of Assumptions Underlying the Various Indications of Change in Crop Acreage." In *Class of the Division*, March 9, Washington, DC.

Blondiaux, L. 1998. *La fabrique de l'opinion*. Paris: Le Seuil.

Champagne, P. 1990. *Faire l'opinion*. Paris: Minuit.

Church, V. H. 1943. *Personal Recollection of the Government Crop Reporting Service*. Washington, DC: National Agricultural Statistical Service.

Cronon, W. 1991. *Nature's Metropolis: Chicago and the Great West*. New York: Norton.

Deleuze, G. 1968. *Spinoza et le problème de l'expression*. Paris: Minuit.

Desrosières, A. 1998. *The Politics of Large Numbers: A History of Statistical Reasoning*. Cambridge, MA: Harvard University Press.

Didier, E. Forthcoming. *En quoi consiste l'Amérique? Représentativité statistique et administration aux Etats-Unis pendant l'entre-deux-guerres*. Paris: PUF/INED.

Estabrook L. M. 1915. *Government Crop Reports: Their Value, Scope and Preparation*. Washington DC: Government Printing Office.

Gigerenzer, G., Z. Swijtink, T. Porter, L. Daston, J. Beatty, and L. Krüger. 1989. *The Empire of Chance: How Probability Changed Science and Everyday Life*. Cambridge: Cambridge University Press.

Latour, B. 1999. *Pandora's Hope*. Cambridge MA: Harvard University Press.

MacKenzie, D., and Y. Millo. 2003. "Constructing a Market, Performing Theory: The Historical Sociology of a Financial Derivatives Exchange." *American Journal of Sociology* 109(1):107–145.

Massumi, B., Ed. 2001. A *Shock to Thought: Expressions after Deleuze and Guattari*. London: Routledge.

Miller, D. 1998. "Conclusion: A Theory of Virtualism." Pp. 187–215 in *Virtualism: A New Political Economy*, edited by J. G. Carrier and D. Miller. Oxford: Berg.

Miller, D. 2005. "Reply to Michel Callon." *Economic Sociology European Electronic Newsletter* 6(3). Available at http://econsoc.mpifg.de/archive/esjuly05.pdf.

Miller, P. L., and G. Shepherd. 1933. "Cooperation in Agriculture, Livestock Marketing." *Iowa Experiment Station Bulletin* 306:76–95.

Porter, T. 1995. *Trust in Numbers: The Pursuit of Objectivity in Science and Public Life*. Princeton: Princeton University Press.

Tarde, G. 1890/2001. *Les lois de l'imitation*. Paris, Les Empêcheurs de Penser en Rond / Le Seuil.

Taylor, H. C., and A. D. Taylor. 1952. *The Story of Agricultural Economics in the US, 1840–1932*. Ames: Iowa State College Press.

U.S.D.A. 1933. *The Crop and Livestock Reporting Service in the United States*. Washington, DC: Government Printing Office.

Chapter 11 _____

What Does It Mean to Say That Economics Is Performative?

MICHEL CALLON

> L'homo œconomicus n'est pas derrière nous, il est devant nous;
> comme l'homme de la morale et du devoir; comme l'homme de la
> science et de la raison. L'homme a été très longtemps autre chose; et
> il n'y a pas bien longtemps qu'il est une machine, compliquée d'une
> machine à calculer.[1]
>   (Mauss 1960, p. 272)

> Economists have long recognized the importance of technological
> innovation for economic growth; however, economists have
> generally studied only such contributions of the physical sciences,
> overlooking the fact that economics itself has been the source of a
> surprising number of inventions.
>   (Faulhaber and Baumol 1988, p. 577)

Faulhaber and Baumol's Quandary

In 1988 economists Gerald Faulhaber and William Baumol raised a question similar to the one that I raised in *The Laws of the Markets* (Callon 1998).[2] In "Economists as Innovators: Practical Products of Theoretical Research" they indicated their intention to "determine how much economists have in fact contributed to the flow of innovation used in business and government and to judge what this evidence implies about the degree of validity of the standard optimization premise" (Faulhaber and Baumol 1998, p. 580).

To this end, Faulhaber and Baumol selected nine noteworthy innovations (marginal analysis; the use of net present value for capital budgeting; peak load pricing; econometric forecasting; the portfolio selection model and the associated *beta* coefficient and duration analysis; the Black-Scholes option pricing model; Ramsey pricing; and the stand-alone cost test) and studied their history from origins to (non)adoption and diffusion, treating these innovations produced by economics like any other scientific or technological innovation.

Their results were "mixed." While economics did play a part in the conception of innovations, it was less important than they had anticipated. Economics seldom acts alone and is rarely a driver of invention. Their classification of their results (Faulhaber and Baumol 1988, p. 580) shows these findings clearly:

1. Cases in which economists provided the actual invention and may have contributed to the innovation process (e.g., econometric techniques, duration, *beta*, stand-alone costs).
2. Cases in which economists helped in the innovation process, though the idea was initially contributed by others (e.g., discounted present value, Ramsey pricing).
3. Cases in which economists provided an optimality formula for a concept previously introduced by others in an imperfect and intuitive version (e.g., peak-load pricing).
4. Cases in which economists acted primarily as disseminators of the ideas of others (marginal analysis).

This mixed conclusion clearly put Faulhaber and Baumol in a quandary. On the one hand, like many of their colleagues, they were convinced that economics does not have to make any contribution whatsoever to the economy in order to justify its existence. On the other, they were concerned about economic agents' lack of interest in economists' work.

If Faulhaber and Baumol were uneasy about their results, it is first because they had shown that economics (in its most theoretical form) plays a secondary or even tertiary role in innovation. Even the best economists are often content to relay or to rediscover inventions produced by others, sometimes completely failing to impose their most original views, as they did in the case of marginal analysis, one of the cornerstones of neoclassical theory. Economics may be useful but it acts simply as an additional force! In this view, skeptics might see economists as mere parasites, common ideologists, or vile mercenaries in the pay of wicked capitalists.

If Faulhaber and Baumol's quandary was due only to what they consider an unexpectedly weak contribution of economics, it would be easy enough to reassure them. Having dared to treat economics like any other science and to question its contribution to economic life, they have fallen victim of the theory of innovation that they chose to use. According to that theory, innovation is seen as a linear process (research → invention → development → innovation → diffusion), in which basic research can play only one part: a necessarily episodic role in which it is the source of major innovations.

The linear view of technological change was recently superseded by a nonlinear conceptual model featuring feedback loops emanating from each stage (Kline and Rosenberg 1986). In this alternative model, basic science can fit into the process of innovation at any stage. Moreover, the very idea of a source or an origin point of technology is misleading because innovation is an emergent, interactive activity. It involves many actors who cooperate or oppose one another (Akrich et al. 2002). Science and scientists—and especially economics and economists—are no exception. Considered from the point of view of the interactive and iterative model, the four trajectories identified by Faulhaber and Baumol no longer demonstrate the weakness of economics' contributions. To the contrary, what they confirm is the variety of possible contributions economics can make to the economy, as well as its constant presence in technological change. If we take the interactive and iterative model of innovation and apply it to economics, economics' contribution to the economy becomes significant and diverse because, as Faulhaber and Baumol's case studies show, there have been few innovations in which it has not been involved at some stage in one way or another.

We could stop there and be content with developing a sociology of economic innovations based on the interactive model, one that gives a more accurate and more balanced view of the contribution of economics to the economy. But that would only partially solve Faulhaber and Baumol's quandary, since they are tormented not only by the (supposed) weakness of economics' contribution to the economy, but also by a real epistemological concern. Is it reasonable to consider that a scientific theory can alter the nature of the object that it describes? Can economics act on the behavior of real economic agents, which it claims to analyze objectively and from a distance? Wouldn't this be tantamount to claiming that physics and physicists are able to influence the laws governing the course of planets?

These sorts of objections clearly worry the authors. They have them in mind when they clarify the criteria by which they selected the innovations in their study: "We explicitly focus on innovations whose value to those who adopt them is the promise of improvement in their own economic performance in coping with market forces" (Faulhaber and Baumol 1988, p. 577). Faulhaber and Baumol chose innovations that were compatible with the model of rational agents capable of deciding what would provide them with a competitive advantage—in short, innovations that markets and agents should have invented and would eventually have invented on their own. For Faulhaber and Baumol economic theory can play a role in accelerating the processes that it sets out to describe but it cannot change their course.

When addressing the issue of the epistemological status of economic knowledge, Faulhaber and Baumol present two different conceptions of relationships between economics and its object (the economy). In the first, economists are *inventors* who naturally fit into the innovation process and are immersed in the economy; in the second, they are *describers* (or analysts) who produce concepts, theories, and tools and who stand back from the economy.

Faulhaber and Baumol know that the majority of orthodox economists are fervent supporters of the second position and believe that the market, provided it is well organized, prompts agents to conceive of and adopt efficient behavior. The discovery of formulas such as that of Ramsey or of Black-Scholes does not change behavior; it describes and clarifies it, just as Newton's laws have not changed the behavior of falling apples: "Yet strong believers in the market will be skeptical, claiming that competition will force firms and agents to do what is optimal. Consequently, the discovery of a formula for discounting or peak-load pricing will not change behavior but merely describe it" (Faulhaber and Baumol 1988, p. 578). Economic agents don't need economists to conceive of tools and to choose the right behavior. When they use economics, it is because economists correctly describe what will necessarily happen—just as Newton's laws anticipate any trajectory of any bodies in any field of gravitational forces. Basically, for an efficient market, economics is a futile luxury.

The opposition between scientists as describers and scientists as innovators is not peculiar to markets or institutions. It runs through all the disciplines and the philosophy of science, with those who think that theories simply mirror reality on the one hand and those who believe that they can represent reality only by intervening on and transforming it on the other (Hacking 1983).

The reader can sense that Faulhaber and Baumol believe more in the thesis of inventors-innovators than in that of describers. If they fail to state their preferences explicitly, it is because they are aware of the weakness of their positions. Describers dominate economics. Moreover, no proof, no crucial experience allows the two positions to be separated in the short term. In several cases Faulhaber and Baumol—as if they were inspired by a sociology of science à la Feyerabend—concede that it is impossible for them to prove that the use of a formula or a new calculating tool (for instance, the use of a discounting technique that allows calculation of the payment necessary to reimburse a debt earlier than planned) affords a competitive advantage for the agents who adopt it, because "*ceteris* are never *paribus [sic]*" (Faulhaber and Baumol 1988, p. 578). At another point, even though they are sure of having shown that Black-Scholes's formula really did contribute to changes of behaviors and markets—and in a way that markets, left to themselves, would have been incapable of imagining—they observe that some of their colleagues will object. These colleagues will argue that the well-known thesis of beauty contests or self-fulfilling prophecies is enough to explain the effects of the adoption of this tool. The equation per se has no impact; it simply acts as a convention, a common belief that guarantees the coordination of actors in a situation of uncertainty.

Aware that the balance of power is not in their favor, Faulhaber and Baumol downplay the importance of their observations. Yet this does not prevent them from developing killing arguments against an extreme version of the expectation that the market will always get it right. Since the market, simply by its force, is seen as capable of causing actors to innovate, Faulhaber and Baumol rightly say that it ought to have driven firms, on their own, to find the electric, chemical, or biological techniques that guarantee them a competitive advantage. The history of science and technology, however, shows the opposite: "First, if the market is always able to force surviving firms to anticipate correctly (if implicitly) the behavior called for by as yet unborn economists, why does it not work in the case of engineers and physicists also unborn?" (Faulhaber and Baumol 1988, p. 579). Without assistance, economic agents are not able to produce of all the innovations that will guarantee them a competitive advantage. They need chemists, physicists, or biologists working in universities. So why treat economists, who profess to be scientists in their own right, any differently from others of their kind?

If Faulhaber and Baumol refuse to answer this question clearly, it is because they feel that it might introduce a difficulty that is peculiar to economics. To an open-minded economist it poses no problem that chemistry, physics, or biology participates in the construction of markets and their functioning because these disciplines say nothing and have nothing to say about economic markets. As such, they can take part in the economy because their object is unrelated to it. Economics is not so fortunate. By participating in the economy, it would place itself within the object that it is supposed to be studying from the outside, and it would thus run the risk of corrupting or distorting that object. To maintain the parallel with the natural sciences, we need to ask what would happen to chemistry, physics, and biology if they were to participate in the constitution of the "natural" objects that they are purported to describe.

My thesis is that both the natural and life sciences, along with the social sciences, contribute toward enacting the realities that they describe (Law and Urry 2004). The concept of performativity affords a way out of the apparent paradox of this statement. Without performativity we would be destined to sharing Faulhaber and Baumol's quandary. We would have no alternative but to acknowledge economist-describers' point of view. We would have to settle for a comfortable but rather boring life offered by academic ivory towers.

Performativity: Truth as Success

How can a discourse be outside the reality that it describes and simultaneously participate in the construction of that reality as an object by acting on it? To this paradoxical question the concept of performativity
provides a convincing and general answer.

My intention here is not to enter into the details of the debates surrounding this concept. Yet I cannot continue to settle for a metaphoric use and
for the accurate but elliptical definition I gave in *The Laws of the Markets*.
A discourse is indeed performative, as I suggested there, if it contributes to
the construction of the reality that it describes, but we need to go further
than that and at least briefly turn to discourse analysis to understand the
meaning of the verb "to contribute." The idea is to assess the extent to
which the concept of performativity, which implies that any discourse acts
on its object, applies to science in general and to economics in particular.

The Pragmatic Turn

Since the ancient Greeks, reflection on language has been organized
around the dissociation between logic and rhetoric. Whereas logic questions the conditions of the verisimilitude of statements through an
analysis of propositions and their sequence, rhetoric—the prerogative
of sophists and rhetoricians—disregards the question of truth and ap-
prehends discourse as a producer of effects, a power of intervention in
the real. Logic implies the existence of an outside world, populated by
entities that are distinct and cut off from the propositions referring to
them. The ontology of the world of logic is set and independent of the
discourses describing it. Rhetoric, on the other hand, implies relationships of entanglement between propositions and their referents; it acts
on the ontology of the entities to which it refers. Science obviously
seems to be on the side of logic and exteriority (an electron is an electron, regardless of what one says about it), while politics is on the side
of rhetoric (the identity and missions of the United States depend on
what is said about them).

To establish an impervious division between these different modalities
of the functioning of discourse has always been difficult. The two ways
constantly interfere with each other, as in the so-called Port-Royal logic
in which considerations of a strictly rhetorical order are introduced
alongside purely logical developments.

> If we say to someone that they have lied, and we consider only the main
> meaning of the phrase, it is as if we told them that they knew the opposite of
> what they had said. But apart from the main meaning, these words convey an

(accessory) idea of contempt, which makes them insulting. (Arnauld and Nicole 1662/1970).

In this extract the notion of an accessory idea denotes that which, along with the propositional content of a discourse, constitutes what was later called its illocutionary force—in this case, its value as an insult. The mere fact of saying "You have lied" is at once a statement, a description of the state of the world (which may be true or false), and an act through which the enunciator acts on the enunciatee (the receiver) of the statement (by insulting him or her).[3]

Despite these theories and observations, which show the difficulty of separating logic from rhetoric, the interlocutory dimension of language has always been considered as located at the periphery of logic. It was only with the rise of pragmatics that the gap was reduced. There is pragmatics as soon as one gives up the separation between the grammatical structure of the discourse and its use. The use of language is not added to a theoretically self-sufficient statement from the outside. Morris (1938) noted, for example, that any language has a syntax (relations between signs), semantics (relationships between the signs and what they denote), and pragmatics (relation between signs and their use context),[4] which cannot be entirely dissociated from one another. There is no discourse without a speaker and an audience, and no communication without well-formulated sentences and well-articulated concepts. On the basis of these distinctions, several positions seem possible. From a minimalist point of view we can consider that pragmatics is one component of linguistics among others (along with syntax and semantics), or else adopt a maximalist point of view and argue that nothing in linguistic phenomena can escape pragmatics.

Austin's decisive contribution is to have shown, or at least to have suggested, that the very idea of a separation between these dimensions is impossible and that only the maximalist position is defendable. Austin's work is interesting precisely because he starts with a distinction between those statements that describe the worlds to which they refer and those that act on those worlds and help to make them exist. This is his famous distinction between constative utterances (the cat is on the mat; the structure of DNA is a double helix; in the prisoner's dilemma rational agents choose suboptimal configurations) and performative utterances ("I promise," "I baptize you," "I sentence you to ten years' imprisonment," "I marry you"). In the former the object is the outside world; the latter cause the reality that they describe to exist (e.g., being married is the consequence of an act of language). By proposing this distinction and showing the diversity and large number of purely performative statements, Austin wanted to criticize the idea that the function of language is essentially representative. But, in attempting to make this distinction more precise and profound, he seriously considered concluding that all utterances are performative (or illocutionary) and that it is impossible to maintain the hypothesis of the existence of pure constative utterances.[5]

The Semiotic Turn

According to Austin, because it is uttered (what is called enunciation), there is no statement that does not constitute the context in which it functions: there is no language; there are only acts of language. Phrased in Greimassian terminology, to have meaning a statement implies its context of enunciation (at least an enunciator and an enunciatee) (Greimas and Courtès 1982). Although Austin was not explicitly referring to scientific discourse, there is no reason to exclude science from the general rule, as we will see. Scientific theories, models, and statements are not constative; they are performative, that is, actively engaged in the constitution of the reality that they describe.

To explain the scope and reasons for this assertion that all science is performative, which some would consider scandalous, we can conveniently begin with the distinction between universal and singular statements. For its clarity and precision I prefer to adopt Popper's terminology here, and will refer to singular existential statements (SESs) and universal statements (USs).[6]

SESs can be found in all of the scientific disciplines. An SES is characterized by its "indexicality": it explicitly refers to particular circumstances, singular entities located in time and space.[7] For instance, "At *such-and-such* a place, at *such-and-such* a time, *such-and-such* a thread can be observed, that breaks when we apply *such-and-such* a force over x kilograms." This statement describes the existence of an *event* (the thread breaks) whose spatiotemporal coordinates are provided (the event is observable at a particular time and place) and whose operating mode is indicated. One of the characteristics of SESs is that they contain what semioticians call "shifters," words in the statement which refer (or shift) to situations, contexts, or operations that can be described and observed. In the example given, the statement includes phrases such as "at *such-and-such* a place, at *such-and-such* a time." The statement also indicates precise devices, operators, and operating modes which are not directly described but have to be describable (for instance, through the addition of other statements that complete the SES and clarify what it implies). In other words, the statement contains its own context.[8]

The epistemological question concerning the conditions under which the observation is considered valid and the mechanisms through which witnesses are convinced, as well as the equally epistemological question concerning relationships between the SES and other USs (for example, of the type "threads subjected to a force exceeding their breaking strength will break") are of no interest, even if they have fueled fierce controversies.[9] The only thing that matters here is that in a scientific theory or model there is necessarily a place for SESs. Science cannot exist without the possibility of formulating statements that describe singular events localized in time and space, without describable sociotechnical devices that produce events described by singular statements.

This implies that the verisimilitude of the statement (i.e., does the event occur or not?) cannot be dissociated from the context denoted by and built into the statement. The SES is not a statement outside the world or worlds to which it refers; it requires that very world. Conversely, the world to which it refers is meaningless without the statement that puts it into action. A thread on which a weight is hung and which breaks is not an intelligible and interpretable event; under no circumstances can it be associated with a scientific fact if it is not, at least, accompanied and framed by the singular existential statement announcing that its breaking stress has been exceeded.[10] The SES is entangled with the device that produced what it describes; the device and the series of actions undertaken are shaped by the statement, and vice versa.

Last Turn: The ANT Turn

To understand the strange relations of exteriority and interiority that are implied by the semiotic turn consider, as an example, a set of operating instructions and the device to which they refer (Akrich 1992). Without the material device the operating instructions are meaningless: the gaze needs to constantly *shift* from one to the other. Likewise, the machine without the instructions is likely to be opaque, unusable, and passive. At the heart of science lies this two-way relationship between description and action. When I say "this thread breaks," I am referring to all the actions that cause the break in the thread and that cause my statement to be true, to actually happen (or not). It is because the statement describes a singular course of action still to happen—and not a preexisting word out there—that it is performative. A scientific statement can be compared to the instructions for use (that is, for action) with which we grapple when we try to get a VCR to function.

This helps to explain why I prefer to refer to the relationships between statements and their worlds as sociotechnical *agencements*.[11] The term *agencement* is a French word that has no exact English counterpart. In French its meaning is very close to "arrangement" (or "assemblage"). It conveys the idea of a combination of heterogeneous elements that have been carefully adjusted to one another. But arrangements (as well as assemblages) could imply a sort of divide between human agents (those who arrange or assemble) and things that have been arranged. This is why Deleuze and Guattari (1998) proposed the notion of *agencement*. *Agencement* has the same root as agency: *agencements* are arrangements endowed with the capacity of acting in different ways depending on their configuration. This means that there is nothing left outside *agencements*: there is no need for further explanation, because the construction of its meaning is part of an *agencement*. A sociotechnical *agencement* includes the statement(s) pointing to it, and it is because the former includes the latter that the *agencement* acts in line with the statement, just as the operating instructions are part of the device and participate in making it work. Contexts cannot be reduced, as in semiotics, to a pure world of words and interlocutors; they are better conceived as textual and material assemblages (Latour 2005).

We can now see why the concept of performativity has led to the replacement of the concept of truth (or nontruth) by that of success or failure. In Chapter 3 Donald MacKenzie shows, for instance, that Black and Scholes's famous formula, so basically simple, has meaning and effect only in its own world. MacKenzie rightly talks of "an equation and its worlds" (MacKenzie 2003). One world implied by the equation—without which the equation would not function and which would not function without the equation—is a world in which prices can be observed to follow a random walk. It is a world in which "skewnesses" (a new variable for taking into account non-Gaussian distributions) will later be calculated and reinjected into pricing formulas, a world in which software (Autoquote) will allow the production of continuous quotation even for options with low liquidity. It is a world which has its vocabulary, its evaluation criteria, a world in which the notion of implied volatility, a simple mathematical variable, becomes observable and calculable. What MacKenzie describes with surgical precision is the gradual actualization of the world of the formula: a formula that progressively discovers its world and a world that is put into motion by the formula describing it; a formula that previously functioned in a paper world, which was perfectly real (for what could be more real than paper or equations?), subsequently functions, after many investments, in a world of computers and silicon, algorithms, professional skills, and cleverly adjusted institutions. We could say that the formula has become true, but it is preferable to say that the world it supposes has become actual.[12] The supposed world has gained in precision, weight, robustness, and extension through the intense work of articulating, experimenting, and observing that has been required to produce the gradual, mutual adjustment of sociotechnical *agencements* and formulas. The actualization process is a long sequence of trial and error, reconfigurations and reformulations. But what makes this process possible is the performative dimension of the statements and the trials that they allow. For if the statement could be dissociated from the world in which it functions, if it could be denied as an utterance pointing or shifting to supposed worlds, no trial, learning, or adjustment would be conceivable. The conditions of felicity of a (performative) statement, that is, its success, depend on this adjustment, an adjustment that is never given in advance and always requires specific investments.

As MacKenzie shows in his chapter, at a certain point in time, in certain places, the world of the formula is actualized, in such a way that it can be said that the formula describes and represents its world correctly. We are no longer in the register of truth as a reference but—to stick to the same word—in that of truth as success or failure, in truth as fulfilled conditions of felicity. The formula that is born performative, and remains so, seems to be constative when the world (finally) acts according to it. Yet failure can occur when events take place that are incompatible with the formula and its world. Financial crisis is a crisis for the formula. New adjustments are made; the formula is given a new twist (volatility skew) that translates into an alteration of the sociotechnical *agencements* (dedicated professionals and observation tools are required to carry out the calculation of this parameter daily). And the game is never over, for new framings are always possible, always involving a *bricolage* of both the *agencements* and the statements. This, at least, is what the notion of performativity, enriched by the semiotic and the ANT turn, makes visible.

From Self-Fulfilling Prophecies to Performation

One of the main benefits of the notion of performativity is that it rids us of what Pickering (1995) calls the representational idiom, in terms of which the purpose of science is to create representations of reality. But we have to go further. We would be wrong to sum up the debate as the opposition between performativity and constativity. Many concepts are proposed, especially in this book, to describe the strange relations between the social sciences and their objects. I am now going to discuss some of them. This will enable me to further clarify the meaning of the notion of performativity.

Self-Fulfilling Prophecies

One way of describing the effects of economic theories on agents is through the notion of self-fulfilling prophecies proposed by Robert K. Merton, the father of the option theorist whose work is discussed in chapter 3. If everyone is persuaded that Bank X is on the verge of bankruptcy, then to avoid being ruined, all of its clients will rush to withdraw their money before everyone else does and bankruptcy will inevitably ensue. Likewise, if we are convinced that women do not have the capacities required to practice certain occupations, those occupations will effectively be closed to women and the assertion will be verified. The concept of a self-fulfilling prophecy seems to apply to economics. Economics—and this is where it derives its strength—is a constructed, logical discourse based on a number of irrefutable hypotheses. As discourse it can change into a system of beliefs that infiltrate agents' minds and colonize them. For example, neoclassical theory is based on the idea that agents are self-interested. If I believe this statement and if this belief is shared by the other agents, and I believe that they believe it, then what was simply an assumption turns into a reality. Everyone ends up aligning himself or herself to the model and everyone's expectations are fulfilled by everyone else's behaviors. To predict economic agents' behaviors an economic theory does not have to be true; it simply needs to be believed by everyone. Since the model acts as a convention, it can be perfectly arbitrary. Even if the belief has no relationship with the world, the world ends up corresponding to it. We can thus consider that the famous Black and Scholes formula has no truth value, that it says nothing of real markets, and that it is simply a coordination tool that allows mutual expectations. It constitutes a false but effective representation, and can be seen as pure convention. This is what Faulhaber and Baumol suggest in their article.

Those who support the thesis of the self-fulfilling prophecy or that of prescription explain that if an economic model or formula can act as a convention (by nature arbitrary), it is because its object is human beings, whose actions and behaviors depend entirely on their beliefs and the meanings that they attribute to the social world surrounding them. Could one say that the universal law of gravity is a self-fulfilling prophecy? Of course not. We justifiably believe that it is not enough for human agents to behave as if they believed in the law for it to govern the course of planets. A law in $1/d^3$ would not become true if everyone believed in it, simply because celestial bodies follow their nature, regardless of what the humans who observe and interact with them think and say. In contrast, the Black-Scholes-Merton model can be self-fulfilling because it is all about the behaviors of human beings, and human beings depend on beliefs and expectations that planets do not have. In the final analysis it is the humanity of human beings that allows self-fulfilling prophecies and, more generally, the effectiveness of conventions. Society has thus opposed nature since Aristotle.

This 2,500-year-old conception is not convincing. The case of the Black and Scholes equation is a typical example of the limits of the theory of self-fulfilling prophecies applied to the social sciences and especially economics. Imagine, as MacKenzie proposes, a different formula, for instance, one with a calculation error or a statistical incoherence. Would it have had the same impact? This question is obviously difficult to answer directly since no one has ever tried the experiment. Fortunately there is another, indirect, way of answering the question. MacKenzie shows that the use of the Black and Scholes formula led to a situation of crisis that can be explained in a plausible way by the technical shortcomings of the formula. These shortcomings amplified the crisis, since the formula induced behaviors that challenged the distribution of the very course of action on which the formula itself was based. To be sure, the Black and Scholes formula does successfully organize agents' coordination, at least for a certain time. But, as the 1987 crash (briefly discussed in MacKenzie's chapter) shows, it cannot for all of that be considered an (arbitrary) convention. The content of the formula matters.[13]

The Black and Scholes formula implies a world without which it cannot function and the realization of that world is at stake. Clearly, as seen above, it is not the formula itself that can cause that world, a sociotechnical *agencement*, to exist. Other forces, other interests, are involved. It so happened that the adjustment took place—Donald MacKenzie explains how—and lasted a few years, but it was unable to withstand the 1987 events. This was due not to a lack of belief in the formula but to the incapacity of the formula to forecast the events and the behaviors they triggered.

Whereas the notion of a self-fulfilling prophecy explains success or failure in terms of beliefs only, that of performativity goes beyond human minds and deploys all the materialities comprising the sociotechnical *agencements* that constitute the world in which these agents are plunged: performativity leaves open the possibility of events that might refute, or even happen independently of, what humans believe or think.

MacKenzie proposes the notion of counterperformativity to denote these failures, because in this case the formula produces behaviors that eventually undermine it. This analysis applies equally to the natural sciences and to the human and social sciences. What Popper called refutation is another name for counterperformativity or what I have called overflowing. The fact of imposing devices designed to realize a statement causes other worlds to proliferate in reaction to that performation. Any act, even of language, produces effects that might strike back. The history of science is nothing but the long and interminable series of untimely overflowings, of sociotechnical *agencements* that have been caught out, unable to discipline and frame the entities that they assemble. Just as, through their very actions, a badly calculated boat, an ill-adjusted missile, or a wrongly formulated theorem reveals unsuspected worlds, the Black and Scholes formula sets in motion events that without it would not have happened and that, once taken into account, lead to new sociotechnical *agencements*. What is at stake is the success or failure of the performation, what is at stake is the realization of the sociotechnical *agencement* inscribed in the statement.

The notions of representation, convention, or belief and, with them, that of self-fulfilling prophecy do not enable us to study failures because they give no principle of reality. The Black and Scholes formula has a world to impose, sociotechnical *agencements* outside of which it cannot survive. A formula that would index share prices on sunspots (Guesnerie 1986), that is, that would be pure convention, would last no more than a second, simply because not a single element can be mobilized to rapidly produce a sociotechnical *agencement* linking sunspots to share prices in an observable and stable manner.

Prescription

The notion of "prescription" is not very far removed from that of "self-fulfilling prophecy." It is also frequently mobilized to describe the mechanisms through which a conformity between economic theory and economic reality is achieved. Whereas self-fulfilling prophecies imply (similarly) formatted human minds ready to believe in the truth of certain categories or assumptions proposed by economic theories, prescription implies a medium, an intermediate device between theory and behavior, between economics and the economy. Generally this medium is taken to be institutions and the norms that they impose (Ferraro et al. 2005). Consider the role of economic theories and their hypotheses in institutional design. We can say that the creation of a European central bank, directly inspired by the monetarist theses of Milton Friedman, helps to make real monetary markets correspond to the descriptions and analyses proposed by theories or models qualified as abstract. Similarly, enforcing incentives inspired by economic theories and their assumptions about human or organizational behaviors causes these behaviors to fit the theory's predictions. When workers are paid on the basis of performance, they end up complying with the anthropological models that fit the incentives imposed on them. If we consider that a firm is a nexus of contracts, and we set up procedures to make these contracts explicit and to ensure their enforcement, the firm does become a nexus of contracts. One of the contributions of the prescription thesis is that it highlights the importance of what I have called sociotechnical *agencements* in comprehending relations between economics and the economy. To understand how statements become true and describe the world as we see it, one has to take into account institutions and the constraints and incentives that they impose. The difference between self-fulfilling prophecies and prescriptions is slim: from the point of view of prescription (as in that of self-fulfilling prophecy), economic theory says nothing about the real economy. Economics does not have to describe reality; its mission is to say what the economy is supposed to be and to propose solutions and devices to make it that way.

Since it is often said that economics is prescriptive rather than descriptive, it is worth devoting a few lines to the difference between prescription and performance. I am going to show that the notion of prescription denotes a particular case of performance.

A convenient way of proceeding is via Sahlins, who introduces the opposition between performative and prescriptive structures to describe the attitude of Hawaiians who are reported to have offered Captain Cook and his crew the opportunity of having sexual relations with them (Sahlins 1985). How can this type of behavior with strangers be explained? Sahlins notes that the case shows, above all, Hawaiian society's faculty for invention when faced with the unexpected. He argues that Hawaiian women showed their strong ability to adapt and to react when Cook and his crew landed, adding that these faculties of adaptation and change were nevertheless framed by references to well-established beliefs and norms that were not questioned. If Cook was considered to be a God and Hawaiian culture encouraged women to have children with gods, then Hawaiians can be said to have adjusted to a new situation without disregarding the norms of their culture.

Based on this observation, Sahlins develops a more general reflection. To account for this framed inventiveness, he proposes that some societies have performative structures,[14] while others have prescriptive structures. In the former, identities are performed by the actions undertaken by individuals (when they are in situations of uncertainty); in the latter, the actions are prescribed by cultural codes that imply well-established identities and roles: these are the cold, repetitive societies described by Radcliffe-Brown.

All in all, Sahlins posits a dialectical relation between prescription and performance. An unexpected event—in this case the arrival of those strange Englishmen—is interpreted in terms of existing categories (Cook is considered as a God) which prescribe behaviors and practices (the norm is that since he is a god, the women should want to be pregnant by him) that perform Cook as a veritable god. But the performation can be successful only if Cook—and especially his sailors!—fulfill the role ascribed to them, which is not the case. Neither Cook nor the sailors behave as gods ought to. In reaction to this inappropriate behavior, the Hawaiians then set about devising new categories and practices. Hawaiian society is heated up again.

Sahlins, almost unwittingly, shows us why the notion of prescription is futile. The distinction is not between prescriptive and performative structures, but between closed situations and open ones, between situations of repetition, where events that occur are known and treated as routine, and situations where events are unexpected (Cook arrived in Hawaii out of the blue) and trigger behaviors and analyses that tend to reduce them to known categories and events. We can therefore say that Radcliffe Brown–type societies, those that remain closed in on themselves because they aren't fortunate enough to cross paths with a Cook, have performative structures, just like Hawaiian societies and their unexpected encounters. But in one case the performance is repetitive—it is always the same roles, the same behaviors, that are enacted in identical situations—whereas in the other, when faced with unusual situations, it seeks adaptation, absorbing differences and turning them into novelties. Prescription is simply a particular case of performation, a borderline case corresponding to pure repetition, in what Sahlins rightly calls closed situations.

The same applies to economics: it does not alternate between prescriptivity and performativity; it is always performative. In certain cases the sociotechnical *agencements* and the worlds corresponding to its models have ended up existing and producing recurrent events, for example, that share prices scrupulously follow a random walk. When this type of adaptation occurs, the performation becomes a prescription. But the performation may well fail, and the conditions of felicity may not be fulfilled. In that case the existing *agencements* have to be rearranged or even profoundly transformed: what MacKenzie calls counterperformativity prevails. The distinction, therefore, is not between prescriptive and performative structures; rather it is between performations that manage to produce regularities and repetition and performations that are constantly faced with unexpected events, which they sometimes—only sometimes—absorb for a while. The Hawaiians made a God out of Cook, but only for a while. The market follows Black-Scholes, but only for a while.

Expression

Redefined by the pragmatic turn, the notion of performativity cannot be reduced to a mysterious mechanism (the "*Fiat lux et lux fit*" of the Old Testament)[15] which would cause the reality to which the statement refers to exist, without an addition of forces. The notion of enunciation underscores the fact that any statement defines its context and has meaning only in relation to that context. The question of the actualization of this context is therefore open. Moreover, enriched by science and technology studies, the notion of enunciation takes into account materialities: the context is not reduced to institutions, norms or rules; it is a sociotechnical arrangement. Exit the idea that everything is a matter of language and that the performativity of statements is to be found only in the statement. Neither the notion of self-fulfilling prophecy nor that of prescription makes sociotechnical arrangements visible.

The notion of expression, illustrations of which are found in the chapter by Didier, shares the same critique of the closely linguistic definition of performativity. A statement does not create the object to which it refers *ex nihilo*; the notion of performativity is relevant only if it is further refined by the semiotic turn and the ANT turn. Why not therefore opt for the notion of expression, rather than maintaining a term, performativity, that can be misleading? Despite frequent misunderstanding, I prefer the notion of performativity (and performance) to that of expression, which might underplay the importance of the contribution of models and statements in the shaping of economies.

The notion of expression does have the advantage of emphasizing that there is no *tabula rasa*. Not everything is feasible. The notion of expression guards against the idea that the economy could be created from scratch by economics. Very specific work, new material arrangements, the implementation of tools such as shingling and the manipulations that these tools allow are necessary. To produce merchandise from things that are not yet completely economicized one has to use what exists, edge one's way in, articulate. This oblique work is highlighted by the notion of expression, which shows the multiplication of elements and actants already there, who are involved and have to be taken into account. The notion of expression is a powerful vaccination against a reductionist interpretation of performativity; a reminder that performativity is not about creating but about making happen.

Employing the notion of expression nevertheless bears an inherent risk, that of overplaying material practices and leaving linguistic and textual practices in the background—in short, in our case, of underestimating the models and elements of economic theory. Didier's chapter illustrates these difficulties. On several occasions he evokes the "out-thereness" of the world and the innerness of subjects: the pickles are there, outside the statistics that apprehend them; the subjectivity of farmers, their beliefs, and their convictions, explain why statistics prove to be effective. The notion of expression tends constantly to recreate the divide between an object-reality that is expressed and the subject expressing it. As for the notion of performation, it has the advantage of focusing on a question that is essential: it rejects the distance between the object and the discourse about it. That is the inner meaning of the notion of an act of language. When the mayor says "I hereby pronounce you man and wife," he is not expressing something that is already there; he is making it happen. And for that act to be successful, the appropriate *agencements* have to exist; the felicity conditions have to be met. Caricaturally and generally speaking we could say that the economy does not exist before economics performs it, and that when economic (or economicized) elements are already there it means that economics (at large) has already been that way. I prefer the risks of overinterpretation of this statement (which can be pushed so far as to become a caricature; some criticize me for saying that economics creates the economy from A to Z!), rather than risking the underinterpretation favored by the notion of expression (the idea that there are economic practices per se which exist and existed before economics put words to them). To be sure, it is unquestionable that things exist, that the discourse of economics, when successful, does not make the economy exist *ex nihilo*! But to understand this process of economicization (Callon 1998) in which economics at large participates, it is preferable to use the concept of performation rather than that of expression, which erases the process by which acts of language contribute to the occurrence of radically new events.

Expression is a crucial *component* of performation, but it is not *all* performation. Talking of the combination, the association or the networking of existing elements, all concepts and metaphors that Didier uses, is insufficient. I prefer the concept of sociotechnical *agencement* and opt for a description of these *agencements* that includes, primarily but not only, the elements of theories, models, and so on. Each element of an *agencement*—and among these, hypotheses and models have to be included—contributes to the performation of the whole. The wedding ceremony is a sociotechnical *agencement* that will demonstrate, for example, two beings' wish to be married. But in that *agencement* the marriage pronounced by the official plays a crucial part: entangled with all the other elements composing the arrangement, it causes that which did not exist before to exist and to last, at least for a certain time—the event and the matter of fact that we call marriage.

Performation

My discussion of the relations between performativity and sociotechnical *agencements* (agreements which include the statements that describe them and contribute toward putting them into action) echoes Annemarie Mol's discussion of the use of the notions of performativity and performance in sociology. A long footnote in her book *The Body Multiple* is highly instructive in this respect: "When people present themselves to each other, Goffman said they present not so much themselves but a self, a persona, a mask. They act as if they were on stage. They perform" (Mol 2002, p. 34). We thus dissociate that which happens backstage and concerns psychology from that which happens front stage and concerns sociology—the personal identity on the one hand and the public identity on the other. Regardless of the actor's adherence, the role she performs is therefore perfectly real and produces effects: it defines the social as such.

Authors like Judith Butler have extended Goffmanian reasoning: all roles are performances; there is no backstage or back office: "There need not be a 'doer behind the deed' but . . . the 'doer' is variably constructed in and through the deed" (quoted in Mol 2002, p. 37). People's identities do not precede their performances but are constructed in and through them. Butler is concerned about gender identity. She maintains that this identity is constantly reconfigured and realized through accomplished acts. We must therefore talk of contrasting identities as they are performed in a variety of sites and situations. Yet Mol is not convinced by the Butlerian analysis. According to her, this conception brackets off the crucial role played in the production of identities by entities such as the vagina, which have come to be considered as natural and therefore outside the social. Even if the vagina does not make a woman, it contributes to making her, at least in certain circumstances, just as the penis contributes to the constitution of a man: "Bodies thus do not oppose social performances, but are a part of them" (p. 40). As showed by Stefan Hirschauer they are also reshaped, restyled, redesigned.

It is because the notion of performativity has been linked to that of performance, which tends to ignore the sociotechnical and especially the corporeal elements composing *agencements*, that Mol, wanting to avoid Butlerian-type culturalist excesses, proposes the notion of enactment. Identity is a process; even though it is constructed, the construction has no end, it is constantly under way. In this approach, there is no reason to apply a different analysis to so-called objects. Criticizing the use—by sociology or by cultural (gender) studies—of the notion of performativity when it is equated to that of performance, Mol notes that (1) the (sociological or anthropological) analysis of the shaping of entities and of the expression of their identity must take into account so-called natural entities, the body, for example, and, more broadly, all the materialities composing what I call sociotechnical *agencements*; and (2) the identity of each entity, human or nonhuman (including the vagina), is never set for once and for all, definitively constructed: it is a flow. Situations of closure, as assumed by Sahlins, are not situations in which identities are mechanically prescribed. As in situations of openness, they are under trial. Stability is a constant struggle which stems from the involvement of, but is not determined by, materialities.

Emphasizing the role of materialities—or of what I call sociotechnical *agencements*—leads to the notion of performation. Statements and their world are caught in a process of coevolution. The Black and Scholes formula or the theory of general equilibrium, confined to the academic world, can find its appropriate milieu, its felicity conditions. But when they move over to the Chicago derivatives exchange or to ministries responsible for economic planning, they may encounter or even trigger resistance, for their felicity conditions are not filled. The sociotechnical arrangements that would have enabled them to survive in these strange worlds are not present or prove to be difficult to put in place. We can agree to call *performation* the process whereby sociotechnical arrangements are enacted, to constitute so many ecological niches within and between which statements and models circulate and are true or at least · enjoy a high degree of verisimilitude. This constantly renewed process of performation encompasses expression, self-fulfilling prophecies, prescription, and performance.

Performation's Struggles

The success (or the failure) of an act of language becomes clear only at the end of the tests to which it is put, through the cooperation it triggers, the oppositions and controversies that it generates. Statements can survive and prosper in one particular place and at one particular time, and disappear in other places and at other times. Within the academic world, marginalist analysis thrives without any problem. As soon as it leaves that world of textbooks and students, which suits it so well, it gets into trouble. Yet marginalist analysis has not, for all that, been invalidated, simply "de-realized" in some settings—which does not prevent it from surviving and even prospering in the academic world (at least in some U.S. universities). All of the economists who say that the unrealism of their propositions are of no concern to them have chosen their world, a world of papers, colleagues, and students—the one that suits their theories. That is where they remain and do everything to ensure that it survives. On this note, it is to the process of adjustment of statements and their associated world (what I call the process of performation) that I now turn.

Economics at Large

"The thread breaks when subjected to a force greater than its breaking strength"; "the human being is moved by her interests and knows her preferences and their hierarchy"; "the Black and Scholes formula gives the price of an option." Each of these statements can survive and be taken into account only if accompanied by its own world: its diffusion is possible only if the environment that the statement requires is available throughout its circulation and in all the places to which it leads. To move a statement from one spatiotemporal frame to another and for it to remain operational (that is, for it to be capable of describing situations and providing affordances for them), the sociotechnical *agencement* that "goes with it" has to be transported as well. In the process of circulation of a statement there are tests and trials that will determine its realization or de-realization, the fact that it remains set in its original world or, alternatively, spreads out and spreads its world with it.

Whether we are dealing with the natural or the social sciences, the case of no doubt or ambiguity as to the world being mobilized by the statement is obviously rare. Many rehearsals are required (that is the purpose of experiments and laboratories), many trials, to know what those worlds in which the statement will succeed are made of. Under which conditions can two threads be considered as identical? What exactly does the phrase "apply a force to a thread" mean? What are the possible causes of the break? Is the recording of the deformation not influenced by other phenomena? Or: how can we construct the data needed to calculate the price of a particular option? How can the price obtained be used to negotiate a deal? In which situations, with which equipment, does a human being become able to assess her own interests and to calculate them in such a way as to determine an optimal behavior? All these questions are futile when statements remain confined to their paper world: no more than a few words are required to mention the possibility of observations. They become crucial and tricky when statements start to travel, to shift out of their initial location, to be translated from one frame to another.

The full answer to these difficult questions is rarely known before many experiments and trials have been completed. In other words, any shift of the statement reveals problems, causes the appearance of misfits, maladjustments, untimely overflowings. During these successive displacements and the consequent trials, the statement's world becomes more complex. Just as one discovers only progressively, through replications and movements, why an experiment succeeds (or fails), an equally long process is required to explore the sociotechnical *agencements* that a statement or model needs to function in such-and-such a spatiotemporal frame (see the chapters by MacKenzie and Holm). In the paper world to which it belongs, marginalist analysis thrives. All it needs are some propositions on decreasing returns, the convexity of utility curves, and so forth. Transported into an electricity utility (for example, Electricité de France), it needs the addition of time-of-day meters set up wherever people consume electricity and without which calculations are impossible; introduced into a private firm, it requires analytical accounting and a system of recording and cost assessment that prove to be hardly feasible.

This does not mean that marginalist analysis has become false. As everyone knows, it is still true in (most) universities.

Between perfect adaptation and total inadaptation, there is a wide range of intermediate configurations. Sometimes one simply has to amend statements, models, and formulas to ensure their survival, by taking into account the reactions to their circulation in exotic and hostile places. MacKenzie shows that, for it to have been able to absorb the crisis that showed it to be wrong, the Black and Scholes formula could have been amended, for instance by choosing Lévy-type probability distributions rather than log-normal distributions. This did not happen, because many other programs were competing to impose other statements, other worlds, and other sociotechnical *agencements*. The alternative proposed by Leland and Rubinstein ("sunshine trading"), with would have made it possible to provide the Black and Scholes formula with an environment better suited to its functioning,[16] was finally excluded because the Chicago exchanges were opposed to "sunshine trading" and imposed their own solution. The performativity approach makes it possible to exhibit the struggle between worlds that are trying to prevail;[17] it makes the struggle for life between statements visible. Each statement, each model, battles to exist. But the Darwinian metaphor stops there. In reality this struggle between statements is a struggle between sociotechnical *agencements*. It is not the environment that decides and selects the statements that will survive; it is the statements that determine the environments required for their survival.

By examining the confrontation between sociotechnical *agencements*, we have to take into consideration statements other than those produced by scientists, in our case other than those produced by academic economists. To understand the failure, from 1987, of attempts to adjust the financial world to the Black and Scholes formula (which, despite its partial de-realization, continues to survive, although hidden, since it is a part of the informational infrastructure of markets), we need to take into account the programs with which the formula enters into competition. Some of them, probably the majority, are produced outside academic circles. To understand the effects of (academic) economics on the economy is impossible if we fail to consider the formula—with its statements, models, and analytical tools—in the context of the struggles opposing it against all of the other actors who also perform the economy, format it, produce their own statements and models, and organize their own trials.

Academic economics does not have a monopoly on performation. It is only one possible source of transformation of the economy. Many historical studies emphasize the role of economist engineers (Hughes 1983; Porter 1995). The contribution of accountants, marketers, and, more generally, market professionals has now been amply documented (Barrey et al. 2000; Clark and Pinch 1995; Cochoy 1998; Cochoy and Grandclément 2005; Hopwood and Miller 1994; Kjellberg 2001; Power 1996; Strathern 2000). One might imagine that by shifting from the theoretician economists' world to that of practitioners (including economic agents themselves), we would change to another register, because it would no longer be a matter of economics but of regular engineering and social technology, and the notion of performation would loose its relevance in the process. But that is not the case.

First, the distinction between science and techniques is often used only to disqualify certain practices (qualified as techniques), which are not fundamentally different from those considered to be theoretical and supposed to be the monopoly of academic research. Preda (forthcoming) gives a striking evidence of this when he shows that technical analysis or financial chartism, which developed alongside the use and diffusion of the stock ticker, is entirely theoretical in the most classical sense of the word. It produces concepts and interpretations, proposes models, clarifies causal relations, and organizes experiments. The so-called experimentalist economists who help to design spectrum auctions (see the chapter by Mirowski and Nik-Khah) produce as much theory as do game theorists. In both cases the words "technique" (or "technology") and "theory" serve more to impose social hierarchies and scales of legitimacy than to describe practices and types of production.[18]

Second, transporting a theoretical statement from one point to another and implementing it requires the intervention of new actors who will contribute to (or oppose) the actualization of the sociotechnical *agencements* implied in the statement. These sociotechnical *agencements* can be explored, created, tested, and tinkered with only if engineers and practitioners are mobilized. To make a formula or auction system work, one has to have tools, equipment, metrological systems, procedures, and so on. To establish relations that "exist" between monetary masses and price levels, to act on the one in order to control the others, there have to be institutions, systems of observation, codification and data collection, tools for analyzing large numbers, and so on. A host of professions, competencies, and nonhumans are necessary for academic economics to be successful. Each of these parties "makes" economics. They are engaged in the construction of a world described and performed by statements and models that we readily agree belong to the world of economics, in the strict sense of the word. The world conveyed by the statement is realized only after a long collective effort, which one could call economic research, involving 90 percent engineering and 10 percent theory.

There is a third reason for expanding the meaning of the word economics: the statements and models that perform reality (in our case the economy) are not limited to the propositions formed like ordinary sentences ("the thread breaks," "the price rise is caused by variations in monetary masses and flows," etc.). As the Black and Scholes example shows, a formula or equation effects the same articulation or performation as a statement in ordinary language, but with even more precision and effectiveness. With the help of a few signs, the Black and Scholes formula encapsulates the financial market (its variables provide its constituent elements) and causes it to function (when one calculates the formula one obtains the market price). Applying the formula and calculating the price means making the world that the formula articulates and describes exist.[19] Any tinkering with the formula can have considerable consequences because it changes the world that the formula is supposed to activate. It happens that practitioners are often producers of formulas. Some, like accountants, are even specialized in this type of activity. The formulas that they devise are not different from the statements and models of professional economists. And they have the same fate as classical linguistic statements: they can succeed or fail. They are entirely economics, as I use the term, and as economics they perform the economy.

What I just said about formulas applies to operating methods, calculation tools, and technical instruments. They are statements like any others. Like all statements (that which is stated can be an ordinary sentence, a formula, or a technical device), they are "uttered," put into circulation, sent out, and like all statements they convey a world. Rather than being made with words or reduced to simple equations, they are composed of tables, abacuses, preprogrammed series of operations, assemblages of silicon, and software packages.[20] The case of automation of the Paris Stock Exchange, analyzed by Fabian Muniesa (2003), shows that behind the choice of quotation algorithms and data transmission procedures, it is the concept of an efficient and fair market that is at stake. The decision to install electricity meters and the choice of the technical characteristics of meters imply an economic world that differs from the one in which such meters do not exist. Madeleine Akrich has demonstrated this in detail in the case of an African country: conceiving of electricity meters and uttering them (putting them into circulation) means creating consumers, citizens, and a market for electricity (Akrich and Law 1996). As she showed, the resistance triggered by the initiative was not resistance to change or to progress, but was a struggle against the economy of meters, that is, against a particular form of economy among many others that might exist. Economics can be inscribed in the hardest technologies, and when they are put into circulation those technologies manage or not to impose their world.

All in all, I simply apply to economics what everyone agrees with in respect of ordinary technoscientific innovation: that it is collectives that innovate.[21] In these collectives there is no point in opposing those who articulate statements to those who make them function. Everyone does economics with different means, and through different modalities of enunciation (models, theorems, formulas, or technical devices). I have suggested the term "economics at large" for this collective (joint) performation, this co-performation of the economy.

Co-performation as a Historical Process

With the concept of performation, observable reality is considered as the temporary outcome of confrontations between different competing programs, including scientific ones. The historical dimension of processes is emphasized, as well as the fact that history matters and that the economy and markets are the temporary and fluctuating result of conflicts and the constantly changeable expression of power struggles. The history of these struggles is incorporated into markets, just as a living organism retains traces of its evolution. As MacKenzie and Millo say in their description of the transformation of markets due to the application of the Black and Scholes formula: "By the late 1970s, then, Black and Scholes was widely used by CBOE (Chicago Board Options Exchange) traders, and in the 1980s it began to be incorporated into the CBOE's informational infrastructure. Gradually, 'reality' (in this case empirical prices) was performatively reshaped in conformance with the theory" (2003, p. 127). Once it has been accomplished this incorporation is no longer challenged. The Black and Scholes formula was transformed into an element of the market and of its functioning. The theory has become part of the market. But the story does not end there. The skew calculation (at least in the United States), coupled with the Autoquote system, adds an additional layer which enhances and alters existing performations, without challenging them. There is nothing extraordinary about this historical process; it is no more than a trivial matter of lock-in and path dependency. But instead of lock-in being produced by a hard technology, it is produced by a soft technology that directly concerns the market organization and the formatting of agents' calculative capacities (and that readily resorts to hard technologies to consolidate and perpetuate its effects). The dead grips the living. Taking the struggles between programs into consideration—what I have called co-performation of the economy by economics at large—enables us to study the incorporation of theories, statements, and tools which, transformed into algorithms, into routines, become infrastructures and revive the possibility of a new cycle of performations and counterperformations.

Marie-France Garcia's postscript to her article—an article (finally available in English in this volume) which was so useful to me for proposing the thesis of the performativity of economics—shows how actors can reformat a pure and perfect competitive market. The performation of this perfection required heavy investments, so that ironically it ends up becoming more like the market described by economic sociology (in the manner of Granovetter or Fligstein). What seemed to be verified because it was actualized at a particular point in time and a particular place is "de-realized" when circumstances change, that is, when other sociotechnical *agencements* are established for a variety of reasons.

The other chapters in this book help to further our understanding of the historical process of co-performation of the economy by economics. These chapters show the diversity of configurations, from a pure and simple complementarity of programs to their open opposition resulting in compromises, both within "confined (or academic) economics" and between "confined economists" and "economists in the wild." Since I use the word "economist" to denote all agents who participate in the analysis and transformation of economic markets, an economist may be an academic researcher whose job is to produce theories on the market and to collect data in order to demonstrate statistical regularities that reveal laws or causal links. He or she may also be the head of an international institution or a central bank who applies economic theories, sometimes enhancing them with his or her own analyses, for the purpose of making decisions or designing regulations or institutions. Or he or she may be a market professional who designs market devices, algorithms for comparing supply and demand. Finally, the economist may be a consumer union that sets up tests to qualify products.

Having effaced the distinction between all these agents who participate in the analysis and collective configuration of markets (in a more or less abstract, more or less direct and professional way) and who cooperate simultaneously in the production of economics at large, I do find it convenient to distinguish between those working in laboratories and those engaged in scale-one activities. Thus I will introduce a new distinction between what I call "confined economists" and "economists in the wild."

COOPERATIVE PERFORMATION

Do Norwegian fishermen fit the anthropological model proposed by certain confined social scientists? Are they calculative by nature and motivated by their own interests? Are they inclined to put their own welfare before the common good? The history of fishing in Norway shows that the answers to these questions depend on the period under consideration. Community regulation requiring powerful entanglements between human beings and the fish with which they live—entanglements that are so strong that the survival of the one depends on that of the other—is obviously a falsification of the anthropological program that affirms the universality of selfish human beings. Yet this does not allow us to say that the statement "human beings in general and Norwegian fishermen in particular are selfish, calculating beings" is false. History shows that it can become "true" if the circumstances change and if the environment needed by such a being starts to exist. The history described by Holm in his chapter shows precisely how we go from one *agencement* to another, how the world supposed by neoclassical economics is actualized.

This neoclassical *agencement* was made possible by the spectacular metamorphosis of fish, by what can be seen as nothing less than their ontological mutation. The initially invisible and slippery fish, to which it was difficult to attach property rights, were progressively transformed into identifiable, graspable fish that accommodated such rights. They became "distributed" fish, which Holm suggests calling cyborg fish. Cyberfish are traceable, identifiable, predictable, and controllable. They correspond to a new stage in the ongoing process of evolution of the species. This latest mutation has required a huge effort involving documentation, fleets of boats to observe catches, cohorts of statisticians to implement the models and make them work, airplanes for watching the fishermen, traceability tools so as not to lose the elusive fish along the way, international institutions and negotiations to ensure that the calculations were right and to take the "necessary" decisions. To achieve all of this, it has been necessary to transform the dark and mysterious ocean into a transparent aquarium. When fishermen turn into *homines economici*, they are able to live well only when seas are reconfigured as aquariums.

Without this new fish the Norwegian fisherpeople would not have been able to calculate their interests. Once the cyberfish had been performed by the technosciences (halieutics, marine biology, population dynamics) and by politicians, the scene was set for the entry of *homo economicus*. Economics, then, had only to propose the tradability of fishing quotas, for the Norwegian fisherman to become calculative and selfish. The convergence of technosciences, politicians, and economics, and their co-performation of the fishing world, has resulted in the invention and "implementation" of a new cosmos inhabited by new animal and human species whose coexistence has been made possible. This new cosmos is a radical innovation which is both destructive and creative. Its case history shows that the contribution of economics is productive insofar as it participates in the actualization of a world in which it becomes or is true. But this story also underscores the importance of the verb "to contribute" in the sentence: "Economics contributes to the construction of the reality that it describes." Without economics the market would not exist (it is the individual transferable quota—ITQ—concept that makes this market operational, and the fishermen's calculative and maximizing rationality cannot be investigated as long as this market does not exist). Yet economics alone is not enough to make it exist. All of the investments, models, observations, calculations, and institutions so accurately described by Holm are also necessary. In short, the cyberfish is needed. In this case as in many others, economics as such is necessary but not sufficient.

The importance and specificity of what I have suggested calling "economics in the wild" are evident here. Economics in the wild is not pure economics; it is mixed with engineering, life sciences, and management science—its complexity and heterogeneity constitutes its strength and makes it irreplaceable. But it is also about calculations, optimizations, and the management of rare resources. It is imbibed and impregnated by the anthropological program of "confined economics". Moreover, as Holm so neatly puts it, there is constant traffic, continuous interaction, and endless coordination between those who perform the cyberfish and those who perform *homo economicus*. The alliances that this cooperation implies and the *agencements* that it allows obviously include the law. Property rights support what has *already* been assembled and arranged. As Mitchell shows in his chapter, and contrary to what is often said, property rights neither constitute the cornerstone of markets nor provide the foundations on which it can be built.

In a sense, Didier's story echoes that of Holm. Didier focuses on a particular time in the process of reconfiguring a market and the different entities comprising it. At the origin of this transformation we find not academic economists but an economist in the wild concerned by pickles, whose obstinacy soon led to a reconfiguration of the pickle such that that it became a sort of *cyberpickle*, which was visible and could be counted.

The performance of the cyberpickle was achieved after a series of manipulations which perfectly illustrate the process of disentanglement/reentanglement that I explained in *The Laws of the Markets*. Initially the farmer and his pickles could hardly be dissociated. This close entanglement made the pickles invisible at a distance and precluded their circulation. Gradually the pickle became autonomous; its ability to circulate increased. Its standardization and the comparisons and aggregations that it allowed paved the way to its economicization and to that of the agents who produced, packaged, traded, and consumed it (the farmers who filled in questionnaires on their production, the cooperatives who commercialized the pickles, the federal agencies that centralized the data and decreed regulations, etc.). The stage had to be prepared for categories such as supply and demand to be enacted, for the market to be unified, and for prices to be set in relation to the (aggregated) demand and the (aggregated) supply. The basic categories of economics are present in this reconfiguration. What is striking here, as in the case of Holm, is the cooperative aspect of these mutually complementary interventions.

Didier does not tell us the rest of the story, but we can imagine that an acceleration of the economicization became possible once this infrastructure was in place.

Such cooperation and the irreversibilities that it produces are by no means ineluctable. The co-performation of the economy by economics at large is not always smooth sailing. As Mitchell shows in his chapter, in Egypt, farmers have been successfully resisting programs inspired by neo-classical economics. We will now turn to situations in which intersecting performative programs, rather than being openly complementary (as in the case of fish and pickles), clash and end up reaching compromises.

COMPETITION BETWEEN CONFINED ECONOMISTS

Guala's work on the organization of spectrum auctions by the Federal Communications Commission (FCC), as well as the follow-up by Mirowski and Nik-Khah, highlight situations in which different programs developed mainly by confined economists confront one another. This is a particularly interesting case, primarily because it illustrates the increasing role of experimentation in market engineering (discussed below) but also because it describes episodes in which different programs clash and end up reaching a compromise.

The story begins with the FCC's decision to discontinue the traditional practice of granting communication spectrums on the basis of bilateral arrangements. As a government agency, the FCC's aims were multiple and partly contradictory since it wanted to reconcile economic efficiency, technological innovation, and social justice. To design the market for frequencies it understandably turned to economists privileging the most theoretical of them all, game theorists (GTs). What makes this affair complicated and interesting is that the difficulties posed by the market in question caused these economists to recognize that they had no ready-made solutions at their disposal. Known types of auction were ill-suited to the nature of the goods and the multiple constraints imposed by the FCC: "Game theory supplied no global discipline with regard to the type of recommendation tendered." Game theorists could certainly contribute to auction design, either formally by using explicit models (for example, to invalidate certain solutions) or more informally by applying tacit knowledge, know-how, and informed intuitions. But what they were unable to do was to provide a turnkey solution. One of the reasons for their difficulty stemmed from the fact that auctioned goods are interdependent, a condition ignored by game theory.

As in any acceptable innovation history, there was soon a proliferation of actors, all defending their own programs. A point of key interest in this case is the fact that another family of economists, experimentalist economists (EEs), entered the game, simply because they were able to persuade the agency to launch real experiments using computer technology. It was then that the story started to take unexpected turns.[22] The sociotechnical *agencements* proposed by the experimentalists coincided only very partially with those that should have been deployed to make the GTs' statements, models, and recommendations actual.

Mirowski and Nik-Khah show the gap between the two worlds proposed by GTs and EEs. They show the depth of opposition between the anthropological programs and the sociotechnical *agencements* presupposed by the different models proposed. These differences related to the agents' assumed competencies (Are they capable of Bayesian learning or not? Are they prepared to revise their preferences?) and, further to the manner of conceiving of the role and effects of algorithms for organizing the encountering of goods and agents (EEs, who represent markets as combinatorial optimization procedures, are interested in "the attainment of a competitive equilibrium," whereas GTs represent markets as Bayes-Nash games). Theoretical models lead GTs to favor the increase of "the amount of information" provided to agents, while leading EEs to seek improvements in "the capacity for information processing." Mirowski and Nik-Khah's striking translation of this opposition is as follows: for GTs, "the bidder who would create the most value from owning the license wins it," while for EEs, "the bidder who values the license the highest at the outset acquires it." The differences can be summed up in this way: EEs think that it is the algorithms that do calculations, while GTs locate them in agents' heads. Alternative theoretical positions cause the two groups to favor different organizations of auctions, two different socio technical *agencements*. EEs are in favor of combinatorial auctions while GTs support the idea of simultaneous–multiple round–independent (SMRI) auctions. Mirowski and Nik-Khah describe in detail the alliances formed between the multiple actors (operators, economists, federal agencies, etc.) engaged in the design of auctions. In this history there are familiar elements, such as hierarchical relationships formed between theoreticians and experimentalists, or coalitions of interests between groups of scientists and economic or political actors. Economists are everywhere: people employ their own economists to defend the models assumed to be compatible with their economic and political objectives. There is even a fierce struggle to attribute the success of the operation to a particular group (in this case GTs proved to be the strongest and cleverest), a group which, as in any history of innovation, was simply one of the many protagonists responsible for the final design.

We would be unable to understand what was happening in the design of the FCC spectrum auctions if we reduced its history to a mere clash between existing interests. All these actors, especially the economists,

strive to construct the sociotechnological *agencements* that they believe
are compatible with their own models, statements, and assumptions.
To be in line with the overall argument I am putting forward here, and to
avoid sociologizing or psychologizing interpretations, it would be more
accurate to say that the confrontation takes place between sociotechnical
worlds that are struggling to exist, at the expense of other sociotechnical
worlds. What is original in this story is that none of the protagonists is
able to push his or her own program through to the end, for none of them
is able to completely frame the world that they create. They can only
adopt a logic of compromise in which some elements of their world are realized and others are not. For example, EEs cannot avoid the adoption of
the solution proposed by GTs (the simultaneous–multiple round–independent auction), but in the implementation of algorithms and procedures
they reintroduce elements of their own world by imposing technical solutions drawn from experimentation that GTs initially exclude because they
do not fit with their game-theoretic models.

In the final workable compromise, which translated into a sociotechnical *agencement* consisting of bits and pieces, and which partially, but only
partially, made the assertions of both GTs and EEs true, we find elements
of the different competing sociotechnical *agencements*. The world that
ended up existing was a patchwork, cobbled together with elements from
competing worlds. Of course there is no point in asking whether the models were true. The only criterion is failure or success. In this case of two
rival programs the result was mixed. But Mirowski and Nik-Khah are
right to point out that other programs did not have the possibility of joining the struggle. The worlds excluded a priori are the losers in this affair.

In the history of the spectrum auction an important role is granted to
academic economists, whether they are GTs or EEs. One of the advantages
of the co-performation concept is that it establishes a symmetry between
all of the categories of economists. Whether they are in the wild or confined, whether they state a formula, build a piece of software, or devise an
accounting technique, they all give themselves a world or worlds so that
the formula, model, or software that they put into circulation (utter) finds
an environment, *agencements*, enabling it to function.

COMPETITION BETWEEN ECONOMISTS IN THE WILD AND
CONFINED ECONOMISTS

Preda (forthcoming) examines the constitution of a theory of financial
markets that was developed very early on, outside academic circles, and
that was able to stand up to rival theories by being established as a theory in its own right (financial chartism, or technical analysis). This
"vernacular" theory, the product of authentic research in the wild and a

clear illustration of the importance of the concept of economics at large, draws its strength from its previous and continuing capacity to make the world that it describes, and that makes it true, exist. It is closely linked to the sociotechnical *agencements* with which it interacts closely and tirelessly: to instruments (tickers) that make it possible to continuously record price variations and that produce those inscriptions, so useful to theoretical construction and to its performance; to professionals who specialize in the observation of those variations and in their interpretation; and, finally, to users with interests and an identity that are well-established and taken into consideration. This world is closely linked to the tracing of price variation curves, and therefore to tickers. Without this technology for representing markets (curves traced with data from the ticker are both real and artifactual), the very idea of transforming forms into instruments of analysis and interpretation would be inconceivable. These inscriptions impose a principle of reality; they constitute an obligatory point of passage, a perfectly material reality to be taken into account. Chartism is neither reducible to a convention nor reducible to a belief or even a superstition outside the market that would enable it, once diffused and shared, to coordinate actors by making their expectations possible. It is not disconnected from the market; it is articulated to sociotechnical *agencements* that produce the traces that it uses to describe the world in which it is a participant and on which it will, in turn, make it possible to act.[23] The curves to interpret are there. Analyzed by chartists, they belie the hypotheses in terms of which price variations are correlated with political or economic events. As tools of refutation in a Popperian style, they furthermore make it possible to affirm the existence of regularities, of collective patterns, where others talk of random walk.[24]

Theoreticians in the wild are often engineers, well trained in statistics, and they invent concepts to reveal regularities hidden by sudden movements: the normal line concept, for example, describes underlying trends hidden by short-term variations. The ticker and its curves are an intellectual technology which enables the human mind to see things that it is otherwise unable to see and to conceive of (Goody 1977). An epistemic community is formed, manuals are written and disseminated, traders are turned into users of these techniques and of this knowledge. Preda concludes that "technical analysis becomes simultaneously a theory of financial markets, a theory-based technique for forecasting prices, a set of instruments, a commodity sold by the members of the group, a commodity around which data processing firms emerged, a media discourse, and a narrative."

Financial chartism is being actualized. As its world is unfolding, groups, techniques, inscriptions, and courses of action are becoming necessary.

Theory performs in the precise sense that I have given to this term. And what explains the deployment of this world is the ticker and its circulation. As shown by Preda, the theory underlying technical analysis is highly elaborate. It was only with the Black-Scholes-Merton model that academic science reached the level of this theory in the wild, that is, not equally true, but powerful enough to make a world exist, its own world, one that is able to withstand the comparison with the world of tickers and to enter into a performation struggle.

Convergences?

The cases analyzed in this book correspond to situations in which the different programs that participate in the performation of the economy eventually prove to be compatible, even if they differ on a number of points. Just as we formerly posed the question of the so-called convergence of industrial societies—whether socialist or capitalist—we can now pose that of the convergence of performating economics—whether academic or in the wild.[25]

The thesis that I present in this section is the following: a certain sort of convergence exists and is organized around an anthropological program that is not very different from the neoclassical one (broadly speaking). This explains why common sense refers to "the market economy" to talk about the economy, and why notions such as "neo liberalism" are currently used to capture what seems to be an overall logic.

I argue that this shared anthropological program has three main features. 1) it promotes the disentanglement of things and humans; (2) it asserts the centrality of individual human agencies; and, finally, (3) it tends to underplay the uneven distribution of calculative equipment and capacities among agencies.

Disentanglements (and Reentanglements)

The different chapters in the book all recount stories of disentanglement through which, with growing force and clarity, a world exists in which entities are transformed (and retransformed) into things and then goods (Callon, et al. 2002) that can circulate, passing from hand to hand, alternating between detachments and (re)attachments, and in which a deep divide has been created and maintained between these objectified things and the generally human agencies that produce, exchange, and consume them.

Holm analyzes the mechanisms through which two new beings were simultaneously brought into existence: the cyberfish and its (ocean) bedfellow, the *Norwegian economicus* fisherpeople. This performation started with an initial series of disentanglements that broke up the fishing community—a community in which fish and fishermen had coexisted, attached to one another until they became strangers. The fish were disentangled from the sea in which they had always hidden. They were reduced to bar codes, quotas that could be sold and taken advantage of, "stocks" of populations to conserve and develop, a dissuasive weapon in international power struggles. At many junctures, economics intervened decisively in this process. It allied itself with the forces that performed these new ontologies, bringing in its own, strategic one when it was a matter of organizing markets, that is, of attaching appropriately formulated property rights, creating the relevant incentives, and defining control procedures and devices. The selfish-er-man could then develop and prosper. This performance is no more miraculous than is the fishing that it allows. Didier, in a story reminiscent of Cronon's (1991) work on the market in "futures" on grain, likewise describes the manipulations that allowed the constitution of the cyberpickle (albeit a cyberpickle produced by technologies that predate the digital computer) and that so marvelously illustrate the required disentanglements. As time goes by the divide between calculative agencies and calculable goods grows wider and establishes a market based on an anthropology well described by economics, especially neoclassical economics. It is clearly a convergence that is announced and initiated here.

A series of disentanglements is also found in the history of spectrum auctions. The first disentanglement was the one wanted by the FCC, which imposed a reshaping of all the old Mafia-like networks within which licenses were granted. In the terms of economic sociology à la Polanyi-Granovetter, the auction aimed to disembed firms and administrations, and to bring new interests into play. The second disentanglement brought GTs and EEs into contact and triggered a lot of controversies. The definition (which I call "qualification") of goods to be auctioned generated debate. The question was whether to disentangle the frequencies that applied to different geographical areas, and consequently to multiply goods (GTs), or rather to entangle them in order to form a single good (EEs). The GTs won the battle and pushed the disentanglement process a step forward, deploying the market world further and further. Without economics (that of GTs) this deployment would have been simply unimaginable.

Financial markets also supply numerous examples of this convergence that deepens the disentanglement (reentanglement) mechanism and allows the production of things and goods. For a long time and until recently, options were seen as barely disguised forms of gambling. Their development has perpetually been submitted to scrutiny on moral grounds. Millo (2003) showed how these financial products were gradually disentangled from such moral issues and dissociated from gambling. MacKenzie noted that with the Black-Scholes-Merton model this disentanglement is complete. The Black-Scholes formula defends the legitimacy of the very idea of an options market on which rational calculations can be made. It imposes the market that it describes, by transforming options and derivatives into economic goods whose prices can be calculated objectively. The accusation of gambling and immorality automatically falls away. MacKenzie adds—and this point is strategic—that a difference is thus created: the new market is different from the preceding one. Economists do not simply legitimize, reveal, or express practices and existing models: "The Black-Scholes-Merton model did more than simply express price patterns that were already there: . . . the use of models altered price patterns."

Of interest from the point of view of convergence, under consideration here, is the fact that a competing economics, born before and outside academia (an economics in the wild), helped to lay the ground by furthering this disentanglement. The economics in question was chartism, the history of which has been studied in detail by Preda. Apart from competition between the two forms of economics (chartism assumes the existence of significant regularities in the forms of price variations, whereas the Black-Scholes-Merton model posits a random walk), there is profound agreement on the economic nature of options (which no longer risk being likened to gambling). This might explain why chartist practices are still being used in the field, in parallel with or as a complement to the Black-Scholes-Merton model.

These cases indicate how economics plays a crucial role in making this convergence possible and in accelerating and finalizing it. All in all, what dominant economics does, in close collaboration (even when it is conflicting) with the leading productive forces of modernity that the natural sciences are, is to perform disentanglements which cause market goods to proliferate while dissociating them from the agencies that are in a position to produce and trade them (for a wonderful historical analysis of such a process see Mitchell 2002).

Human Individual Agencies

It is not enough to separate goods and agencies. One also has to profile the latter, and the options available for that profiling are obviously multiple. A second feature common to most performative programs of economics (confined or in the wild) is that they share an identical choice, that of producing individual human agencies capable of calculating their interests in one way or another. They tend to localize agencies in (individual) human corporeal envelopes and to equip them with tools, instruments, prostheses (obviously distributed but under the control of particular individuals), and rights, enabling them to construct something like individual interests (likened to income, indexes of satisfaction or welfare, or degrees of recognition of their legitimate dignity), and granting them the resources to calculate them. What "human" means in the term "the human being" is the outcome of co-performation in which economics plays a key part. The human being is not a starting point.

The "individualization of the agency," that is, the performance of a self-interested agency obsessed by the calculation-optimization of his or her own interest, is clearly visible in the case of the Norwegian fisherpeople. Petter Holm shows that once all the scientific, material, technical, and institutional investments have been made to transform the sea into an aquarium and the wild fish into a cyborg fish, the ground has been cleared for the conception and construction of a market in which fishermen are transformed into selfish individual economic agencies. The convergence is evident here: different groups of professionals, experts, institutions, scientific disciplines, and public national and international bodies implicitly agree to enact this anthropological model.

The same convergence can be observed at a micro level in the economic experiments analyzed by Mirowski and Nik-Khah. Economists (GTs or EEs) as well as federal agencies share a general hypotheses: the agent has preferences (whether they are revisable or not) and the challenge is to equip that agent so that she or he is able to calculate and defend them as well as possible. Each player is thus supported by his or her computers, algorithms, and favorite economists! This convergence is even clearer in the case studied by Lépinay: mathematicians, financiers, engineers, and traders calculating with their bodies all contribute in their own way to the production of a calculation that enables them to qualify and price a disentangled product.

At this point we need to consider a question raised by MacKenzie and Millo (2003). They say that certain selfless behaviors of traders (who agree to integrate into their calculation a parameter—skewness—whose value is supplied by a designated primary market maker, and to refrain from engaging in free-rider strategies that would enable them to increase their profits) can be explained only by means of conventional economic sociology. These traders behave in a moral way, with a sense of solidarity, because they are entangled in social networks and communities.

Hence, MacKenzie's question: "How should one theorize the articulation between performativity and markets seen as networks, culture and moral communities?" (MacKenzie and Millo 2003, p. 140). Reset in the terms of this chapter, the question becomes: does the convergence of anthropological programs not encounter limits? Can it go so far as to produce a monolithic agency that is entirely calculative, to the point of imposing a *homo economicus* who is so well framed that he no longer overflows? MacKenzie and Millo's answer to this question is a resounding no: "With the aid of economic theory, of technology and of much else, a passable version of *homo œconomicus* can be and has been configured cognitively, so to speak. Whether he can be configured morally, out of real men and women, remains an open question" (p. 141).

MacKenzie and Millo are right to answer in the negative. Humans in their somatic envelope, made of neurons, genes, proteins, and stem cells, are constantly overflowing. A total, unambiguous configuration is impossible. There is always a remainder, something that hasn't been taken into account. But this must obviously not lead us to consider that moral behaviors are not framed and arranged in the same way as selfish ones. What MacKenzie and Millo observe is that the trader alternates between different framings, passing from one configuration of *agencements* to another. The question that they ask seems to be able to be formulated as follows: how can traders' alternation between calculative and noncalculative *agencements* be analyzed and described? This question is largely unexplored, but partial answers have been proposed. First, the symmetry between selfish and altruistic *agencements* has been shown; both involve material, textual, procedural, and other investments. When *homo economicus* becomes altruistic "again," he does not rediscover his true nature; he changes his equipment. Second—and this point is even more fundamental—calculative and noncalculative *agencements* are mutually interwoven. Thus they cannot be conceived of as exogenous, exclusive, or even hostile. They share elements, which makes alternation resemble the cross-dissolves in the movies: noncalculation implies elements of calculation and vice versa. In other words, economic markets cannot exist without moral *agencements* or, conversely, any altruistic *agencement* is calculated (Callon and Law 2005). In any case, the question is crucial for the performativity program: the anthropology of economics is constantly confronted with other, equally performative, anthropological programs.

Finally, this work of performation of individual agencies and their calculative capacities translates—and this is a strong point of convergence—into a very high level of asymmetry between those individual agencies which are almost totally deprived of the prostheses and rights that would enable them to negotiate, calculate, and defend their interests and those which, by contrast, have immense calculative capacities. This inequality is due to the fact that performation of the economy by economics is always a co-performation, and that the programs represented in co-performation favor the agencies whose competencies are already firmly established. (A history of economics should be written, which shows up the mechanisms through which the strongest—that is, the best equipped—agencies become stronger by performing the very world in which they can thrive.)

Unequal Calculating Capacities

We have shown (Callon and Muniesa 2005) that economic markets are
better described as collective calculating devices where sociotechnical algorithms organize and, very often, facilitate encounters between agents
endowed with unequal calculating capacities. The recent dissertation that
Koray Caliskan (2005) devoted to the functioning of the global cotton
market illustrates this point. It shows how dominant economic agents design and impose modalities of encountering, and consequently sociotechnical algorithms of pricing, that produce asymmetries and guarantee the
domination of certain agencies over others. These asymmetries, Caliskan
tells us, can be explained by means of the notion of prosthetic prices. At
any point in time a large number of different prices exist in the cotton
market. In the transactions that occur on various sites (in the Turkish or
Egyptian countryside, in Izmir or Alexandria, or in the New York Board
of Trade) certain agents have access to a wide range of existing prices that
they transform into "prosthetic prices," that is, into inputs into a calculation that only they master and that enables them to decide on the price in
the transaction in which they are engaged. The strongest agent is the one
who can play with the largest number of prosthetic prices to calculate
and set the price of the transaction. Caliskan notes that this calculative
capacity is unequally distributed. The Egyptian farmer is soon sub-
merged; the price he offers is reduced by his interlocutor to a prosthetic
price among many others, and he loses control. He is calculated by one
stronger than he as he delivers his bales of cotton, and at the same time
he is rendered incapable of choosing another partner.

These asymmetries, which scale-one markets produce and reproduce,
are at the center of the negotiations and compromises punctuating the design and implementation of the electronic economy. Muniesa, analyzing
the automation of the Paris Stock Exchange, has shown that the choice of
computer algorithms and digital equipment constantly raised questions of
accuracy, fairness, transparency, and equity. Existing balances of power
frequently lead to options that favor certain asymmetries. Other authors
have shown how the technologies used to make labor markets more
transparent or to "rationalize" calls for tenders (in the case of B2B markets) could sometimes deliberately result in an inversion of the balance of
power between suppliers and buyers, just by reallocating calculating capacities (Mellet et al. 2005; see also Lindberg and Bergström 2005).

The different anthropological programs developed—sometimes con-
currently but very often in a convergent way—by economics at large,
and in particular by the different professionals and experts who equip
markets, tend to overlook inequalities in calculating equipment and even

more frequently are actually busy trying to produce such inequalities. They likewise disregard or, even worse, promote the fact that the organization of encounters, for instance, between buyers and suppliers, directs badlyequipped agencies toward well-equipped ones. In the bracketing off of these issues, economics particularly in its most abstract and formal parts has played and still does play a decisive role in producing and reproducing inequalities.

———————

This triple convergence (a disentanglements of goods and agencies, a shaping of individual agencies, either an ignorance or production of uneven distributions of calculating capacities) does not lead to the imposition of homogeneous markets. It does nevertheless impose a certain form of economy that, increasingly, is reduced to nothing but a question of "the" market and tends to confuse the possible plurality of markets and forms of competition with an anthropological model that is highly compatible with neoclassical economics.[26]

Behind convergence, divergences obviously exist. As shown in great detail in the different chapters of this book, actual markets are heterogeneous assemblages that are integrated to a greater or lesser degree and are always capable of disassembling locally. The good news is that there is no overall logic, thanks to the struggles of performation. It is precisely these power struggles between competing programs which make the disassembling and reassembling process possible, necessitating investments that measure up to those by which actual markets were formatted. Only carefully prepared and organized experiments can achieve such a concentration of resources. They form an obligatory point of passage for a perpetually local production and exploitation of differences.

On Economics Experiments

The failure of so-called planned economies has helped free us of the belief in Kapitalism and of the myth of Revolution as the only alternative.[27] We are no longer in a period when the only choice was between a program aimed at performing an entirely state-controlled economy and a symmetrical, equally monolithic, program of performation of self-regulated markets. It is time indeed, as Gibson-Graham suggests, to unpack the notion of markets as self-regulated institutions and to think of projects in which models or programs are experimented with for constructing multiple axes of economic diversity (Gibson-Graham 2003).

Future societies will probably have to be pluralistic in all of their organizations, including the economy. There is no pre-given path to follow. Saying that the economy is performed by economics (at large) means implicitly highlighting the existence of a plurality of possible organizations of economic activity and of several programs than can be conceived of and tested, that is, (co)performed. The notion of performation leads to that of experimentation.

Experiments can be organized in many ways. A first strategy consists of choosing the laboratory as a starting point. Guala's chapter perfectly illustrates this point. For him, the remarkable development of experimental economics in recent years has gone hand in hand with its profound evolution. Initially designed to test the hypotheses of academic economics, experimental economics has gradually turned into an institution-building program. As Guala notes, it is by becoming aware of its performative dimension that experimental economics accomplished this transformation and is now both legitimate and influential. "Building new institutions" means aiming at constructing what I have proposed calling sociotechnical *agencements*. That means also organizing trials of strength in order to validate assumptions and to enact procedures. The looping process can then take place; new hypotheses can be tested, new sociotechnical *agencements* proposed, and, in return, lessons learned that revive theoretical analysis. The design of laboratories where new forms of economic activities can be tested and experimented is a strategic site for those interested in the performativity thesis.

Economic experiments include experimental economics, as redefined by Guala, but are obviously not restricted to it. Gibson-Graham (2003) describes in detail experiments in the wild aimed at constructing cooperative economies and an economics of cooperative actions. The Mondragón cooperative, criticized from all sides, devised and applied original rules and devices that inspired experiments in other countries. The organizational innovations that were tested and progressively enhanced took into account a series of requirements, real terms of reference: choosing products that would link the cooperative to the regional economy; defining rules for calculating the surplus production and its distribution; testing original forms of savings. These innovations in the field were made, it seems, without the help of academic economists and sometimes even against them! The strategy followed was to abandon the project of substituting a new form of economy for another (replacing Kapitalism), instead creating sustainable niches. The cooperative does not propose *the* alternative solution to a general problem but *a* particular solution to a series of very specific problems. In so doing it does not help to strengthen the illusion that global forms of organization of the economy exist. The thesis of performativity pays justice to these strategies which strive to experiment with new settings, new forms of *agencements*, and which raise the question of their transpositions.

Moreover, by inviting us to consider actual economic organizations as the outcomes of explicit or implicit performation struggles, the performativity thesis incites us to get rid of epistemological considerations and to adopt a more pragmatic stance. Mitchell's chapter perfectly illustrates how the change that Guala sees in experimental economics could be extended to in vivo experiments and economics in the wild. Property rights theory is one of the cornerstones of neoclassical theory and of . . . Hernando de Soto's program. Instead of privileging epistemology (is neoclassical economy true or wrong?) and considering the (relative) failure of this program as a proof of its lack of realism, Mitchell describes it as the unpredictable outcome of a battle between two opposite (performative) programs, that is, as an (even if involuntary) actual scale-one experiment. Lessons can be drawn from this (unequal) trial of strength, in particular about the assumption of the existence of clear boundaries between markets and nonmarkets and also about the role of property rights in "formatting a form of exclusion-inclusion" by causing property transfers from the poor to the rich.[28] By highlighting the confrontation between two property-rights theories, one produced by confined economics and the second by economics in the wild, Mitchell's chapter invites us to go further and to raise the more general question of the emergence, conditions of survival, and extension of certain forms of economy that are born outside academic circles and that illustrate the inventiveness and audacity of economists in the wild, especially when they are confronted with stubborn professional economists.

The variety of experiment sites and forms of organization (as illustrated by Guala's and Mitchell's studies of very contrasted settings) raises the question of their typology. The chapter by Muniesa and Callon proposes several analytical categories to grasp the diversity of modalities of experimentation, linked to different types of economics at large. They thus distinguish three types of site for experiments: laboratories, platforms, and in vivo experiments. They note that an interesting question is the choice of a particular type of site, as well as the categories of problems that are posed. One of the challenges for the future, they tell us, is the networking of these sites and their organization.

This networking should probably facilitate the cooperation/confrontation between different populations of economists, including confined economists and economists in the wild. Why not conceive of economists in the wild, who have been running experiments on cooperative economy for decades, conducting laboratory experiments in cooperation with academic economists, for instance, to test different rules of distribution of surplus or different modalities of setting wages? Gibson-Graham (2003) points out, for example, the "lack of an appropriate economic analysis for building new cooperative economics" and more particularly "the underdevelopment of an economics of surplus labor distribution." Why not envisage, symmetrically, that laboratory economists may be invited to continue their work in vivo, or even to start it in vivo where relevant. These joint experimental networks should facilitate the appearance and evaluation of a wider diversity of forms of organization of economic activities[29] and introduce within academic economics more theoretical variety. Convergence will be no longer our only fate.

The territory that is opening up to the social sciences is vast. All the social sciences, not just economics, can contribute to this research program, alongside the agents engaged in economic activities (Barry and Slater 2005). We no longer have to choose between interpreting the world and transforming it. Our work, together with the actors, is to multiply possible worlds through collective experimentations and performances.

Notes

1. "*Homo economicus* is not behind us, he is ahead of us: like the moral and dutiful person; like the person of science and of reason. The person has long been something else, and only recently has the person been a machine, complicated by a calculator" (my translation).

2. This chapter was prepared during my stay as an invited member at the International Center for Advanced Studies (NYU). I benefited greatly from Tim Mitchell's insights and support. I thank all the participants in the 2004–2005 ICAS seminar, and in particular Koray Caliskan, Julie Graham, Vincent Lépinay, Fred Myers and Steven Lukes for their comments and criticism. I am also grateful to Donald MacKenzie, Fabian Muniesa, and Bruno Latour for their suggestions and to Martha Poon for her cautious reading.

3. The opposite is also true. The best specialists of rhetoric (Perelman 1982) have pointed out its close relations with logic. The notion of demonstration, useful to both the rhetor and the scientist, serves to explain the articulation of these two dimensions of discourse (Barry 2001; Rosental 2002). Moreover, Cassin (1995) shows how the *epideixis* (through which the speaker tries to convince his or her audience) is always articulated to the *apodeixis* (by which the speaker indicates and qualifies the objects to which he or she is referring).

4. Pragmatics derives from *pragma*: action, a deed or intentional act.

5. In his twelfth lecture, Austin says: "Stating, describing, are just two names among a very great many others for illocutionary acts" (1962, pp. 147–48).

6. The obvious limit of Austin's work is that his analysis does not depart from discourse per se, as his work on the different categories of verbs and performativities shows. Consequently, he can explain neither the force of statements nor their meaning. These limits have led certain authors to complete the Austinian analysis, either by highlighting the importance of the interlocutors'

subjectivity (as Grice and Searle for philosophy and Butler for sociology do) or by noting the need to take social and cultural context into account (Bourdieu). But these critiques simply continued Austin's error by accepting an insurmountable boundary between discourse and that which lies beyond it (either in the form of the psychology of subjects or of society). To extend Austin, we have to go in another direction and question the actualization of the contexts and subjectivities that are implied by the utterance. In the case of science, this implies the study of the relationships between SES and sociotechnical arrangements (*agencements*). The critique of Austin should not exclude the notion of performativity but rather should enrich and complete it, first, by insisting more on the fact that the context of enunciation is included in the enunciation (semiotic turn) and, second, by taking into account the materialities composing that context (ANT turn).

7. An SES perfectly illustrates the thesis of Cassin in terms of which any discourse articulates *epideixis* and *apodeixis* (see note 3).

8. Shifters are traces or marks of the enunciation. They point to the world presupposed by the utterance.

9. See Callon (1994).

10. This is what epistemology highlights when it asserts that facts are always theory-laden.

11. See Deleuze and Guattari (1998).

12. Deleuze has proposed distinguishing between two sets of relations he calls virtual/actual and potential/real. The latter refers to processes in which events could be reduced to the causal consequence of preexisting configurations; the former to events that could be said to be dependant on but not causally determined by preexisting configurations. In one case, framing (and repetitions) prevail, whereas in the second case overflowing and differences impose their destabilizing logic (Deleuze 1968).

13. From this point of view, a major issue is arbitrage conceived in a sociotechnical sense: see Beunza, et al. (2006). Some formulas are more vulnerable than others to the counter program of the arbitrageur. For example, an option formula that has as its result half the Black-Scholes price, or twice the Black-Scholes price, would have succumbed in this way, just as, in fact, the practitioners' rules of thumb prior to Black-Scholes succumbed to Black-Scholes–based arbitrage (MacKenzie, personal communication).

14. Sahlins uses the notion of performativity in a purely Austinian sense. Taking the example of friendship, and of assistance that a person in difficulty can expect from a supposed friend, he says that "the relationship is even more certainly created by the performance, than is the performance guaranteed by the relationship."

15. A usual translation is: Let there be light and there was light.

16. "'Sunshine trading . . . could be seen as an attempt to repair the Black-Scholes world, to create a world in which the mere placing of 'informationless' orders did not affect prices" (MacKenzie 2004, p. 323).

17. In the following discussion, I use the terms programs, worlds, and sociotechnical *agencements* interchangeably.

18. The situation is the same in physics; see Galison (1997) and Knorr Cetina (1999).

19. It is amusing to note the problems involved with putting into ordinary words a mathematically simple formula describing a new product conceived of by engineers rather than economists (see Lépinay's chapter). The formula's signification is contained entirely in its calculation and in the result of that calculation.

20. As MacKenzie shows in chapter 3, the Black and Scholes formula ends up being all that at once.

21. I could simply have referred to the work on innovation that highlights the role of non academics and particularly the role of research in the wild, and of research collectives. For a recent illustration of this point see Hippel (2005).

22. For the analysis of these changes of direction, typical of any innovation process, see Akrich, et al. (2002).

23. Inscriptions are crucial elements in the chain of translations which organize the shifting out and the shifting in of scientific statements (Latour 1987).

24. Preda notes that those who, like Bachelier, maintain that the probability clause is adapted to price analysis are precisely the same ones who had no instrument for observation and recording. Without adequate technology, they were in a sense limited to the probabilistic hypothesis.

25. Convergence must be understood as the construction of more or less extended compatibilities and not as the elimination of any difference.

26. This model assumes the obviousness of the three elements described in this section (nonhuman/human divide; individual agency; competition between equal agencies).

27. I use the word Kapitalism, with a capital K, to denote the reality imagined by everyone who considers the Western economic system to be a homogeneous reality, endowed with its own logic. The assumption of a homogeneous economic reality is made by those who criticize capitalism, thus defined, as well as by those who defend it by talking of the market and its laws, in general. Experiments in past decades have shown that Kapitalism could only be a fiction: no program has managed to make Kapitalism exist nor to overthrow it. There are only capitalisms; see Barry (2004).

28. See also Elyachar and her analysis of NGO's micro-lending programs in Egypt (Elyachar 2005).

29. This evolution could be related to the growth of what Thrift (2005) calls "knowing capitalism."

References

Akrich, M. 1992. "The De-Scription of Technical Objects." Pp. 205–224 in *Shaping Technology/Building Society: Studies in Sociotechnical Change*, edited by W. Bijker and J. Law. Cambridge, MA: MIT Press.

Akrich, M., M. Callon, and B. Latour. 2002. "The Key to Success in Innovation." *International Journal of Innovation Management* 6:187–225.

Akrich, M., and J. Law. 1996. "On Customers and Costs: A Story from Public Sector Science." In *Accounting and Science*, edited by M. Power. Cambridge: Cambridge University Press.

Arnauld, A., and P. Nicole. 1662/1970. *La logique ou l'art de penser*. Paris: Flammarion.

Austin, J. L. 1962. *How to Do Things with Words*. Cambridge, MA: Harvard University Press.

Barrey, S., F. Cochoy, and S. Dubuisson. 2000. "Designer, packager et merchandiser: Trois professionnels pour une même scène marchande." *Sociologie du Travail* 42:457–482.

Barry, A. 2001. *Political Machines: Governing a Technological Society*. London: Athlone.

Barry, A. 2004. "Ethical Capitalism." Pp. 195–211 in *Global Governmentality*, edited by W. Larner and W. Walters. London: Sage.

Barry, A., and D. Slater, Eds. 2005. *The Technological Economy*. London: Routledge.

Beunza, D., I. Hardie, and D. MacKenzie. 2006. "A Price Is a Social Thing: Towards a Material Sociology of Arbitrage." *Organization Studies* 27:721–745.

Caliskan, K. 2005. "Making a Global Commodity: The Production of Markets and Cotton in Egypt, Turkey, and the United States." PhD diss. New York University.

Callon, M. 1994. "Four Models for the Dynamics of Science." Pp. 29–63 in *Handbook of Science and Technology Studies*, edited by S. Jasanoff, G. E. Markle, J. C. Petersen, and T. Pinch. London: Sage.

Callon, M. Ed. 1998. *The Laws of the Markets*. London: Blackwell.

Callon, M., and J. Law. 2005. "On Qualculation, Agency and Otherness." *Environment and Planning D: Society and Space* 23:717–733.

Callon, M., C. Méadel, and V. Rabeharisoa. 2002. "The Economy of Qualities." *Economy and Society* 31:194–217.

Callon, M., and F. Muniesa. 2005. "Economic Markets as Calculative Collective Devices." *Organization Studies* 26:1129–1250.

Cassin, B. 1995. *L'effet sophistique*. Paris: Gallimard.

Clark, C., and T. Pinch. 1995. *The Hard Sell: The Language and Lessons of Street-wise Marketing*. London: HarperCollins.

Cochoy, F. 1998. "Another Discipline for the Market Economy: Marketing as a Performative Knowledge and Know-How for Capitalism." Pp. 194–221 in *The Laws of the Markets*, edited by M. Callon. Oxford: Blackwell.

Cochoy, F., and C. Grandclément. 2005. "Publicizing Goldilocks' Choice at the Supermarket: Political Work of Shopping Packs, Carts, and Talk." Pp. 646–657 in *Making Things Public: Atmospheres of Democracy*, edited by B. Latour and P. Weibel. Cambridge, MA: MIT Press.

Cronon, W. 1991. *Nature's Metropolis: Chicago and the Great West*. New York: Norton.

Deleuze, G. 1968. *Différence et répétition*. Paris: PUF.

Deleuze, G., and F. Guattari. 1998. *A Thousand Plateaus: Capitalism and Schizophrenia*. London: Athlone.

Elyachar, J. 2005. *Markets of Dispossession: NGOs, Economic Development and the State in Cairo*. Durham, NC: Duke University Press.

Faulhaber, G. R., and W. J. Baumol. 1988. "Economists as Innovators: Practical Products of Theoretical Research." *Journal of Economic Literature* 26:577–600.

Ferraro, F., J. Pfeffer, and R. Sutton. 2005. "Economics Language and Assumptions: How Theories Can Become Self-Fulfilling." *Academy of Management Review* 30:8–24.

Galison, P. 1997. *Image and Logic: A Material Culture of Microphysics*. Chicago: University of Chicago Press.

Gibson-Graham, J. K. 2003. "Enabling Ethical Economies: Cooperativism and Class." *Critical Sociology* 29:1–39.

Goody, J. 1977. *The Domestication of the Savage Mind*. Cambridge: Cambridge University Press.

Greimas, A. J., and J. Courtès. 1982. *Semiotics and Language: An Analytical Dictionary*. Bloomington: Indiana University Press.

Guesnerie, R. 1986. "Stationary Sunspot Equilibria in an n-Commodity World." *Journal of Economic Theory* 40:103–127.

Hacking, I. 1983. *Representing and Intervening*. Cambridge: Cambridge University Press.

Hippel, E. von. 2005. *Democratizing Innovation*. Cambridge, MA: MIT Press.

Hopwood, A. G., and P. Miller. 1994. *Accounting as Social and Institutional Practice*. Cambridge: Cambridge University Press.

Hughes, T. P. 1983. *Networks of Power: Electric Supply Systems in the US, England and Germany, 1880–1930*. Baltimore, MD: Johns Hopkins University Press.

Kjellberg, H. 2001. *Organising Distribution: Hakonbolaget and the Efforts to Rationalise Food Distribution, 1940–1960*. Stockholm: EFI.

Kline, S., and N. Rosenberg. 1986. "An Overview of Innovation." Pp. 275–306 in *The Positive Sum Strategy: Harnessing Technology for Economic Growth*, edited by R. Landau and N. Rosenberg. Washington, DC: National Academy Press.

Knorr Cetina, K. 1999. *Epistemic Cultures: How the Sciences Make Knowledge*. Cambridge, MA: Harvard University Press.

Latour, B. 1987. *Science in Action*. Cambridge, MA: Harvard University Press.

Latour, B. 2005. *Reassembling the Social: An Introduction to Actor-Network-Theory*. Oxford: Oxford University Press.

Law, J., and J. Urry. 2004. "Enacting the Social." *Economy and Society* 33:390–410.

Lindberg, K., and O. Bergström. 2005. "Transforming Buyer–Supplier Relationships: B2B System as a Boundary Actant." Working Paper.

MacKenzie, D. 2003. "An Equation and Its Worlds: Bricolage, Exemplars, Disunity and Performativity in Financial Economics." *Social Studies of Science* 33:831–868.

MacKenzie, D. 2004. "The Big, Bad Wolf and the Rational Market: Portfolio Insurance, the 1987 Crash and the Performativity of Economics." *Economy and Society* 33:303–334.

MacKenzie, D., and Y. Millo. 2003. "Constructing a Market, Performing Theory: The Historical Sociology of a Financial Derivatives Exchange." *American Journal of Sociology* 109:107–145.

Mauss, M. 1960. "Essai sur le don." Pp. 145–279 in *Sociologie et anthropologie*, edited by Marcel Mauss. Paris: PUF.

Mellet, K., E. Marchal, and G. Rieucau. 2005. "Job Board Toolkits: Internet Matchmaking and the Transformation of Help-Wanted Ads." Working Paper.

Millo, Y. 2003. "Where Do Financial Markets Come From? Historical Sociology of Financial Derivatives Markets." PhD diss. University of Edinburgh.

Mitchell, T. 2002. *Rule of Experts: Egypt, Techno-Politics, Modernity.* Berkeley: University of California Press.

Mol, A. 2002. *The Body Multiple.* Durham, NC: Duke University Press.

Morris, C. W. 1938. *Foundations of the Theory of Signs.* Chicago: University of Chicago Press.

Muniesa, F. 2003. "Des marchés comme algorithmes: Sociologie de la cotation électronique à la Bourse de Paris." PhD diss. Ecole des Mines de Paris.

Perelman, C. 1982. *The Realm of Rhetoric.* Notre Dame: University of Notre Dame Press.

Pickering, A. 1995. *The Mangle of Practice: Time, Agency, and Science.* Chicago: University of Chicago Press.

Porter, T. M. 1995. *Trust in Numbers.* Princeton: Princeton University Press.

Power, M., Ed. 1996. *Accounting and Science: Natural Inquiry and Commercial Reason.* Cambridge: Cambridge University Press.

Preda, A. Forthcoming. "Where Do Analysts Come From? The Case of Financial Chartism." In *Market Devices*, edited by M. Callon, Y. Millo, and F. Muniesa.

Rosental, C. 2002. "De la démo-cratie en Amérique: Formes actuelles de la démonstration en intelligence artificielle." *Actes de la Recherche en Sciences Sociales* 140–142:110–120.

Sahlins, M. 1985. *Islands of History.* Chicago: University of Chicago Press.

Strathern, M., Ed. 2000. *Audit Cultures.* London: Routledge.

Thrift, N. 2005. *Knowing Capitalism.* London: Sage.

Contributors

Michel Callon is a professor at the Ecole Nationale Supérieure des Mines de Paris, and a researcher at the Centre de Sociologie de l'Innovation. He works on the anthropology of markets and the study of technical democracy, and he is completing research with Vololona Rabeharisoa on French patients' organizations. His books include *The Laws of the Markets* (Oxford: Blackwell, 1998); *Le pouvoir des malades: L'Association Française contre les Myopathies et la recherche* (Paris: Presses de l'Ecole des Mines, 1999); *Agir dans un monde incertain: Essai sur la démocratie technique* (Paris: Le Seuil, 2001; English translation forthcoming from MIT Press). In 2002, the Society for Social Studies of Science awarded him its highest honor, the Bernal Prize.

Emmanuel Didier is a researcher at the Centre National de la Recherche Scientifique (CNRS). He is a graduate of the Ecole Nationale de la Statistique et de l'Administration Economique (ENSAE) and the Ecole Nationale Supérieure des Mines de Paris. He was a visiting scholar in the Department of History of Science at Harvard University, and then a postdoctoral fellow at the Max Planck Institute for the History of Science in Berlin. He works on the social studies of statistics. His next book will be *En quoi consiste l'Amérique? L'invention de la représentativité probabiliste aux Etats-Unis pendant l'entre deux guerres* (Paris: Presses de l'INED, in press).

Marie-France Garcia-Parpet is an anthropologist and senior researcher at the Institut National de la Recherche Agronomique (INRA) in Paris and member of the Centre de Sociologie Européenne (CNRS and EHESS). She has studied the social construction of markets in France and in Brazil. She is currently working on the globalization of wine markets.

Francesco Guala is an associate professor of philosophy at the University of Exeter. He received a PhD in philosophy at the London School of Economics, and he has held visiting positions in France, Italy, and the United Kingdom. He is the author of *The Methodology of Experimental Economics* (Cambridge University Press, 2005) and of several articles in philosophy and social science journals (including *Philosophy of Science, Studies in History and Philosophy of Science, Economics and Philosophy, Journal of Philosophy, Experimental Economics, Journal of Theoretical Politics*). He won the 2002 History of Economic Analysis Award and the 2002 International Network for Economic Method Prize for best article written by a young scholar.

Petter Holm is a professor of fisheries management at the University of Tromsø. His work in the sociology of science includes "The Dynamics of Institutionalization: Transformation Processes in Norwegian Fisheries" (*Administrative Science Quarterly* 40, 1995:389–422); "Crossing the Border: On the Relationship between Science and Fishermen's Knowledge in a Resource Management Context" (*MAST* 2[1], 2003:5–49); "Creating Alternative Natures: Coastal Cod as Fact and Artefact" (with Stein Arne Rånes and Bjørn Hersoug in D. Symes, ed., *Northern Waters: Management Issues and Practice* [Oxford: Fishing News Books, 1998], pp. 79–89); and *Community, State and Market on the North Atlantic Rim: Challenges to Modernity in the Fisheries* (with Richard Apostle, Gene Barrett, Svein Jentoft, Leigh Mazany, Bonnie McCay, and Knut Mikalsen [Toronto: Toronto University Press, 1998]).

Vincent-Antonin Lépinay is an assistant professor at MIT in the Science and Technology Studies program. He graduated from the Ecole Normale Supérieure, the Ecole Nationale Supérieure des Mines de Paris, and Columbia University. He completed a PhD in anthropology of finance, investigating how traders, engineers, customers, and regulators deal with highly innovative financial products. He has collaborated with Ellen Hertz on a study of insider trading regulation by U.S. courts and the question of financial fraud. He is now studying the controversy over personal banking of stem cells.

Donald MacKenzie holds a personal chair in sociology at the University of Edinburgh, where he has taught since 1975. His books include *Statistics in Britain, 1865–1930: The Social Construction of Scientific Knowledge* (Edinburgh: Edinburgh University Press, 1981); *Inventing Accuracy: A Historical Sociology of Nuclear Missile Guidance* (Cambridge, MA: MIT Press, 1990); *Mechanizing Proof: Computing, Risk, and Trust* (Cambridge, MA: MIT Press, 2001); and *An Engine, Not a Camera: How Financial Models Shape Markets* (Cambridge, MA: MIT Press, 2006). His current work on social studies of finance is supported by a U.K. Economic and Social Research Council Professorial Fellowship.

Philip Mirowski holds the Carl Koch Chair of Economics and the History and Philosophy of Science and is a Fellow of the Reilly Center, University of Notre Dame. He is author of, among others, *Machine Dreams* (2002), *The Effortless Economy of Science?* (2004), *More Heat than Light* (1989), and the forthcoming *ScienceMart™: A Primer on the*

New Economics of Science. His recent article in *Studies in History and Philosophy of Science* attempts to revive interest in the ways in which philosophies of science are linked to the political economies of their respective eras, while that in *Social Studies of Science* describes the novel institution of the contract research organization. He has undertaken this research, in part, because he worries that STS itself is in danger of becoming co-opted to the modern regime of globalized privatization of science. Some members of the Society for Social Studies of Science must feel the same, since they awarded *Effortless Economy* the Ludwig Fleck Prize in 2006. Outside of the commercialization of science, he is collaborating with Wade Hands on *Agreement on Demand* (2006), a history of the theory of demand in the twentieth century and with Dieter Plehwe on the history of the rise of neoliberal doctrines in the postwar era.

Timothy Mitchell is a professor of politics at New York University. He served as director of the university's Center for Near Eastern Studies and is currently directing a project on "The Authority of Knowledge in a Global Age" at NYU's International Center for Advanced Studies. He is the author of *Colonizing Egypt* (University of California Press, 1991) and *Rule of Experts* (University of California Press, 2002) and the editor of *Questions of Modernity* (University of Minnesota Press, 2000).

Fabian Muniesa is a researcher at the Centre de Sociologie de l'Innovation, Ecole Nationale Supérieure des Mines de Paris, where he teaches economic sociology. He was trained as a sociologist at the Universidad Complutense de Madrid (Spain). In 1999 he joined France Télécom R&D's social science laboratory, where he worked on a PhD on the computerization of the Paris Bourse, completed in 2003 at the Ecole Nationale Supérieure des Mines de Paris. He was also a postdoctoral fellow at the London School of Economics. He is the author of several articles on the social studies of finance and the anthropology of calculation.

Edward Nik-Khah is an assistant professor of economics at Roanoke College. He recently completed a PhD in economics at the University of Notre Dame; he has also studied at the Erasmus Institute for Philosophy and Economics (EIPE) in Rotterdam. His dissertation examines the use of economics in the U.S. electromagnetic spectrum auctions. He is currently researching the emerging consensus around the implementation of public policy through the reengineering of markets.

Lucia Siu worked as a journalist in technology and finance in Hong Kong for seven years and has written extensively on the electronic forms of money, cyber culture, telecommunications regulation, environmental policies, and the dot-com bubble. She holds a BSc in Computer Science and an MSc in Science and Technology Studies (STS), and she is currently conducting postgraduate research at the University of Edinburgh in China's commodity futures markets. She is a freelance writer and has edited eleven publications (print and online) for academic, business, and community organizations.

nonsatiation, 140

normative utterances. *See* utterances, normative

norms, 153, 288, 293, 297, 324–325

objectivity, 278, 295, 299

object-oriented programming languages, 110–111

objects, of experiments, 166–168

odd lots, 179–181

Olympic fishing, 235–236

ontological boundaries, 134–135, 152–153, 155n14, 194–195, 296, 299, 315, 337

openness, 173–174, 178, 183

open-outcry, 60, 179

operations research (OR), 195–196, 216

option (pricing) theory, 8, 56–59, 79, 97. *See also* Black-Scholes model

options, 56–57; American, 57; call, 56, 60, 91; European, 57–58; gambling, 344; put, 56, 76

overcapacity, 235–236. *See also* fisheries

overexploitation, 235. *See also* fisheries

overflow, 179, 183–184, 229–230, 234, 323, 331, 346–347. *See also* disentanglement; embeddedness; framing

overregulation, 250

over-the-counter (OTC), 75, 93, 116

Pacific Bell, 212. *See also* telecom firms

parallel existence, 265

parallelism (validity), 137, 140, 156n23, 165–167, 179, 182–183. *See also* experimental economics

Pareto efficiency, 133, 138

Pareto optimum, 134, 208–210

Paris Bourse (Paris Stock Exchange, PSE), 179–181, 334

Paris School, 190, 193. *See also* science studies

path dependence, 7, 335. *See also* lock-in phenomena

payoffs, 92; distribution, 134; functions, 91; individual, 133; maximization, 142. *See also* returns

PCS licenses, 206

Peirce, Charles S., 3

perfect competition, 20, 25–28, 30, 45

performance, 328–330

performation, 15, 182–183, 239–241, 245, 282, 305, 323–324, 329, 334–336, 338,

343, 349; expression, 328; prescriptions, 325–326. *See also* co-performation

performative idiom, 3

performative utterances. *See* utterances, performative

performativity, 3, 5, 72; Austinian, 56, 69; Barnesian, 9, 55–56, 66–69, 76–80, 153, 280; versus constativity, 321; creative, 136; Darwinian metaphor, 332; destructive, 136; effective, 55–56, 59–60, 64–66, 76–78, 280–281; experimental, 184; versus expression, 307–308, 327; feminist theories, 3; generic, 55–56, 59–60, 64–66, 76–78, 153; genuine (Type-2), 153–154; linguistic, 3, 5, 14, 56, 69, 78, 294–295, 303, 308, 327; as magic, 69, 276, 295–296, 300; materialities, 323, 326–327; mobilizing power, 269; normative, 153; paradox, 316; postwar context, 195; priest model, 296–297; as problems, 136–137, 294–295; as research practice, 241; resistance, 277, 295–296, 330; as resource, 10, 130, 134; in science, 318; versus self-fulfilling prophecies, 324, 330; spurious (Type-1), 153–154; as tautology, 191, 198–200. *See also* co-performation; counterperformativity; performation; self-fulfilling prophecies

pharmacovigilance, 164

Pickering, Andrew, 3, 190, 321

pickles, 48, 283–294, 298, 302, 304, 306–307, 327–328, 338, 344

platforms, 164–170, 173–178, 182–184

Plott, Charles, 129, 132, 147

plurality, 350–352

policy making, 7, 139, 173, 176, 203, 207, 213; influence, 250

political ecology, 215

polls, election, 136

Popper, Karl, 318, 323

porous legality, 246

portfolio, 75; riskless, 58

portfolio insurance, 56, 76, 79, 96–97. *See also* Leland, Hayne

Port-Royal logic, 316

poverty, 260; household, 251; ILD's solution, 249

power: abstract, 267; balance, 36–37, 39, 45–46, 348; discourse, 296–297; foreclosure, 264, 267; physical eviction, 267;